The Testament of
LAZARUS

The Testament of
LAZARUS

THE PRE-CHRISTIAN GOSPEL OF JOHN

JANET TYSON

Pirištu Books
Norwich, Norfolk, UK

©2023. Janet Tyson. All rights reserved. No part of this publication may be reproduced, stored in a retrieval system or transmitted, in any form or by any means, electronic, mechanical, photocopying, recording, or otherwise, without the prior written permission of the author.

Images: Cover images licensed through AdobeStock.com. *Madonna and Child with Mary Magdalene and Donor* by Lucas van Leyden is in the public domain. All other diagrams drawn by the author or free clipart.

ISBN 978-1-7393154-0-5

British Library Cataloguing in Production Data. A catalogue record for this book is available from the British Library.

Contents

Introduction **i**

1. Samaritan Foundations **1**
A brief discussion on the cultural context of the Jesus' mission, with respect to the mentioning of Jesus as "a Samaritan," i.e., the schism at Sinai, the northern tribes and their belief in their own messiah, and the basis of the Remnant motif that permeates Jesus' theology.

2. The Meeting near Qumran **14**
Jesus and John first meet across the River Jordan out on the salt flats that form a symbolic starting point for Jesus' campaign. The first disciples are introduced and their significance within the "twelve" is demonstrated by deconstructing their names. Time references in the gospel are vital to its interpretation; they reveal an intentional pattern.

3. Statements of Intent **36**
The wedding at Cana is Jesus' first open declaration of his mission to symbolically reunite the tribes. Ezekiel's Bride of God theme is introduced. Jesus' attack on the temple institution is explained.

4. Martha **53**
The character of Martha is assessed in terms of mythology and of her relationship to Jesus.

5. Nicodemus and the Son of Man **58**
The entire scenario of Jesus' discussion with Nicodemus is an echo of that between Uriel and Ezra/Salathiel in 2 Esdras. The 'Son of Man' concept is discussed.

6. The Meeting at Qumran **72**
Jesus moves closer into John's territory and tensions build; he is seen by some to be a dubious upstart but John is initially supportive.

7. Samaritan Woman **76**
The Bride of God theme is acted out in the chief female character of the gospel; her first entry into the narrative is as the representation of the 'adulterous' Israel. Jesus comes to Jacob's Well in search of this woman; she has a specific destiny. The idea of a child of Jesus is put forward.

8. THE SON OF THE MAN **87**
Continuing this theme, the Bride of God pattern demands that in preparation for the new kingdom, she must be reunited with her 'lost' companions; she represents the northern tribes, and the next male character represents the southern tribes. The identities of the 'sick boy' and his father are discussed; the lad will become Jesus' protégée.

9. LAME MAN **92**
No cure takes place in this scene; it is a metaphor for the corruption and impotence of the extant priestly institution. The 'lame man' is one of Jesus' more troublesome disciples.

10. SAMARITAN REBELLION **100**
Historical evidence provides a probable explanation for the feeding scene and the subsequent turmoil; the gospel's chronology is questioned.

11. STUMBLING BLOCKS **120**
Jesus' strange speech about his flesh and blood, which creates confusion and dissention is explained. Peter shows his true colours; Nicodemus exploits his position to assist the cause.

12. ADULTERESS **128**
The adulteress is the same Samaritan woman Jesus 'elected' at the well. This is a testing of Jesus' apparent claim to high-priestly status. He demonstrates a keen knowledge of the law and of scripture, turning the tables on the accusers. The question of marriage arises.

13. ESCALATION **137**
Jesus' mission takes on a new level of intensity; he challenges the temple priests in their own territory and castigates their lack of duty and honour. Jesus' birth-year is potentially discovered.

14. THE BEGINNING OF THE END **144**
Jesus' protégée submits to an arcane initiation rite; he proves himself worthy of becoming Jesus' right-hand-man and deputy. This angers the Pharisees and initiates a precarious aftermath for the young man.

15. LAZARUS **157**
Knowing his time is nearly up, Jesus must make one final effort to show 'the world' what he means and what is at stake. Lazarus is not dead; he is incarcerated by the Sanhedrin.

16. MEAL 1: SIX DAYS BEFORE PASSOVER **181**
The first meal scene is one of celebration and preparation for the last day; Mary's actions are explained. Judas shows his disdain; the entry into Jerusalem through a symbolic gate is a demonstration of Jesus' Samaritan roots.

17. MEAL 2: THE DAY OF PREPARATION **192**
The second meal scene focuses on the ritualistic preparation for the disciples' anticipated entry into the new kingdom. The 'beloved disciple' is named; Peter shows his true colours; the Iscariot is explained; the *parakletos* is defined.

18. LAW AND ORDER **204**
Many clues lead us to where Jesus is, physically, within Jerusalem, challenging tradition. The mutilation of Malchus is given new meaning; Peter's denials are discussed.

19. TRUTH AND CONSEQUENCE **221**
The 'custom' of release is clarified. Pilate seeks a reason for killing Jesus without implicating himself; the "Jews" provide one. Jesus is mocked as a false king but the symbolism is often underestimated. Herod fears for his own position. Someone else is crucified on Pilate's command. Vestments are described.

20. CULMINATION **244**
Mary is now esteemed and is named "the Magdalene." Clopas and his wife are explained. Jesus makes his last will and testament, handing over the responsibility for his family to his right-hand-man. Jesus receives a drug that makes him appear dead; the piercing of his side is unexpected. The identity of Joseph of Arimathea is revealed.

21. SECRETS AND SURVIVAL **253**
The myrrh and aloes are both symbolic and therapeutic. The plan for Jesus' escape is discussed; the site of Golgotha and that of the makeshift 'tomb' are revealed. The transference of authority to Jesus' 'deputy' takes place. Jesus survives. Peter is tested.

22. EPILOGUE AND PROLOGUE **280**
The gospel's epilogue is written by another hand, i.e., someone close to the inner circle of disciples, in an effort to reiterate Jesus' determination for who would succeed him. Peter is tested. The prologue is written by a later author.

23. CONSIDERATIONS **293**
Many aftereffects of Jesus' mission appear in the historical record and in other texts of the New Testament, yet scholars seldom discuss them. Paul protests against this gospel and has a dubious motivation for allying with the character we know as Lazarus. Thoughts on Shiloh, where Jesus may be buried, and what might have happened to his son.

EXCURSUS: NOTHING NEW UNDER THE SUN? **322**
Many aspects of this interpretation have been found in various works of literature and art. A sixteenth-century painting and the legends of King Arthur are offered as proof.

APPENDICES **339**
Potential FG Historical Timeline; External References; Parallels to the Exodus Story; Parallels to the Story of Joseph; How Many Cubits?; Mary and Lazarus Parallels; Table of Chief Characters; Siloam Tower; Carpenter

SUGGESTED READING **357**

INDEX **359**

It is impossible for a man to learn what he thinks he already knows.

–Epictetus

INTRODUCTION

> At the present moment, many sense that the quest of the historical Jesus is lurching towards a cul-de-sac which will soon be requiring us to wheel around and try a different route.[1]

THERE IS NO ACADEMIC MONOPOLY on the story of Jesus. You can either accept the traditional interpretations and theories put forward by others, or you can do as Jesus himself advises Nicodemus in the Gospel of John (commonly and here referred to as "the FG") and start from the beginning, as a child, learning for yourself. It is not an easy journey.

During my final year as an undergraduate and throughout my graduate degree, I consumed every scrap of information out there but conventional, mainstream interpretations of and commentaries on the FG left me frustrated with the overwhelming lack of answers to the questions I was asking. My approach, therefore, was more like a scientific experiment, in that I had a few of my own theories but I needed to put them to the test. The original audiences of the Gospel of John, however literate or 'in tune' with the author's methods, still had only the testament itself and their cultural history to draw upon. The entire meaning and purpose of the text must be decipherable from that foundation alone. Like Nicodemus, I chose to start with a clean slate.

The FG has gone down in history as an enigmatic, esoteric, almost metaphysical entity that all but defies complete understanding; I will attempt to prove that this is because the 'same old' interpretations, the familiar translations, and the comfortable perspectives have all but blinded us to its reality. I proudly saw *myself* as an academic for many years. I got straight As at university and won a much-coveted graduate fellowship—but when my own reading of the FG started to take shape, I felt I had to completely ignore my Christian upbringing and attempt to get into the headspace of a first-century Jew or Samaritan, which was not an easy task (and, to this end, I acknowledge the profoundly important early Jewish sources that I discovered late in the process, when I sought confirmation or clarity). I was,

---

[1] Nicholas Perrin, *Jesus the Priest* (London: SPCK, 2018), 33.

initially, akin to a Pharisee, saying "I've read everything, therefore I *know*"; I soon learned I knew very little. This was the best possible place to begin a quest to comprehend the enigmatic Gospel of John.

If the FG is such a mysterious text, and seemingly so different in nature to Mathew, Mark, and Luke, why do we persist in trying to make it comprehensible *in light* of these other versions of the Jesus story, rather than allowing it, simply, to speak for itself? This rigid juxtaposition between the Synoptics on the one hand, and the FG on the other is inevitably restrictive, for focus is drawn away from the most meaningful internal elements and placed on such matters as its chronology, authorship, dating, and ethnicity (i.e., Judean or Hellenistic). Although these *are* significant to a full understanding of the gospel, I argue that these concerns 'fall into place' when the *narrative* of the text is first comprehended. By this I do not mean the precise translation of every word by linguists; I mean understanding the subtleties of homophonic puns, wordplay to infer alternative meaning, symbolism, repetition, numerology, etc. The language of the gospel, though Greek, follows the same patterns of expression and the same literary techniques as many of the Hebrew texts of the Old Testament. Finding these patterns is necessary, as they allow the text to lead you to where you need to be, mentally; this is basically what Jesus tells Nicodemus, i.e., 'open your mind and see the way'.

One of the strongest patterns is the constant and consistent use of intertextuality, where the gospel's words relate directly to a precedent in the Hebrew texts. Many commentators find the allusions but then fail to draw out the intended meaning because the original *context* is not assessed. There are no gratuitous "quotations" of scripture in the FG. There were no chapter-verse delineations in Jesus' day, so relevant context can span a few lines, or a few pages; sometimes it is a pointer to what a person says, or to what is done to them. When you 'see' the necessary allusion, it makes complete sense. The FG uses this technique so much, I *did* begin to wonder if the entire gospel and its testament of Jesus' campaign was invented purely from the precedent passages; it would be possible. In the end, however, I decided that the author, Lazarus, was simply a proficient, imaginative, and skilled scribe, using the Old Testament texts to convey his assertion that everything Jesus said and did *was* "written."

The FG is also known for its emphasis on duality, i.e., its use of contrasts, such as light/darkness, truth/lies, above/below, etc., encouraging its readers to delve deeper into the meaning of the text that tells the story. There is not one meaning, the author urges us, there are (at least) two, and this also holds true for names, places, and relationships. This is one of the most vital clues to unlocking the FG narrative, which is written almost as a cypher, a challenge to those 'with eyes to see' to crack and thereby truly "follow" Jesus. The original gospel was *not* intended for everyone; there is a definite winnowing going on within its text. Several times in the FG there are instances where Jesus could just declare himself outright, declare his intentions, his affiliations but he doesn't. That would defeat the purpose, be too easy.

The gospel records far more about who Jesus was, what he attempted to do, and the repercussions of his actions than has ever been acknowledged; it is an attempt by Jesus' right-hand-man, Lazarus (other hands are also evident in the narrative), to preserve the truth about the man he followed … all the way to the 'new kingdom'. It is a chronicle of an attempted coup that went horribly wrong and yet, thanks to Lazarus' scribal skills and ability to act as a spin-doctor, Jesus' mission became *symbolically* profound and scripturally vindicated. This mission, to be clear, was *not* to herald the dawn of Christianity. This investigation will demonstrate that the Gospel of John, the FG, proved so at odds with the new Christian tenets being promulgated by Paul, he all but outlawed it. This suggests that the FG is not the "Fourth Gospel," but the "First Gospel." It *is* also, despite opposition to this claim, a truly gnostic gospel; it reveals secret knowledge to those who have learned how to find it.

I realised about ten years ago that I was *not* the only one seeing certain patterns and apparently alternative 'facts' in the FG; for centuries there have been poets, artists, mythmakers, who took from the gospel most of what you will find in this book, and turned it into works of art that served as hiding places for the "truth." I discovered several over the years.

Although the approach taken in developing this investigation is somewhat maverick, challenges orthodoxy, and probably challenges credulity at times, it has reaped profound results. It has been a once-in-a-lifetime project. I do hope the ensuing opus is testament to the perseverance of a curious mind and inspires others to pursue any loose ends I might leave, or any parallel trains of thought that could further enlighten us. When you look through only one eye you see one image; when you look through both you see two, slightly offset. The brain does its magic and understands the three-dimensional world. The FG has been read with one eye, so to speak; a post-Synoptic, non-historical type of eye. Now I propose an alternative vision, in the hopes that we can at least agree that there is something far more three-dimensional going on in this ancient document.

Prepare to leave the cul-de-sac!

(The NRSV is used for English quotations; translations of the Greek are attributed to *Strong's Concordance*.)

1
SAMARITAN FOUNDATIONS

[T]he suggestion that Jesus and his disciples were Samaritans [is] a view that could hardly be entertained seriously—and has accordingly been assigned to the limbo of scholarly footnotes.[1]

THIS IS PRECISELY THE SENTIMENT that has kept the search for the historical Jesus running around in circles (in that 'cul-de-sac') for years. Rather than accepting that something more has to be done to make sense of the Samaritan elements in the FG, scholars seem to find it simpler to ridicule the notion that Jesus may, in fact, have Samaritan blood running through his veins. Most wash their hands of it, for fear it may jeopardize their own careers, or perhaps because it forces them to rethink the entire history of Christian faith in the Davidic messiah.

Jesus is notoriously difficult to pigeon-hole conveniently into the available options. It has generally been decided that he does not qualify as one of the many self-appointed kings of the time (such as described in Josephus, *Wars*. 2.4.3; 2.13. 5, etc.) because these kings are so obviously militant, self-imposed leaders who wreak violence. Can Jesus possibly be associated with such political display? Well, actually, yes, to a degree, and although he rejects one sort of kingship (in the FG), he fully accepts another.

Neither, it is generally claimed, does he fit well into the familiar mind-set of the Zealots, who condone the use of *extreme force* to remove the current ministers of the temple priesthood and replace them with influential partisans who support Jewish independence and autonomy. The FG Jesus is not *overtly* violent toward the cultus though, again, there is reason to doubt a complete passivity, and his political agenda is different to that of the Zealots'. He does not bump off the priests, he attempts to convert them! However, there is evidence to suggest that Jesus might have bitten off a little more than he can chew late in his campaign, when violence does lead to some serious consequences.

---

[1] James D. Purvis, "The Fourth Gospel and the Samaritans," *Novum Testamentum* 17.3 (1975): 161–98, here 169, citing H. Hammer, 1913.

Despite common tradition, the Christian tradition, Jesus does not even reflect the accepted perception of the Davidic messiah, i.e., one who is from the house of David and who emancipates Israel from oppression (in this context, from Herodian/Roman dominance) through military or political means. The FG, in fact, is conspicuous by its total *lack* of interest in a Davidic representation of Jesus. There is only one reference to a Davidic messiah in the FG and this appears in John 7:42, where the *expectations* of such a figure are emphasized. At no stage does the FG Jesus refute these expectations but consistently throughout the narrative he demonstrates his aversion to the role for himself.

That Jesus is not successful in his role as deliverer in the *Davidic* sense does not seem to be an obstacle for the author of the Matthean gospel but one can discern elements of caution and confusion in the Gospel of Mark, evident in the so-called 'messianic secret' device, where the rationale behind Jesus' mission is somewhat obscured (e.g., Mark 1:34, 44; 3:12; 5:43; 7:36; 8:26, 30; 9:9). Indeed, Jewish literature of the Mediaeval Period preserves a view of Jesus the Nazarene that precludes his possible contention for the position of the Davidic messiah *because* he had failed to free the nation from its oppressors. To the later Jewish mind, Jesus was *one of many* who were to make the way straight for the messianic king.

The Remnant of Joseph
The Samaritan link in the FG *must* make sense; it is there and cannot be swept under the carpet. I suggest the answer lies in the ancient tradition that Joseph had succeeded in preserving a "remnant on earth" (Gen 45:7) of the original, divinely ordained Israel. By appointing only one family as the beneficiary of the new hereditary priesthood, Aaron is challenged and ultimately rejected by those who initially agree to accept him (and Moses) into their tribe, on the understanding that "all the congregation" will be considered holy (Num 16:3).

Consequently, the fact that Aaron is stripped of his vestments on Mount Hor (Num 20:22–8) suggests something more than a mere handing over of the vestments of office. The Hebrew word employed here is *pashat*, which means to plunder, to deploy in hostile array, to invade, etc., thus implying a stronger, more violent image than, perhaps, *sheylal* (to strip naked) would have done (see 1 Sam 19:24, Job 19:9). What seems to be implied, then, by the use of *pashat* in Numbers 20 is that Aaron is forcibly (and surreptitiously, it seems) removed from office, killed, and replaced. Korah and his fellow conspirators are obliterated because they dare to question the primacy of Aaron.

Joshua and Eleazar, then, lead the entry into the Promised Land while

Moses and Aaron are both denied access to the new Israelite home. The priesthood inaugurated at Sinai, however, persists under Eleazar, Aaron's elected heir, effectively his son. Those who reject this priesthood, the followers of the ancient Josephite tradition, are comparatively less significant in the biblical traditions to follow. Amalgamated in the general area of Samaria, these Israelites see themselves as *the* Remnant, the loyal descendants of Abraham, Isaac, and Jacob, through Joseph, who worship a god untainted by the Egyptian pantheon.

It seems that Joshua takes the Remnant idea literally and devotes himself to the ideal of Joseph's pre-Egyptian religion (Josh 24:1–15), while the majority of the Israelites who head south to Jerusalem seem satisfied with the now familiar synthesis of beliefs.

Evidence for the schism at Sinai being based on differing religious beliefs and not just political squabbles, for instance, lies in the preservation of references to solar worship maintained in the southern kingdom: "He removed the horses that the kings of Judah had dedicated to the sun, at the entrance to the house of the Lord" (2 Kgs 23:11); "the bones of the kings of Judah ... shall be brought out of their tombs and they shall be spread before the sun and the moon and all the host of heaven, which they have loved and served" (Jer 8:1–2). Given all the disparaging remarks in the OT pertaining to the northern tribes, not one mentions solar worship. Even in the time of Ezekiel, the wrath of God is focused against *Judah* for permitting the abomination of sun worship in the temple (Ezek 8:16–17).

Joshua, in praying to God to make the sun and moon halt in their paths across the sky (Josh 10:12–14) provides a symbolic (and exploitative) show of divine supremacy, following the example of Moses and Aaron before Pharaoh of course, but this time between the god of Abraham and the sun/moon-deities of the Amorites. "Put away the gods that your ancestors served beyond the River and in Egypt, and serve the Lord" (Josh 24:14); Joshua instructs the tribes who follow him to Shechem, where all contact with the religion of Moses and Aaron is severed. The concept of the Sinai covenant is nevertheless retained, reiterated, and re-codified for the people who see themselves as the true Remnant of Israel, the Samaritans.

The schism of the tribes is effectively finalized by the fact that although Joshua and Eleazar are both buried in the "hill country of Ephraim," Joshua is buried in Timnath-serah and Eleazar is buried in Gibeah, a town allotted to Benjamin. The north/south divide is also symbolically depicted in Num 26:63–5, where Caleb of Judah and Joshua of Joseph are reputed to be the only members of the Sinai enrolment to enter the Promised Land. As it is elsewhere recorded that Eleazar and Ithamar (at least) also enter the territory, what must be concluded is that the legend of Caleb and Joshua is intended as a representation of the inevitable tribal division.

So, it is Joshua the Josephite, not Eleazar, who is hand-chosen by God to replace Moses. It is Joshua, the Ephraimite, who is granted an audience with the divine and the honour of leading his people into the land of their inheritance.

It is on this allegiance to the original religion of Abraham, Isaac, and Jacob, preserved through the Remnant of Joseph, that the Samaritans base their claim to primacy. The Taheb figure, their messiah, is said to live to 110 years old, the same age as both Joseph and Joshua when they died, supposedly. In symbolic numerology, this threefold repetition represents perfection, a neat, cyclical fulfilment: Joseph represents the patriarchs, Joshua the new beginning after the split from Egypt, and the *anticipated* Josephite, the Messiah ben Joseph, will be the culmination of the present world order and the beginning of the new priestly kingdom, which is just what the FG is all about. There will be a new schism, a new covenant in the North and, most importantly, an in-gathering of the faithful that will reverse the scattering of Israel and bring them to the true Promised Land.

> *Judah became prominent ... and a ruler came from him,*
> *yet the birthright belonged to Joseph.*
> 1 Chr 5:2

> *God sent me ... to preserve for you a remnant on earth ... Joseph.*
> Gen 45:5, 7

> *It may be that the Lord, the God of hosts, will be*
> *gracious to the remnant of Joseph*
> Amos 5:15

Messiah ben Joseph Tradition

Sometime *after* the events that founded the Christian faith, another messianic phenomenon arose, i.e., the complex Messiah ben Joseph tradition. The earliest reference to this specific tradition is in the third century CE Talmud (Succah 52a). This cites Zech 8:6 (which mentions the Remnant) and 12:10 (which mentions the "firstborn" and being "pierced through"). Midrash fragments refer to Gen 30:24, relating to Rachel who, on giving birth to Joseph, entreated God that she have another son; this is thought to be a prophecy concerning a future Josephite messiah. The Midrash also points to Deut 33:17, the blessing conferred upon Joseph that "majesty" will be his.

This is the main gist of the Messiah ben Joseph, or more specifically, the Messiah ben Ephraim expectation (bear in mind it grew over the centuries from a few short sentences to quite a detailed description):

★ He would arise from the children of Joseph but would live in Jerusalem.

★ He would perform many signs while gathering the nation, a gathering which would start in Upper Galilee, though many of Israel would be scattered and unaware of his coming.

★ He would be responsible for the downfall of the procurator of the King of Edom.

★ His followers would rally around him but many would be killed in a conflict with occupying forces, otherwise known as Armilus (later referred to as the Antichrist).

★ He would be slain by Armilus but would be revived by the Messiah ben David (after his body had been left in the streets for 40 days, with nothing unclean touching him).

★ He is referred to as Messiah, Son of God, Son of Joseph, King of Israel, Messenger of the Lord, and Comforter.

★ In some versions of the legend he is a suffering messiah, e.g., he is said to await his divine calling at the gates of Rome, winding and unwinding the bandages of the sick and poor. He is said to be wounded because of our transgressions.

★ In others, he is the military messiah anointed for battle, come to prepare Israel for the advent of the Davidic messiah.

Remember, these are ideas from Jewish, not Christian texts. What seems to have happened is that many, unconvinced *during* Jesus' active campaign, were soon so impressed by his uncanny timing and political impact (you will see what I mean), that they assumed he *must* have been a 'man of God' all along but they had missed the 'signs'. In fact, one document tries to justify this apparent messiah's death:

> And when Messiah ben Joseph and all the people with him will dwell in Jerusalem, Armilus ... will go up and wage war against Israel, and will defeat Messiah ben Joseph and his people, and will kill many of them, and will capture others, and divide their booty .... And he will slay Messiah ben Joseph and it will be a great calamity for Israel.... Why will permission be granted to Armilus to slay Messiah ben Joseph? In order that the heart of those of Israel who have no faith should break, and so they will say: "This is the man for whom we

have hoped; now he came and was killed and no redemption is left for us" ... they will leave the covenant of Israel, and attach themselves to the nations, and the latter will kill them.

Hai Gaon, Responsum, Hai ben Sherira, 939–1038 CE

Several things to note here:

★ This passage seems to infer that the rise of the Christians was due to a schism after the Messiah ben Joseph was killed—those who lost faith in the covenant (the new Christians) left the motherland (Israel) and were ultimately persecuted. Does this not imply that ben Sherira equated Jesus with the Messiah ben Joseph?

★ The forces that kill the Messiah ben Joseph are said to kill many and take others captive, dividing the booty between them. The first half of this reference will have to await a later discussion but the latter suggestion echoes the dividing-up of Jesus' garments at the crucifixion.

★ Perhaps the root of this legend stems from a fear that such a significant event had been catastrophically mistaken for just another 'failed messianic contender' leaving a wake of disruption and disappointment. In other words, some Jews later wondered if Jesus *was* a messiah, much like the one anticipated by John and the Essenes, and the prophecy was adapted to include other signs and portents, based on the history of the Jesus phenomenon, lest a future visitation be missed also.

★ The 'procurator of the King of Edom' is an intriguing reference. The royal Herodian family was of Edomite descent[2] and were seen to be if not puppets, certainly protégées of the Roman Senate. When all the various territories of Palestine came under Roman rule in 44 CE, they were redefined as the procuratorial province of Judaea. Before this date, rulers such as Pontius Pilate were called prefects, though Tacitus refers to Pilate as a procurator.[3]

---

[2] The Edomites were the descendants of Esau, Jacob's brother. The tension between the two brothers (see Gen 27) forms the basis of a history of antagonism and confrontation between the Israelites and the Edomites but what was the original dispute about? It concerned the rights of the firstborn, one of the central themes of the FG. Some versions of the Messiah ben Joseph tradition stipulate that he will do battle against the sons of Esau (cf. Obad 1:18).

[3] Pilate was a *praefectus civitatium,* appointed by the governor of a province to rule a part of it; he was of equestrian rank. Procurators were more involved with financial, taxation matters etc., while the prefects were military men in charge of the army, the construction of roads, etc.

★ We must not forget that a messianic hope based on a 'son of Joseph' is recorded in texts found at Qumran and we will have reason to consider this in more detail.

Jesus, Son of Joseph
The name Jesus is the Hellenized form of Joshua (Yeshu/Yeshua) and although this seems a rather obvious thing to say, it does have quite a significant bearing on the overall understanding of the FG. The original Joshua, son of Nun, is of the Josephite house of Ephraim and becomes the right-hand-man and successor to Moses but his name is Hoshea initially, which means "salvation." On the eve of the entry into Canaan, Moses gives Hoshea the commission name Joshua, which means "Yahweh is salvation." The Hebrew verb, *yasha*, from which the name derives, actually means "to remove someone/thing from oppression, distress," and this is *just* what Jesus, the new Joshua, intends to do.

Whether Jesus/Joshua *is* the real name of the chief character in the FG is impossible to say but it serves as a commission name in the narrative and is actually mentioned for the first time only *after* the meeting with John (below), which is, itself, depicted in light of the Joshua tradition. The Jews[4] later say they know of his mother and father; this is not a claim to know them personally but a very direct indication that Jesus' heritage is known. Jesus is explicitly called a "son of Joseph" (John 1:45, 6:42).

After the Babylonian exile, Israelite men often adopted for surnames the names of the patriarchs of the twelve tribes and once the Israelites returned to their homeland, there was an exerted effort to write down all the genealogies for posterity and for the division of properties, etc. Although the northern tribes were never really accepted into the fold down in Judaea, there were some of the tribes of Ephraim and Manasseh (the "sons of Joseph") who lived in and around Jerusalem (1 Chr 9:1–3), so it may be that Jesus ultimately descends from one of these families. Genealogies, however, were kept active and were stored in the archives near the temple right up to the War in 70 CE, when the archives were destroyed.

Jesus is actually called a Samaritan to his face (John 8:48), yet Christian interpretation has handed this down to us as nothing more than a derogatory accusation, for the Samaritans are traditionally reviled by the

---

[4] The term 'Jews' is not meant to disassociate the FG author from the Hebrew tradition, as some interpreters have claimed, but is a commonly made distinction between Samaritans and Jews, used even by the Samaritans themselves, Josephus, and other early historians, e.g., *Ant.* 13.3.4.

Jews.[5] Individuals claiming descent from any of the so-called 'lost' tribes are almost non-existent in the Bible but one in particular stands out, i.e., Anna, the prophetess in Luke 2:36 who belongs to the tribe of Asher, and who heralds the coming of Jesus "to all those ... looking for the redemption of Israel." Here we have a northern prophetess, quite distinctly described in terms of her heritage, claiming not that Jesus is the messiah but that those who wish to see Israel 'redeemed', i.e., in the sight of God, should pay attention.

"Joshua, son of Joseph" is hardly the most Davidic sounding name and there is no hint in the FG of Jesus having affiliations with the tribe of Judah.

Samaritan Perspective

There are a few things about the Samaritans that should be mentioned, though there is not much to tell, as little is known of their ancient history; although about two to three hundred, or so, still live at the base of Mount Gerizim, their religion and literature have been deeply influenced by Islam. Both the Samaritans and the Jews accuse the other of falsifying the scriptures to emphasize primacy, so getting to the core of the Samaritan mentality of Jesus' day is difficult. We do know that their traditional language is Aramaic, written in the archaic Hebrew alphabet. Most pertinent, however, is that they see themselves as the *remnant of the true Israel* (which is supported by a reference in 2 Chr 34:9), calling themselves either Samaritans i.e., *keepers* (of the faith), or Hebrews, rather than Jews, hence the distinction so clearly demonstrated in the FG. Their influence is seen in some of the writings of the Dead Sea Scrolls.

The Samaritans are monotheistic and traditionally refer to their god as El, or Ela, though the more familiar (to us) Yahweh is also used. One aspect that distinguishes a Samaritan from a Jew, however, is the superstition about pronouncing the holy name; the Jews do not invoke the name, while the Samaritans do.

They are a religious community, governed by a high priest and they observe the festivals of Passover, Pentecost, and Tabernacles on Mount Gerizim, the mountain they claim to be the original site chosen by God to be his home. The mountain, according to Samaritan tradition, is the navel of the earth, an oasis in the wilderness; in the end days, rivers of "living waters" will pour out from it. It is the site, they claim, of Jacob's vision of the ladder

---

[5] According to Ezra 4:1–3, the northern tribes are considered adversaries and are prohibited to partake in the construction of the Temple; and in Neh 13:28 the Samaritan priests are considered an abomination to the priesthood of Jerusalem.

to heaven and the site of the sacrifice of Isaac. Beneath its summit, they assert, lies the Ark of the Covenant, buried in a cave, awaiting discovery at the time of the great reunion with God and the coming of the Taheb, or prophet-messiah. The Samaritan version of the Ten Commandments includes the divine order to build this sanctuary at Gerizim but given the rivalry between the northern and southern tribes, such a definitive annotation would seem almost inevitable.

In the FG, we see how Jesus exploits the various festivals to promote his own agenda, emphasizing those "of the Jews" and thereby suggesting he adheres to an alternative calendar. We also learn how he perceives the significance of the Samaritan heritage and what role Gerizim will or won't play in the end days.

The Samaritans adhere only to the law of Torah, the first five books of the Hebrew Bible (HB), though they show an interest in other texts, especially the Book of Joshua, which tells of the original migration of Israelites into Samaria after the Sinai schism. Their claim of descent is from Joseph, through Ephraim and Manasseh, and they refer to themselves as the "sons of Joseph." Jesus is not only called a Samaritan outright in the FG (which he does *not* refute), but the authorities also refer to him as a "son of Joseph," which most interpreters don't think to link to the Samaritan theme. The FG narrative also substantiates the link to Ephraim, though it is cleverly disguised!

Moses, to the Samaritans, is a unique human being, an exalted prophet who is, in essence, a representation of the light of God. As such, he is not truly of this world but has his origins in heaven, with God. He existed before the Creation, and was sent to earth in corporeal form to intercede on behalf of the righteous and deserving. Intercession on behalf of the just is also attributed to the ancestral saints in whom the "light of holiness" acts as a force of inspiration, or prophetic authority; it is handed down from one generation to the next, from Adam, through Abraham, Isaac, Jacob, Moses, Joshua, etc. A subtler theme, perhaps, this concept of a hereditary authority, or sanction, does prove integral to the story of Jesus' mission as it unfolds.

The Samaritans also believe that there has been a time of favour and a time of wrath; they were in God's favour for only about two-hundred and sixty years, and have been suffering his wrath ever since. They do anticipate a final judgement day, however, when rewards and punishments will be dealt out, and the Remnant will be reinstated. The righteous will wear fine garments and will smell of sweet perfume, while the wicked will be in rags and will stench, i.e., their fate is to be relegated to the devouring fire where Cain, the murderer, is said to dwell. The strongest allusion to this ideology, of course, comes in the FG scene where Martha visits the tomb of Lazarus and anticipates a "stench," perhaps alluding to some sort of guilt attributed to him.

I suggest that Jesus is, indeed, a true "son of Joseph," i.e., a Samaritan. His genealogy, so often an issue of debate in the early Christian writings, is deemed suspicious because he is not of Judaean birth, which makes him, automatically, an outsider, if not an enemy of the Judaean clans in Jerusalem (and as such, not a Davidic messiah). He dares to confront and challenge the Judaean authorities from the perspective of a disdained Samaritan, provoking ridicule and name-calling, evidence for which is found not only in the FG (John 8:48) but also in extra-biblical texts, where his Samaritan roots are used against him (see Appendices).[6]

It is worth noting how uncanny the Messiah ben Joseph tradition seems in retrospect, yet how little attention Christian scholarship has afforded it. With a new perspective, perhaps the mystery of Jesus' non-Davidic, pro-Samaritan depiction in the FG can be better understood.

Remnant and Priesthood

Perhaps the most dramatic and obvious goal for Jesus, which is fairly widely accepted, is the denunciation of the Judaean priestly cultus that dominates, indeed controls the Israelite nation via the temple, and of its associated rituals, rules, and traditions. Rather than breaking away from the faith of his forefathers to create what we now know to be Christianity, Jesus' intention is to highlight the distinction between Jewish and Samaritan faith, a distinction that proves both crucial and provocative. That is not to say he wants to negate all that is Jewish and impose a purely Samaritan ideal; rather, he wants to demonstrate how the two factions must find common ground, if the children of Abraham are ever to find peace and know freedom again. This common ground is to be reached through Jesus, via the Remnant.

The entire mission Jesus embarks upon, according to the FG, is one that is rooted in the eventual reunion of the twelve tribes, the withdrawal from worship from both the temple at Jerusalem *and* the site on Mount Gerizim, and the return of the sanctified, pure priesthood, along with all the sacred accoutrements, *including the Ark,* to the last site of authentic, Josephite-led devotion, i.e., Shiloh.

Worshipping the "Father in spirit and truth" (Jesus' comment to the Samaritan woman in John 4:23) is thus simply a rephrasing of Joshua's order at Shechem to "revere the Lord, and serve him in sincerity and faithfulness," which is to be done by putting away the gods of the ancestors, destroying

---

[6] The *Toledot Yeshu*, an alternative 'history' of Jesus (see Appendices, 3C) suggests the interest in Jesus' genealogy is based on the Jewish claim that he was born of an adulteress who was menstruating.

the idols and altars, etc. (Josh 24:14). Only the tabernacle and the Ark are to be the physical foci/loci of worship.

The concept of the Remnant, as we have seen, has its foundation in the legend of the exodus and was originally predominantly a north/south division. Over time, however, the Remnant was scattered and disowned by the dominant Judeans. Followers of the original non-Egyptian, Abrahamic/Josephite faith, be they converts from among the Jews, Samaritans, or believers lost in the diaspora, these are Jesus' congregation, his flock. The priesthood he will inaugurate is thus not a means of usurping the authority of the temple in Jerusalem, nor does it initiate a new branch of Judaism, let alone a new religion. It is a means of reinstating the *old* religion, the faith of Abraham. Jesus' function as high priest, which becomes evident as the gospel progresses, does not rival that of the extant high priest, it *nullifies* it (symbolically).

This is powerful propaganda and the authorities in Jerusalem soon know precisely what Jesus is doing. It is a revolutionary approach supporting the underdog and offering the long-neglected Remnant a chance to become strong once again, if they unite. Jesus' plan to reinstate Shiloh with its own priestly dynasty is something the Jews in Judaea simply cannot tolerate. His Samaritan heritage is thus brought into the fore in their bid to discredit him and, ultimately, it is this association with Samaria that gets him arrested and crucified.

The Ark

Invoking such a sense of ancient patriotism and long-suppressed religious fervour would naturally spark more enthusiasm amongst the Samaritans than the Jews, for the gospel suggests Jesus *does* know where the Ark is. How else could he hope to return the seat of worship to Shiloh? This is, in part, why he gains such a following in the north: if he can return the Ark to its rightful site, the firstborn (Ephraim) will be reinstated and no longer subject to ridicule and humiliation (there is much more to be said on this, obviously).

There is a slight hitch, though. The Samaritans consider Shiloh somewhat suspect, as they believe the eventual loss of the Ark was the fault of the high priest Eli, who allowed the sacred object to be taken onto the battlefield, where it was seized by the Philistines. Suffering a terrible sickness soon thereafter and thereby believing the object to be cursed, the Philistines returned the Ark not to Shiloh but to Jerusalem, where it would become ensconced in the temple. The northern tribes suffered further alienation and those who maintained that the true sacred site was Mount Gerizim were isolated. So, although Jesus is sympathetic to the Samaritans, he doesn't merely pander to their desire to see Judaea proven wrong—he still has to prove to *them* that his vision of the new kingdom is worth fighting for. The conversion of many Samaritans is made simpler by virtue of the northern primacy issue but is not contingent upon Jesus' promising to acknowledge Gerizim as the home of the Ark and thus the divinely ordained kingdom. This is vital to understanding why certain repercussions occur and to locating references to Jesus' movement in certain extra-biblical texts. (We should also be aware of the fact that the term used to define the Ark of the Covenant, *arown*, is also used in Gen 50:26 to define the "coffin" [ossuary] in which Joseph's bones are interred and later buried. Perhaps this isn't such a coincidence.)

Kingship

The FG thus implies that Jesus fulfils the Genesis prophecy concerning the advent of a Josephite messiah, i.e., Gen 30:24 (where Rachel requests another son). A second prophecy, and one far more profound and specific, is fundamental to the theology of the FG: "The sceptre shall not depart from Judah, nor the ruler's staff from between his feet, *until tribute comes to him and the obedience of his people is his*" (Gen 49:10). The English translation loses what is most significant about this short stanza. In fact, it makes it rather awkward, for it infers that Judah will lose the position as ruler when tribute is made to him; it doesn't make sense. In the Hebrew/Syriac versions, however, the phrase "until tribute comes to him" is rendered, remarkably, as "until *Shiloh* comes," "until he comes to *Shiloh,*" or "until he comes to whom it belongs" (i.e., the ruler's sceptre). This *does* suggest a future fall of the ruler of Judah in some connection with the true ruler returning to Shiloh!

When Ezekiel is commissioned to preach against the sanctuaries in Jerusalem, he warns that Judah will be destroyed, the "turban" and the "crown" removed "until he comes whose right it is" (Ezek 21:26–27); to this mysterious figure God will give the kingdom. The turban could be seen as the representation of the priesthood, and the crown of kingship, but in the FG the two concepts are interchangeable, for the priesthood Jesus envisions is also a kingly dynasty, as exemplified by Melchizedek (this will discussed again).

In the FG, Jesus does not reject Nathanael's *tribute* to him as the "King of Israel," though he does reject other impositions and expectations of kingship elsewhere in the narrative. Blend this with the blessings of Jacob and Moses and you can begin to see where Jesus gets his ideas:

> Joseph is a fruitful bough ... shot at ... and pressed ... hard ... by the name of the shepherd ... by the God of your father, who will help you ... the bounties of the everlasting hills; may they be on the head of

Joseph ... who was set apart from his brothers.
Gen 49:22–6

Blessed ... be his land, with the choice gifts of heaven above ... with the rich yield of the months ... and the favour of the one who dwells on Sinai. Let these come on the head of Joseph ... the prince among his brothers ... *firstborn* ... majesty is his!
Deut 33:13–17

Not only would a return to Shiloh act as a reinstatement of ancient Samaritan worship practices and thus qualify as the anticipated act of restoration, it would also give added meaning to Jesus' declaration that "the ruler of this world has been condemned" (John 16:11). The ruler of the world Jesus speaks of is not the Roman Empire, nor Satan, as some would suggest but the corrupt seat of Judah, the usurper, the body of Israelites who travelled south from Sinai. The legitimate royal seat is at Shiloh (2 Kgs 15:13–14), so only a return to that site will fulfil prophecy and complete Jesus' mission.

It will be prudent to bear in mind throughout this analysis that the common translation of Shiloh is "peaceable or pacific" and "gift of God"; the symbolic numerical value given to the Hebrew letters forming the word Shiloh (i.e., its gematria) is equal to that given to the word "messiah."

2
THE MEETING NEAR QUMRAN

VERSES 1:1–18 OF THE FG constitute a Prologue which appears to be from a different hand, written some time after the events of the ensuing narrative; these shall be discussed at the end of the investigation. The FG 'proper' begins at 1:19, with the meeting of John and Jesus on the dry salt plains near Qumran.

John appears only briefly in the FG; he is said to *be* baptising which, in the Greek, means "to make overwhelmed; to wash, to immerse in water." His presence, though, is essential not to the theological message (for any character, actually, could say what he says) but to the *historical* background of the FG narrative, which becomes evident only much later.[1] The Greek for John, *Ioannes*, is derived from the Hebrew, *Yehowchanan*, which means "Jehovah favours"; *chanan*, which generally means "to show favour," stems from *chanah*, "to decline, grow to an end." John is heard to say in John 3:30: "He must increase, but I must decrease."

John "that was called the Baptist" appears in Josephus' writings only once (*Ant.* 18.5.2); the passage should be treated with the same discretion as those concerning Jesus, for it is a little too convenient, yet it contains intriguing details that suggest an original, authentic core to the scenario. It interjects the story of the fall of Herod at such an opportune moment, i.e., between the introduction of Herodias and her illicit union with Herod, and Tiberius' ordering of the head of Aretas, the King of Arabia. Josephus goes on to relate how, although Herod's defeat in battle against Aretas was caused by the "treachery of some fugitives," many Jews considered his downfall to

---

[1] An interesting PhD dissertation offers the following insight: "Jesus' own praise of John as recorded in the Fourth Gospel is very grudging when compared with that given in the Synoptics ... So violent is the opposition of the fourth Evangelist to John that he will not even allow that he is Elijah" (Joseph Carter Swaim, 1931, *The Historical Character of the Fourth Gospel*, Candidate for the degree of Doctor of Philosophy in Theology University of Edinburgh, 132). I posit that there are *specific grounds* for the FG's lack of overt support for John that really only make sense once the FG is re-examined.

be the result of his slaying of John.[2]

The account in *Antiquities* suggests that John had a remarkable hold over masses of people who would, seemingly, do just about anything for him, so where is this affirmed in the New Testament? Yes, he has followers but one doesn't get the impression his group is of any real threat to Herod, who, we are told, actively seeks John's death to avoid public mischief. In the FG, emissaries are sent from the authorities in Jerusalem to sound John out but is this really a precursor to his assassination? In Josephus' writing there is no explicit mention of John's alleged beheading, or the confrontation concerning Herod's new wife, suggesting either his unfamiliarity with the tradition on this matter, or that subsequent Christian writers inserted the account of the 'Baptist' at this point (which I think is more likely).

With the strengthening *modern* theory that John did have a connection to the Essenes, it seems strange that Josephus, having sampled life in the Essene community before choosing to become a Pharisee (*Life*, 2), never mentions this apparently awe-inspiring gentleman in any of his accounts of the Essenes, whom he praises consistently but rather, relegates him to a sub-story about Herod. This acts against the passage being genuine. So, too, the claim that some of the Jews considered Herod's downfall as divine justice for the slaying of John; after all Herod had done to build up such an ill reputation, the one thing this Romanized historian recounts so emphatically, in terms of retribution, is his involvement in the death of Jesus' predecessor? It is just too neat.

When John first makes himself heard, in John 1:23, he is declaring that he is the embodiment of the figure alluded to in Isa 40:3, i.e., "the voice crying out in the wilderness, 'Make straight the way of the Lord.'" The context of Isaiah 40 is one of an anticipated deliverance from oppression and captivity for those who attend the 'word' of God and have patience in awaiting his support. The wilderness imagery is significant, representing not only a geographical setting but also the state in which the captives exist, i.e., in a spiritual wilderness. Recall that in Exod 17:1 the Israelites are said to wander in the Wilderness of Sin (Zin) for an entire generation, in a symbolic purging of one life and preparation for another; in Hosea (2:14) the vision of the restoration of Israel is in the context of a wilderness. For Jesus' own mission to have its foundation in the desert helps to signify what kind of mission it is and gives it the air of legitimacy it requires.

---

[2] In *Ant.* 18.7.2, Josephus suggests that God punished Herod for "giving ear to the vain discourses of a woman," i.e., Herodius. In other words, he was not a politic ruler. This sounds more like a rather obsequious Josephus, pandering to Roman sentiments!

Suffering Servant

The Jews send out emissaries (priests and Levites) to enquire about John's intentions. Already we get a sense of insecurity back in Jerusalem. Who is this man?

Although I have explained that there is an intentional distinction made between Jews and Samaritans, the FG takes this one step further. By "Jews" the FG often implies a certain *section* of the Jewish people, i.e., the leaders, the decision-makers, the priests, Levites, Pharisees, scribes. When it mentions others, it uses phrases like "the world" or "crowd." From this conglomerate of authority, and specifically the Pharisees, some priests and Levites are sent to discover what all the fuss is about out here in the desert.

Unable to comprehend why John is preaching redemption, if he is not one of the three agents of God promised to Israel (the Davidic messiah; Elijah, the prophet; or the prophet "from their own people" mentioned in Deut 18:18), they demand explanation, which John provides in a sort of code: "Among you stands one whom you do not know, the one who is coming after me" (John 1:26). In the precedent of Isa 40:3, the 'one' who comes after is the "suffering servant," the figure Christianity has identified with Jesus.

The "suffering servant" discussion is too lengthy and convoluted to present fully here but a few things do need mentioning. For instance, there are at least *two* servants mentioned in Isaiah, i.e., this one, who is seemingly portrayed both as Israel *and* as an individual, and an earlier one, Eliakim son of Hilkiah (Isa 22:20). Eliakim *is* associated with the house of David but the servant who first appears in Isa 41:8 is simply referred to as "the offspring of Abraham." What makes Isaiah's "servant" significant to John's declaration in the FG is the fact that he will:

come from the north[3]
(Jesus comes from Galilee/Samaria)

exist, in essence, from the beginning of time
("before Abraham I am")

be granted the divine spirit
("I saw the Spirit descending")

---

[3] There is a serious ongoing debate concerning the north verses east direction for the coming of the "servant"; some scholars argue this character is the Persian King Cyrus, who is mentioned elsewhere as a servant (military tool) of God, but others claim the Hebrew text has to be adjusted to make the "east" designation work, as Cyrus advanced southward to Babylon, not westward.

be a "light to the nations"
("I am the light of the world")

make the blind see, and release prisoners
(blind man/Lazarus)

have his sins redeemed
(discussion on 'purity' in John 3)

glorify God
(his 'works' glorify the Father)

'raise up' the tribes of Jacob and bring them back to God
('raising' of Lazarus / 'gathering' of the sheep)

be "lifted up and shall be very high"
(lifted up as King of Israel/ascending to the Father)

come from an unlikely place
("can anything good come out of Nazareth?")

be granted a "portion with the great"
(will be 'glorified')

These may seem to pertain to an individual but, especially once other information becomes apparent, each can also allude to the Remnant of Israel. In Isaiah 53, the passage in which Christianity is primarily interested, the 'servant' is compared to a young plant, a "root out of dry ground," just as the Remnant is so envisioned elsewhere in the OT *and* in the FG. The servant, although despised and rejected, crushed by the iniquities of others and taken away by a perversion of justice, somehow rises to a new status ("Who could have imagined his future?") because he "pours out himself to death." This phrase actually implies that he "pours his *soul* out to death," which seems to indicate a spiritual, rather than a physical death, for it is not clearly stated that the 'servant' *physically* dies.

The grave and tomb references pertain to the actions of the servant's oppressors: "*they*" make his grave with the wicked, etc., and this apparently is the will of God *but* there is a twist: "When you make his life an offering for sin, *he shall see his offspring, and shall prolong his days*" (Isa 53:9). In other words, ***the suffering servant survives*!**

Making intercession for others, a significant aspect of the Samaritan saints and also Jesus, of course, can only be done by the righteous and the

Remnant *are* the righteous. Samaria, in the FG (as will become clear), is the rightful home of the Remnant and *it* has all the qualities of the 'suffering servant', for it, too, is (effectively) "cut off from the land of the living," despised, and held "of no account." The Remnant will, eventually, be "allotted a portion with the great" just as the individual 'servant' will receive his glorification.

The idea doesn't end with Isaiah 53 but continues straight into 54, with the concept of the Bride of God and her return to glory, i.e., the subsequent major step in the FG narrative, also. So, although Christianity tends to focus on the suffering and (apparent but not fulfilled) death imagery, this multi-faceted personification of the devout Israel and each of these anticipated eventualities are paralleled in the FG.

What John is saying, then, is that someone from the north has been divinely chosen to re-establish the righteous as God's elect—but John isn't the one. Jesus "ranks ahead" of him because he is "before him." The eternal "light of heaven" that is sent to imbue God's chosen one is part of both the Samaritan belief system and the description of the servant.[4]

Bethany

John is said to be baptising in a place called Bethany, which means a "house of affliction." This is the first example of the duality of names I mentioned earlier, for there are two Bethanys within the FG, i.e., this one (in John 1:28) and the one mentioned in 11:1 as the home of Lazarus. The subtle allusion to "affliction" is significant and intentional, making the name, potentially, a commission name invented for the FG narrative (and adopted for the subsequent Synoptics). In the first case, John's declaration concerning the voice in the wilderness relates to Isaiah 40, where the "voice" heralds the advent of divine favour and the spiritual healing of the nation after the devastation of the exile; in the second, Bethany is the home of the man who is first said to be "sick" then "dead." The former implies a "wilderness" setting, the latter a village near Jerusalem.

However, there is a somewhat confusing history concerning this name. The Christian theologian Origen (c.185–253 CE) argued that although the earliest manuscripts he had read did, indeed, say "Bethany," no such site could be found "across the Jordon" in his day; there was a local legend pertaining to one called Bethabara, however, where John was said to have baptised. The debate continues but I suggest the name Bethany is a commissioned place name anticipating the symbolism that is yet to reveal

---

[4] Moses is God's 'servant' (Num 12:7), as is a prophet in the general sense, e.g., Amos 3:7.

itself in the gospel—and this is directly linked to Lazarus, so the duality within the narrative will prove deliberate, even if the geographical site bore an alternative name.

There is a Beth-barah in Judg 7:24, for instance, where Gideon is fighting the Midianites in Lower Galilee; he sends messengers down to the Ephraimites to "seize the waters" against the enemy as far as Beth-barah and the Jordan, the south-east boundary of their territory, near the tip of the Dead Sea. This is corroborated by a place called Beth-arabah, in Josh 15:61 and 18:18, which is listed as being close to the "City of Salt." At the junction of the River Jordan and the tip of the Dead Sea lies a large, sterile salt flat, i.e., a true wilderness.

On the other side of the River Jordan (where John is) is the Abarim range (the Beyond Mountains) i.e., the end of the Wilderness of Sin (Zin) and the end of the exodus, at least for Moses. One can see the famous Mount Nebo from the salt flats. He is told by God to climb to the top of this range so that he can see the Promised Land, after which he will die. Before dying, however, Moses is to commission someone to lead the people (Exod 27:17); he is to "lay his hand" on the man "in whom is the spirit" and thus give him authority. This someone is Joshua, son of Nun. This is precisely what *seems* to happen to Jesus, our Joshua, son of Joseph, i.e., there is a definitive recognition and transference of authority. So, Bethany, aka Bethabara, is a perfect setting to open the narrative of the FG, where Jesus receives his divine commission in the same land his predecessor took his commission from Moses.

An intriguing, almost imperceptible reference to this area comes in Ezek 39:11; Ezekiel is told by God that when Israel is restored and the old age has come to an end, the oppressors and invaders of Israel (under the name Gog) will be destroyed, and that the Israelites will have to search for their bodies for seven months, cleansing the land of its defilement. The place where all these bodies will be buried is called the Valley of the Travellers or, 'Valley of the Abarim', east of the sea. Thus, the site of Abarim becomes the "sign" (39:15) of Israel's victory over its oppressors—a powerful political concept that Jesus is all too aware of.

As well as on Isaiah however, John's response to his visitors is founded on Jer 17:5–6, where it is stated that those who put their faith in 'mortal' leaders are led into a wilderness and will be unable to "see when relief comes." The representatives of the temple institution have been led into a wilderness that is both physical (they have been 'sent' into it) and metaphorical (the spiritual wilderness created by ineffectual and illegitimate leaders); they can't even see that relief is needed, let alone who will bring it! Among them stands one they do not know, they don't recognise: what can this mean, on a practical level?

Jesus doesn't actually appear at Bethany until the next day; he is in the vicinity of Jerusalem. This is why he is said to be 'amongst' them, i.e., the priests and Levites, not physically, right then and there but *dwelling* amongst them; he is the one they 'do not know' (do not *recognise*) because he is a Josephite. (Remember, according to the post-Jesus Messiah ben Joseph tradition, the chosen one would be a Josephite, living in Jerusalem). A Josephite cannot be a priest of the temple, yet in John's strange statement, there is the insinuation that *he* recognises Jesus as a priest and it is to *this* the confirmation in John 3 relates (discussed at that juncture).

What we also need to be aware of is the fact that in the FG Jesus *does not* receive any form of baptism *from* John. Look at the sequence of events in the scene: John is questioned, he sees Jesus coming and declares him the "lamb of God"; he testifies that he saw the Spirit descend upon Jesus, and that he was told by "the one who sent" him to baptise that this conferring of the Spirit would be the sign of the one who would be "revealed to Israel." Thus, John is apparently *not* intimately familiar with Jesus (which forces us to question the familial relationship that is traditionally accepted, i.e., as cousins), and there is *no* intimate baptismal scene between Jesus and John.

Who is "the one who sent" John to "baptise"? If John is a leading figure at Qumran, who would have the authority to order him to the other side of the Jordon to perform this rite? Does he mean God told him? Why not say that, for authority; why be evasive? Retaining the cultural context of the scene, however, the act of 'baptising with water', rendered using the Greek verb *baptizó*, actually implies a very Jewish spiritual-purification ritual, i.e., the ceremonial dipping of the body in the mikvah. Mikvot (plural) are most efficacious when the waters are naturally flowing (called "living waters" in the Mishnah [Mik. 1:1–8]), hence the Jordan River is the best mikvah (this anticipates the FG's scene with the "blind man" in John 9). As the investigation proceeds, it becomes evident that it may be Jesus himself who instigates this meeting with John; he proves to have 'friends in high places' who are able to pull strings in the background.

Twice, John declares that he does not "know" Jesus, and with the added statement that the emissaries do not know him, this is a threefold (here, negative) declaration, a motif that permeates the FG and one that will come to influence the reader's understanding of the relationship between Jesus and John.

One of the most familiar connections between Jesus and Isaiah's servant is John's designation of Jesus as "the lamb of God who takes away the sin of the world" and Isaiah's servant being "like a lamb that is led to the slaughter" who bears "the sin of many" (Isa 53:7, 12). In both instances, "sin" is singular and refers to a communal state; it is not, as some assume, the sins of each of us against one another but the sin of the *nation* against

God. It is the sin of illicit worship, of pride, of deception, in full knowledge of the divine Law.

Jesus' identification with the 'lamb' has two potential implications. One is fairly conventional, suggesting a connection to the Passover animal because Jesus is crucified at this time of year, which would make John's speech a true prophecy. John, however, is not a prophet; he is a priest who preaches *concerning* prophecy. Also, the original wording for the Passover animal in Exod 12:5 (LXX) is *probaton* (sheep), not *amnos* (lamb), as in the FG. Some scholars, regardless, take this passage to imply that John must be baptising in April, around the time of the Passover. I don't think this is justifiable and will provide further argument, in due course.

John's words simply mean: "This is the man who will redeem Israel." The 'lamb' reference, along with John's own claim to being the one who heralds the servant, identifies Jesus as the embodiment of this mysterious character from Isaiah, the suffering servant. The 'lamb to slaughter' imagery in Isaiah 53, recall, culminates in the *survival* and elevation of the servant, *not* in him being sacrificed; the simile is used by Isaiah to describe the "silence" of the servant during his ordeal (just as Jesus remains silent when being interrogated by Pilate). The *Brown-Driver-Briggs Hebrew and English Lexicon* states that in Isaiah 53, the term is not intended as a "sin-offering" (as per the NRSV) but as a self-offering of the servant "in compensation for the sins of the people, interposing for them as their substitute." It is not the same thing. We will see this reflected in the Jesus-Barabbas scenario.

The Passover sacrifice does not expiate sins. It is a commemoration of *redemption* from spiritual slavery, as the first event had been, back in Egypt, where the blood of the animal was brushed over the doors of the Israelites to protect them from death. Only in *this* context would the Passover lamb concept make sense and this *does* have an unusual bearing on Jesus' arrest and crucifixion but this *isn't* what John says (see "Temple Business" in Chapter 18).

An offering specifically to ameliorate sin/guilt is never stipulated as being a male lamb. If the congregation or the anointed priest sins, the sacrifice must be a bull; for everyone else a *female* sheep or goat, or two birds (if the people are poor), according to Leviticus 4. The beast that actually 'takes away' the sin of the nation is an adult male *goat* which, on the Day of Atonement, is released into the desert after the high priest has laid his hands upon it, transferring the guilt of the congregation—*a second goat is offered up as a sacrifice* (Lev 16). It is in this context that the allusion to Jesus' *expiation* of sins will be found and in this context the crucifixion scene will reveal its most dramatic secret.

Son of God

Very generally speaking, the Qumran community anticipate a messiah of Aaron, a high-priestly messiah, as well as a lay, or temporal messiah of Israel but in some of the DSS texts the description seems to combine the two, making it appear that they expect one messiah, who is both priestly *and* 'of Israel' (i.e., of the northern tribes).

The sign of Jesus' commission comes down from heaven like a dove (John 1:32) but a metaphorical dove, for such is the traditional symbol of God's beloved, Israel (e.g., Isa 60:8; Hos 11:11; Ps 74:19, and 2 Esd 5:26). According to Exod 4:22–3 and Hos 11:1, Israel is God's symbolic 'son', his legal representative on earth (i.e., not meant as "offspring"); by associating Jesus with the symbol of the dove coming to rest upon him, the implication is made that Jesus is God's chosen representative, his authorized agent. Both Joseph and Ephraim were hand-chosen by God to become the symbolic *firstborn*. The dove, the 'spirit' of God, is simply a metaphor for the laying of the hand on the head in a ritualistic election, e.g., "Israel stretched out his right hand and laid it on the head of Ephraim" (Gen 48:14).

A son, according to the apocryphal Sir 30:4–6, is a continuation or reflection of the father; he is a living memory of a father who dies, or is absent; he takes on the role of avenger and benefactor in his father's absence. As the representative son of God, Jesus becomes the authority *within* Israel, amongst the "children of God" (Deut 14:1). As Solomon is supposedly chosen by God to be his son for the sole purpose building the temple (1 Chr 28:6), so Jesus is made a son by virtue of his (perceived) divine authority to raise up a purified priesthood and re-establish worship in the true house of God. This won't be the last time such a parallel is drawn between Jesus and Solomon. This is the moment of recognition of the divine 'spirit' that imbues Jesus with the authority he will claim in the subsequent narrative; following in the footsteps of Moses and Joshua, Jesus is seen as receiving the "light of heaven."

More germane to the Jews' perception of Jesus is the use of "son of God" to imply kingly descent, as prescribed in 2 Sam 7:14. This will crop up again during the discussion of Jesus' arrest.

Unnamed Initiate

Perhaps the most intriguing of the initial characters of the FG is the unnamed companion of Andrew. All we learn of him is that he is initially a disciple of John (John 1:35). Even his apparent claim to recognise Jesus as an authoritative figure (by calling him "Rabbi" in 1:38) is somewhat of a red herring for he speaks in unison with his companion, concealed in the anonymity. The only other instance of one disciple appearing in close connection with another, while remaining so explicitly incognito, is in John 18:15, where it is implied that this shadowy character is actually known to the high priest. In 20:2 however, another unnamed disciple is verified as the "one whom Jesus loved," purposefully distinguishing him from the character in John 1 and 18.

A very common symbolic technique, be it literary or visual, is to represent ignorance, evil, or the potential for either, by referring to darkness, furtiveness, mystery, etc. The elusive trial of Jesus in John 18:3f is held at night; Josephus tells of Pilate's desecration of the temple occurring during the dark hours (*Ant.* 8.3.1); under the cover of darkness come murderers and thieves (Job 24:14); and it is a general maxim that one must be on one's guard for trouble at night (Ps 119:148). The FG author intends for his readers to be on their guard with respect to this mysterious figure, whose nature is so obviously concealed, first by the lack of a name, then by the ambiguous recognition of Jesus, and finally by the nocturnal events of John 18. His identity becomes evident later in the FG narrative but, like Jesus, we are not supposed to recognise him yet.

Andrew
Along with the unnamed disciple comes Andrew, of whom also very little is related, other than that he is the "brother" of Peter, and that he, along with Peter and Philip, is from the town of Bethsaida. Andrew and the unnamed man are directed by John to go to Jesus and the two remain with their new leader for a day of enlightenment. Andrew, it should be noted, introduces Peter to the group and it is with Peter that the unnamed disciple is connected in John 18:15. In effect, Andrew acts as a mediator, a general assistant or messenger in the narrative, i.e., he introduces Peter, he raises the question of Jesus' identity (1:41), he is the disciple through whom the feeding in John 6 is finally initiated, and in 12:22 he is the one Philip approaches with the request to introduce the Greeks to Jesus.

A subtle pattern arises when we compare the fate of Jesus' associates who have singular Greek names, with those who bear more traditional Hebrew names: the former tend to fade out of the narrative, the latter prove to be highly significant. "Andrew" is a Greek name (meaning "virile, manly") and, like Philip's, his is a very mundane nature. The theological complexity of Jesus' mission proves to be too much for this disciple and he gradually disappears from the main plot of the narrative, though he serves his purpose.

Jesus' disciples, most interpreters agree, represent the twelve tribes of Israel, so each *should* provide us with a clue as to which tribe he represents. I'm not implying that each individual's genealogy is traced to confirm heritage before Jesus takes them on (though this is a possibility). It is a symbolic gesture that helps to create the *impression* of the high priest, who wears the symbols of the twelve tribes upon his chest, in the form of twelve stones. This representation can take the form of ideology, traits, or actions.

The Greek name Andrew does, ultimately, derive from the Hebrew term, *'aner* (meaning "young man") and there are only two precedents for this name in the OT. The only person named Aner is an Amorite, one of three brothers who are allies to Abraham; this is fitting (if we substitute Jesus for Abraham, which is actually hinted at in the gospel, and Andrew, Peter, and the unnamed disciple as the three 'brothers').

The other Aner is a place, mentioned in 1 Chr 6:70: though originally within the land allotted to the half-tribe of Manasseh, it is actually given to the Kohathites, who are of the tribe of Levi. Andrew, then, may be affiliated with the tribe of Levi and although this seems an arbitrary interpretation of his name, it proves to have further support in the symbolic representation of the *other* characters, as we shall see.

Together, then, Jesus, the unnamed disciple, and Andrew effectively echo the situation at Sinai, with Eleazar, Joshua, and Caleb as their parallel characters in the OT. Eleazar and Andrew are Levites, Caleb and the unnamed disciple are of the tribe of Judah (bear with me for a while), and Joshua and Jesus are Josephites.

Combined with the *site* of John's baptising, we get a clear allusion to the end of the exodus and the imminent entry into a new Promised Land.

Peter

The third disciple to be introduced in John 1 is Simon Peter. He has both Greek and Hebrew names, so his fate is more complicated. He is brought to Jesus, quite without ceremony, by his brother Andrew. "Brother," though, may mean blood-relative, something analogous to 'kin', or simply that the two men are from the same town. Elsewhere in the NT, "brothers" is used to indicate fellow believers. The point is, Simon Peter is to be affiliated with *Andrew* in some way, rather than with Philip.

"Simon" derives from the Hebrew name Simeon, the *second* son of Jacob, i.e., *not the firstborn*. He *is* the brother of Levi (represented by Andrew). Simeon is rebellious and impressionable (Gen 34:25–30) and his descendants become strongly associated with the tribe of Judah (Judg 1:3), eventually becoming the weakest of all the tribes and *this will become a significant factor in the FG story, so it is worth remembering*. Peter and Andrew are 'brothers' I submit, by virtue of their mutual priestly profession, as mentioned in the discussion on Bethsaida, below. "Simon" also stems from the Hebrew word *shama*, meaning "to hear attentively" that is, to understand, obey, etc., and this, too, becomes a major factor of Peter's subsequent depiction.

This disciple, in fact, has *four* names, i.e., Simon, Peter, Cephas, and in the NRSV translation, "son of John." "You are Simon the son of John. You are to be called Cephas," Jesus states, in the only direct and explicit renaming in the FG (John 1:42), confirming the use of commission names in the gospel. Although "Peter" is, in Greek, *Petros,* and *can* be translated to mean "rock" as in bedrock (a classic interpretation based upon the supposed primacy of Matt 16:18, where Jesus claims that Peter is the rock upon which the Church will be built), this cannot be said of Cephas. The FG makes a vital distinction.

The word *kephas (keph)* is Aramaic and means "a hollow rock." This in turn stems from *kaphaph,* "to curve, bow down." In several OT uses of the *keph/kaphaph* terms what is represented is the humbling action of prostrating oneself before, or 'bowing down to' another, sometimes physically, but usually metaphorically. In the context of Isa 58:5, for instance, it is claimed that outward signs of faith, humbling oneself publicly by bowing down, etc., mean little if, inwardly, one is not sincere; and in Mic 6:6, it is stated that arrogance and ignorance preclude intimacy with God. The term thus implies humility, a humility that must come from complete subjugation and repentance. A strange name to bestow on the supposed leader of the Church, wouldn't you say? There's more.

The FG doesn't *actually* call Peter the "son of John"; in the original Greek, it calls him the "son of Jonah," which makes a profound difference to our understanding of the man. The OT precedent for Jonah is from the book of the same name and as the son must reflect his father (he inherits traits, fulfils expectations, perpetuates identity, just as Jesus does, as the "son of Joseph"), Peter must reflect Jonah in some way.[5]

Jonah is a proud, arrogant man, who initially defies the will of God; he is cast into the belly of the leviathan in order to subdue him, to *impose humility* upon him, so that the intended mission can be carried out (i.e., the conversion of the Ninevites). In this state of bondage Jonah prays to God for deliverance, thus reiterating the need for true repentance in anticipation of freedom from one's own personal prison. Humbled and penitent, Jonah is delivered and he accepts his commission to be a missionary to Nineveh. Jonah, however, rejects the will (i.e., word) of God three times (Jonah 1:2–3; 4:1; 4:9–11); so too will Peter thrice reject Jesus and the word, or will, of God (John 13:38). Like Jonah, Peter must be humbled.

---

[5] Some scholars compare the vision of Peter in Acts 11:1–18 and its ultimate effect on the transformation of Peter's attitude to the inclusion of 'outsiders' into the divine plan to the similar general concept of the Jonah narrative.

Thus, we see the importance of retaining the Greek text of John 1:42. The only other gospel to use "son of Jonah" with respect to Peter is Matthew (16:17), where the common Jewish way of naming is used, i.e., Simon Bar-Jonah. What is interesting about this is the fact that in Matt 12:38f Jesus warns that the "sign of Jonah" will be the only sign Jesus will show the Pharisees, i.e., the *necessary* rejection of arrogance and pride. What does the "sign of Jonah" mean to the Pharisees (or to anyone, for that matter)? The answer: "Change your ways, or else!"

Peter's renaming echoes that of Abraham (Gen 17:5) and Jacob (Gen 35:10), in that the name is confirmed by the 'voice' of God; Jesus acts as God's representative in this, the only verbal renaming in the FG. Where both Abraham and Jacob were ideals of unadulterated Israelite piety, however, Peter now represents the Israel of Jesus' day; proud, self-assured, and in danger of losing sight of God in the glare of its own arrogance. This is the 'world' Jesus must overcome if he is to inaugurate the new kingdom.

With this allusion to the humbling of the spirit in order to fully accept the will of God, Peter is the one who *must* "hear attentively" and he is the one who *must* "obey." As the "son of Jonah," he is identified as one who is rebellious and obstinate, and as Cephas he is destined to be disciplined.

> *[P]repare the way, Remove every obstruction*
> *from my people's way.*
> Isa 57:14

Philip

The Greek for "Philip" is *Philippos*, with the prefix *Phil-* meaning "a lover of" and *-ippos* meaning "horse," i.e., "a lover of horses." The first part of the name, *Phil-*, is significant because it surfaces again, in the form of *phileo*, in connection with two other disciples, i.e., Lazarus and Peter.

Philip is from Bethsaida, a village expanded upon by Philip, the brother of Herod Antipas, in whose tetrarchy it lies. It thus has to be on the eastern side of the Jordan. The most popular position for scholars is on the northern tip of the Sea of Galilee (note that this is very close to "Bethany/Bethabara") supposedly because there is a thriving fishing centre there (hence, the name translates as "house of fish") but one has to wonder if this is not a post-Jesus attribution, especially when just at this location, at the juncture of the Little Jordan and the Sea of Galilee, is the ancient town of Ain (Num 34:11); some scholars suggest that Ain became the city of Bethsaida sometime later in its history. I suggest the significance lies in "the house of fish" idea, which links directly to Jesus. In Josh 19:7, however, there is another Ain, said to be in the land allotted to Judah but it is given over to the Simeons. It then becomes a Levitical town provided for the Kohathites, the descendants of Aaron's branch of the Levite tribe, as a specifically priestly town (Josh 21:16).

This is interesting. There are two Ains mentioned in the OT; one seems to be in the north, the other in the south. The FG author *exploits* this traditional ambiguity to serve his own purpose, reiterating the schism of north and south, of Judah and Joseph, of Judaea and Samaria. Andrew emulates the Kohathites (Levites), Peter the Simeons; both are linked in a way that suggests a hereditary affiliation (i.e., "brothers") and both are connected (symbolically) with the priestly aspect of the town.

Philip is the only disciple in John 1 who is sought out and chosen by Jesus; he is "found." This may suggest that Jesus is looking for a protégée of some sort, a second-in-command perhaps, or at least a *special* disciple (and this is supported by subsequent events). Perhaps Jesus knows Philip already; it may be that Philip is actually Jesus' own relative, considering the high expectations, the profound disappointment but continued affection for this character that the FG depicts (which will be revealed in due course). I am willing to bet this is the case; in fact, I shall propose that Philip is Jesus' son. There is no concrete evidence to support this assertion but when you see the patterns I have been seeing for the last thirty years, the familial intimacy becomes obvious. It is my opinion that Philip, the only male disciple to a) earn the bestowal of the special *phileo* word for "love," b) be tested for his suitability for the role of Jesus' right-hand man, and c) be retained within the inner circle right to the end, despite being unsuccessful (to be discussed), is Jesus' initial choice for the heir to the kingdom. *Philip is the firstborn.*

Philip is also the only disciple (except for Peter, in the epilogue of John 21) to whom Jesus directly says, "Follow me." He is the one who finds Nathanael (echoing his own experience of being sought and found), and it is he who declares that the one "about whom Moses in the law and also the prophets wrote," Jesus son of Joseph from Nazareth has been found. This distinction is paramount to the understanding of the FG throughout: Andrew, Peter, and the unnamed disciple all refer to Jesus as "the messiah," to which there is no response on Jesus' part; Philip declares *exactly* what Jesus *wants* him to declare. It is almost as if he has been coached to say this. The phrase actually gives us much of what we need to unlock the gospel, i.e., the Torah, the Prophets, the Samaritan/Josephite connection, and the role Jesus is to play. *However...*

The horse, according to Ps 32:9, is "without understanding," and in Ps 33:17 (and Ps 147:10; Hos 1:7 and 14:3) the horse is associated with the idea of battle against an enemy. God, it is implied, will save Israel *not* by "war, or by horses, or by horsemen" (Hos 1:7); Israel "will not ride upon horses." Philip, associated with the "lovers of horses," both lacks understanding (as we shall see) and is affiliated with the Greeks (see John 12:20f), who also revere the horse as a weapon of war.

For all intents and purposes, then, Philip comes to represent the Israelites who have undergone too profound a change under the Hellenistic influence to revert back to the old way of thinking. The fact that Jesus has to seek him out, only to find he is not cut from the same cloth, reveals a distinct *lack* of divine foresight, also apparent in the (previous) acceptance of the dubious unnamed disciple. This works to depict a very human, fallible Jesus, as the mistake costs him valuable time, forcing him to prolong his stay in the 'world' (amongst the general population) and to rethink his strategy.

Nathanael
Nathanael means "Given of God" (*nathan*, "to give" plus *el*, meaning "god"); it is a Hebrew name. It is Nathanael who is at the centre of John 1:45–51, *not* Jesus; it is Nathanael who questions *Jesus'* significance, reacting to the idea of something 'good' coming from Nazareth with dismay (1:46). Jesus responds by making what some Christian interpreters understand to be a clairvoyant declaration; he claims that he has already seen Nathanael "under the fig tree," before he is called by Philip.

The fig tree in the OT has several interconnected meanings. It describes the ideal of God's protection and mercy (e.g., Jer 24:1–8 and Dan 4:10), the ideal nation (e.g., Joel 1:7, 12), and conveys the idea of peace, prosperity, and unity (1 Kgs 4:25; 1 Macc 14:11–12, etc.). The most profound instance of this theme, as far as the FG is concerned, is that expressed in Zech 3:10, where God promises that *on the day when the old priesthood is cleansed of its iniquities and the new high priest crowned*, each man shall invite his neighbour under his "vine and fig tree," presumably as a sign of harmony and unity. By seeing Nathanael under the fig tree, Jesus is simply assuring him that this ideal time will come, soon.

The imagery of John 1:51 draws on Jacob's vision of the ladder between heaven and earth, upon which the 'angels' are seen ascending and descending (Gen 28:10–17). In this precedent, God declares that he is the god of Abraham and Isaac, he promises prosperity for Jacob's descendants and he confirms the promise of a return of the land to its rightful inheritors, i.e., Jacob and his offspring. God claims that he will be with Jacob and will 'keep' him wherever he goes until the promise is fulfilled. Jacob responds to this dream by pronouncing that God has become manifest at the site and that it truly is the "the gate of heaven." He seems surprised at his own ignorance of the sanctity of the place (Bethel, in what is later Samaria).

Comparing this to the FG, the similarities become clear: Nathanael is promised a vision paralleling Jacob's; he reflects Jacob's astonishment and subsequent conviction; after his encounter he reacts in a respectful and devout manner; and his exclamation, "you are the Son of God," echoes Jacob's affirmation of God's presence (in this case, through Jesus).

Jesus is acting as God's representative, his son, purposefully reflecting his father, the divine King of Israel who stood beside Jacob and promised him an ideal future and a helping hand in the meantime. Nathanael recognises Jesus' authority and exclaims his faith in Jesus' word; unlike the emissaries from the Pharisees, he 'sees', he understands.

The word for "you" in John 1:51 is plural, suggesting a representative depiction of Nathanael, but a representation of what? Why, too, does his initial impression of Nathanael cause Jesus to remark on his lack of "deceit" (1:47)?

The link between Jacob, whose subsequent commission name is Israel (Gen 35:10) and Nathanael, whose name infers those given to Jesus by God, e.g., to re-establish as the foundation of the *new* Israel, is provocative and hardly coincidental. Both incorporate the early 'El' designation ("god") and, recall, this is something rooted quite firmly in the Samaritan religion. What makes Jesus' connection to Nathanael most profound (and this will have a bearing on Jesus' crucifixion) is Nathanael's declaration that Jesus is the King of Israel. This will be the *only* affirmation of kingship Jesus acknowledges.

The lack of deceit becomes significant because the only Israelites that are not deceitful, according to the scriptures, are those chosen, the elect, i.e., the Remnant. Nathanael, therefore, represents the Remnant of the ideal Israel, the descendants of Abraham and Jacob who were not tainted by the Egyptian influence. It seems fair to ascribe to Nathanael the role of "true Israelite." Jesus hints at this again in John 17:6–8, when he says:

> I have made your name known to *those whom you gave me* from the world. They were yours, and you gave them to me, and they have kept your word ... the words that you gave to me I have given to them and they ... know in truth that I came from you; and they shall have believed that you sent me.

"Those whom you gave me" alludes to the Remnant (those who have kept God's word), and is also the meaning of the name Nathanael.

Jesus' enthusiastic reception of Nathanael has a precedent in the suffering servant passages of Isaiah 53, where the Remnant is described as having "no deceit in his mouth." It also has a precedent in Ps 32:2: "Happy are those to whom the Lord imputes no iniquity, and in whose spirit there is no deceit." The original context of this psalm is one of deliverance and the promise of instruction of a new 'way' for those who will humble themselves and admit their sins. The "Lord imputes no iniquity" to the Remnant for in it (in Nathanael) there is no deceit. Everyone else has to earn his or her redemption.

Nathanael, with his Hebrew name, is there, at the end of the gospel.

> *Blessed are the solitary and the elect,*
> *for you will find the Kingdom.*
> *For you are from it, and to it you will return.*
> Gos Thom 49

Nazareth
Why is Nathanael surprised that anything good can come from Nazareth?

The name Nazareth is not attested in the OT, the Talmud, Midrash, or Josephus, and the current estimated location, about four or five miles southeast of Sepphoris, is based on a second-century reference cited in a fourth-century historical account (Eusebius), making it, to say the least, fallible. In Matt 2:23, Jesus' association with this northern town is rationalized by claiming that it is a fulfilment of some obscure prophecy, which scholars insist must refer to the Davidic messiah mentioned figuratively in Isa 11:1 through a play on the word *neser*: "A shoot shall come out of the stump of Jesse." What few interpreters mention is that there is *another* use of the word in the OT, in Isa 49:6, where the "suffering servant" is described as *the one who will restore the Remnant of Israel*, the tribes of Jacob (in the NRSV the word *nesurim* is translated as "survivors"). If Jesus is to be identified with the servant, he must also be the restorer of the "survivors," the Remnant.

To make matters even more intriguing, in Deut 29:28 there is a word that is translated as "another land," a mysterious place beyond the Euphrates (metaphorically, out of sight). Moses has been warning about the tribes' necessary devotion to the *one* god and about the curses that will be invoked if the Israelites allow the other gods of Canaan to lure them away. He tells them that in future days, when people ask where all the people have disappeared to, the legend will be that God "cast them into *another land*" because of their deviant ways. Then Moses adds: "The secret things belong to the Lord" (Deut 29:29), inferring that this place is not so much a geographical site, as a metaphor for limbo, with the scattering a direct punishment. This secret, mysterious place, "another land," is Arzareth.[6] I suggest *this* is the theological basis for Nazareth. It is no wonder Nathanael doubts that anything good can come from there, yet there is optimism in

---

[6] Josephus mentions it, also (*Ant.* 11.5.2). In the Talmud, the realm is interpreted as the 'world to come' and the *ten* tribes are only allowed to have a share in this new world if they repent.

Jesus' message to Nathanael that overrides the negative implication of Arzareth and hints at the re-gathering and future prosperity after a return to God, which is the FG's message throughout.

This strange realm is also mentioned in 2 Esdras. Ezra is granted an interpretation of one of his visions—a man coming down from a mountain, who gathers a multitude before the end days. The man, Ezra is told, is God's son, and the 'peaceable' multitude represents the scattered nine tribes who have *chosen* to disassociate themselves from the rest of the world in order to live according to the statutes of their own religion. The place to which they, the Remnant, journeyed, Ezra is told, is Arzareth (2 Esd 13:45).[7]

So, is Nazareth simply a play on Arzareth?

I really think this is the most fitting explanation of Jesus' mysterious origins, an explanation of how the Jews can both "know his mother and father" (John 6:42) and yet "not know where he is from" (9:29). If Nazareth was listed as his birthplace, why the mystery? Perhaps there was no such town and the obscurity is mentioned solely for the purpose of identifying the Remnant from the Jews, the sheep from the goats, i.e., the Jews who cannot 'see' cannot follow Jesus.

The FG isn't really interested in Jesus' birth, as nothing is mentioned of it, other than this remark telling us that the authorities have checked his genealogy. As was the case with the original Josephite families that returned to Jerusalem after the exile, Jesus' birth would have been a matter of record but as a Samaritan, his genealogical record would have proven (politically) insignificant to the authorities. They may know his bloodline, which is why they taunt him with the supposedly derogatory "you are a Samaritan" (John 8:48) but he is a stranger to them.

In the FG, Jesus sees himself as having been chosen to *represent* the people of Arzareth, those scattered Israelites who fled in order to protect their true identity and beliefs, and so he associates himself with them (as their spiritual "shepherd"). This is precisely how the connection between Salathiel and his mission is made, in 2 Esdras: "… do you not know that Israel has been entrusted to you in the land of their exile?" (5:17). Thus, perhaps, Jesus is not born in a town called Nazareth, rather, he is from this representative group, i.e., he is one with and of the Remnant.

According to a fourth-century inscription at Caesarea found in 1962, Nazareth is listed as one of the villages in which priestly divisions took up residence after the War in 70 CE. One wonders why such a place name was

---

[7] This is a more optimistic concept of the place, where the northern tribes make it a conscious decision to detach themselves. This sounds more like the version in the Book of Joshua, where there is a concerted effort to detach from an Egyptian heritage.

chosen, if it had such potentially negative connotations, especially in terms of a non-Jewish priestly pretender a generation earlier. Is this evidence of the post-Jesus Messiah ben Joseph idea that many had failed to recognise his role until it was too late—was this town so named after its significance in the FG was comprehended?

What of the Synoptic version of Jesus' birthplace, Bethlehem? This is assumed to be the site of Jesus' birth in Judah because the Messiah ben David must come from Judah. *This* particular town is not mentioned in the tribal allotment in Joshua's account but appears later, in the story of David fighting the Philistines. The original Bethlehem, in Josh 19:15, was actually allotted to the tribe of Zebulun, in Galilee, bordering Asher.[8] Not surprisingly, this northern town is given little or no attention in most mainstream interpretations.

Searching for any clues to a geographical (as well as a symbolic) Nazareth, I came up with two potential places. The first is Zarethan, a simple phonetic inversion, with the '-an' ending reversed and placed at the beginning. Most atlases base their location of Zarethan on the description of 1 Kgs 7:46, combined with that in Josh 3:16, making it somewhere along the Jordan, just north of Succoth (the site of which is also ambiguous), on the eastern bank. However, a few chapters earlier, in 1 Kgs 4:12, Zarethan is said to be a boundary marker between two of the twelve districts in the kingdom of Solomon. It is said to lie "below Jezreel, beside Bethshean" only a few miles south of the present-day, *estimated* position of Nazareth, yet no one questions this!

At the time of Jesus' birth, Zarethan would have been right on the border between Samaria and Galilee. It was only in 6 CE, when the tetrarchy imposed a redefinition of borders that Zarethan would have become a town in the district of Galilee; before this time, it was a town of Samaria. If Jesus was born here, he would definitely be a native of Samaria. What is more significant, though, for Jesus tends to be rather nostalgic in his ideas, is the fact that this lies in the original tribal territory of Manasseh, i.e., Josephite land. The name is easily adapted to invoke symbolic meaning and to link it with Arzareth, the mythical home of the exiled followers of the religion of Abraham.

This is close but if the alternative to "Messiah ben Joseph" is "Messiah ben Ephraim" and not Manasseh, there must be a stronger connection to the Ephraimite tradition; and what of Jesus' apparent

---

[8] Yet again, there is a duality here—two Bethlehems, one in northern territory, one in the southern but to make matters even more interesting, the southern site can also be identified as Ephrath (from Gen 35:19, 48:7), the site of the burial of Rachel. Compare this to what I say about Rachel in "The Road to Shiloh."

identification with Joshua, the Ephraimite? There *is* a town that marks one of the boundaries of the territory of Ephraim. In Josh 16:7 it is called Naarath (or Naarah) and in 1 Chr 7:28, Naaran.

In the word Nazareth is the term *nazar*, meaning "to set apart/to consecrate" and *eth*, meaning "the self," which stems from *'owth*, meaning a sign or omen. This, in turn, stems from *'uwth* which means "to come." Jesus is thus the one consecrated, just as Joseph is the one 'set apart' in Gen 49:26 ; he is the *sign* (cf. Zech 3:8), he is the one who has 'come': "I stirred up one from the north and he has come" (Isa 41:25).

Jesus is, in effect, a Nazarite (a consecrated one), i.e., "a Nazarite to God from birth ... who shall begin to deliver Israel" (Judg 13:5; cf. Isa 1:22). Both the Samaritans and the Qumran sect had Nazarites and this is the reason why the FG describes Jesus as the *christos*, the 'anointed one', for it simply means he is God's chosen, his representative; it is *not* contingent upon the Messiah ben David concept. It may refer to Jesus' status as the King of Israel (which becomes more probable in light of the crucifixion/burial scenes) but it just as likely refers to his (unorthodox) high priestly status, which is depicted throughout the FG.

The prophecies of Jer 30:18–21, Ezekiel 37, Daniel 7, and Zechariah 3 each allude to the salvation of many through the actions of just one figure. In Jeremiah, this figure is a *high priest* who rises from the "tents of Jacob,"[9] and in Zechariah, most significantly perhaps, he is Joshua, the *high priest* who wins for his people the right of access to the Lord's new (purified) house.

Time

Jesus and John do not meet at Passover in John 1, which really would be a relatively ineffectual time to preach *repentance*, but just before the Day of Atonement, when such matters are at the forefront of priestly and prophetic concerns, i.e., the tenth day of the seventh month, Tishri (October).

Jesus and his first disciples stay/rest together, indoors, from "about four o'clock in the afternoon." The English translation loses some of the meaning here, however, for in the Greek, Jesus is inside by "about the tenth hour." Traditionally, the Jewish civil day runs from sunset to sunset. If this is the Day of Atonement, it is designated as a day of fasting (hence no Passover feast is mentioned) and of sabbatical rest (Lev 23:26f), i.e., they

---

[9] The interpretation of the 'prince' in Jer 30:21 as a 'high priest' is legitimate, for none other could approach God so closely, as the poem itself suggests; the context is messianic but a distinction is made between the 'king', David, and the 'prince', who remains unnamed.

stay put. According to Josephus (*Ant.* 16.6.2), the day of preparation for Sabbath lasts up to the ninth hour, or about 3 P.M. Jesus and the disciples, then, are inside *just* in time to observe *their* Day of Atonement Sabbath, according to the law (Lev 16:29–34).

The Hebrew fascination with numbers is legendary; appreciating the use of gematria, for instance (i.e., the assigning of numerical value to the letters of the Hebrew alphabet and thereby encoding or extracting hidden information), is a vital tool in the biblical historian's toolbox. I propose that this number "ten" is *intended* to allude to the tenth day (e.g., of Tishri), purposefully directing our attention to the Day of Atonement. The ancient way of dividing the day was to allot a period of three hours per division; this allowed plenty of time for people to get to the temple for services. The third 'hour' of the day was (roughly) 6 to 9 A.M., the sixth hour 9 to 12 midday, the ninth hour 12 to 3 P.M., and the twelfth hour 3 to 6 P.M. (The night, broken down into first, second, third, and fourth 'watches', was likewise divided. Although the twenty-four-hour timing system was in everyday use by the Romans, the Talmud, written between the first and fourth centuries CE, still makes reference to the 'watches' of the night.)

The "tenth hour" is thus incongruous with the average allocation of time; why not simply say they were inside by the ninth hour? Would a single hour really have made that much of a difference to the narrative? Well, yes, but o*nly* if a Sabbath is implied, or some other symbolic meaning is intended. The "tenth hour" invites us to make the connection to the Day of Atonement on the *tenth day* of the month (Lev 23:32 stipulates the 'ninth day of the month at evening,' making it, in effect, the beginning of the tenth day). The Passover lamb, on the other hand, although *selected* on the tenth of Nisan (Exod 12:3), is not actually *killed* until the evening of the fourteenth (effectively, the fifteenth; traditionally, a Friday).

Each time a specific hour is mentioned in the FG, then, it corresponds to a calendar date, i.e., a day on which a special event takes place. An 'hour' that deviates from the regulated divisions of time indicates a *precise* day of the month, while that which is phrased according to the standard divisions (third, sixth, ninth, twelfth) suggest a *symbolic* day that is otherwise not mentioned, and this can fall *within* a three hour/day division. For example: the 'third hour' (not mentioned in the FG) could mean 6–9 A.M. *or* the sixth to the ninth day of the month; the "tenth hour" indicates the tenth day of the month and a vague sense of the time, i.e., between 3 and 4 P.M. The following table illustrates how significant and *consistent* this code is in the FG, though the other entries are yet to be discussed.

Table of Hours

Citation	Hour	Day	Festival	Month
John 1:39	Tenth (4 P.M.)	10th	Day of Atonement	Tishri
John 4:6	Sixth (9–12 noon)	9th to 12th + "two days"	Passover	Nisan
John 4:52	Seventh (1 P.M.)	7th	Pentecost	Siwan
John 19:14	Sixth (9–12 noon)	9th to 12th Precedent escape (Zedekiah)	Passover	Nisan
		10th day (symbolic)	Day of Atonement (symbolic)	

3
STATEMENTS OF INTENT

IN THE MESSIAH BEN JOSEPH traditions, the anticipated in-gathering of the nation begins in Upper Galilee. If Jesus' initial meeting with John takes place on the far side of the Jordan, not far from Qumran, Jesus must now return to the north to begin his work.

One of the most confusing and difficult issues to deal with in the FG is its timeline. I provide further discussion on this where I feel it necessary and offer an overall time chart in the Appendix to help explain how I see the flow of FG events on a pragmatic level. The wedding scenario of John 2, the feeding episode of John 6, and the entry into Jerusalem are the three areas of concern. I only realised the timeline issue when nearing the completion of my research, so I was forced to do a rethink when it came to describing these scenes. Rather than disregarding what I was convinced was a valid interpretation on a theological level, I chose to *add* commentary, where needed, concerning the potential shift in the narrative's chronology.

Each of these three scenes has a theological significance that the FG author deems more significant than their historical contribution to the narrative. They are manipulated and exploited for symbolic ends, though deep within their depiction are buried away the clues we need to follow the physical, rather than the spiritual story of Jesus. It can seem a little overwhelming at first but even this is the intention of the FG author as part of the winnowing process that we see enacted within its narrative. There are secrets to be kept from getting into the hands of the wrong people even though the 'good news' must be disseminated.

We are invited to a wedding (John 2), one of the most profoundly symbolic events in Israelite society, in which the seven-fold blessing culminates in a prayer for the reunification of the nation. Here at Cana of Galilee the first of Jesus' seven "signs" occurs (*semeia*, as the original Greek text of the FG calls them, as opposed to "miracles" in the Christian tradition).[1]

---

[1] The seven traditionally noted are in John 2:1–11 (water into wine); 4:46–54 (healing the boy); 5:1–15 (healing the lame man); 6:5–14 (feeding the multitude);

Cana

Cana is an example of a name that has a certain degree of contextual significance, yet it, too, is seldom given due attention. We have to remember that there is a symbolic aspect to such names, as well as a geographical one. The name itself (*Kana* in the Greek, *Qanah* in Hebrew/Aramaic) has several meanings. Traditionally, it is "the place of reeds" but it can also mean "creation," with the connotation of recovering, redeeming, or restoring. It is also a play on, or an abbreviation of Canaan, the land promised to Abraham, Isaac, and Jacob, the land the Israelites would again possess in the *ideal* future.

Geographically, Cana has been allocated a position quite close to the modern-day *estimated* position of Nazareth, about eight miles north-east (though some scholars prefer to place it about nine miles due north). I am in agreement with Eusebius, however, who reckoned the FG Cana to be the Cana mentioned in Josh 19:28, which is just south-east of Tyre. Not only does this allow for OT corroboration, it places Cana in the tribal territory of Asher, the very tribe from which the only openly-declared northern person in the NT comes from, i.e., Luke's prophetess, Anna, who hails the imminent redemption of Israel.

Again, people taking the gospel literally consider the time frame of John 1–2 and deduce that Cana has to be within a certain distance, if Jesus is to make the journey relatively quickly. Although interpreters often mention that Josephus *lived* in Cana of Galilee, which he tells us in *Life* (16), they tend to omit that later in his account, Josephus tells of an arduous overnight trek to Tiberias (on the western shore of the Sea of Galilee), from Cana. Had he been travelling from the site near Nazareth, Josephus's journey wouldn't have taken more than a few hours, traversing only about ten miles but from the Asherite Cana the journey would be about thirty miles. This sounds more like Josephus' long haul.

Also, in *Life* (71), Josephus describes a blockade set up near Julius, on the northern tip of the Sea of Galilee, intended to "hinder the inhabitants from getting provisions out of Galilee" via Cana and Gamala. Gamala lies to the east of Julius, east of the Sea. The traditional site of Cana is not on a major trade route but rather, up in the hills north of Sepphoris, a major city of the day, which *does* lie on the trade route from Ptolemais (which is on the shore of the Mediterranean). The Cana in Asherite land, however, *is* directly on the main trade route from Tyre, also on the coast, and more directly enroute to Upper Galilee and the area around Julius. So, if provisions are sent south, Sepphoris would be the aim of the blockade, not some village in

---

6:16–24 (walking on water); 9:1–7 (healing the blind man); 11:1–45 (raising Lazarus).

the hills further south. This more northern Cana allows for Jesus' messianic mission to begin in Upper Galilee, just as the Messiah ben Joseph tradition prescribes.

Symbolic Union

The character of Nathanael, the representative of the Remnant of Israel, comes from Cana (John 21:2). In terms of the twelve tribes, he represents Asher and is intrinsically linked to the wedding scenario that is about to take place. It is the third day; in the Jewish calendar the third day is a Tuesday. The FG also uses the "third day" phrase as a literary device, a symbolic rendition of an ancient biblical motif. If you count the Day of Atonement in John 1:35–9 as the first theological 'day' of Jesus' mission, 'day two' is the day he declares himself to Nathanael, the Remnant, and 'day three' is the day in hand. We have no way of knowing what length of time separates these events, as this was not significant to the gospel author at this point. As there are at least five other 'days' implied before this verse of the FG (e.g., John 1:28–9 suggesting two days, 1:35 another day, 1:39 a period of a day, and 1:43 a trip to Galilee of unknown duration), obviously we are looking at a case of theological symbolism, where there is a build up to a momentous "third day."

A wedding is a form of covenant and the sealing of a covenant on the third day provides a sense of *gravitas* and sanctity; the idea of performing a sacred, or special, act on such a day first appears in Gen 22, where Abraham prepares to offer his son Isaac as a burnt offering to God. It is God who directs this action, chooses the site, and ensures the outcome; Abraham simply obeys and as a result receives an everlasting covenant for his descendants. In Exod 19, too, the third day is sacrosanct; it is the day Moses ascends the mountain to meet with God, in preparation for the inauguration of the priestly kingdom of Israel. The granting of the commandments and the covenant of Sinai are the result.

The third day, then, is a day of union and ceremony. It is a day of consecration, where the divine and the mundane meet in anticipation of some mutual covenant.[2] It is just the same in the FG. The wedding takes place on the third day, not only because it is a ritual of union in its own right, nor because the Jewish marriage ceremony is a symbolic reflection of the

---

[2] In the Jewish tradition the most propitious day for a wedding is on a Tuesday (as we call it), for this is the third day of Creation and God is heard to say not once but twice how good it was. So we might deduce that this particular wedding *actually* takes place on a Tuesday. Though this may seem purely incidental, there is cause to return to this suggestion later.

marriage between God and Israel but because this is *Jesus'* moment of union with the will of God and with the Remnant. Having received the spirit of authority, Jesus has already assumed his role as God's representative; as Abraham and Moses had both received divine commissions *before* their 'third day' encounters with God, so Jesus follows this tradition. He is the "bridegroom" of John's vision (John 3:29), not the physical groom at this wedding.

As festivals seem to play such an important role in the FG's depiction of Jesus' signs, and as these tend to be reflected in the actions and the dialogue, it is possible that certain festivals are *inferred* in the text, where none is explicitly mentioned. This current scenario is one example, e.g., there is a covenant made on the third day and there are references to purification and to supplying people with sustenance. We know that the Passover festival follows shortly in the narrative, so this wedding is probably in the early days of Nisan (April), when the exodus and the Sinai covenant are celebrated. With the Remnant an implicit factor of the scene, there is also the idea of emancipation.

Many interpreters now consider the *possibility* that this is actually Jesus' own wedding but I doubt that it is probable. In Jesus' society a boy becomes a man at age thirteen; legally, though perhaps not emotionally, he is ready to marry, though usually he waits until he is about seventeen, or eighteen. Even those who undergo temporary vows of chastity, be they Nazarites or Essenes, etc., are usually married by the age of twenty. One of the prime directives of the HB is, of course, to multiply, and the devout Hebrew would deem it a failure on his part if he didn't produce a family as soon as possible. According to the Talmud, an unmarried man is but half a body, incomplete as Adam without Eve.[3] Jesus is, I suggest, *already* married (explained in due course). This wedding *could* be that of Jesus' daughter. If she is marrying Nathanael, Jesus' significance and association with Cana becomes even more important.

As mentioned earlier, *Beth + ab + ara* (the alternative to Bethany) translates as "house of the father of Ara," who was an Asherite, the descendants of whom amalgamated with the Josephite tribes through marriage. Here it is in action! Nathanael, representing the tribe of Asher, makes an alliance with Jesus' Josephite family. This is the *beginning* of the reunion of the Remnant, in Cana-an, the Promised Land. It may explain why Luke's prophetess, Anna, comes from Asher.

It may also explain why, when Jesus is called upon to supply more

---

[3] "God utters a curse against those who remain single after they are twenty years of age; and those who marry at sixteen please him, and those who do so at fourteen still more." *Kiddushin*, fol. 29, col. 2.29, col. 2.

wine, he reacts to the request as if to say, "Why me?" Traditionally, it is the *groom's* house in which the marriage feast is prepared and it is thus the groom's responsibility to provide his guests with enough victuals (and the "master of the feast" who calls the bridegroom [*not* Jesus] to enquire after the wine is generally the groom's, not the bride's, father). If Jesus were the groom, the request would have been anticipated. Jesus, then, becomes father-in-law to Nathanael and the sense of his responsibility for the Remnant is heightened (symbolically).

The Jars
There are no miracles in the FG. What Christianity preserves as supernatural acts that prove Jesus' divinity are, in the FG, simply metaphors, or scriptural allusions that turn what is probably a very deliberate, even planned situation, into a theological statement of intent. This is the first of a certain type of sign, a 'wonder', which is to be interpreted in terms of Jesus' overall message, although there are seven of this type (see note 1, above), there are other signs, too, which must not be ignored (e.g., the storming of the temple).

As other interpreters have suggested, there are probably *six* jars of purification water in order to infer a certain discrepancy, as the number seven is a fairly universal symbol of perfection. I suggest, however, that it has nothing to do with the legitimacy of the *rite* of purification, per se, as some Christian schools of thought hold but rather, that it pertains to the *difference* between the establishment's idea of purification and Jesus'.

Water would be present for purifying the hands before the meal, the wedding couple themselves, etc. There is nothing unusual about such jars being there, though current archaeological research suggests only wealthy families owned stone jars like this, at least until the middle of the century when, one Talmudic source states "purity broke out among the Jews" (Tosef. Shab. 1:14). Thereafter they became popular as part of the domestic mikvah, or immersion pool. Waters of purification are a complex topic but suffice it to say that purification water, especially at a wedding, is not to be drawn water, as earthen vessels are not ritually pure, but as new stone vessels become available, these are deemed sufficiently pure to convey and hold mikvah water.

It is difficult to discern if the jars are only partially full (and thus have *room* for more water), or are standing empty, not being used. The jars are not full, *that* is the point. The partially empty jars are like the "cracked cisterns" of the relapsed Israelites that "can hold no water" (Jer 1:13). Jesus orders these jars to be "filled to the brim," to overflowing, like the fountain of "living waters" that only complete loyalty to God's word can bring. *That* is all he does. It is the theological implication of this order (not even an *action* on Jesus' part) that creates the 'sign' within the narrative: Return to the original laws, the original worship, and life itself will be overflowing with joy and prosperity.

> *It is a time of distress for Jacob,*
> *yet he shall be rescued from it.*
> Jer 30:7

Remember, numbers in the FG are always significant; the author does not include them without intending the reader to learn something from them. The term *metretae* ("measure") is understood to mean approximately forty litres of liquid, but this is not the important aspect here; we need to use the numbers, i.e., 2, 3, 6.

The FG's numerology is fairly basic but it is there. It can be as simple as adding or multiplying two numbers, or implying a certain number within the text. The most significant numbers in the gospel are 3, 7, and 12. In this case, we can have (2 x 3) (i.e., 2 to 3 measures) + 6 (jars) = 12, the number of tribes. As this is the moment of union between the tribes of Asher and Joseph, heralding the gathering-in and reunion of *all* the tribes, I think this is a perfect use of number symbolism that just about anyone can appreciate.

There is, however, another option: 2 + 3 + 6 = 11. How could this be meaningful in the context of the FG's symbolism? Well, I think there may be a foreshadowing here, which actually forms a powerful inclusio with Jesus' burial scene, where the number 11 becomes a very significant allusion to the final assembly of Jesus' ministers. I shall explain at the appropriate juncture.

When full, the jars hold about 240 litres of water that supposedly becomes wine. Jesus doesn't just create new wine out of thin air; this is not a miracle. The FG author has used this scenario to show Jesus' intent, i.e., he is metaphorically replacing the *contents* of the jars with something better, just as he intends to replace the *temple* with something better, i.e., a new, *pure* priesthood!

In vino veritas

The 'sign' at Cana serves to further illustrate the degraded moral condition of Israel, as it introduces the concept of an alternative way of life by echoing the drunkenness ideology of the OT. There are three types of wine, or strong drink, in the OT: a) wine that offers solace, or is used for celebrations, etc., such as in Exod 10:19, Judg 9:13, and Ps 104:15; b) wine which dulls the senses to the imbiber's disadvantage, making the will weak, as in Gen 9:21f, Prov 4:17, 20:1, 31:4–6, Hos 4:11, etc.; and c) wine which acts as the medium for God's wrath or mercy (e.g., Job 21:20, Ps 11:6, Jer 25:15). The basic implication is that the drunken state is self-imposed; there is a subsequent lack of knowledge and understanding, followed by an opportunity to re-establish oneself on a righteous path.

Here in John 2:9 the guests are too intoxicated to appreciate the good wine and there is confusion about where it has come from, reiterating the 'inability-to-see-relief-coming' theme of 1:26, and emphasizing the mysterious origins of Jesus' authority. The good wine itself, of course, represents the righteous path, an almost identical depiction to that set out in the Gospel of Thomas: "I took my place in the midst of the world ... I found all of them intoxicated; I found none of them thirsty ... for the moment they are intoxicated. When they shake off their wine, then they will repent" (Gos Thom 28).

Such an opportunity for redemption, however, demands a certain degree of moral agency; it demands a *choice* between good and evil. This is precisely the situation portrayed throughout the FG; a choice has to be made between Jesus, metaphorically the 'good wine', 'the light', the righteous path, etc., and the current establishment (the bad wine) with its tendency toward personal advancement, arrogance, and even deceit. (According to Isa 1:22, 'wine mixed with water' i.e., bad/weak wine, is a sign of a debauched society.) The choice will be set before the people through the mission Jesus is about to undertake. It will culminate in the scene involving Jesus and Barabbas, in John 18.

The seventh blessing of the Jewish marriage ceremony is a prayer for the reunification of Israel, reflecting on the original marriage at Sinai between God and his chosen 'bride'. This will be discussed shortly but it is vital that we recognise Jesus' first major demonstration of intent, here. Israel's history is replete with covenants made, broken, and remade. The FG has its own version of this pattern that permeates the entire narrative and involves two *other* special characters. The marriage scenario at the outset of the gospel draws our attention to the importance of this ancient motif and helps set the foundation for what is to come. So, the six water jars may also represent all the blessings up to but not including the one most important to Jesus. By highlighting the lack of a seventh blessing there is scope to have Jesus 'step in' and demonstrate that through him reunification will be the very least the nation can hope for; like *comparing* water to wine. What Jesus can offer with the new kingdom is likened to good wine (e.g., *old* vintage wine, echoing the idea of a return to the *old*, better ways).

When the marriage is over, Jesus and his family go "home" to Capernaum (there is no indication how long Jesus stays there).

Bride of God
The original marriage between God and Israel occurs at Mount Sinai, when the priestly nation is betrothed to the divine will through the Ten Commandments and the covenant of the priesthood. Since then, however, Israel has failed to maintain its side of the bargain and has fallen out of favour.

In Ezekiel 16, the anticipated rescue and restoration of Israel is depicted in terms of a female foundling thrown out to die in the wilderness. Completely helpless, the foundling is inspired (in the literal sense of the word) by the passing "spirit" (breath) of God, and lives (i.e., an echo of the Creation story). She grows to be a beautiful woman and becomes the beloved of God, his elect. A covenant is made between the husband (God) and wife (Israel); she is cleansed, anointed, and elevated to the highest status. Although married to God, she is seduced from her loyalty to him by the attractions of other (e.g., Canaanite) gods, who are depicted as her illicit lovers. She has become as a "whore" in the eyes of God, and suffers the consequences of his wrath.

> Have you seen what she did, that faithless one, Israel, how she ... played the whore...? And I thought, 'After she has done all this she will return to me' ... I had sent her away with a decree of divorce.
> Jer 3:6–8

The bride, according to Jeremiah, is the "sister" of Judah, i.e., northern Israel, Samaria. She is charged with adultery and is prepared for trial. It is the act of repentance that determines whether the harlot wife is to be forgiven or stoned. If she is truly ashamed of her behaviour, she will be restored to her former glory and reinstated as the beloved companion of God. If she is stubborn, nothing can save her. She is, in the end, forgiven, and the entire process begins again, ending with the ideal of the perfect marriage between humanity and the divine.

In Ezek 20:33f, the theme is taken up once more but in pragmatic terms. This time, the elders of the nation are the focus of indignation and the adulterous action that of defiling *themselves* with idols. The emphasis is upon the jealousy of God and the need for complete fidelity. Even the idea of the final re-marriage is apparent in the action of passing "under the staff" (symbolising the renewed covenant).

Ezekiel 23 reiterates the "whoring" element through the personifications of Samaria and Jerusalem. As capital cities of the northern and southern kingdoms, they once held a place of honour and responsibility. When they forfeited this position through the sinful ways of their inhabitants, they brought the rest of the nation down with them. The hitherto vague nature of God's wrath is clarified as an invasion from hostile neighbours and includes plunder and, most significantly, rape. As the "whore" has allowed these strangers to enter her, now they will do so regardless of her consent; she has, according to the allegory, brought this upon herself.

This collective, national responsibility for fidelity and purity, left in the hands of the priests, prophets, scribes, etc., has been neglected. Thus the male influence of the nation, which should have protected and taught, instead ruins and leads astray. The harlot theme is thus used as a device to emphasize the profound guilt of the male populace, in a way that humiliates them, emasculates them, i.e., *they* become as harlots prostituting what should be sacred.

It is Ezekiel 16's pattern for the Bride of God, the depiction that singles out so clearly the inevitable and sequential rise of Israel (Samaria) to its original glory that the FG seems to emulate, i.e., through the character of the Samaritan woman.

In Hosea's account, God openly claims that when reparation is made between himself and his people he will take them as his 'wife' forever. The prophet is told to find a woman who is an adulteress and to love her, as God has loved the inconstant Israel; but this woman is to be maintained on a sort of probation, until she has proven herself morally sound for a rise in status to 'wife.' She is not to see other men, nor have relations with her new partner; she is left utterly to her own devices. So too with Israel; she is to lose the security of civil and religious institutions (e.g., through foreign occupation) until she turns away from her evil ways and returns to a true faith in God.

Hosea returns Israel to the wilderness where the first marriage (or election) had taken place (i.e., the inauguration of the priesthood at Sinai), and tars it with the very brush used to castigate the Canaanite worshippers of Baal, namely, illicit sexual behaviour. Hosea casts a profound doubt on the suitability, or even the right, of Israel to call itself the "chosen of God." Israel is thus cast into a spiritual void out of which there can be but one means of escape—a return to absolute faith (shown by Abraham, for instance).

In Isaiah's depiction the spiritual aspect of the divine/mundane marriage is stronger than in any other text, and its positive anticipation of the ideal future state is unequalled. Where Ezekiel concentrates on the current weaknesses and ill favour of Israel, with its redemption contingent upon a difficult and humiliating moral transformation, Isaiah emphasizes the glory of the reunion with God, and the ideal is related in enticing, encouraging terms. Isa 61:1, specifically, calls the message of reunion "good news" (the meaning of "gospel") and suggests that it is aimed at those who most require, and therefore will most readily accept, the hope it brings (the Samaritan anticipation of Taheb, the Restorer, is also called "the good news"). Trials and tribulations will be reversed; mourners will exchange their ashes for garlands; the priestly nation will be reinstated; and the people will be decked in garments of 'salvation' which are interpreted as marriage adornments. Yahweh speaks to his people, Israel, saying, "you shall be called My Delight is in Her (*Hephzibah*), and your land married (*Beulah*)" (Isa 62:4–5). The desperation of the age, the wickedness, the fear, will all pass away, and in that day Israel shall become once more the beloved Bride of God

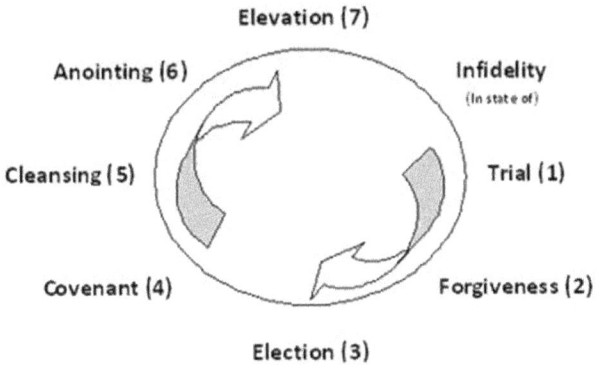

Ezekiel 16's Bride of God

> ....*you will not suffer disgrace...*
> *For your Maker is your husband....*
> Isa 54:4, 5

Thus, the Bride of God motif from the Hebrew Bible begins in state of infidelity, for the female figure is initially on *Trial*; *Forgiveness* follows; then her *Election*; a *Covenant* is made; there is a *Cleansing*; an *Anointing*; and then the ultimate *Elevation*. There are *seven* stages. The jars at the wedding feast, representing the status quo, once again prove insufficient. The final elevation of the Remnant is contingent on Jesus' success.

Malachi, on the other hand, hails God as "King" (1:14) and "husband" and the diatribe is against the "sons of Levi" to whom the rights of the priesthood were originally granted. It is this covenant, *this* marriage that has been defiled. The priests are male and symbolically take on the role and responsibility of a husband, e.g., protecting and caring for the sacredness of the deity. It is the charge given to the priests (just as the Ark was the charge given to the Sinai priesthood) that takes on the symbolic role of 'wife.' The priests have abused and/or neglected their duty as 'husbands', as caretakers of the priesthood, protectors of the glory of God.

Temple Tirade

One of the most common interpretations of the temple scene in John 2 is that Jesus is demonstrating, or foreshadowing, the nullification of the sacrificial system but this is a wholly Christian perspective. No devout Israelite would have considered the worship of God *without* sacrifices, at least, not in Jesus' day. The *concept* of sacrifice is fine; the problem lies more with how and where it is performed and who performs it.[4] Just as the *rite* of purification itself is *not* repudiated at the wedding, the *rite* of sacrifice, here, is not rejected as a means of worship. The Samaritan perception of sacrifice, recall, is that it is not legitimate *as practised in the temple in Jerusalem*; the return of legitimate sacrifices is an anticipated obligation of 'the Restorer'.

In the FG the temple scene occurs at the very outset of the mission, not at its end, as in the Synoptic accounts. Many scholars find the Synoptic sequence of events much more acceptable because it provides a convenient justification for the anger and animosity of the chief priests and, therefore, the arrest of Jesus soon afterward (though the accusation is one of blasphemy). The FG's placing of the demonstration immediately after the marriage/commission scenario, however, is *theologically* sound and necessary, given the apparent nature of Jesus' mission; so far, *Jesus* knows what his mission is, the Remnant (represented by Nathanael) knows, but Jerusalem does not. Jesus must declare himself, and his intentions, to 'the world'. There is sufficient cause for the Synoptic authors to make this significant change in chronology, as will be explained.

It is often suggested that Jesus' display in the temple is a partial fulfilment of Zech 14:21, where it is prophesied that in the days of the glorious return to God and the coming of the messiah, no "traders" will be in the "house of the Lord." There is, though, more to this than meets the eye, and the careful reader will gradually come to realise that even the concept of "traders" is exploited to fit the FG author's specific tale.

The timeframe of this episode is rather intriguingly vague, with the FG simply stating that Jesus remains with his family in Capernaum for "a few days" (John 2:12). The possibility that this scene might be repositioned to fit the theology rather than the true chronology of the movement could be the reason for this lack of detail, where in other places we get very specific depictions of time. That the festival is designated "of the Jews" reinforces the schism between the Samaritan practices and the Jewish (in Jerusalem).[5]

---

[4] Josephus (*Ant.* 18.1.5) states that the Essenes, the sect now associated with Qumran, refused to offer regular sacrifice at Jerusalem and chose to offer their own, 'more pure' sacrifices. Evidence of the Dead Sea Scrolls suggests prayer and purity were considered sacrifices of a sort.

[5] Josephus tells us of the Samaritans who profaned the Jerusalem temple (during the term of the procurator Coponius, 6–9 CE) by bringing dead bodies into it on the

That Jesus attends such festivals isn't so much proof of his devotion to the laws concerning attendance at the sanctuary, as evidence of his determination to stir up a hornets' nest there during religiously and politically sensitive times.

The observance of the Passover, of course, is described in Exod 12:1–28, and Jesus' behaviour in the temple is, in part, linked to this precedent. Moses, on seeing his people worshipping the golden calf, destroys the sacred tablets of stone (Exod 32:19f); likewise, Jesus performs *this* violent act of defiance against the impropriety of current worship. The temple has, in effect, become but another 'golden calf'; destroy the false (tainted) image of God and the true God will forgive and return.

> *Return to me, and I will return to you....*
> Mal 3:7

The final destruction of the Nehushtan, the brazen serpent raised in the wilderness by Moses (Num 21:4f), offers another precedent. According to 2 Kgs 18:4–6, Hezekiah tears down and demolishes the object, which has become an idol in its own right, i.e., the people are concerned more with making offerings to *it* than to God, whose power it represents. The temple, by extension, with all its legal debates, and its concentration on making money from sacrifices, etc., means little if the worship of God is forgotten.

It is also just before Passover that Joshua prepares the new generation of Israelites for the entry into the Promised Land (Josh 5:10f); the 'wicked' generation has perished in the wilderness and those who are born *out* of bondage receive the circumcision of the flesh, marking them as the new, cleansed, elect of God. Likewise, Jesus is to lead the *new* elect into the spiritual Promised Land, where a "circumcision of the heart" will allow them entry into the kingdom of God (see Deut 30:1–6). Surely, though, Jesus does not suppose that forcing the moneychangers and the men who sell sacrificial animals out of the temple precinct will be enough preparation for the coming of the messiah, or the return of God's blessing? No, this is a sign of intent, not fulfilment. So, why must these "traders" be expunged?

In his only overtly violent outburst in the gospels, Jesus wields a whip against the men in the outer courts of the temple, the *hieron*; when he mentions the *destruction* of the temple and when the Jews react, however, the term *naos* is used, and this is the word that denotes the sacred inner area

---

festival of Passover. Whether this is true, or hyperbole, we don't know but whatever actually occurred, the Samaritans were thenceforth excluded from the temple and security was stepped up (*Ant.* 18.2.2). Apart from anything more damning to exclude him, Jesus' mere presence as a Samaritan, let alone his actions, would be enough to warrant his arrest and expulsion from the temple precinct.

of the temple, not the outer courts (i.e., they recognise the significance of his 'sign' though they mock it). Jesus' hostility is *directed*, that is, toward the temple *proper*, the *naos* built by priests for priests, not toward the actual tradesmen, though they take the brunt of the violence.

Naos is also used in the Septuagint version (LXX) of Mal 3:1, where it is declared that once the "messenger" has prepared the way, God will return to his sacred place, the holy centre of his house. If the sanctified area of the temple, not the precinct, is identified with the "house of merchandise," its so-called "traders" *must* be the priesthood.

That the priesthood of the temple in Jerusalem is corrupt is not a new idea, e.g., "... oppression and fraud do not depart from its *marketplace* (i.e., implying "traders"; Ps 55:11); "No one who practices deceit shall remain in my house; no one who utters lies shall continue in my presence" (Ps 101:7).

This offers a very satisfactory precedent for Jesus' storming of the temple but it also gives us a clue to the identity of the "father of lies" mentioned in John 8:44–5, which I shall have reason to discuss again. If the priesthood, the caretakers of God's house, are the ones who "utter lies" then the "father of lies" must be the incumbent high priest, in this instance, Caiaphas.

> *The priests did not say, "Where is the Lord?"*
> *Those who handle the law did not know me ....*
> Jer 1:8

> *They have held fast to deceit ... How can you say, "We are wise,*
> *and the law of the Lord is with us," when, in fact,*
> *the false pen of the scribes has made it into a lie?*
> Jer 8:5, 8

In Jeremiah 8, God is denouncing the false worship and misleading "wisdom" of those who claim authority falsely, "from prophet to priest" (Jer 8:10).

The Book of Malachi, however, offers an even stronger potential source for the *ideology* behind Jesus' demonstration, as the emphasis is upon the cessation of meaningless, or *tainted*, sacrifices (*not the ritual itself*). The covenant with the priests, Malichi 2 implies, was a covenant "of life"; this has been corrupted and Israel has lost favour in the eyes of God (i.e., symbolically, it is dead). Israel, the once priestly and holy kingdom, has been unfaithful to the "wife of his youth" (i.e., God's essence) and has been rejected. Divorce (spiritual death) is not the ideal state, so Israel must amend its ways and work for reconciliation, but in order for God to return to "his temple" (3:1), a "messenger" must first "purify" the sons of Levi (the priesthood) of their inherited iniquities, i.e., "from the sins of the fathers" (see also Job 36:8–9 and Isa 5:18–23). Only when the house of God is cleansed (and the actual job of ritually cleansing the temple, on a day to day basis, falls to the priests, making Jesus' actions even more inflammatory to the extant cultus), will its incumbents' "burnt offerings and ... sacrifices ... be accepted on [the] altar" (Isa 56:7). Whether that altar remains in Jerusalem or is reinstated in the 'true Israel' is another matter!

The impulsive and forceful nature of Jesus' action and his words, "Destroy this temple" (John 2:19), reflect Isa 10:20–7, where the situation being depicted is one of dire circumstance; the Remnant of Israel is oppressed and weary. "Destruction is decreed" but this destruction is one that will, ultimately, allow the Remnant to escape the torment of its enemies. God will turn his wrath toward the oppressors, "wield[ing] a whip against them" (Isa 10:26), just as Jesus wields a whip against the "traders," the corrupt priesthood that oppresses its own people. This concept of emancipation surfaces again, in the context of the temple priests, when we take a look at Jesus' healing signs.

The decree of destruction preserved in 1 Sam 2:27–36 is even more interesting. The priesthood is threatened with imminent demise because of its iniquities. It is declared that a new, "faithful priest" will be *"raise[d] up,"* who will work according to God's will, who will have a *new* "house" built for him, and who will minister "before" the messiah.

The most intriguing precedent, however, comes in 2 Kings 23, where Josiah storms into Jerusalem and throws out the paraphernalia of the "sun worshippers" and the illicit sacrificial altars. He defiles the high (sacred) places in the surrounding countryside by taking the bones out of the tombs and burning them on the altars, including one at Bethel. When he spies a tomb that has been made into a monument, he asks whose it is, and the Samaritans say that it is the tomb of a "man of God" who came up from Judah (Judea) to prophesy that this destruction would happen. Josiah refers to him as the "prophet who came out of Samaria" and leaves his tomb intact. This itinerant prophet is Ahijah, a *Josephite from Shiloh* (1 Kgs 11:36). Just as the Messiah ben Joseph tradition would later stipulate, here we have an allusion to a northern man of god coming out of Judea, in the context of the destruction of temples. Can this really be mere coincidence, or might Jesus have visited this tomb on his travels and been inspired?

Jesus declares that the new temple will rise three days after this one's destruction (John 2:19); again, the author uses the 'third day' motif, implying that the creation of the new temple will involve a union (reunion) with the divine, i.e., the anticipated eventuality of Malachi 3. In preparation for this, Mal 4:2 brings the promise of 'healing' and emancipation for the righteous. The mission of Jesus in the FG is thus *apparently* prophesied (i.e., it intentionally 'fulfils' prophecy) but not in the sense that makes him the

Davidic messiah. He is the prophet-priest, come to destroy the iniquitous priesthood of the temple, in preparation for the new kingdom at Shiloh.

John 2:21–5 is an addendum, very obviously trying to explain to non-Jewish readers how this episode relates to the Christian ideal. The format of Jesus' words in 2:19 is not one of a conditional phrase, e.g., 'If you destroy this temple ...'; it is, rather, an imperative, an order. In other words, 'Give up this folly! I will show you the *real* house of God'. The 'three days' reference is, I agree, an intended allusion to *a* death and *a* resurrection but not, as the addendum implies, to Jesus'. It applies, rather, to the death of an age, the passing of an era, and the resurrection of the true Israel and the holy priesthood. This will make more sense once I discuss the Samaritan woman and Jesus' declaration to her.

A Vital Clue

The reference to "forty-six years" (John 2:20) is so precise it begs the question: is the FG author trying to provide us with a true chronology for his account? Why not just tell us outright the year according to the Jewish, or indeed, the Samaritan calendar? We will see in due course that the author has good reason to avoid certain historical associations. If we take the reference at face value, however, we will be able to discern the year of Jesus' temple demonstration. The only source we really have for any corroboration of dates regarding the temple is Josephus' *Antiquities*.

In *Ant.* 15.11.2, having first told us that Herod began his great project of refurbishing and extending the original temple of Solomon in his eighteenth year as ruler, which would have been c.20 BCE, Josephus goes on to suggest the following preparations before any work was actually carried out: 1000 wagons were constructed to haul the stone from the quarry; 10,000 skilled workmen were hired; 1000 sacerdotal garments were commissioned for the priests who insisted they construct the inner temple; these priests were trained as stone-cutters and carpenters; the old temple was then razed and cleared before any work commenced. We can only estimate the time this impressive preparation must have taken but two or three years would not seem improbable. For argument's sake, let's say the first stone was laid sometime around 18 BCE.

Scholars often suggest there was constant titivating right up to c. 64 CE, so anything near an accurate dating from this comment would be all but impossible. I suggest, however, that this 'titivating' comprised quite a distinct programme of *renovation*, not new construction. Josephus remarks (in *Ant.* 15.11.3) that the Jews were hoping, "in the days of Nero," to "raise again" certain sections of Herod's structure that had sunk quite dramatically in its foundations, allowing some to fall down completely. He states quite clearly that the inner temple, the *naos*, took only eighteen months to complete and that the rest of the temple complex proper, i.e., "the cloisters and outer enclosures" (*hieron*) took eight years (from around 18 BCE). This brings us to 10 BCE; a simple calculation that becomes a common tool in deciphering the FG's numerical symbolism.

Now this is an interesting point: If you search the Internet for references to "forty-six" in the FG, you will find page after page of Christian translations and interpretations explaining that the number is merely an estimate (pretty precise estimate!) or symbolic (of?), or that it refers to ongoing construction, etc. Most date the building from c. 20 BCE, to arrive at the year 26 CE for the temple scene, which is too early to sit comfortably with their preconceived dating of the gospel and/or Jesus' actions.

One comment, in a published book on the FG (which I will not cite) literally states that readers need not be concerned with this exact number, for it doesn't "fit the facts" (which *are*?) and because it detracts from Jesus' message! As it was my method to try to unlock the secrets of the FG *without* reference to secondary sources, I battled with this conundrum for years, arriving at a variety of possibilities but each affected several other elements in the gospel text. It was only toward the end of my research that I allowed myself to investigate a little further. I had come to the conclusion that "forty-six years" refers to the time elapsed from the *completion* of the temple to the time of Jesus' tirade therein, for that is how the Greek reads, to me.

Apparently, much celebration and fanfare marked the final construction of the temple and the timing of the event made the festivities even grander, for it occurred on the very anniversary of Herod's inauguration, the first of Nisan (April), i.e., the month of Passover (thus the anniversary of the temple's completion would be in the minds of the Jews just at this time, making their specific reference in context).

The words *naos* and *hieron* can be used interchangeably to a degree, but it is the FG author's clever technique of placing the truth on the antagonists' lips that we see in action in this scene. By using the former, *naos*, the Jews reveal that they comprehend perfectly well Jesus' insinuations but in their reference to the dating of the temple, they allude to the entire complex, for which there *is* an historical record; the inauguration of the temple in Jerusalem *was* celebrated in 10 BCE, the same year Herod's building programme in Caesarea was completed. Look to Christianity for this information and you will be hard-pressed to find it. Look to the Jewish historical documents and you can find it in one click of the mouse. The author of the FG expects his readers to know this significant historical detail and indeed, they would have. This may sound obvious but 10 BCE plus "forty-six years" equals 36 CE. What can Christianity do with *that* date, when tradition maintains a crucifixion in about 33 CE? It *must* be wrong—

right?

I will argue the case that this is one of two precise historical reference points in the gospel. It gives us the year Jesus made a violent demonstration in the temple at Jerusalem (the second appears in John 5). Ironically, it also proves the Synoptics *right* in their unified tale of Jesus entering the city and disrupting the temple courts just prior to his arrest. This *is* the correct positioning of the scene. Scholars have been correct in their claim that the FG author has his own agenda and manipulates events to make his theological message clear but this is because the historical detail of what *actually* occurred is simply too provocative and potentially damning to include in his testimony.

For now, we must continue with the FG narrative but it will soon become clear that there are other examples of this literary licence. The author of the FG provides this exact dating as part of his duty to record the *history* of the original movement, though his obligation to bear witness to Jesus' spiritual mission takes precedence.

4
MARTHA

AFTER STRUGGLING WITH THE QUESTION of Jesus and Mary's relationship for several years, I finally had to face the evidence that was staring me in the face all along, i.e., Jesus is, indeed, married in the FG. The persistent duality of the gospel, so much an element of its composition, provides us with two of almost everything, reflecting both the mundane facts and the esoteric nature of its theology. This aspect is no different; there are two 'wives' in the story. Before we go any further with this idea, and for lack of a more appropriate juncture to explain her character, we need to give Martha a chance to be recognised, for she is perhaps one of the most understated women in the Bible. Martha is Jesus' wife. This strays somewhat from the current popular debate about Jesus and Mary Magdalene. The theory that Jesus and Mary have a sexual relationship is no longer ground breaking and much has been written and surmised on the subject but what has not come to the fore, in any satisfactory way, is how Martha fits into this equation.

The Christian tradition can cope, I think, with the idea that maybe, in his humanity, Jesus *did* have the need for a physical relationship but can it handle the notion that in having such a relationship with Mary he is, in fact, becoming an adulterer, or even a polygamist? These are questions that inevitably arise as we progress but the gospel author has anticipated such a reaction and deals with the delicate subject most adeptly.

The FG holds many clues to the complex interrelationships between Jesus, Mary, Lazarus, and Martha. The first three form the central nexus that links the entire theology of the gospel but Martha seems to be somewhat of an odd, misplaced, uncomfortable character. She has come down in tradition as the slightly resentful, perhaps jealous 'servant' who plays second fiddle to Jesus' favourite, Mary.

Martha is mentioned in the Synoptics only in Luke 10:38–42. She is either not considered important enough by the others to warrant a mention, or they knew nothing of her at all, as the focus of their gospels was not the same as the FG's. It is interesting that Luke seems to suggest that the Jesus/Mary/Martha/Lazarus group were living farther north, in Galilee, before moving down to Bethany (near Jerusalem), as this is precisely what occurs in the FG; the house at Bethany is a strategic location for Jesus' plan down in Judea but this external verification of the northern 'family unit' is important to bear in mind. Also similar is the fact that both Luke and the FG portray Martha as a rather fussy, anxious character and this figures in the overall assessment of her role.

Martha Myth
In mediaeval legend Martha takes on a strange, almost fairy-tale portrayal as a veritable dragon-slayer! She is said to flee Palestine with Mary and Lazarus, settling in Avignon, France.

According to the legend, there existed in the area of Nerluc, Provence, a terrible, Grendel-like monster called the Tarasque. It was a chimera, with six bear's legs, an ox's body, a spiked turtle's shell, and a scaly tale that ended in a scorpion's sting. It had the head of a lion but horse's ears, and the face of an old man. The Tarasque was said to have been the offspring of a creature called the Onachus (from Galatia, a place in central Anatolia, now Turkey) that burned everything it touched, and the Leviathan of biblical fame.

Just as in *Beowulf*, the king of Nerluc and his knights were losing an extended battle against the tormenting, destructive beast, until along came a saviour, in this case Saint Martha. With hymns and prayers Martha lured the Tarasque into the town, where the local residents killed it. She proceeded to preach, converting the town to Christianity. She supposedly ended her days in this same town, now called Tarascon, and the local Collegiate Church is said to house Martha's tomb. Every June, the people of Provence gather to celebrate Martha's victory over the Tarasque with games, parades, and re-enactments.

The first evidence the legend is in a manuscript in the Oxford Library and is attributed to Archbishop Raban Maur, of Mayence, who lived in the ninth century and claimed his sources stemmed from the fifth century. What makes this legend appear to have some basis in historical fact, however diluted, is the fact that the crypt at the church in Tarascon *does* attest to a *first century* Christian community.

Another tradition suggests that fourteen years after Jesus' death, Mary Magdalene, Lazarus, Martha, St. Maximin (who is said to have baptised Mary Magdalene), Sidonius (the 'blind man'; this will prove an interesting correlation), Sera (the maid of Mary Magdalene, suggesting an esteemed status), and the body of Anne (Jesus' grandmother in the Synoptic tradition) were put into a boat with no sails or oars *by the Jews*. They were set adrift and came to rest on the shores of Southern France. There is wisdom in heeding myths, so I'll come back to this.

Martha as Wife

The image of the proselytising dragon slayer may have its roots in the unusual strength of the character illustrated so subtly in the FG. This is not a strength that involves good deeds, or strong faith, or obvious suffering, for Martha is not depicted in such terms. She is very pragmatic, very much a woman who is at her best in the family home. She has such an intimate association with Jesus and later, with Mary and Lazarus, that she demands more attention than has been given her.

There are at least twelve separate clues to Martha's role as Jesus' wife that few biblical scholars take the time to analyse individually, let alone in concert. Perhaps the consequences are just too provocative for mainstream researchers but here, we will throw caution to the wind and assess the evidence with an open mind:

★ Jesus' theological mission is instigated by the figure called his "mother" at the wedding in Cana. Although Jesus is supposedly invited to this celebration, his mother seems to think it is his responsibility to procure more wine for the other guests. The Greek word for "mother" is *meter*, which can mean a *mother figure*, not necessarily one's biological mother, i.e., it can be used in a figurative rather than a literal sense. In various cultures one might call one's wife "mother" if there are children.

★ Jesus' reaction to this demand is as if to say "Why me?" and this is fitting, given that it is the duty of the *groom's father* to supply the venue and the food for the wedding. Thus, Jesus begins his work with the order of a woman and will come to end it in the same fashion, i.e., with an order from Martha (for Jesus to come and deal with the Lazarus issue, John 11:20–27), the last of the seven signs in the gospel.

★ Jesus' curtness in John 2:4 is almost striking: "Woman, what concern is that to you and me?" Although such a response would have been considered reprehensible behaviour had Jesus been replying to his *mother's* request or direct order, it *would* suit a husband/wife context, especially where a fastidious and apparently overburdened wife is stepping beyond the bounds of her defined duties.

★ The "mother" in John 2, the Samaritan woman, the adulteress, and Mary are all referred to by Jesus as "woman," using the Greek word *gune*, which tends to (though not always) infer a wife. As we will soon discover, there is ample evidence to link Mary with the woman at the well and the woman caught in adultery, but there is also reason to believe that the term "mother" is inextricably linked to Martha. The references to Jesus' mother might well be an amendment by an early Church uncomfortable with the depiction of a married saviour. How much simpler to change just one word than to have to explain the convoluted relationships, sexual intimacies, and inevitable offspring of a divine, unsullied icon (rather like getting rid of all the awkward characters by setting them adrift in a boat without an oar?).

★ The name Martha means "mistress," as in "mistress of the house." This is why, in Luke's rendition, she is such a homemaker, perturbed by Mary being in 'her house' earning Jesus' attentions with no more than what might be construed as fawning subservience, while *she* is left to fetch and carry. Depicted as being concerned with *serving* in both the marriage scene in John 2 and in Luke's account, Martha plays the ideal role of wife.

★ By the end of the gospel (John 11:5) we learn that Jesus "loves" Martha. The Greek term *agapao* is used to imply something more than mere respect or fondness. It implies a love of the *heart*, not merely the mind. The others, Mary and Lazarus, are mentioned as extensions of this tender affection, that is, as Jesus' family. This is precisely how the group at Bethany is supposed to be understood and it is the construct on which the legal and spiritual legacy of Jesus' mission will come to depend.

★ Martha speaks her mind to Jesus with an unparalleled familiarity. She takes it upon herself to go out into the streets to meet him as he returns to Bethany. She practically chastises him, blaming him for Lazarus' demise and then has the effrontery to get into a theological debate with him (arguing the finer points of the *eschaton*, the 'end days'—something women would not normally do, unless in private, with a husband, father, or brother, say).

★ Both Mary and Martha call Jesus "lord" or *kyrios*, which is the title granted the head of a household, i.e., the husband or father. The ambiguity that makes the FG more a riddle than a gospel permeates every aspect, every relationship, and this one in particular will find culmination in the post-crucifixion scenes.

★ Martha mourns Jesus. When Lazarus lies in the tomb and Jesus finally arrives it is she who goes out of doors to meet him, while Mary remains indoors to mourn. When she believes Jesus has died, however, it is Mary who ventures out to be at his side while Martha, the wife, conducts her mourning, as per tradition, in private.

★ Martha is conspicuously absent from the crucifixion scene itself. Why, given Jesus' admission of his love for her, given their apparently intimate relationship, and especially given her constant, dutiful presence throughout the gospel, is she suddenly cast aside, without further thought, just when you would have thought she would be at the centre of everyone's attentions?

★ Lo and behold, just at this crucial juncture we suddenly have Jesus' "mother" appear again. Living up in Capernaum (John 2:12), a fair distance to travel for an aging woman, let alone in such a short space of time (consider how long it would take for a message of Jesus' arrest to reach her and then for her to trek on a donkey, or on foot, all the way down to Jerusalem). Nevertheless, the received text of John 19:25 would seem to suggest she manages it. If, however, we remove the word "mother," assuming it, just for argument's sake, to be a later alteration, the entire scene makes much more sense, especially in light of the following points.

★ This "mother" seems to have brought along with her a "sister," a character whom we have never met, whose name is also Mary. The FG follows very specific rules of presentation, with no name, measure, character, or place introduced without a direct link to the central symbolism of its theology. In other words, nothing is gratuitous. This sudden appearance of Jesus' long-since absent and aging parent, along with his obscure aunt jars with the consistent style of the document. It is even more perplexing for the author to suddenly insert another 'Mary' into the plot without explanation or symbolic significance. The only "sisters" to be depicted in the FG are Mary and Martha. In order for the gospel text to be coherent in style and content, which I believe it is, the mother character who stands under the cross is none other than Martha, the motherly figure who made her first appearance at the wedding in Cana and who has been by Jesus' side throughout. Martha's role as mother in the FG does have further potential basis in the narrative, as we shall see.

The FG thus preserves no unequivocal record of Mary the Virgin (or otherwise), mother of Jesus. She is purely a Synoptic phenomenon. It is possible that if the Synoptics do post-date the FG, the problems surrounding Jesus' genealogy, which even Paul denounces as a waste of time trying to make sense of in terms of the 'gospel' to be preached, might have been swept under the theological carpet. By having a virgin as a mother and God as a father, there is no reason to seek out an authentic lineage, as one has been divinely preordained (i.e., for the Davidic messiah).

What we have in the Gospel of John is the consistent, well-rounded, persistent presence of a woman who meets all the criteria of a *wife*. Where the FG now reads "mother," it once read or implied, I suggest, "wife."

5
NICODEMUS AND THE SON OF MAN

BECAUSE OF THE UNUSUAL NATURE OF John 3:1–15, scholars have argued from one extreme perspective to another about what is actually going on here, with many analyses concluding either that Nicodemus is ignorant of the truth in Jesus' words/actions and that his spiritual progress is thwarted at this early stage or, that the construction of the narrative itself presents complications which require elaborate justifications or readjustments of the text.

Nicodemus, I suggest, is actually one of the clearest *success* stories of the entire gospel and his significance is profound, for through his story is disclosed the *means* by which the Remnant can return to God.

The name Nicodemus means "conqueror/victor for/of the people"; how can that inspire such negative interpretations? To support such a negative appraisal, perhaps, we must consider that he is a "leader" of the "Jews" (John 3:1), a Pharisee; he is also described as "the teacher of Israel" (3:10), a designation originally granted only to priests (Deut 31:9–13, 33:10), subsequently assumed by the Levites and ultimately, usurped by the Pharisees. The Jews of the FG, the leaders, appear as the antagonists throughout the narrative, so Nicodemus' is an exemplary case. Like Philip's declaration in John 1:45, which gives us everything we need to decipher Jesus' identity, Nicodemus' depiction provides us with all the information we need to *comprehend* Jesus' (and the FG's) theological message. The victory Nicodemus' name implies is not only a conquest over his own ignorance, I suggest; it is also Jesus' victory, for this Pharisee's experience becomes a reflection of Jesus' own conquest over the "world."

Nicodemus' story is told on three distinct levels, though he is present in the narrative elsewhere, under an alternative commission name. The first level depicts an almost mystical conversation between him and Jesus (John 3); the second reveals the first hints of defiance against the establishment that has hitherto been his life (John 7), and the third finds him completely unreserved in his allegiance to Jesus (John 19). The first stage is given the greatest attention and is strikingly similar to the enlightenment tale of Ezra, in 2 Esdras.

The day of judgement is imminent, according to 2 Esdras, a judgement that will separate the faithful from the corrupt and the "dead" from the "living." This is a diatribe against a wilful and wicked people, whose neglect of God has brought them despair. Ezra questions the declined moral status of Israel in God's eyes; he is under the impression that Israel has been loyal and true and that it has not been rewarded justly for its goodness. (Noting the Pharisaic context of Nicodemus' depiction, the echo of this presumption, indeed arrogance, is fundamental to the FG's general portrait of the proud Pharisees, especially in their attitude in John 9:40–1). In response to this, the angel Uriel is sent to offer Ezra a path to enlightenment.

At the outset, however, Ezra's understanding is weak, he is ignorant and blind to the truth; this corresponds to the description in John 19:39, of Nicodemus first coming to Jesus "by night" meaning, simply, that as a Pharisee, he walked in a spiritual "darkness" (though this also alludes to his *secret* meetings with Jesus). "You cannot understand the things with which you have grown up; how then can your mind comprehend the way of the Most High?" demands Uriel (2 Esd 4:10). This is simply paraphrased in John 3:12: 'If I have told you about earthly things, and you do not believe, how can you believe if I tell you about heavenly things?'

Only those whose origins are "in heaven," the angel continues, can truly understand heavenly matters (4:21, cf. compare John's argument concerning Jesus' "purity" i.e., Jesus' authority is "from heaven," as is Uriel's). Nicodemus, a Pharisee, is not considered "from God" (see John 8:47), and thus cannot comprehend heavenly matters *unless* he is reborn from "above" (3:7). The Greek word for "you" here is plural (as in vv.11 and 12), inferring that Nicodemus (like Nathanael) is representing a group, e.g., all those who walk in metaphorical darkness (e.g., the Pharisees). Being "born from above" simply means being *chosen* as, or *choosing* to become, a member of the new order that has its authority 'in heaven'. It also implies a shedding of presumption, of arrogance, of assumed knowledge.

Ezra is confused, claiming he doesn't desire knowledge of heavenly things, he merely wishes to understand why Israel appears to have been forsaken. Uriel responds by insisting that the root of 'evil', the "place where evil has been sown," must pass away before the "field where the good has been sown" can "come" (2 Esd 4:29). This theme is apparent in the sign of the old/new wines and the public declaration concerning the old and new temple in John 2, the latter of which Nicodemus is, undoubtedly, fully aware.

Beginning to perceive that the fault may lie within Israel itself, a fault that prolongs the advent of the new era, Ezra demands an explanation. In John 7:5–1, Nicodemus perceives a fault in the rash behaviour of his fellow Pharisees, requesting clarification (this acts as the second stage in Nicodemus' depiction, which I will discuss again).

Uriel uses the imagery of a woman giving birth at the end of her term, insinuating that the destruction of the old world is an *inevitability* and that the evil will be eradicated and the righteous reborn from the 'womb' of Hades (2 Esd 4:41–2). The earthly woman cannot return the child to her womb but the implication is that God can (i.e., where the child is understood to be the spiritually pure Israel). The reproduction theme is echoed within the basic premise of the 'rebirth' discussion between Jesus and Nicodemus, and in Jesus' own birth analogy in John 16. For Ezra and Nicodemus the central element of interest is the matter of *signs* pointing to a new truth or reality that is not easily comprehended. *Seeing* the signs and understanding them requires a degree of humility and difficulty; the rebirth (the rite of passage) is a painful one.

Ezra is asked, "why are you disturbed ... why have you not considered in your mind what is to come ...?" (2 Esd 7:15–16). Such a question is reflected in Jesus' astonishment over Nicodemus' initial lack of understanding, even though he represents those who claim to 'teach' Israel (John 3:9–10). The inadequacy of these teachers is, once again, brought to the fore of the narrative. The underlying order to Ezra, then, is a commission for him to convey what he has learnt to others; he is to *teach* from his experience (cf. 2 Esd 14:22), to show people the path to Life.

The overall essence of this debate on earthly versus heavenly matters is that in order to recognise the 'kingdom of God' and in order to return to it, one must remove all preconceptions and convictions. Everything Nicodemus *thinks* he knows will not earn him a place in the new order; he must accept that he is ignorant of the Truth and be willing to be enlightened. Once granted the wisdom of the Spirit, such an enlightened one must teach (not preach to) others, and show them the path to God. This is the first lesson of the gospel, a lesson in humility and concentration. It teaches us how to proceed through the gospel, how to 'see' the signs, and how to 'follow' Jesus.

Jesus and the 2 Esdras Parallels

How does Jesus come to the knowledge that *he* is the one to challenge the establishment and herald the dawning of a new era for Israel? There is a potential answer within the profound parallels of 2 Esdras; in fact, I will go as far as to suggest 2 Esdras is, at least partially, another record of the trials and tribulations of Jesus, and that this account is either a first-hand testament written by Jesus himself, or another, perhaps slightly earlier rendition of the FG, written by the same gospel author. It may, indeed, be a united effort, for it bears the same stamp of ambiguity inherent in the FG, where one identification suits two people, or places, etc., and the distinction between the protagonist and the author is intentionally made unclear.

Take a look at the following list of *selected* parallels (there are many more than Christian exegetes suggest) between 2 Esdras and the FG (including some concepts retained in Luke's gospel). The similarities are astounding, if we are to take them as coincidental. (Naturally, most of the FG scenarios have yet to be explained but you can refer back to this list once you have finished reading the book and verify what I suggest.)

2 Esdras	Jesus Story
"The word of the Lord that came to Ezra son of Chusi"	The only similar name in the NT is in Luke 8:3, where Chuza is a "steward" of the king; cf. the "royal official" (John 4:46). Lazarus (FG) is the son of the royal official
The story opens with an allusion to the wandering in the wilderness and the lack of appreciation for the Promised Land	The FG opens with a symbolic parallel to the wilderness, the entry into the Promised Land, and the corruption of the covenant
The author is called Salathiel ("I have asked of God") and/or Ezra ("help")	Luke's genealogy of Jesus includes a "Salathiel." Jesus claims to have spoken to the Father. Lazarus becomes "one who is helped" (by Jesus) and one who helps (as the *parakletos*); both Lazarus and Jesus have echoes of Ezra, reflecting FG ambiguity
Salathiel begins his mission thirty years after the "destruction of the city"	In Luke, Jesus' age at the beginning of his mission is "about thirty"
He disappears for forty days and nights before beginning his work	In the Synoptics, Jesus spends forty days/nights in the desert before beginning his work
Children of the Father	Children of the Father
A certain "chief of the people" comes to Salathiel/Ezra, at night; his name is Phaltiel, meaning "deliverance of God"	Nicodemus (meaning "victor for the people," teacher, or leader) comes to Jesus by night
"Recently, you also laid hands on me, crying out before the judge's seat for him	John 19

"to deliver me to you, and you delivered me to death by hanging on the tree"	
"if I have not done the things my Father commanded, I will contend in judgement with you"	John 5:36–8; 18:19–23, etc.
"they do not see me with bodily eyes, yet with the spirit they will believe the things I have said"	"Blessed are those who have not seen, yet have come to believe"
"And I will raise up the dead from their places, and bring them out from their tombs, because I recognise my name in them"	The "raising" of Lazarus
"I will send you help"	The *parakletos*; general concept of healing the nation; help in the 'storm'; Lazarus' name implies help
Consecrated twelve	Twelve disciples/ministers
"Not one of the servants whom I have given you will perish"	John 17:6f
"Remember your children that sleep"	Jesus' adopted 'son' Lazarus is (symbolically, as Israel) "sleeping"
"When I came to them they rejected me"	Self-explanatory
"Wait for your shepherd"	John 10:1–18
A "perpetual light" will shine on the righteous.	"...the light of the world...of life."
The converted are robed in white	John 4:35; 20:12
On Mount Zion: those "who have put off mortal clothing and have put on the immortal, and have confessed the name of God" are "crowned, and receive palms"	Jesus returns in triumph; followers hail him with palms
Many "wonders" have been seen (cf. 9:6)	"Unless you see signs and wonders"
"My spirit was greatly agitated"	John 11:33

"…what was good departed"	The Remnant concept
"…you raised up for yourself a servant"	Jesus as servant / Israel 'lifted up'
"You may find individuals who have kept your commandments, but nations you will never find"	Nathanael (the Remnant)
Uriel/Ezra discussion	Jesus/Nicodemus discussion
Sowing, reaping, harvesting; evil must pass away before good can come, etc.	John 4:35f; 12:24f
"Stand at my right side, and I will show you the interpretation"	Lazarus is at Jesus' right side, and is privy to 'secret' knowledge
"And one shall reign whom [they] do not expect"	John 1:26, 8:48f, 19:5, etc.
"…do you not know that Israel has been entrusted to you in the land of their exile?"	Nazareth = Arzareth
"…do not forsake us, like a shepherd who leaves the flock in the power of savage wolves"	John 10:12
A seven-day confinement	Lazarus and disciples undergo seven-day confinements
The "chosen vine"	"I am the vine"
"…one dove"	John 1:32
"…this people whom you have loved"	Lazarus/Israel ("the one whom Jesus loves")
"…why have you handed the one over to the many …?" (and read on)	Martha questions Jesus' decision to let Lazarus 'die' (it is the will of God)
God visits his creation / the 'plan' is prepared before Time / see note regarding Son of Man	Son of Man
"Jacob is the beginning of the age that follows"	Abraham's children, the 'house of Jacob'; the firstborn, and the rightful

	heir
"…when the humiliation of Zion is complete"	Storming of the temple, conversion of priests and Pharisees, triumphal entry, seat over the stone pavement
"…corruption shall be overcome"	"I have conquered the world"
"…greater things than these"	"…greater things than these"
Ezra is granted this insight because God has seen the 'purity' he has maintained from his youth	Jesus' purity debated; there is no deceit in Nathanael, or the Remnant
"As for the other nations that have descended from Adam, you have said that they are nothing … they are like spittle"	Blind man washes away 'world' by washing off the dust and spittle
"…how will the heir receive the inheritance unless by passing through the appointed danger?" / "unless the living pass through the difficult … experiences, they can never receive those things that have been reserved for them"	Lazarus, Mary and Jesus all have to undergo great tribulation before the 'kingdom' can be inaugurated
The disobedient do not perform God's 'works'	Jesus does the 'works' of the Father; Peter does not
The time will come, when the city ('bride') "that now is not seen shall appear, and the land that is now hidden shall be disclosed"	"…the hour is coming when you will worship the Father neither on this mountain nor in Jerusalem"
"…to you alone I have shown these things"	The secrecy between Jesus and Lazarus/Nicodemus
"…who among the living is there that has not sinned?"	"Let anyone among you who is without sin be the first to throw a stone"
"…the Most High has made not one world, but two"	Throughout the FG, Jesus alludes to the duality of existence (good and evil, light and darkness, above/earth, flesh/spirit, etc.); also, John 19:36

Honour God's name	John 12:28
The seven blessings of the righteous after death, including glorification, inheritance, faces that shine "like the sun"	Lazarus' seventh sign is for the glorification of Jesus and God, it is the culmination of the uniting of the tribes and the reinstatement of the 'rightful heir'; his face is covered with a veil to suggest a shining face
The righteous dead will have freedom for seven days in order to witness what has happened	Jesus flees to Shiloh after the crucifixion, in order to inaugurate the new order; his period of purification lasts seven days
The "righteous will be able to intercede for the ungodly, or to entreat the Most High for them—fathers for sons"	Martha believes Jesus can intercede for Lazarus, his 'son'
The 'contest' of choosing 'life' over 'death' (cf. 8:56)	John 3:19–21; 18:40
The "world to come [is] for the sake of only a few"	Throughout the FG this is a running theme. Only those who hear Jesus' 'voice', 'see' the signs, etc., get to enter the new Promised Land
Ezra is "taken up" from humankind after his mission is complete	Jesus retreats and then expects to go to the Father after his mission is complete
Ezra humbles himself / compared to those who "walk in great pride"	The story of Lazarus and Peter
For the righteous, "paradise is opened"	"…under the fig tree"
"…illness is banished… death is hidden"	Lazarus and Jesus 'conquer' both
God saved and laboured over the Remnant	Jesus tells the disciples that they are benefiting from "others' labour" / the Samaritans are part of the Remnant
The vision of the mourning woman	John 11
The vision of the temple being destroyed and the raising of a divine 'city' in its place	John 2:13–22 (and the raising of Lazarus, etc.)

The Testament of Lazarus

"Stand up like a man, and I will instruct you"	The lame man is told to get up
"…you have been called to be with the Most High as few have been"	"The Father and I are one"; calling of the twelve, and "the one"
"Twelve kings shall reign," each of equal duration	The 'twelve' are to be equal (foot-washing and Peter's story in the FG epilogue)
The Messiah ben David will come later, at the end of days	Jesus is not the Messiah ben David (cf. John 7:41–3)
"judgement seat"	"judgement seat"
The man from the sea	John 6:16–21
"…carved out for himself a great mountain" but the place from which it is carved cannot be seen	Shiloh is Jesus' 'holy mountain'; it cannot be 'seen' because it isn't a physical mountain but a symbolic one
A violent crowd gathers against him; many are killed	Jesus' group is attacked by Pilate's men (Samaritan tumult)
He comes down from the mountain with a "peaceable" crowd	Shiloh means 'peaceable'
Where he is, is a site of worship	Jesus establishes the 'house of God' at Shiloh
This figurehead is sent to "direct those that are left"	Jesus the 'shepherd,' the 'way,' etc., for the Remnant
This figure is the "Son of God"	Jesus is the "Son of God"
He shall declare the iniquities of the world from Mount Zion	Jesus begins his tirade against the world from the temple and does so repeatedly
The "nine tribes" are in Arzareth	Jesus is "of Nazareth"; the northern (scattered) tribes are in 'limbo'
No one can see the "Son" until his hour comes	Many do not 'see' Jesus; his 'hour' is anticipated throughout the narrative

"On the third day"	"On the third day"
"...the age is divided into twelve parts, and nine ... have already passed"	"Twelve hours of daylight ... night is coming..."
Ezra is "lying there like a corpse" because a vision has confounded him; he seeks understanding and is subsequently 'raised'	Lazarus is 'sick,' imprisoned, and metaphorically 'dead'; Jesus rescues him and he rises a new priest
Darkness vs. light	Darkness vs. light
"...send the holy spirit into me"	Jesus receives the Holy Spirit
Secret teachings for the 'wise' are the "fountain of wisdom, and the river of knowledge"	Jesus confides certain mysteries to his chosen ones, and the gospel itself tells a secret

The concept of Jesus' own enlightenment before his mission in Judea and Israel does seem logical. On the basis that 2 Esdras is, in fact, a parallel tale of our man, Jesus, I suggest that we can glean a rationale for Jesus' mid-life compulsion to stir up trouble in Jerusalem from the explanation provided in 2 Esd 3:28–36. Having spent thirty years travelling the world (just the period of 'missing years' scholars are so intent on explaining), Salathiel begins to realise that the rest of the nations seem to do very well, in a materialistic sense, even though they are unmindful of the commandments. He questions the long-believed in supremacy of (the Jerusalem-based) Israel and its unique relationship with the divine because the nation has failed so dismally in its attempt to attain, or retain, the Promised Land ideal. In other words: If God's way is so fickle as to allow his chosen people to fall into despair, while the ungodly foreigners seem to reap all the rewards, how can anyone hope to comprehend, and follow, the path to righteousness?

As he lies on his bed one night, so Salathiel describes (2 Esd 3:1), his emotions get the better of him, and he demands explanation. The ensuing text reveals how he is granted enlightenment and this forms the very foundation for the parallel discussion between Jesus and Nicodemus in the FG. Salathiel (Ezra) is convinced by one wiser than himself (the angel, Uriel), that the salvation of Israel lies in the advent of one who will bring the 'secret knowledge' (cf. 8:62) of the divine will back to the devout Israelites. The visions of a man going up a mountain, coming out of the sea, etc., are visions of his own future (albeit with the benefit of hindsight); these, too, are episodes depicted in the FG.

Salathiel is called to Mount Horeb, another name for Mount Sinai (where Elijah is also to be found, in 1 Kgs 19:8), from which he is ordered by God to 'go to Israel' (2:33), e.g., as the new Moses. As we have already seen, in the gospel, Jesus is formally commissioned in the shadow of Mount Nebo, where Moses dies, having passed on the office to Joshua.

It is perfectly feasible that Salathiel, our Jesus, leaves Palestine (for whatever reason) while still quite young, and travels. The more he sees, the more he thinks of his homeland, his people, and his heritage. He returns with knowledge few of his peers can match ("How does this man have such learning ...?" John 7:15), and a zeal for the revivification of Israel, i.e., the cultural inheritance of his forefathers.

So, it may be that Jesus, just like Moses before him, finds himself in a foreign land, under the patronage of an advisor (e.g., a Jethro-figure), a guru; he perceives things his peers back in Palestine have no hope of perceiving, being so close to the cause of the problem for an objective understanding. His passion for God and for the apparently forgotten roots of the Israelite religion leads him back to the land of his birth and the people of his blood. Jesus believes he has been sent from God for a purpose—to return his people to the Promised Land, once and for all, and to return the crown to the sons of Joseph.

In Luke's genealogy for Jesus, which contains the significant FG names of Joseph, Joshua, Eliezer, Melchi (i.e., Melchizedek), is also the unusual name Salathiel (Shealtiel in the NRSV). If Matthew's account was already in circulation, why would Luke choose to vary the lineage so greatly? There is no logical means by which he could have discovered Jesus' lineage after 70 CE (when most records were destroyed), so I think the only feasible answer is that Luke was influenced by the FG and/or the 2 Esdras legacy.

The second and third stages of Nicodemus' story (John 7 and 19) will be explored at the appropriate junctures.

Raising the Son of Man

The "son of man" phrase occurs in the OT, in one or other of its variant forms, one hundred and seven times. In most instances it refers to humans in a generic sense, either in the singular or the plural. Obviously, this is not the easiest of topics to discuss briefly but, once I uncovered what seemed to me to be the overall gist of the FG's message, and realised the context into which the "son of man" phrase is set, I returned to the OT precedents to see if anything in particular stood out.

In the Greek FG, the phrase in John 3:13 is ambiguous and doesn't appear as an obvious title as it does in the English versions, where the 'S' and the 'M' are capitalized (again, a Christian practice, to show respect for what is perceived to be a pseudonym for Jesus). The literal translation of the Greek is actually "the son of the man" or, "the man's son." This becomes a clue, in fact, to the identity of a significant character later in the narrative, so it is important to recognise this subtle distinction.

My search for a precedent to suit Jesus' apparent usage of the phrase led me to this, taken from a direct translation of the Hebrew text: "O Shepherd of Israel, you who lead Joseph like a flock! ... let your hand be upon the man of your right hand, upon the son of man whom you made strong for yourself" (Ps 80:1, 17). The Hebrew term for "right hand" is *yamin*; some commentators hazard a guess that a potential allusion to Benjamin may exist here (which is itself translated as "son of the right hand"), but no further explanation is offered. Benjamin, of course, is one of the tribes to head southward to Jerusalem after the Sinai schism, along with Judah (hence, "Benjamin" can also be translated as "man of the south"). The son of Jacob, Benjamin, is not only the youngest, he is said to have been born in Canaan; he is falsely incriminated and imprisoned (for theft) but proves to be Joseph's favourite brother and is exonerated. The midrashic Book of Jasher suggests Benjamin and Joseph shared secret knowledge. We soon discover that the disciple symbolically linked to the tribe Benjamin is none other than Jesus' right-hand-man. Coincidences?

There is more to Psalm 80 that proves germane to our interpretation of the FG; it is a song praising the stalwart nature of the "vine" God had taken "out of Egypt" (in Jer 6:9 the 'vine' is equated with the Remnant). Despite the humiliation and degradation at the hands of its neighbours and the threat of extinction, this vine remains hopeful of some future restoration. The Hebrew word first used for "man" is *'iysh,* which is a formal or dignified term that is often used to denote a 'house' (i.e., a hereditary lineage), family, etc.; it is, effectively, a collective plural. As Joseph is likened to a "flock," we can conclude that the vine being referred to is the Remnant of the house of Joseph (see 2 Chr 34:9).

The "son of man" phrase is, in its Hebrew form, *ben 'adam* and this signifies an individual, a human being. It appears in the Manual of Discipline (DSS) as "one born of a woman." In the blessings of Jacob, it is Joseph who is depicted as the strong one, the one made "agile" and the one "helped" by God; it is Joseph who receives God's blessings on his head (Gen. 49:22f). It is also Joseph, this younger brother, who receives the special robe from his father, *not* the actual firstborn, who *normally* would have inherited this honour, as Deut 21:16 stipulates.

The placing of the right hand of God upon this representative indicates forgiveness and sanction. That the person/group is already situated on the 'right' side signifies a prominent and authoritative position; they were once 'made strong' by God for *himself*. This is an apt description of Ephraim, the firstborn of Joseph (Jer 31:9), God's *beloved* son whom he "taught to walk" (Hos 11:3):

> When Joseph saw that his father laid his right hand on the head of Ephraim, it displeased him; so he took his father's hand, to remove it from Ephraim's head to Manasseh's head. "Not so, my Father! Since this one is the firstborn, put your right hand on his head."
>
> Gen 48:17–18

Echoing his father's unconventional rise in status, Ephraim effectively becomes the firstborn in the eyes of Jacob, and of God. Ephraim's strength, however, has since been "devoured" by foreigners (Hos 7:7), and it is *this* concept that lays the foundation for the ensuing FG narrative.

> *...for I have become a father to Israel,*
> *and Ephraim is my firstborn.*
> Jer 31:9

In John 15:1–6, Jesus declares that *he* is "the vine"; he actually makes, in v.6, a clear reference to Ps 80:16, e.g., the branches of the vine will be cut down, gathered and burned, if the chosen do not follow him—reference, that is, to the long beleaguered house of Joseph. In other words, *now* is the time for the Remnant to make itself strong again, or it must resign itself to extinction.

In comparison, the wicked tenants of the parable in Luke 20:9f and Gospel of Thomas 65, the evil shepherds of John 10, and the 'unsound' grapevine of Gospel of Thomas 40, all seem to refer to the corrupt, Pharisee-ruled, priestly establishment of Jerusalem. They resent the coming (or return) of the rightful heir and plot to kill the "son" of the "landlord" in order to keep their ill-gotten inheritance. The return of the northern Remnant, remember, restores Ephraim (and thus, the house of Joseph) to the position of firstborn, and there are many with vested interests who would not wish to see this become the case. In Ps 78:67–8 the boasting of Judah is explicit: God rejected the "tent of Joseph" and "chose the tribe of Judah" as his "sanctuary." This is pure (and common) Davidic propaganda.

The raising of the "son of man" in the FG, then, has a dual implication, just as in the precedent. It suggests the rise of the Remnant of the house of Joseph, the true Israel (see 2 Esd. 16:74: "my elect ones") but also, the raising of an individual. In its general context, the "son of man" must be lifted up in a sense that evokes the meaning of Moses' raising of the Nehushtan (Num 21:4f). In both Numbers 21 and the FG, the fundamental theme is the reconfirmation of the power of God. Just as God and his people triumphed over the Egyptians, so the Nehushtan, in the former instance, stands as a reminder that even in a spiritual "wilderness," where temptations abound, the saving power of God is there for all who seek it out. It is a beacon of salvation.

> ... *lift up an ensign over the peoples ... see, your salvation comes.*
> Isa 62:10–11

> *I have made you a sign for the house of Israel.*
> Ezek 12:6

A son of man must be raised up and set before the nation as a sign by which others may see the way to an everlasting 'life'. Where the alternative is a spiritual death under the influence of contemporaneous "serpents" (i.e., the Pharisees, and the corrupt cultus), Jesus, as the divinely sanctioned agent for Israel, offers himself, and "those given" to him, as the new Nehushtan, the righteous, pre-ordained alternative. The "son of man" symbolism is linked to Nicodemus' scene because the one to be 'raised' is intimately associated with him, i.e., it is *not* Jesus.

6
THE MEETING AT QUMRAN

Aenon near Salim
JESUS BAPTISES AT THE SITE CALLED Aenon near Salim (John 3:23). Most modern scholars place the two sites where Eusebius suggested, about nine or ten miles south of Scythopolis, on the western banks of the Jordan. Others place them nearer to Shechem, with Aenon at the Wadi Far'ah, and Salim some ten miles away. I suggest there is an alternative understanding of the name.

From the Hebrew, the name Aenon derives from *'ayin*, meaning "eye," figuratively understood to mean "fountain or spring" (e.g., as the focal spot of a landscape, etc.) and this is usually how it is translated. From the Greek, however, it comes from the word *aineo*, "to praise." "Salim" echoes the name Salem, the city commonly identified with Jerusalem, from which Melchizedek came to meet Abraham in the desert (Genesis 14); John 3:22 states that the site is in Judea. One of the most ancient sources of a reference to Jerusalem is the collection of Amarna Letters (c. fourteenth-century BCE letters from foreign rulers that include many details on Canaan and the Hebrews' entry and settlement there), where it is referred to as Urusalim. In Assyrian texts there is a similar spelling of Urusalimmu. There may be an intended play on the Hebrew word, *shalem,* which means "to make ready, to complete, restore," etc., but scholars have a difficult time accepting the shift from the 's' sound to the 'sh'; there is also an inherent meaning of "peace," where *shalom* is inferred, making Jerusalem, traditionally, the "city of peace" (which, despite the 'sh', is seldom debated).

The word used in the Greek text of John 3:23 to denote "near" is *engus*, which has the connotation of being ready, being at hand. The ordinary application of "near" (proximity), such as in John 4:5 ("Sychar, near the plot of ground ..."), uses *plesion*; the reader is thus intended to interpret *engus* as being not only (necessarily) physically near but also, strategically 'ready'.

The three words taken together offer an interesting picture of where John and his disciples are in John 3:

Aenon + near + Salim

The place of praise + ready + Jerusalem / restored

Or: The place of praise which is ready for the restored Jerusalem

Other information comes from John 3:23, i.e., "water was abundant there"; if we take Salim to be a possible play on the Greek term *saleuo*, which means, "to destroy, disturb by shaking," this would suggest something to do with an earthquake. Earthquakes are rarely mentioned in the OT and are usually described in fairly generic terms as a punishment of God, or a sign of his presence, etc. They are, however, fairly common in Palestine and a few extremely damaging ones have been recorded in sources external to the Bible; there is *one* specific biblical source, however, i.e., Amos 1:1, in which an earthquake is mentioned in a historical context. The prophet Amos, who is also sent to warn the Samaritans that the time has come for them to return to God, is given his message from God at Jerusalem, "two years before the earthquake." This only precedent (cf. Joel 4:16) is thus a historical account of a physical phenomenon and is directly associated with the vicinity around Jerusalem. There is only one place that we know of that fits these various elements: the place we now refer to as Qumran.

Qumran is a place of worship (praise), whose inhabitants see themselves as the elect few who are prepared for the day when Jerusalem will be purified. Here we find copious supplies of water, specifically for cleansing rituals, etc., but there is also the Wadi Salim only six miles northeast of Jerusalem, lying between the city and the Dead Sea. To complete the picture, Qumran has previously been abandoned due to an earthquake, probably the one in 31 BCE that is well attested.

It would seem that Jesus has approached the sect *at* Qumran; he has taken it upon himself to emulate John, who is now back in his own territory. Is this a challenge? It certainly is not a peaceful joining of forces to ensure a mutually satisfactory outcome, for there is a degree of antagonism in the narrative, a sense of resentment and/or imminent rejection even.

In John 3:25f, there is a debate taking place concerning purification, specifically the level of purity Jesus can claim in taking on the role of baptiser (3:26). This purification theme echoes the description of the six jars of purification water at the wedding; we are invited to make the connection. The Manual of Discipline (DSS) specifies that there must be a complete submission of the soul to the will of God before the waters of purification can sanctify the individual; the water itself symbolises the conferring of the "spirit of truth." One intriguing rule is emphasized, though: No one can use baptism to assume the purity of holy men. This would seem to be the crux of the debate concerning Jesus.[1]

> *O Jerusalem, wash your heart clean of wickedness*
> *so that you may be saved.*
> Jer. 4:14

Bridegroom
John, in the context of ritual cleansing, attempts to quell the debate on purification by launching into a strange analogy of the bride and bridegroom; what is the connection? There must be two sides to the argument; *presumably*, the disciples are defending Jesus' purity, and the Jew is questioning it (at least, that is how the FG preserves the event but I have more to say on this) but why is this emissary from Jerusalem concerned with Jesus' purity at all? Jesus has made his intentions known to the priesthood in Jerusalem; he has declared that he is going to see the current order destroyed and a new one rise in its place. People are already converting to his way of thinking, so the emissaries are in pursuit, in order to learn more about this man's credentials.

Priests according to law, do the ritualistic cleansing of anything, e.g., people, temple, etc. John *is* a priest, but Jesus? Remember that the Jews claim to 'know' Jesus' genealogy; at some stage they must have checked him out (it isn't until John 6:42 that they reveal they have done this). *Records are scrutinized if anyone claims descent from the priestly families* (see Neh 7:64), so judging from their reaction, Jesus obviously doesn't meet the criteria. What right *does* he have to act this way? John's intercession is profound and damning: "No one can be given anything except was has been given from heaven" (John 3:27), he begins, referring of course to Jesus' earlier election as God's representative (the hand of God, remember, symbolically coming to rest on his head [as the 'dove'], granting him authority, e.g., "I have put my spirit upon him" [Isa 42:1]).

Such a granting of authority and the debatable level of purity for the role, echoes Isaiah 6, which tells of the prophet being chosen to give the people of Israel a message. Isaiah questions his own suitability for the job, suggesting that he is not pure enough to speak the word of God; a seraph (a winged creature; cf. 'dove') brings a burning coal from the altar and touches his lips, both purging his guilt and conferring on him his commission. He is then told to go to the people and to tell them that they must *close their eyes*

---

[1] Note how John 3:22 states Jesus "baptised" but in 4:2, which is clearly an addendum, this is contradicted, claiming it was not he who baptised, but his disciples. I suggest this is a direct reaction to the purity debate, i.e., the "Jew(s)" consider that Jesus, as a man of history (not a divine entity) cannot be seen to assume the purity of John, the priest, especially as he is a Samaritan.

and ears, e.g., to the iniquitous world and turn their hearts back to God, who will save (heal) them. This is precisely what Jesus has to (and will) do.

In the presence of the Jew, John *apparently* reconfirms Jesus' commission and at the same time he rails against the ineptitude and illegitimacy of the present cultus, the representative of which is standing right there, i.e., *it* has not received authority from heaven. This endorsement of Jesus at such an early stage in the mission, however, is valuable propaganda for the FG author but notice how rapidly John disappears from the story.

To John, Jesus is the "bridegroom" because he *seems to be* the authorized, sanctified high priest of God, come to restore Israel to her rightful place at God's side. John must retreat, so that Jesus can take over, so the gospel suggests. John's rejoicing over the bridegroom in turn echoes the sentiment of Isa 62:5, where the bridegroom rejoices over the bride and God then rejoices over Israel. We are led to suppose that this pattern will be followed, progressing from the bridegroom's friend, to the groom, to God, with the ultimate effect being restored relations between God and Israel (the sentiments expressed in the marriage ceremony).

> The spirit of the Lord is upon me, because the Lord has anointed me; he has sent me to bring good news to the oppressed, to bind up the broken hearted, to proclaim liberty to the captives, and release the prisoners; to proclaim the year of the Lord's favour, and the day of vengeance of our God ... he has clothed me with the garments of salvation, he has covered me with the robe of righteousness, as a bridegroom decks himself with a garland, and as a bride adorns herself with jewels.
>
> Isa 61:1–2, 10

This is fighting talk to any security-minded informer who may be listening; a coup must be in the works, a challenge to the *status quo*. That the information gets back to the Pharisees is no surprise; their appeasement policy helps keep Jerusalem in bondage to the Romans but if they can be of any assistance in quelling a potential uprising, the better for them.

John, remember, claims not to know Jesus; he claims someone told him to baptise, told him to authenticate 'the one on whom the Spirit landed'; his initial ratification of Jesus' mission, we shall see, is short-lived. The overwhelming aftermath of Jesus' visit to Qumran is ultimately detrimental.

7
SAMARITAN WOMAN

ISRAEL IS IN A SORRY STATE when Jesus begins his mission. In the cycle of events prescribed in Ezekiel 16 for the divine bride, the nation is currently in a state corresponding to that of *infidelity*. The very next scene in the FG, not surprisingly, is the story of the woman with many ex-husbands *and* a current lover!

Sychar
Jesus and the disciples are said to travel from Aenon near Salim to Galilee, through Samaria (John 4:3–4), apparently following in the footsteps of Joseph in Gen 37:13–15. Instead of arriving at Shechem, however, they come to a place called Sychar, around which there is much debate concerning its possible identification with, or distinction from, Shechem. Most interpreters tend to identify Sychar with Shechem because it is akin to the Hebrew word *cakar*, which can mean "purchase," and to *karah*, which is more specifically the purchase of land; this is justified by the fact that Jacob purchases a plot of land from Shechem's father (Gen 33:19).

Shechem is significant for other reasons, however, e.g., it is where Jacob erects an altar to the God of Israel; Joseph's bones are buried there (Josh. 24:32); and it is the site of the renewal of the covenant in Joshua 24. It is the location of the blessings and the curses, according to the Law of Moses (Deut 11:29, 27:11f), and in the allocation of territory, it is given to 'the house of Joseph' (Joshua 16). It is this affiliation through Jacob to the house of Joseph that John 4:5 makes clear but we are told only that Sychar is '*near*' this plot of land, i.e., 'near' as in physical proximity (not 'readiness', as in "near Salim"). Besides, the tale of Shechem in Genesis 37 is one of the incarceration of Joseph (in a dried out well) by his brothers; this negative imagery, though germane to later episodes in the FG, is not what is required or intended at this point in the narrative. The current scenario is ultimately positive and hopeful, so although the site may indeed allude to Josephite territory, and to important cultural precedents, the name

"Shechem" is purposefully avoided and Sychar is inserted to provide further theological impetus.

In attempting to decipher the symbolic significance of this specific place name, taking into consideration any possible corruptions but assuming the original was never explicitly written as "Shechem,"[1] we must see if there are any other biblical words, apart from *cakar*, that could be the subject of allusion. I offer the following suggestions:

> **Shachar (verb)**: Meaning "to go about a task early; to seek, enquire, etc., diligently"—the woman is at the well early, and the first thing she does is ask Jesus a question. This term is used in Pss 63:1, 78:1, and Prov 1:28, 8:17, in the context of searching for God. In Hos 5:15, however, it is used in a direct diatribe against the illicit practices of both Judah *and* Ephraim. God is the one saying, "I will return again to my place, until they acknowledge their guilt and seek my face." What Jesus is about to do and say reflects this sentiment.
>
> **shekar (noun) / shakar (verb)**: Meaning "strong drink / drunkard; "to be intoxicated." In John 2, Jesus is presenting himself to an intoxicated world, a world in which the inhabitants have been seduced by cheap wine but have remained parched. The concept is used first in Lev 10:9, where the priesthood is warned not to drink before entering the tent of meeting. From Num 6:3 (regarding Nazarites), to Mic 2:11, it is employed almost exclusively in a pejorative sense.

Ephraim is full of "drunkards" (Isa 28:1), so we are led to believe, and this has made it weak (Hos 7:7). Hellenism, foreign idolatry, kingship, illegal marriages, etc., have all seduced God's children away from their birthright, away from the clear path to, and promised position with, God. The northern tribes, whose assimilation with the indigenous peoples of Samaria has brought nothing but damnation from their southern relatives, are seen in Hosea's passionate verses as the "prostitute" (9:1), the whore who has "bargained for lovers" (8:9) and has broken the covenant with God (see Isa 1:21; 57:8 and Jer 3:1).

Still, there is another potential allusion to be recognised, here. Joshua

---

[1] The only other mention of Shechem in the NT is in Acts 7:16 and this is in its Greek form, Sychem. The ancient Greek manuscript evidence for Sychar, on the other hand, is overwhelming. Only the Sinaitic and Syriac translations of the FG employ Sychem for John 4:5.

(son of Nun) is buried at a place called Timnath-serah (Josh 24:30) in the hill country of Ephraim, north of Mount Ga'ash, i.e., in his *own* territory from within the lands of the Israelites (19:50). The burial site is referred to in the LXX, however, as *Thamnasachar* (Gk). Mount Ga'ash has never been located; the name appears first in the Book of Joshua (and then in Judg 2:9, 2 Sam 23:30, and 1 Chr 11:32) in connection with a torrent, or wadi. The word *ga'ash* is commonly translated as "earthquake" but is more of an agitation, a troubling or stirring up of something, rather than a trembling earth. It may be a play on *ga'al*, and/or *ga'ar*, both of which have negative connotations ("to reject or rebuke"). On the other hand, "Gerizim" means "to cut off"; all these terms suggest an upheaval, a change, an agitation. Is Mount Ga'ash the same as Mount Gerizim? As the hill country extends all the way up to include Shechem (Josh 20:7), the site may lie very close to Sychar. The wadi (a tributary of the Jordan is close by) is, perhaps, that which supplies Jacob's Well.

We can glean more information from Timnath-serah:

Timnath: Meaning "portion assigned" or "manifestation."

serah/cerach: Often translated as "overhanging," and thus taken literally to mean that the town was on the edge of a steep declivity; however, it generally refers to something that extends, or is in excess and thus suggests the possibility of a "remnant."

This creates a very interesting possibility:

Timnath + Serah/Cerach

portion/manifestation (of the) Remnant

Joshua saw himself (and his people) as the Remnant of Joseph and this was *his* land, *his* 'portion'. Jesus' mission is to restore the 'portion' to its rightful owners, i.e., the Remnant.

So, Sychar is probably Timnathsachar/cerach, the burial place of Joshua, Jesus' namesake, north of Mount Gerizim, *near* Shechem.

The Virgin Harlot

Jesus happens upon this supposedly shameless woman at Jacob's Well. The introduction of a well/water scenario allows for Jesus to offer himself as the bearer of a satiating alternative, e.g., "With joy you will draw water from the wells of salvation" (Isa 12:3), echoing the overflowing water at the wedding in Cana but there is much more to this scene than meets the eye!

In both Genesis 24 and 29, there is a basic thematic structure: A man arrives at a well; he meets a woman; there is a discussion concerning the water of the well; there follows a discussion concerning 'kin' and marriage; the woman runs home to tell her people; the man stays with his new found family for a time. In Genesis 29 the man marries the woman at the well but in Genesis 24, the woman follows the servant *to* her future husband.

The Samaritan woman is at the well at about "noon" or, in the Greek, "about the sixth hour." In the explained reckoning of time, however, this "sixth hour" (one of the designated "hours") runs from 9 A.M. to 12 midday, so it is, generally speaking, morning. In Genesis 24, Abraham's servant arrives at the well "toward evening," while in Genesis 29, Jacob arrives in "broad daylight." It is the echo of this latter scene to which the "sixth hour" time frame, and the explicit mentioning of Jacob in the FG alludes; it is a signal for us to return to the precedent for further insight (there is no other biblical precedent for "Jacob's Well" than this).

Jacob is advised that the sheep cannot be watered until "all the flocks are gathered together, and the stone is rolled from the mouth of the well" (Gen 29:7–8). This is a very cryptic clue, employed in the FG as an allusion to the culmination of Jesus' mission and which you will only appreciate much *later* in the gospel's narrative but it makes the symbolic allusion to Genesis 29 very strong indeed. From Genesis 24, on the other hand, are almost verbatim repetitions of dialogue in the request for a drink of water and the refusal to eat until Jesus has completed the work he has been sent to do. There is also a similar testing of the woman concerned; the servant in Genesis 24 decides that the woman who gives him a drink *and* offers to water his camels will be the one he will choose to be the wife of Isaac, his master's son.

Jesus sets up the Samaritan woman for a 'test' by telling her to fetch her "husband"; if she is a "virgin, whom no man [has] known" (Gen 24:16), she can become a suitable wife. Her first response, as Rebekah's in the precedent, is to confirm the man's expectations, i.e., she has no husband. This becomes the basis for another theological expression of intent in the FG. The woman at Sychar has no husband, yet she has known many "husbands," i.e., five, in fact.[2] It is clear that this character is now a

---

[2] In the story of Tobit, the man from Naphtali, there is a woman by the name of Sarah who is said to have had seven husbands, though she remains a virgin, for each of them has died before she 'took on their name' in the 'bed chamber'. This is not the only parallel between Tobit and the FG, for there is also a blindness that is miraculously cured, a wedding feast, emphasis on heritage and remnant, and the testing of the young couple by an angel. Tobit, like the FG author, is also

representative of Samaria, just as Nathanael is the representative of the Remnant, and Nicodemus of the Pharisees.

Originally, I interpreted the number five in light of 2 Kgs 17:24f, where, after the mass deportation by the Assyrians, Samaritan Israelites are assimilated with peoples from Babylon, Cuthah, Avva, Hamath and Sepharvaim. A marriage of thought and of culture ensued which was officiated, or supervised, by an Israelite (Samaritan) priest, and because of this apparent sanctification, the idea of Yahweh as "husband" during this time *seems to be* compatible. The current immigrant into Samaria, who is *not* considered a husband, for there is no marriage, would then be Rome. This union is *not* sanctified by the legitimate priests of, and therefore cannot include, God.

Then I asked myself, would *this* Jesus, a man so devoted to returning Israel to its original priestly and exalted state, truly consider these foreigners as husbands? Is this in keeping with the FG's perception of the bride/groom, and does it truly tally with the concept of Ezekiel's Bride of God idea? In the end, I had to say no. It would also make the subsequent statement, concerning the worship on the mountain, a *non sequitur*. The two concepts must be linked and they must result in Jesus' being able to declare himself the 'one' who is expected. So, let's try something else.

When Jesus first arrives, from the south, he is recognised as a Jew (the "you" in 4:20 is plural, indicating that the woman perceives Jesus as a representative of the Jews) but in Jerusalem he is referred to as a Samaritan. Like Nathanael, though, who bases his declaration that Jesus is "the Son of God" and the "King of Israel" on the concept of a *future* restoration (the fig tree idea), so the woman is convinced Jesus is Samaritan (a northerner) *only* when he makes a similar, cryptic declaration to *her* concerning her husbands and, in an *apparent* shift in thought, the *future* concept of worship. It is almost as if Jesus is using key words, secret passwords that define him as a fellow subversive, like a cautious member of a resistance community.

The Samaritan messiah, whom the woman anticipates, is to re-establish worship on Mount Gerizim, yet there seems to be a contradiction of this in the well scene of John 4:19–24. The woman declares that her ancestors worshipped on this mountain but Jesus tells her that there will come a day when the Father will be worshipped *neither* on this mountain *nor* in Jerusalem! How can this be?

Jesus goes on to suggest that the Samaritans worship what they don't know and that he and his disciples worship what they do know, isolating the Jews, yet again, as the source from which salvation comes. Hang on ... isn't

---

commissioned with the writing of a testament to the deeds/words of God. This warrants far more attention than I can provide here.

Jesus *opposed* to the Jews? Why then, are they seen as the means to salvation? If we say that Jesus must be referring to the original concept of the pure and devout (united) Israel being the means of salvation for the rest of the world, then why doesn't he say this, instead of singling out the Jews, who are so obviously the antagonists of the FG?

Remember, as far as Jesus is concerned, Samaria is currently in a state of divorce from God; it is full of 'drunkards' that no longer remember how to worship properly (the sentiment in Amos, too). Jesus needs to bring them back to their roots. The ancestors the woman mentions are, I think, her relatively *recent* ancestors, who worshipped on Mount Gerizim when a temple stood there, between c. 330 BCE and 128 BCE (when it was destroyed by John Hyrcanus, the Jewish high priest). This is why Jesus says she worships what she does not know, i.e., she doesn't know the *true* religion of Abraham, Isaac, and Jacob, and thus worships falsely.

The Samaritan woman, in her role as the representative of Samaria, *has* had five (metaphorical) husbands, five true loci of worship to the god of Abraham:

1. **Bethel**, the sacred site of Abraham and Jacob (though once in Benjamin territory, it became Ephraimite soon after).

2. **Shechem**, the site of Jacob's altar (Gen 33:1 –20).

3. **Gilgal**, which is the site of Joshua's circle of twelve stones and the circumcision of the Israelites; a holy sanctuary of northern Israel in 1 Sam 15:33; Amos 4:4, 5:5; Ho. 9:15, etc.

4. **Mount Ebal**, where Joshua sets up his altar (Josh 8:30f) and there writes the law on stones while in the presence of both the Israelites and their sacrificial offerings.

5. The fifth, and last locus of worship, is **Shiloh**, where, throughout the history of the Books of Joshua and Judges, the tabernacle is established. It is from Shiloh that the Ark of the Covenant is taken by the Philistines (1 Sam 4:5f). It never returns to the territory of Israel but is eventually sent to Jerusalem.

The woman responds to all this by saying, in effect, "the messiah is supposed to tell us these things" and Jesus claims this is his role. The term "messiah" stems from the Hebrew word *mashiyach,* meaning a consecrated person, or an 'anointed one' and, as with the Greek *christos*, this can apply equally to a priest or a king (or even a Nazarite). This specific term is used here, in John 4:25 but also in 1:41, where Andrew declares that the messiah has been found. (Remember that there is a schism being represented in the calling of the first disciples, a schism which will culminate in *two orders of priests*, which is why, I will argue, John 21 is added.

The Samaritan messiah is one who will rise from their own people, i.e., the northern tribes of Joseph (Deut 18:15; also interpreted by the Jews as Elijah). He is the Taheb, the Restorer. This messianic figure will, it is said, purify the priestly cultus so that sacrifices can once again be made according to the law of Torah; give the Samaritans all the rights and blessings that are their legitimate inheritance; convert the unbelievers; and restore the temple on Mount Gerizim.

So why, if Jesus doesn't intend to fulfil this ultimate aspect of the role, does the woman accept his claim to be the 'one' who has 'come'?

The Sceptre and the Ark

The answer lies in the unexpected significance, or profundity, of Jesus' claim. The last legitimate site of worship in Israel was Shiloh, in the heart of Ephraim territory, about ten miles south of Shechem; its hereditary priesthood is unquestioned until the time of the high priest Eli, whose iniquitous ways are blamed for its destruction in about 1050 BCE. The Prophets allude to this loss in terms of a punishment, implying that the northern tribes lost their claim to the rights of the firstborn and to their sacred union with God (cf. Ps 78:60f).

The tabernacle is merely a mobile sanctuary for the divine presence, i.e., the Ark of the Covenant; the priesthood becomes holy *only* by association. If the Ark is not there, no priesthood can be legitimated; Jerusalem, because of its iniquities no longer has the Ark, so the cultus there is all but defunct.[3] What Jesus seems to be suggesting here (and elsewhere in the gospel he reaffirms this perspective) is that the worship of God must be performed according to the ancient ways, before assimilation, before corruption, etc.

There is to be no structural temple; even the altar that Joshua erects on Mount Ebal is said to be of unhewn stones, meaning that it was a natural, temporary structure, not a permanent edifice. Jesus can say, without contradiction, that he can raise up a new holy temple in three days, for the new sanctuary is *not* a building, in fact, it isn't even made of stone!

We must also remember that traditionally, the Ark was *intended* to be housed in the tabernacle, i.e., a tent. Even when David takes the Ark to Jerusalem, he pitches a tent for it, and despite his audacious plan for a

---

[3] Traditionally, the Second Temple lacked five major aspects that made the original site holy: the Ark, the sacred fire, the Shekinah, the Holy Spirit, and the Urim and Thummim.

temple, this is supposedly realised only years later, by Solomon, the king ultimately castigated for his ungodly ways and his pride. In the depiction of Nathan's prophecy, in 2 Samuel 7, it is clearly reiterated that God is unconcerned with having a permanent sanctuary; the temple is a purely human, rather egocentric notion, to tell the truth. The Sinai construction of the tabernacle is the first and therefore the definitive will of God concerning his 'dwelling place' and we find that even in Hebrews 8, the concept of the ideal *tabernacle* and Jesus' new priesthood go hand in hand.

The lover Samaria has *now*, therefore, which is not a husband, is Mount Gerizim. It is, in part, because the Samaritans have copied the Jews, erecting a permanent site on Mount Gerizim, which has no authority in Torah to justify it (although the Samaritans, today, claim otherwise), that they have lost touch with their true heritage. According to Josephus (*Ant.* 12.5.5), the temple was actually rededicated as the Temple of Jupiter Hellenius, in an effort save the Samaritans from the wrath of Antiochus, who had just stormed the temple in Jerusalem (but the anti-Samaritan zeal of the time might have influenced Josephus to make this incident more damning than it really was); the 'other gods' aspect of the Ezekiel 16 'bride' precedent certainly would be an issue if this were true.

Salvation then (ironically), comes in the form of Hyrcanus, *the Jew* who destroys the temple and, albeit unwittingly (which is another motif of the FG narrative, throughout) prepares the way for a return of the Samaritans to true worship. The destruction of the temple on Mount Gerizim is thus a blessing in disguise.

The "White" Harvest

Refusing to eat, Jesus enigmatically refers to food the disciples do not know about; it is easy to suggest that they take it to mean physical food but Jesus, of course, is implying the sustenance he gets from doing the will of God, and that his purpose includes dealing with this woman. It seems, however, that some disciples do not comprehend Jesus' *intentions*, which is actually the case throughout the narrative.

Jesus' words to the disciples, in John 4:37–8 are an allusion to God's in Joshua 24:13, where the Israelites are gathered at Shechem just before Joshua dies: "I gave you a land on which you had not laboured, that towns that you had not built, and you live in them; you eat the fruit of the vineyards and olive yards that you did not plant." This immediately precedes Joshua's order for everyone to worship God in "sincerity and faithfulness" and to decide whom they are going to follow and worship; there is an intended connection here between Joshua and Jesus.

The whole point, I suggest, is that just as the Israelites who first entered into the Promised Land, to take possession of the territory "flowing with milk and honey," yet who had no part in planting the vineyards or olive groves, so the disciples (as representatives of the tribes) now have the opportunity to benefit from the Samaritans' long and arduous history *as the firstborn*, i.e., the first 'home' of the god of Abraham and therefore of the Israelite nation.

The time is coming for the disciples to make a choice, and soon we find that some simply do not want to be a party to Jesus' scheme.

Jesus makes a point of contrasting the mundane with the spiritual harvest just as he does with the water and the food. A very subtle aspect of the Greek text, here, which is altered in the NRSV, is the phrase: "they are already white to harvest" (John 4:35); the Greek word for "white" is replaced with the English, "ripe." The concept of 'whiteness' however, as we will see in the discussion concerning Jesus' burial, is integral to the whole theology of the FG; whiteness alludes to purity and is a strong element of Samaritan ritualistic symbolism. What Jesus is insinuating, is that the Samaritans who are keen to hear his word are pure enough to be 'harvested'—to be gathered. The ingathering of the nation (the gathering of the "sheep"), one of the expected duties of the Restorer, is to begin here, in the land of Joseph. It is during Passover, in John 6, that this intended gathering of the nations is made most emphatic.

There is also another cryptic calendar clue here, i.e., the "sixth hour.' Jesus mentions that there are four months until harvest (John 4:35); in the region of Shechem/Sychar, the produce consists, primarily, of nuts, olives, pomegranates, and grapes (not wheat and barley), and these become ready for harvesting in the months of Ab and Elul (roughly August/September), so four months prior to this would be about the time of Passover, in Nisan (April).

If Jesus arrives at the "sixth hour," this should correspond, according to our "Hours" calculations, to the 9–12 Nisan. The specific stipulation of a "two" day stay means that Jesus is invited to partake of the Passover with the Samaritans, on the evening of the fourteenth. He leaves, *symbolically*, on the "third day," though this is not a precise calendrical date, it is mentioned so that we can see him beginning his 'work' in his own territory, Galilee, on the significant and divinely-sanctioned day of "union."

The Wife
So, is Jesus coming to Jacob's Well, like his predecessors, to find a wife? If so, for himself, as in Genesis 29, or for someone else, as in Genesis 24? That the disciples do not question Jesus' conversation with this woman (John 4:27), even though they are surprised, might suggest they anticipated this

'search' but were simply amazed it happened so quickly (and this is one of many such 'coincidences' throughout the FG that hint at Jesus having connections and string-pullers throughout his 'constituency').

I struggled *intensely* with the question of Jesus' marital status for several years, mainly because I was reluctant to jump on any bandwagons. The persistent duality of the FG, so much an element of its composition, provides us with two of almost everything; why should the most significant and central figures not be treated in the same manner? Maybe the sheer ambiguity is a clue to the reality, as will prove the case with Lazarus. Although Jesus is already married to Martha, his religious convictions are such that he takes on *another* female to serve as a symbolic fulfilment of many of his ideals. This woman is the Samaritan woman; she is Mary Magdalene.

Jesus meets Mary, at Jacob's Well, the well of Gen 29, where Jacob meets Rachel. Finding a wife of his own kin, which both of the Genesis precedents emphasize, will ensure a Josephite King of Israel, one of the most important elements of Jesus' entire campaign. The ideal priesthood itself *must* be hereditary, an aspect of the presiding cultus somewhat lost in the translation between bickering factions, ambitious sycophants, and Roman occupiers!

In Hosea 3, the prophet is told to seek out an "adulterous" woman and to love her. He is to do this in order to symbolise (and understand) the tolerance and forgiveness of God's loyalty to Israel, who has turned against him. By purposefully depicting Jesus as inviting this woman (and her kin) into the 'fold' (and she is only *symbolically* an adulteress by virtue of her heritage, not by virtue of her *personal* sexual exploits, which could explain the subsequent myths about her being a prostitute, a sinner, etc.; the metaphor is lost on many from the start); it would also explain the emphasis on Mary and Martha being sisters, just as Rachel and Leah are in Genesis, i.e., one much older and married first. The ties of sisterhood in the FG might have been invented purely for the allusion's continuity, i.e., it is Rachel, the younger, second wife who bears Joseph and is thus the "mother" of the Josephite tribes. Martha might be getting beyond her childbearing years and, as will become evident, she is not exactly on the 'same page' when it comes to Jesus' self-identification.

Jesus is on an errand of sorts, doing the work he has been given to do, the will of the one who 'sent' him (John 4:34), and although he seems to make reference to "the Father" everywhere else in the FG, he does not at this juncture, which is odd (and this tallies with John not identifying the "one" who sent him to baptise, i.e., in both instances this could suggest a very human, not a divine "someone"). This is the beginning of the ambiguity that will define the ensuing personal relationships in the gospel, for we are given the subtle clue that Jesus *may* be at the well in order to find a wife for *someone else*, just as in Genesis 24, where a servant of a father (Abraham) is 'sent' out to seek a wife for a son (Isaac). In preparing ideal priesthood, Jesus *must* also unite the tribes so the priesthood can be a legitimate representative of the *entire* nation, something Korah had petitioned for back at Sinai but for which he was reviled. Although Jesus first ensures the conception of a male heir through his own lineage, i.e., with Mary, she is destined to be *the wife* of another man; this is proven a theological necessity as the narrative unfolds.

Mary first appears in the gospel, then, as the symbolic 'harlot-wife' of God, who is to undergo a complete transformation before she can aspire, or return, to her rightful position (the sevenfold cycle in Ezekiel 16, hence the "seven demons" in Luke's depiction of her?). In reality, she is a virgin, probably only twelve or thirteen years of age.

8
THE SON OF THE MAN

THE ACT OF 'HEALING' IS a necessary factor of the renewal and emancipation promised in the books of the Prophets, most especially, Malachi. The sign in John 4:46–54 is not a physical healing but a spiritual one. The return to the site of Cana, where the marriage of Nathanael took place is provocative, reiterating the theme of restoration and symbolic union.

> *Why then has the health of my poor*
> *people not been restored?*
> Jer 8:28

The event is described as the "second sign," making it one of the seven special, or wondrous, 'signs' that reveal Jesus' intention but also, his authority. When Jesus reaches Cana, a royal official comes out to seek his help; he asks Jesus to "come down" to heal his son who is sick, i.e., dying. This request for Jesus to "come down" to Capernaum corroborates the suggestion that Cana is up in the northern territory of Asher (as does the inference that it takes the man about a day to get back home—the same time it takes Josephus to make the journey).

The word used in the Greek to denote this character is *basilikos,* which means, "belonging to the king," that is, in *service to* a king. This cannot be an officer attached to the court of Herod; Antipas is not a king, he is only a tetrarch. The Synoptics mention certain "Herodians" who seem to be political supporters of the Herodian family but this has no *apparent* connection to the FG's "royal official." We need to look, rather, at the role Jesus has accepted for himself, i.e., the "King of Israel." All Jesus' disciples are referred to, at one time or another, as "servants" and it is *this* particular sign that will initiate Jesus' "work" and lead to his final victory over "the world."

We should also read these passages while bearing in mind the "father/son" factor; the use of *paidon,* the Greek word for "little boy" in John 4:49 implies a child under the age of *legal responsibility* (i.e., under thirteen), a child who is still under the authority of his parents. A son, remember, is his father's living image, the inheritor of his traits, beliefs, nature, etc. The son of the official in John 4, then, is *destined* to follow in his father's footsteps, i.e., to be a servant of a king.

The word used to describe the condition of the boy is *astheneo*, a word that will crop up again with the 'healing' scene in Jerusalem and in the story of Lazarus. It means "to be sick." The vocabulary of 'life' and 'death' used throughout the FG is metaphorical, as it is in the OT. Deut 4:4 explicitly equates 'life' with a steadfast devotion to God; adhering to the commandments brings 'life' (Deut 6:24); the "circumcision of the heart" to God brings life to the believer and his descendants (Deut 30:6); the search for wisdom is considered the path to 'life' (Prov 8:35–6; Prov 13:14); the *true* Israel is seen as the 'land of the living' (Isa 38:11, 53:8, etc.); and in Mal 2:5, the covenant with the priests is said to have been a "covenant of life."

The whole point of Jesus' discussion with Nicodemus was that one has to undergo a *spiritual rebirth* before one can enter into the new world order; a rebirth implies a death of sorts. The boy, perhaps on the brink of manhood (i.e., he is twelve, going on thirteen; the same age as Mary), will soon become responsible for his own path in life, for his own spiritual choices; this symbolic loss of childhood constitutes a 'death' and anticipates a rebirth. By requesting Jesus, in effect, to *save* his son "before he dies," the man is showing his determination to offer his son a life in Jesus' kingdom, right from the start. He offers his young son to Jesus, much in the manner of Samson and Samuel, to be a protégée, a Nazarite (one under oath to another or an ideal cause). According to Josephus, Samuel was (also) twelve when he was called into service (*Ant.* 5.10.4).

Jesus responds with an enigmatic turn of phrase: "Unless you see signs and wonders you will not believe." Christian tradition holds that Jesus is angry, disappointed in the apparent necessity for tricks and 'miracles'. He *is not* angry; he is making a perfectly clear statement of obligation; he is reaffirming the promise he made to Nathanael back in John 1:50–1; the statement implies a belief contingent upon *seeing* and *understanding* signs (an implication repeated in John 6, 9, and 11). *Except* that they (the plural denotes, again, a representative nature, this time of the servant's character) witness the signs and wonders of Jesus' work (as the manifestations of God's will), they *cannot* believe (in his mission).

The performance of "signs and wonders" in the context of anticipated emancipation brings us back, yet again, to the exodus. In Exodus 7:3, signs and wonders are integral to the transformation of the pharaoh's heart; and in Deut 4:34–5, they are recalled as the means by which God had taken one nation "from the midst of another nation," *and* as the incentive for the people to "acknowledge that the Lord is God." Through these signs and wonders,

Jesus will free those under *religious* oppression, or suffering a spiritual "sickness"; he *will*, in effect, be plucking from the midst of one nation (the sinful Israel), another (the believers). Thus, Jesus' words in John 4:48 suggest an *invitation* to witness, rather than an admonition against signs and wonders.

The sign to which the people are now witness is not a physical healing, as it supposedly takes place some distance away (at Capernaum), out of sight; no physical change is evident. The man's open request for Jesus' help and his desire to obtain for his son a better life are a profound risk because of *who* this man is, which I shall get to in a moment, and one which anticipates the rebellious context of the healing of the blind man in John 9. That Jesus addresses his remark to the crowd suggests, perhaps, that *this* selfless, courageous act of conversion is the 'wondrous sign' they must recognise. More importantly, by numbering only this sign, forcing us to enumerate each, it links to and foreshadows the seventh sign, i.e., the raising of Lazarus, which is intended to glorify both Jesus and the Father.

The exodus themes of "signs and wonders" and emancipation support a Passover context for this scene but Jesus has already celebrated Passover in Samaria. There is a strange passage, intentionally solving this dilemma for us, where the officer asks *his* servants when, exactly, his son was "cured," to which they respond: "yesterday, at about the seventh hour" (in the Greek rendition). "One o'clock in the afternoon" simply does not give us any clue, and yet this *is* a clue, for the "seventh hour" is a non-conventional time division, so it alludes, precisely, to the seventh day of the month.

There are seven signs hinted at in this passage and now a seventh hour/day; this is Pentecost. Counting "seven times seven" days from Passover, it is usually falls on the 6–7 Siwan. The seventh day is another symbolic motif that will prove its significance in the tale of Lazarus. The Pentecost celebrations include offering up the first fruits of the harvest to the priests as recognition of God as its giver; what an apt setting for the scene in the FG just described, with the son (the first fruit) being offered to Jesus!

The Son's Father
So who is the "servant of the king"?

I suggest it is Nicodemus. He is, by virtue of his commission name and subsequent depiction in the narrative a victorious, positive character who undergoes a profound conversion. Nicodemus' introduction, back in John 3, places him in the vicinity of Jerusalem. He is in the temple in John 7. As with other characters in the story, however, this does not imply that he lives in Jerusalem continuously. It may be that he comes into the city only for the obligatory festivals or for some other imposed calendar of duty.

As a "leader of the Jews," Nicodemus stands amongst the priests and Pharisees (John 7) just as Jesus stands amongst the priests and Levites in John 1; he is "one of them." Does this mean he is a priest, a Pharisee, or both? It is possible for a priest to become a Pharisee, for the former is an inherited position, while the latter is one of choice. The teaching aspect of Nicodemus' depiction also suggests both.

I am convinced, and will hopefully convince you, that Nicodemus is both priest *and* Pharisee, a revered elder of the upper echelons of society in Capernaum (where the "royal servant" resides). He is a teacher in the synagogue there and probably, given his standing and the influence we see him exhibit in the FG, a member of the lesser Sanhedrin (which governs each town with a population of 120 householders). This would account for his interest in accurately defining the law in John 7.

The most extensive conversation in the FG occurs between Jesus and Nicodemus, recall, and this is an echo of the profound dialogue between Salathiel and Uriel in 2 Esdras. It is a conversation that centres on faith and conversion, thus anticipating Nicodemus' transformation from priest/Pharisee to one of Jesus' staunchest supporters and allies. The main theme of this exchange is the need to remove all preconceptions and allegiances, in order to follow Jesus to the new Promised Land. Thus, Nicodemus, a man of authority, with reputation, position, influence, openly rejects the *inevitability* of his son inheriting what he perceives to be the futile legacy of the cultus of Jerusalem. He stands before the crowd and asks Jesus to make his son well; his bravery and loyalty make *him* the 'sign', not the supposed healing.

Son

Nicodemus, in requesting a new 'life' for his son is, in effect, requesting Jesus take the boy under his wing, i.e., to teach him, to make him his protégée. At the vital age of thirteen the young man will be destined for the priesthood, like his father, and will probably follow in his father's footsteps and become a Pharisee, as Nicodemus would have followed his father's example. Now it is time to break the cycle and hope for something better. He *gives* Jesus his son. The FG doesn't leave it there, for what would be the point? This tale of conversion permeates the entire gospel, for the "official's son" is none other than the young Lazarus.

As the discussion concerning Lazarus evolves, this will become much easier to see but one of the first clues to this identification is the "third day" motif. After Jesus stays for "two days" in Samaria, the very next scene is the appearance of Nicodemus pleading on behalf of Lazarus. Thus, the theological union between Jesus and Lazarus is initiated on a symbolic "third day." This is an important sequence to note. The Samaritan woman, we now know, is Mary, the young girl who represents the hopes and *physical* reality of Jesus' mission. As the symbolic harlot she must rise through a complex testing, to become the Bride of God, the reinstated, re-elevated Israel. The parallel depictions of the elevation of both the young Mary *and* the young Lazarus begin here, in John 4.

Uniting the Rods

Earlier, it was suggested that Jesus' right-hand man would be a Benjaminite; he would play the part of Eleazar, to Jesus' Joshua, and thereby represent the southern tribes who made their way to Jerusalem after the Sinai schism. The ultimate and complete reunion of the tribes, according to Ezek 37:15–23, must occur before the new house of God can become a reality, however, so the prophet is told in a vision to take up a "stick" or "rod" of Ephraim (representing the Josephite, or northern tribes) and a "stick/rod" of Judah (the southern tribes) and unite them. This responsibility, Jesus apparently believes, now falls to him. He begins, as Ezekiel does, with the rod of Ephraim, i.e., the young woman at the well in Samaria, Mary. When Jesus accepts the young Lazarus as his protégée, he elects the rod of Judah.

So Lazarus, the young boy of John 4, is the representative of the tribe of Benjamin. There is much more to disclose concerning the name Lazarus and his profound significance to Jesus' mission and the narrative of the FG but this must await a dedicated discussion when we deal with John 11 (i.e., the use of commission names and multiple identities is one of the greatest secrets of the FG; it is one of the winnowing tactics that limit the gospel's initial "followers" to those who can discern the patterns of representation). The whole episode concerning the separation and reunion of Joseph and his brother in Genesis, however, makes the supremacy of the northern tribes (represented by Joseph) and the ultimate reunion inevitable, and it anticipates the relationship between Jesus and Lazarus that will dominate the FG.

The uniting of Mary and Lazarus, the symbolic rods of Ephraim and Judah, implies that Jesus does visit Jacob's Well with the goal of finding a wife for someone else, i.e., for Lazarus. This suggests the meeting with Nicodemus on the open road in Cana could have been a staged 'promotional' event and Jesus already knew about young Lazarus and his father's desire to have him join Jesus' campaign. Of course, according to Judg 21:19–21, Benjaminites marry the women of Shiloh, i.e., *Samaritans*.

9
LAME MAN

THE TEMPLE IS PROFANED BY the deceit and the meaningless practices of the priests; there is despondency, and there is mounting frustration. The people look forward to the coming of a messiah, the one who will to rid them of the Romans whom they believe to be the root of their problems. Jesus, however, is on a mission the masses cannot easily comprehend.

Some were sick through their sinful ways, and because of their iniquities endured affliction ... and they drew near to the gates of death ... he sent out his word and healed them, and delivered them from destruction.
Ps 107:17–20

The Impotent Priest
When Jesus returns to Jerusalem, it is the time of yet another festival but it is not named, which is intriguing. For a while I considered that this might be the Festival of Tabernacles (in the month of Tishri), as this would balance with Jesus' earlier emphasis on the harvest, reaping, etc. The festival lasts for seven days, which would also be fitting but Tabernacles is alluded to in John 7, where it is named directly, so why would it not be so described here? Then I considered the possibility that this could be New Year (1 Tishri), the only festival that receives similarly scant recognition in the OT, appearing only in Lev 23:24 and Num 29:1–6. Texts pertaining to 'judgment' and the supremacy of God are read out during this festival, and this seems to be the general gist of Jesus' speech later in this section. It is also a Sabbath day, making the argument concerning the Sabbath perfectly in context. Either way, this episode takes place in the month of Tishri.

At the Pool of Beth-zatha await many who are blind, lame, or withered. The blind and the lame appear in the prohibition of Lev 21:18–21 (LXX), where it is stated that no priests who are blemished in such a way may enter the sanctuary of the holy place. Blindness is also used metaphorically in such passages as Ps 146:8, where it symbolises a lack of wisdom (Isa 29:9–10; 35:5, etc.). In Isa 35:6, though, the dawning of a new "Holy Way" will bring the emancipation of the lame, but this new path is intended only for God's people; the "redeemed shall walk there." This new Way is described as being like waters that "break forth in the wilderness"—a salvation for the "ransomed of the Lord."

The third category, the withered, appears in the lamentation for Israel in Ezekiel 19 (vv. 12, 13 especially), and in Joel 1:8–18 (e.g., v.12). In both these cases, Israel is pictured as a once formidable nation now besieged and near ruin. The "withered" description suggests a sapping of strength, a reduced effectiveness, etc., usually attributed to being "parched" (Isa 5:13; 35:7), e.g., not receiving the quenching waters of Truth and Life. In Joel's account, the lament is specifically targeted toward the priests; Ezekiel's is directed toward the rulers, and the consequences of their iniquities (Ezek 18:30).

These three groups fall under the general heading of *astheneis*, or "invalids," a term used in John 4:46, here in John 5, and then again, in John 11. Elsewhere in the NT, it is used as a description of those who lack morality, authority, or dignity (e.g., Rom 6:19, 2 Cor 11:21, 13:4, Heb 5:2, etc.). Each group is also *distinctly* represented in the FG narrative; in John 4:10–15 the people are parched, in need of the "living water" (they are "withering"), in John 5 there is the lame man, and the blind are represented in John 9.

The infirm of the FG, then, are not the *physically* weak, the beggars on the streets, the old, the sick; this is the traditional Christian interpretation. The FG Jesus is far from concerned with personal illness and deformity, with poverty, or individual misery; he is concerned with the illegitimacy of the Jerusalem temple cultus and the oppression of the true heir to the priestly kingdom. Illness and weakness are symptoms of a more profound instability; the *nation* is weak, unclean, blemished, because its *priesthood* is.

The Sheep Gate is alluded to; it is not specifically mentioned in the Greek. The term used is *probatikē* and this simply means "pertaining to sheep" but traditional translations infer that "Gate" is intended. The Sheep Gate is one of the closest of all the gates to the temple itself, built by the high priest Eliashib and his fellow priests (Neh 3:1f); it is the only gate of Jerusalem to be explicitly described as receiving priestly consecration. Far from being the site where everyday shepherds herd their sheep through the city, it is the gate through which the sacrificial sheep are brought to the temple, thus, it is the place where officiating priests and Levites will be congregating when there is a festival. The insinuation is that Jesus performs his act of attempted conversion (for that is what is happening here) within priestly territory and he gradually works closer and closer to the central hub of the temple as the story progresses.

In the Jerusalem of Jesus' day, there are many, many priests, but there are generally only two distinct classes of priest, i.e., the ordinary and the chief priests. Ordinary priests are those who form a community of priestly families that can supposedly trace its genealogy right back to the original priesthood at Sinai. Animosity and resentment forge a great rift between these relegated orders and their superiors, the chief priests; accusations of nepotism, greed, even cruelty and theft are raised against them. With their strong affiliation to the dominant Pharisees, nothing can be done to release the underdog from the oppression of the illegitimate supervisors of the house of God.

> *There is no soundness in my flesh because of your indignation; there is no health in my bones because of my sin ... my iniquities ... weigh like a burden too heavy for me ... I am utterly bowed down and ... prostrate ... My friends ... stand aloof from my affliction, and my neighbours stand far off.*
> Ps 38: 2–11

The impotence of this faction of the priesthood is reiterated in the lame man's response to Jesus' direct question: "Do you *want* to be made well?" (John 5:6). He replies in a weak and ambiguous manner, blaming his failure to "rise" above his infirmity on the lack of a "helper"; this is a clear echo of Amos 5:2, which speaks of Israel having fallen, with "no one to raise her up," and Eccl 4:1, which speaks of the oppressed who have no one to comfort them (see also Pss 72:12, 14; 107:12, and Isa 63:5). Others, he moans, reach the water before him, so his anticipation of true cleansing has been postponed for "thirty-eight years," the period of time some interpreters see as corresponding to the timeframe mentioned in Deut 2:14, during which the sinful generation perished in the wilderness. In the comparable spiritual wilderness, the lame man awaits the coming of the one who can lead him into the idealistic Promised Land.

The Deuteronomy 2 quotation is unique in the OT, for usually the sojourn in the wilderness is referred to in generic (and symbolic) terms, i.e., as "forty years." If we are meant to take note of the context of this *specific* passage, we must recognise the concept of a divine culling of the wicked, of those who retain the 'sin', the guilt, i.e., of Egyptian assimilation. There *is* an FG character, a disciple, to whom a similar but slightly less extreme reckoning applies, and Jesus' own reference to "sin" supports the OT context.

There is something about the way the FG uses numbers, however, that makes me think there is more to this precise measure of "thirty-eight years." It is a clue to a specific date relating to the efficacy of the priesthood itself. If the lame man is a priest, it would make sense for the "thirty-eight years" of his inaction, or inability, to correspond to the length of time his priestly family has been out of a job, so to speak. He has lost the potential for rising to any higher position, let alone to the high-priesthood.

The problem we have here, however, is one of continuity. We shall soon discover that the FG's tale is not as linear, or sequential, as might first appear, so the year reference here must be deciphered once other clues have been revealed. This is a constant issue in this interpretation and can't be avoided but the end result is well worth the initial frustration. To make my point, however, I shall provide the necessary information at this juncture: the "thirty-eight years" refers to the year 4 BCE, when King Herod died.

Upon Herod's death, the kingdom was divided amongst his three sons, with Judea and Samaria going to Archelaus, who proved to be so ineffectual and unpopular his own subjects requested his dismissal. It was the beginning of the end for the traditional and hereditary priesthood, for when Archelaus left and Judea was annexed to Syria (6 CE), so Josephus tells us; "…all sorts of misfortunes" befell the Judeans, i.e., murders, seditions, depositions, and of a loss of "friends, who used to alleviate [their] pain" (*Ant.* 18.1.1). A famine weakened the city, and the temple itself caught fire. He continues by claiming that "the customs of our fathers were altered, and such a change was made"; nothing was the same. High priests were appointed, influential families (such as Annas' and Caiaphas') were favoured, and the lower echelons of the cultus were relegated to virtual "slavery."

This sounds pretty much like the infirm and tired old Jerusalem that Jesus enters into at the time of New Year. With nothing but a commandment to rise, pick up his bundle, and walk, however, Jesus demonstrates the ease with which the dejected priest *can* reject his oppressors, *if* he really wants to:

> Gather up your bundle from the ground, O you who live under siege!
> Jer 10:17

> Stand up like a man, and I will instruct you.
> 2 Esd 2:33

Furthermore, the reference to a precise number of years implies a *specific* priestly event, i.e., the appointment of the high priest Eleazar ben Boethus, also in 4 BCE. My reasoning can only be appreciated once further chapters of the FG have been interpreted but it has to do with the concepts of rivalry and the rights of the firstborn, *and* the use of commission names.

The chronological significance of this for the FG is that this "lame man" episode takes place in c. 34 CE. Already we are made aware that the timeline for the gospel is not as it 'should' be, for Jesus' storming of the temple occurs in c. 36 CE, as noted. The author is telling us, again and again, how to read his gospel; he hints at the number of signs and how we must recognise them, he provides the elucidation of Nicodemus so we know that

The Testament of Lazarus

we must 'start from scratch', and he provides simple but largely overlooked clues on the historical context of his account.

In the lame-man scenario Jesus is *acting* like a priest. It makes sense that the lame man, a weak, ineffectual, pathetic member of an oppressed and resentful order, does as he is told when ordered by an apparent superior. Confirming his association to the extant priesthood, he, like the emissaries of priests and Levites in John 1, seems to reveal an ignorance of the fundamental truth concerning *who* Jesus is. Or does he? The only reason he *cannot* pick Jesus out for the Jews is because Jesus has slipped into the crowd; it doesn't mean the lame man fails to recognise Jesus' face. This is a clue: The lame man is Peter.

When Peter is introduced, in John 1:42, there is no mention of him 'remaining' with Jesus, as the first two disciples had done. There is only the strange commission name that implies his inevitable disciplining. The allusion to the reckoning of the "wicked generation" fits this context and we will see at least two other allusions to Peter's disassociation from the loyal followers of Jesus.

As the professional 'brother' of Andrew, who is also a priest, Peter is possibly in Jerusalem performing his regular duties; ordinary priests are allowed to live in the outlying country but have to be in Jerusalem for their prescribed term of office, so his abode in Bethsaida is justified, as is his location near the Sheep Gate, especially at the time of a festival. His subsequent characterisation, too, fits this nameless figure perfectly, as we shall see!

It is the action of physical labour on the Sabbath, however, to which the Jews react, not to any semblance of a healing miracle, and this reaction anticipates that of the Pharisees in John 9, i.e., there is no physical change, *per se* (and this makes me wonder why the lame man, had he truly been a sick person awaiting a medical cure, would *expect* anyone to "throw ["put" in the NRSV] him" into the water on such a day as it would not have been allowed anyway). When the Jews, the other priests, Pharisees, etc., confront him, it comes as no surprise when the lame man simply squeaks, "he told me to do it," expecting them to realise that he was just following orders. Jesus, meanwhile, slips away, concealing himself in the crowd, obviously not wishing to be made the centre of attention, not wanting the Pharisees to catch him in the act (which is further hinted at, even explained, in the FG narrative). Inside the temple precinct Jesus "finds" Peter; the question is, has he *sought* him out? Jesus' next words sound like a rebuke, a warning, perhaps even a threat: "I have made you well! Do not sin any more, so that nothing worse happens to you" (John 5:14).

The concept of sin in the Hebrew tradition is ambiguous. The Hebrew language actually has no single word to describe what Christianity refers to as theological sin; it is a broad term with many connotations, including failure, guilt, and the breaching of a covenant. The sin to which Jesus refers in v.14 may allude to the sin of the "wicked generation" in the wilderness, or it may just as easily pertain to the lame man's guilt by virtue of his former insipience. His sin would then be one of inaction and apathy in the face of his responsibility, i.e., he has failed to keep the covenant of priests. If he returns to his previous life, now that he has been shown the path to 'freedom', a worse fate awaits him, e.g., the wrath of God and a spiritual death.

> *If you are rising to this same life, you should rather be dead;*
> *but rouse yourself to a better one!*
> Acts of John 52

Why would this warning, so in keeping with the concept of the reinstated priesthood and the demise of the old regime, sound so personal a threat? Jesus *recognises* Peter as the one who was introduced to him earlier; he had the opportunity to follow, yet he is still here, acting as though nothing is different. He still awaits someone to 'help' him. His sin, perhaps, is more to do with his failure to accept Jesus as the path to emancipation. If he sins again, e.g., by giving the Jews the information they want, he will suffer a worse fate than having someone promoted before him.

That Jesus and his disciples are in any way violent has been a matter of denial, or a matter of concern, for all those who broach the subject but it has proven a necessary avenue of investigation, despite its provocative nature. The FG's account of Jesus' apparent desire to replace the temple cultus is not recorded in the FG as an *overtly* militant one, even though his 'first' action within the temple area *is* violent. So many factions are extant in Jerusalem at this time, factions who have their own political or religious agenda, some of whom are armed; it seems unlikely that Jesus, given the enormity and intense nature of his task, does not resort at least to a few verbal threats when needed. He is a man of his time, and a man on a mission. I cannot see him actually setting thugs on the lame man but I can fully accept that in his warning is more than a theological sermon to be 'good' in future.

As his warning anticipated, however, the moment Jesus' back is turned the lame man, Peter, possibly *feeling* threatened, runs off to inform the Jews that he knows who had ordered him to break the Sabbath—Jesus. Jesus, the troublemaker who ransacked the tables in the temple, is now inciting the lower echelons to rebellion by suggesting they can flout the Pharisaic laws. Accusations of breaking the law and of blasphemy abound, and from this moment on Jesus is 'persecuted' and under a death threat. It is from this moment that Peter's role in the FG is set; he is a weak, impressionable, and untrustworthy character.

Again forced into a situation he simply has to make the best of, Jesus repeats, in a long soliloquy, the claim to divine authority, not divinity itself, and again he assures the crowd of greater works to come. He tries to explain that he has been sent from the Father, that he is the representative "son" whose authority must be heeded if Israel is to be saved. The very works that he is doing *should* verify his identity and intention, should win the nation's support; the scriptures prophesied that he would come but the people fail to comprehend. Moses, attributed author of Torah, 'wrote' of him: "The Lord your God will raise up for you a prophet ... from among your own people; you shall heed such a prophet" (Deut 18:15),[1] yet no one believes. They do not truly know the scriptures and, therefore, do not (according to Jesus) have God within them.

Beth-zatha

Returning to the site itself, Beth-zatha is explicitly referred to as being a Hebrew name,[2] so it is from the Hebrew we must find our meaning, and this meaning should be discernible within a biblical context. It may be a play on *zarah,* which can mean "to cast away, or disperse," e.g., "to winnow," which would certainly suit the winnowing effect of the FG itself, but it also anticipates the theme of separation that *will* become a significant aspect of this particular disciple's depiction, especially in John 18 and 21.

I am going to take a bit of a leap forward, however, to my discussion concerning the adulteress in John 8; Jesus turns the judgement of the accusers upon *them,* intimating that it is *they* who are adulterous and whoring, *not* the woman in question. The most damning passage in the FG, the adulteress' story, was 'conveniently' lost from some early translations. I propose that "Beth-zatha," if not suffering a similar fate and thus an altered version of the original, is *intended* to be (at least) a play on 'Beth-zanah,' i.e., "house of the adulterer, of whoredom," etc., where *zanah* is the term employed in almost every OT instance of religious adultery, or idolatry (e.g., Exod 34:15f, Lev 20:6, Ezek 6:9, and many others). The priesthood has not

---

[1] It is to this precedent that John 4:44 seems to allude but the addendum is awkward, for Jesus has just left the welcoming Samaritans to go to Galilee. If he leaves Samaria because "his own people" do not honour him, this both contradicts the preceding scene and confirms his "own people" *are* the Samaritans!

[2] The area Josephus describes as "Bezetha" (*Wars.* 5.4.2) is in this general vicinity; work started on it during the reign of Agrippa I (37–44 CE) and was completed by his son, Agrippa II. It would certainly have been known in the lifetime of the FG author and should also be considered as a potential influence on the name Beth-zatha.

been faithful, remember, to their divine marriage partner, so the intimation would be just as damning but just as clear as in the adulteress' scene.

Even the name Bethesda however, has conflicting translations. The name is composed of *beth* ("house") + *checed*, which, due to the Christian tradition of Jesus' complete benevolence, has been translated to mean "kindness, merciful," etc., but which can also mean "reproach," or a "wicked thing," making Bethesda, potentially, the "house of the wicked."

The *"five* porticoes" symbolise the five tribes of Judah (this is discussed further in relation to John 6), i.e., representing those who followed Eleazar to Jerusalem after the schism at Sinai. The waters of Beth-zatha, near the priestly Sheep Gate, are therefore restricted, symbolically, to those of the southern tribes. That is, the *priesthood* is restricted and is thus impotent, for it represents only a portion of Israel. *That* is why the waters are ineffectual at 'healing' those who bathe in them. Peter doesn't comprehend this, even when Jesus tells him a better life and more freedom awaits if Peter simply gets up and walks away.

Amen

Another interesting thing to mention is the use of '*amen*' in Jesus' response. To the Samaritans, the Torah is also known as "the Verity," i.e., the Truth, and this is how the word *amen* is translated. Almost every instance in which Jesus uses this phrase, he is alluding to something in Torah, such as here, in John 5, where he speaking of judgement, and in the legal deliberations of John 8 and 10.

10
SAMARITAN REBELLION

Passover

JESUS HAS OBVIOUSLY WITHDRAWN FROM Jerusalem by John 6 and we find him up in the north again, this time on the "other side" of the Sea of Tiberias, but where exactly? In Deut 4:43 and Josh 20:9, certain cities spanning the Israelite land are designated as sites of refuge for those fleeing the death sentence until an official trial can be arranged; the city of refuge which seems to tally with Jesus' position is the city of Golan, in Bashan, i.e., the Golan Heights. Jesus *is* under a death threat. Historically, Golan is both a Levitical (priestly) city and a city of the tribe of Manasseh, i.e., a Josephite city; Joshua gives it to the descendants of the priests (Josh 21:27).

Jesus attempts to remove himself from the crowds that keep following him, suggesting a certain reticence is creeping in. He is high on a vantage point, overlooking the plain below, for he can see the throng approaching. In his day the area around the Sea of Galilee, although surrounded by hills, was quite heavily built up, so Golan would be an ideal place both for safety and for the commanding vista required to be able to see such a vast, itinerant crowd.

The place of the feeding in John 6 is described as having "much grass" (John 6:10), and this fits the Bashan area very well; in several OT passages it is referred to in terms of its rich pasture lands (Deut 32:14, Isa 33:9, Nahum 1:4, etc.).

Compare *these* passages:

> I will restore Israel to its pasture, and it shall feed on Carmel and in Bashan, and on the hills of Ephraim and in Gilead its hunger shall be satisfied ... for I will pardon the remnant that I have spared.
> Jer 50:19

> Shepherd your people with your staff, the flock that belongs to you, which lives alone in a forest in the midst of a garden land; let them feed in Bashan and Gilead as in the days of old. As in the days when

you came out of the land of Egypt, show us marvellous things.
                                                      Mic 7:14–15

The Josephites receive the 'forest' lands as part of their inheritance, in Josh 17. In this Josephite and priestly setting, then, John 6 opens with Jesus on a mountain, very near the time of the Passover (Nisan/April), i.e., two strong images that evoke the exodus story. The prevalent FG theme is also to be understood as one of bondage, of imminent freedom, and of God's desire to redeem his faithful people. In the account of Joshua's final Passover in the wilderness there is a link to Jesus' action, for the day *after* Passover the "pure" Israelites enter the Promised Land of Canaan (Josh 5:11). Jesus is trying, *desperately* trying, to convince his followers that a new Promised Land awaits them. His Bashan location and the "marvellous" action that takes place there constitute an *intentional* fulfilment of the OT passages telling of the anticipated emancipation and reconstitution of Israel.

What we are about to witness on the mountain in Bashan *is* a Samaritan-style observance of Passover, not a 'picnic' as some authors have described it. The Samaritan Passover is celebrated just as the first Passover had been (in Exodus 12); it is conducted on the slopes of a mountain (traditionally, Mount Gerizim, and includes the entire community, though men are the only ones permitted to take part in the actual ceremony. Initially, everyone sits for prayer. No Gentiles are allowed, nor anyone who is not ritually clean. Men and women are separated. The young boys offer the sacrificial foods to the officiating priest, who then offers a prayer of thanks, asking God for the forgiveness of sins.[1]

Certain OT texts are read out in Hebrew, in celebration of the emancipation from Egypt through the "signs and wonders" of God, and of the settlement in the Promised Land. The priest has an assistant who is a layman; between them they slaughter *seven* lambs in the first two minutes of twilight. Twelve ministers, dressed in white, perform ritualistic duties. The unleavened bread and the herbs are distributed first; when the lamb is ready for consumption, it is separated into *seven* large baskets, from which the various families are called forth to receive their portion. The feast is eaten on the ground. When they are finished, they gather up every fragment and burn *what is left* on a makeshift altar.[2]

---

[1] Interestingly, this is the only context in which the Passover meal is related to the expiation of sins, and then it is the priest's prayer, not the animal that is the central element. The discussion concerning the meaning of John's 'lamb' is further supported.

[2] The Samaritan and the Jewish Passover fall on different days, even though both prepare on the fourteenth and eat their meal on the fifteenth Nisan. The former count the day from midnight, while the latter, from dusk. Thus, the Samaritan Passover

The emphasis on political correctness in our modern world has actually taken away some of the meaning of these ancient texts, for in the desire to make men and women equal wherever possible, original distinctions are lost. This is a case in point. The NRSV translates 6:10 as "Let the people sit down ... so they sat down." In the Greek, the words for "people" and "they" are actually masculine; *anthropous* and *andres* (men), respectively. Passover is one of the three festivals (along with Pentecost and Tabernacles) that must be celebrated by every *male* Israelite; the attendance of women is voluntary. So, the distinction between the male and female followers *is* significant. It suggests that Jesus' own 'sign' is intended more for the men than the women, and of this it is worth keeping a mental note, for it is actually a common attribute of Jesus' campaign.

In the FG's feeding scene, a boy, just as in the Samaritan Passover ritual, comes toward the priest (Jesus) with *five* barley loaves (barley bread is 'common' bread, usually unleavened, as opposed to wheat bread, which was a luxury; leaven was not to be eaten or touched before the Passover) and *two* (the Greek implies *dried*) fish, a precise number that many interpreters deem insignificant (focusing, as they do, on the supposed 'miracle' of feeding so many with so little) but which actually proves to be *fundamental* to the understanding of this new 'sign'.

On first glance, the basic 'five plus two equals seven' numerology may symbolise the seven baskets of food used for the Samaritan Passover service but there is a much more pertinent symbolism here. *Two* sons were born to Joseph, representing the northern tribes (Gen 41:50) and *five* to Judah, representing the southern tribes (1 Chr 2:4). The dispersion of the food, then, symbolises the scattering of the tribes. The gathering of the fragments into *twelve* baskets (there are twelve ministers distributing the food and Jesus anticipates twelve ministers in his new kingdom) anticipates their reunion and the reconstruction of the *ideal* Israel. In the prophecy of Ezek 39:28, the tribes of Israel will be gathered into their own lands again, and none will be left behind.

Let us draw a comparison. In the days of Elijah the prophet, there is a great famine in Samaria and all but one of the prophets, i.e., Elijah, are killed. A competition between the many prophets of Baal, and Elijah (alone) is set up in order to prove the Israelite god more powerful and, of course, Elijah's god wins. Jezebel, the infamous queen of Israel, takes her misguided revenge on Elijah, who flees into the wilderness of Judah (Judea), from where he travels to Mount Horeb and here he has an encounter with God (1 Kings 19). The context in 1 Kings is one of hunger, a lone prophet, a mountain, and a

---

might fall on our 1 April, and the Jewish on 2 April, yet each would be adhering to biblical stipulation.

divided sense of rightful worship. So far, this parallels John 6 nicely. God tells Elijah that all the Baal worshippers will be killed but, he promises, "seven thousand" will be left in Israel, i.e., "all the knees that have not bowed down to Baal, and every mouth that has not kissed him" (1 Kgs 19:18). Thus, a remnant of "seven thousand" loyal worshippers remains.

There are about "five thousand" on the mountain in Bashan with Jesus[3]; he has just shown them a 'sign' with the union of loaves and fishes:

$$5 + 2 = 7 = \text{Perfection/Unity}$$
$$5 \text{ (loaves)} + 2 \text{ (fish)} = 12 \text{ baskets}$$
$$5 \text{ (sons)} + 2 \text{ (sons)} = 12 \text{ tribes united}$$
$$5 \text{ (loaves)} + 2 \text{ (fish)} = 7 \text{ items of Passover sacrifice}$$
$$5(000) + 2(000) = 7(000) \text{ worshippers of God (Remnant)}$$

When Elijah 'finds' Elisha, his successor, at the rear of a yoke of *twelve* oxen, he gives the young man his "mantle," thus officially recognizing him; he kills the oxen to feed the people. Thus, the hunger of the Remnant is satisfied by a shared meal, in the symbolic numerical context of *seven* and *twelve*, and in terms of a prophet and his protégée.

The fact that only the bread fragments, not the fish, seem to multiply so dramatically in John 6, together with the emphasis on "gathering," serve to reiterate the exodus precedent, where the bread from heaven, the "manna" (Exod 16:15–16) is sent to quell the complaints of the people. "When you see the bread increase in quantity," God tells them, "you will know that it isn't I who keeps you hungry." In fact, Jesus' words in John 6:26f are explicit about this precedent, and his insistence on identifying the 'bread' with spiritual, not physical satisfaction parallels his refusal to eat at the well in Sychar.

The order to collect the fragments so that "nothing may be lost" brings to mind the passage in Jer 23:1–4, where God blames the bad shepherds for scattering the people of Israel, and in his promise to gather them and return them to the fold, he assures that they will not be afraid (cf. John 6:20), and none will "be missing." By John 17:12 and 18:9, Jesus can identify with the good shepherd, for none except the one *destined* to be lost has gone missing (more on this in due course).

Jesus' invitation to the masses, then, to eat the Passover on Josephite land, is politically provocative. The fundamental argument between the Samaritan and Judean peoples has been one concerning the legitimate locus

---

[3] This is also another sign that a Passover meal is taking place here, for the number of 'diners' had to be calculated as closely as possible, so that the food would be neither too much, nor too little.

of worship; Samaritans insist they have a *bone fide* right to worship in the land of their inheritance, and Jesus is now supporting this claim, intentionally evoking the memory of Exod 5:1 and the very oppression of religious worship that supposedly led to the flight from Egypt.[4]

It is during this celebration that Jesus puts his hand-chosen disciple, his son Philip, to the test (John 6:6), a test he fails by completely overlooking the allegorical nature of the situation. Philip, as predicted, is blinded by his pragmatic nature; he sees no further than the necessity for, and the apparent deficit of, food. He sees not with the eyes of an Israelite (he is no Elisha) but with the eyes of a Greek and this will cost him his potential place as Jesus' right-hand-man. Such a result is foreshadowed by the "complaining" in the desert in Num 11:18f, where a similar concern for 'meat' and 'fish' is voiced, a miraculous feeding takes place, and a subsequent disappointment results. It is Andrew, the priest, who at least sees the boy with the victuals but even Andrew fails to 'see' Jesus' meaning completely.

Because of his apparent heritage, i.e., Jesus' Josephite son by Martha, Philip *should* understand. He *should* comprehend the allusion to Arzareth looming in the distance behind them, where all the scattered, disassociated tribes are, waiting for someone to show them the 'way home'. He *should* see the allusion to Elijah and Elisha, and the union of the tribes but he does not. He simply doesn't have what it takes to "feed the sheep"—an idealistic concept that will form the basis of another testing later. This type of testing is consistent, with respect to Jesus' election of his inner circle of followers. He has tested the Samaritan woman, now Philip; he will test Lazarus, and then Peter.

(This FG chapter really introduces the priestly behaviour of Jesus. It is an interesting fact that the priestly benediction, i.e., the blessings during the Passover, etc., were performed with outstretched hands, with the fingers divided between the middle and ring fingers. What is the 'blessing' sign traditionally depicted in images of Jesus? The hand outstretched, with the little finger and ring finger bent downward slightly. One of the earliest Christian illustrations in the catacombs was of Jesus holding both his hands out in this very form of benediction; at the same time, however, the tombs of the Israelite *priestly families* were being similarly decorated!)

> *... not a famine of bread, or a thirst for water,*
> *but of hearing the words of the Lord.*
> Amos 8:11

---

[4] 2 Kgs 23:21, which depicts the storming of the temple by Josiah, also tells of the re-establishment of Passover according to Torah—something that had not been preserved in the temple of Jerusalem.

Let all who are hungry come and eat.
Passover Liturgy

Sea and Symbol
The previous episode, the Passover meal on the mountain, when taken *together* with the following scene rather than as distinct 'miracles', proves to be one of the most difficult and sensitive chapters of the FG and of this investigation because it introduces us to a vital collection of clues that reaffirm Jesus' movement as being one that involves a degree of violence, as was exhibited in the storming of the temple scene. Before we get to the more dramatic version of events that history *has* managed to retain, albeit in scattered fragments, we must first understand the FG author's intention in presenting this version of the story the way he does. I will return to this section of the gospel with a proposed alternative explanation. What results is an astonishing but feasible substitute for the Christian tradition and one that makes complete sense given the overall interpretation of the FG I put forward here, i.e., the gathering on this mountaintop is the primary cause of Jesus' arrest and crucifixion.

The reaction of the crowd, at first, seems to parallel that of Nathanael and the Samaritans, in that they recognise in Jesus a messianic, or prophetic quality, i.e., his authority *is* acknowledged (John 6:14). No sooner is Jesus relieved to see that his 'sign' seems to be working, than his optimism is dashed, for the crowd has apparently misinterpreted. They perceive Jesus to be either the awaited Davidic 'king', the messiah of David who is to lead the nation in a revolt against their oppressors, or a provisional military king, as Josephus describes: "[A]s the several companies of the seditious lighted upon any one to head them, he was created a king immediately" (*Ant.* 17.10.8). After all he has said and done, all he has tried to explain and prove, Jesus still cannot get the people to understand. The 'signs and wonders' seem to be falling on more stony ground than soil!

Jesus runs away, again, accusing the crowd of seeking him out because they "ate [their] fill of the loaves" (John 6:26). Hosea puts it well: "When I fed them, they were satisfied ... and their heart was proud (Hos 13:6). Their immediate desire and the source of their satisfaction has remained on the level of the mundane. The analogy of the crowd taking their fill of physical food corresponds to their mundane expectations and immediate concerns, e.g., a hunger to see Rome destroyed—but it is not the Roman occupation which keeps Israel 'hungry'. This is what the crowd wants, or expects, to see, so this is what they *do* see.

Jesus, however, rejects their insistence to make him their ruler. In fact, the word used to describe their action, *harpazien*, implies that they attempt to "seize" him, to take him by force: "Someone will ... seize a relative, a member of the clan, saying, 'You have a cloak; You shall be our leader and this heap of ruins shall be under your rule.'" (Isa 3:6). In this passage from Isaiah, the one seized to be king of an 'oppressed' nation also refuses, blaming the iniquity of Jerusalem itself for the people's present, degraded state (3:7–8). Jesus has his kingdom mapped out; this is not what he has in mind.

Alone and rethinking his strategy, Jesus sits up on the mountain, while his disciples go down to the sea. Generally known as the Sea of Galilee, this body of water is also called Chinereth, or Chinneroth (the Hebrew form in, e.g., Num 34:11), Gennesar (1 Macc. 11:67), and Gennesareth in the Synoptics. Only the FG refers to it as the "Sea of Galilee of Tiberias" or "the Tiberian Sea," so again the reader is urged to make a certain connection, to arrive at a certain interpretation that is unique to this gospel. For such a Hebrew-orientated gospel, the use of a Roman name is itself worth noting and questioning.

Herod Antipas erected the great city of Tiberias on the western shore of the Sea in c. 23 CE, to mark the sixty-fifth birthday of Tiberius Caesar. It was the showcase of Antipas' tetrarchy, and became his capital but the site was shunned by devout Israelites whose abhorrence of Levitical uncleanliness due to contact with the dead (Num 19:11) prohibited them from entering the city, for it had been built upon the site of a cemetery, thus perpetually defiling anyone living there. Josephus remarks that Herod bribed "poor people" with houses, in order to raise the population, and many country dwellers were brought by force to reside in the city (*Ant.* 18.2.3). In fact, Josephus tells of an incident in which a "great multitude" were led to the outskirts of the city by a Roman commander *specifically* to show to them "the power of the Romans and the threatenings of Caesar" (*Wars.* 2.10.3). Tiberias is thus a *recognised symbol of the power of Rome*. The malevolence of the deep, i.e., the sea, is also an integral part of the interpretation of this scenario and has precedents in many OT passages: "On that day the Lord ... will punish the Leviathan ... the twisting serpent, and he will kill the dragon that is in the sea" (Isa 27:1); "Am I the Sea, or the Dragon, that you set a guard over me?" (Job 7:12); "for the sea was growing more and more tempestuous" (Jonah 1:17). In context, these passages tell of the power of God to defend his people from peril, and the ultimate salvation of those who trust in him. The sea, or the Leviathan, the 'dragon' that dwells in its murky and turbulent depths, is an enemy, an oppressor, etc., which God conquers for the sake of his Israel. Psalms 107 (the same psalm which speaks of the distressed and afflicted at the gates whom God heals, the thirsty wanderers in the desert who are led to salvation by the straight path of God's making, and the bondage of those who claim to have no helper) offers this image:

> Some went down to the sea in ships ... they saw the deeds of the Lord, his wondrous works in the deep. For he commanded and raised the stormy wind, which lifted up the waves of the sea ... they reeled and staggered like drunkards, and were at their wits' end. ... Then they cried to the Lord in their trouble, and he brought them out from their distress; he made the storm be still ... and he brought them to their desired haven.
>
> Ps 107:23–30

What happens John 6:16–21? The disciples go down to the sea, to a boat, the sea becomes rough because a storm is brewing, they are afraid, there is an apparently divine intervention bringing them to their destination.

Have the people confused Jesus' intention? Are his tactics just too subtle and too arcane to work with a crowd so hungry to see Rome vanquished? Jesus, probably disillusioned and tired by now, withdraws from the crowd, and although he turns up on the other side of the water apparently *before* they do, this is not a miracle, just a 'clean getaway'. I can imagine him getting down to the boat first and hiding under the fishing nets, waiting for the disciples, whom the crowd presume to be alone at this point; during the voyage he reveals himself, startling the men. Not exactly the Jesus of tradition but the FG preserves perhaps the only glimpse of Jesus the man, and he is not a natural rebel, i.e., he shows fear, doubt, frustration, and confusion in the narrative. Meanwhile, boats "from Tiberias" are arriving—officials, no doubt, coming to see what this vast crowd is up to, but Jesus is not to be found; he has managed to get himself away to Capernaum, his family home.

This is a *pragmatic* version of events. So, what of the so-called miracle?

The man, Jesus, does not walk on water. The 'sign' is an ancient, traditional but purely literary one, gleaned from what would have been very well-known precedents. It may be that Jesus gives something of a pep talk to his disciples before they leave, and so this 'sign' is a reinterpretation of Jesus' reassurance to them but the scene itself is a literary construct, intended to reaffirm Jesus' priorities.

By symbolically treading upon the waves of the Sea of Tiberias Jesus is placing Rome, and by extension, the insidious Herod Antipas, under his foot, rejecting the *inevitability* of their supremacy, just as God suppresses the Leviathan. Simply destroying the Romans, without perceiving the *internal* iniquity that keeps Israel under oppression, however, is no true victory but in this 'sign' is the key to a future, *eternal* emancipation ('Life').

When the people of Israel again accept God as their true salvation, when they conduct their lives according to the covenant, they will make themselves worthy in his sight once more, the Davidic messiah will appear,

The Testament of Lazarus

and the tools of God's wrath (the enemy) will be effectively destroyed ... this is just what the 'sign' on the mountain was all about.

> *O that my people would listen to me, that Israel would walk in my ways!*
> *Then I would quickly subdue their enemies.*
> Ps 81:1–14

> *Those who love me, I will deliver; I will protect those who know my name.*
> *I will be with them in trouble, I will rescue them.*
> Ps 91:15

"I AM"

Although the NRSV has, at John 6:20, "It is I; do not be afraid," the Greek reads: "I am; do not be afraid." The use of the "I AM" phrase has become one of the most controversial and debatable utterances in the FG. When Jesus employs the 'I AM' what *is* his meaning? Is he implying that he has become convinced he *is* God? No. He only claims to be the representative 'son', the authority, the elected voice of God. Remember that in the Samaritan tradition, there is an inherited prophetic "light" that comes directly from God *within* his chosen ones. Jesus is making claim to *this* unique phenomenon, or office.

The true prophet speaks in the name of God (Exod 5:23; Deut 18:22; Jer 26:20, etc.) and the use of the divine name enforces the divine *authorization* of an agent of God, as in Exod 23:20–1:"'I am going to send an angel in front of you, to guard you on the way and to bring you to the place that I have prepared. Be attentive to him and listen to his voice ... *for my name is in him.*"

There is no superstition concerning the utterance of the divine name in the Samaritan faith; it is an optimistic, worshipful act. It constitutes, after all, the very *credentials* of Moses' mission: "*say* to the Israelites, 'I AM has sent me to you'" (Exod 3:14). If Moses is allowed to utter the "I AM" as a sign to those seeking emancipation, so is Jesus! The tradition of the Psalms, especially, points strongly towards the potent power of the *name* of God itself. Its invocation in such passages as Pss 54:1; 75:1; 79:6, etc., etc., suggests a correlation between keeping the 'name' of God alive and salvation; those who forget to invoke the name of God, perish.

What, though, of the arcane "I AM WHO I AM" phrase (Gen 3:14)? This, to me, suggests a deliberate ambiguity that is necessary for Moses to address the conglomerate of peoples who constitute the exodus. If the migration from Egypt is a historical fact (which I will debate in a future book), the multitude would represent all manner of religious beliefs from the various Egyptian and Israelite faiths, and every possible conflation of these. *Whose* "God" is this? In order to avert all potential quarrels against Moses unilaterally deciding which deity has such authority, he is given this 'name' to impart that more or less implies: "Call me what you will, I am the same for everyone."

The more we understand the nature of Jesus' intentions in John 6, and the more we learn of his overall goals, the greater we can appreciate his identification with the "I AM." His supporters see Jesus' essence, or substance, as pre-established (by virtue of his divine calling), yet his *identification* changes; it is all a part of the theme of mystery and ambiguity. To some he is the "anointed one" (which can have various applications), to the Samaritans he appears as a Jew but then as the Taheb, to the Jews a Samaritan, to some a priest, to others a king.

When, for instance, Jesus asks the soldiers who come to arrest him in the garden *who* it is they are looking for, they say "Jesus the Nazorean" (in the Greek text), and he responds: "I told you that I AM" (John 18:4–8). To make the phrase more 'correct' in the English, "he" has been added ("I am he") but this dilutes the significance of the declaration. Jesus is effectively saying: "I will be who I will be. No matter what you call me, I am, in essence, what God wills me to be." (A certain truth is placed on the lips of these enemies, as usual, but I shall wait until the appropriate juncture to discuss this.)

The same can be said of John 6. Jesus has just been calming his disciples, trying to convince them that all will be well. His use of the "I AM" is thus a double claim, for on the one hand Jesus is stating that he *will* be what he will be, i.e., *nothing* will prevent his fulfilment of his duty to God; on the other, he is suggesting that he will be whatever he *has* to be in order to succeed, and I think this is where some of his followers begin to part company. He is becoming just a bit *too* formidable (or ambitious?) for the average disciple to comprehend or condone.

Still, there is another interpretation of the other "I AM" sayings, when they are predicated by "the door," "the way," etc. The allusion to the name of God is subtler but still there. In Isa 6:8, the prophet uses "I AM" to mean, "Here I am, send me," and in Isaiah 43, we hear God asking the tormented Israel why she has not called on her God; telling her not to fear, God repeats, several times, "I am here," "I am the one who will save you," "I am the redeemer." This all takes place in the context of "passing through the waters," and redemption for those who return to the one 'true' god, the creator, the Holy One. Similarly, Jesus is seen to be *offering* himself as God's instrument. He becomes the door, the way, only in that he acts as the *conduit* between humanity and salvation; *he* is not salvation itself, only God is that, just as Jesus is not "I AM" but can exploit the rights of the 'son' in employing the phrase to suit his cause!

> *Then I said, 'Here I am'; in the scroll of the book it is written of me.*
> *I delight to do your will, O my God; your law is within my heart.*
> Ps 40:7–8

By following so closely the traditional depiction of the 'trouble at sea' scenario, the FG author has already implied that it *is* God who is in control of the situation, not Jesus. Further, by employing the "I AM" phrase, Jesus is merely reminding his disciples that God is *present* in everything he does, and that if they only pay attention and follow him, Israel will be redeemed: "God is our refuge and strength, a very present help in trouble" (Ps 46:1).

Still, though, there is dissension amongst his followers. Jesus reiterates the 'raising of the son of man' concept, referring to Isaiah's declaration that "All [their] children shall be taught by the Lord" (Isa 54:13) but the original version continues: "and great shall be the prosperity of your children." In other words, you may not see the change you want in your own lifetime but if you return to God, your descendants will reap the benefits! Returning to God means following Jesus' lead and this, allegorically, is what is depicted during the feeding and sea 'signs'.

Before we continue with the FG's story, I must interject with perhaps the most provocative suggestion of this entire book. Let's go over the two main 'signs' of John 6 again but this time in light of some *external* evidence. The following section is based on research that accumulated over several years and only subsequently became such a powerful potential 'truth' that I had to admit I was convinced.

The Tumult

At this juncture we are going to start challenging the FG's version of events, blended as it is with a strong sense of theological idealism. After many years of intimate study of this gospel, it became necessary for me to accept that the Jesus' was a rather turbulent mission, with both a degree of violence and a sense of malevolence, though directed at a specific target, not at people generally. Subtle clue after subtle clue emerged until I was in no doubt that Jesus' actions were, indeed, recorded elsewhere than in the Bible. What I discovered, if you are willing to suspend your disbelief until the end of this analysis, is a Jesus of history chronicled in the Dead Sea Scrolls, the works of Flavius Josephus (not in the two passages that refer to "Jesus the Christ"), and other Jewish documents. This isn't the Jesus of Christian tradition. Be warned.

Let's just recap.

Jesus is apparently prophet, king, *and* high priest; he is a man of Josephite heritage, who often returns to the northern territories when his rebellious tactics in Judea get him into trouble. His demonstration in the temple in Jerusalem is a violent protest against the incumbent priests. He is enticing many away. He has attempted to convince the Samaritans that Mount Gerizim is not the sanctified locus of worship for the god of Abraham and, at least once, he is depicted as observing a Samaritan-style Passover in a place that is mentioned in prophecies concerning the ideal future and the reinstatement of the northern kingdom (i.e., Bashan). He has admitted to being the 'one' whom the Samaritans see as their messiah, i.e., the one who would come to restore Samaria to its rightful place as firstborn, but he sets his sights on the "ruler's sceptre" that is somehow linked to the ancient site of Shiloh. According to the Messiah ben Joseph tradition, he must bring about the downfall, or "death" of the procurator. By assimilating his mission with the expected Samaritan Taheb, he insinuates he has possession of (or knows the whereabouts of) the Ark of the Covenant, one of the foundational tenets of the Taheb tradition.

Reviewing the evidence of John 6 in terms of historical references, or clues, we can deduce the following:

★ Jesus is up a mountain *"near"* the time of Passover.
★ A vast group accompanies him.
★ There is a strongly Samaritan flavour to the scene.
★ Jesus conducts a symbolic version of the Passover, insinuating that he has come to unite the tribes, one of the fundamental tasks of the Taheb.
★ The crowd becomes zealous in their support and Jesus *fears* them, i.e., when he realises they are "about to come and take him by force to make him king" he flees, alone.
★ The disciples also leave.
★ Sometime during the voyage Jesus reveals himself, presumably having hidden in the boat to avoid detection (no one sees him board the boat).
★ He offers assurances that all is well.
★ An unexplained and unspecified number of boats set sail from Tiberias, the Roman stronghold, in search of Jesus.
★ There are, apparently two factions to the crowd, i.e., one on the Bashan side, and one on the Capernaum side (John 6:22).
★ Some of the former group take boats and join the hunt for Jesus.

Now take a look at one of the most controversial passages from Josephus, which a *few* scholars have posited *might* relate to Jesus, though they fail to find enough supporting evidence to justify such a late date for his ultimate crucifixion:

> But the nation of the Samaritans did not escape without tumults. The man who excited them to it, was one who thought lying a thing of little consequence, and who contrived everything so that the multitude might be pleased; so he bade them get together upon mount Gerizzim (*sic*), which is by them looked upon as the most holy of all mountains, and assured them that, when they were come hither, he would show them those sacred vessels which were laid under that place, because Moses put them there. So they came thither armed, and thought the discourse of the man probable; and as they abode at a certain village, which was called Tirathaba, they got the rest together to them, and desired to go up the mountain in a great multitude together. But Pilate prevented their going up, by seizing upon the roads with a great band of horsemen and footmen, who fell upon those who were gotten together in the village; and when they came to an action, some of them they slew, and others of them they put to flight, and took a great many alive, the principal of whom, and also the most potent of those that fled away, Pilate ordered to be slain.
>
> But when this tumult was appeased, the Samaritan senate sent an embassy to Vitellius....
>
> *Ant.* 18.4.1

This Samaritan tumult occurs during the Passover of 36 CE, the very year we see Jesus storming the temple in Jerusalem (as described in "Temple Tirade"). The similarities between Josephus' tumult and the mountaintop scene in John 6 are striking even at this early stage of the comparison:

★ Both men are up a mountain at Passover.
★ There is obviously a strong Samaritan context.
★ The crowd is portrayed as a 'multitude' that has two distinct factions (one group arrives then more join them).
★ Romans intervene.
★ The leader of the Samaritans flees, along with some of his followers.

A couple of other things need mentioning: 1) Josephus goes on to describe how the Samaritans claim they were not revolting against Rome but that they had gone to Tirathaba to "escape the violence of Pilate" and 2) the multitude is armed. In claiming that they are attempting to escape the hostility of Pilate, the Samaritans *can* claim they carry weapons for purposes of self-defence (which is permissible) but nothing is mentioned about why they should fear retribution just for going up their own mountain. They are allowed to do so under normal circumstances.

The multitudinous gathering itself, however, would spark concern and would require careful monitoring but, just as the huge gatherings in

Jerusalem at Passover, it would probably be tolerated *if* there were no more to it. A claim to the Ark, the original validation of the Israelite priesthood, however, would *certainly* be reason for heightened security, especially if informants from the temple institution, who want to maintain the *status quo* and appease the Romans, have informed the Romans of the potential danger of this gathering. Judging by the Jews' (attempted) manipulative exploitation of Pilate's conscience during the arrest scenario, it would be in keeping. There is a hint of this in the subsequent verses of John 6, yet to be discussed, where Jesus first accuses one of his own men of being a "devil."

We must realise that this is Josephus' perspective on the event. As one wholly connected with the 'blind' who fail to comprehend Jesus' message and intent (i.e., the Pharisees), he sees only the bandit, the troublemaker apparently trying to reinstate Mount Gerizim but, as in the FG, what the Pharisees presume to know is not necessarily the truth. We must recall from our earlier discussions, however, that one of the functions of the Samaritan Taheb *was* to release the Ark from its hiding place (beneath the mountain), to prepare for the coming of the (Davidic) messiah. Josephus' account of the tumult, therefore, reaffirms that the rebel Jesus is assuming that role; there is no other renegade or pretender to this position who fits (again, a post-Jesus augmentation to the Taheb description should be considered).

Jesus has been trying to return people to the *original* way of worship, and his mission has included threats to the temple in Jerusalem, and not just verbal threats. He has been saying much the same thing in Samaria, from the moment he met Mary at the well. Although the Gerizim temple itself has been razed, there is still a cleansing that must be done before the people can worship according to Torah.

When Moses tells Joshua what he must do when he leads the Israelites into the Promised Land, one of the *first* duties is to "demolish completely" all the extant sacred sites "on the mountain height," so that worship of the one god of Israel can be untainted (Deut 12:2f). They must be wary of assimilation and imitation, and if they manage this, they will be granted a paradise wherein God will reside, and they will 'eat' with him in peace and prosperity. Jesus, it seems, is leading a party of followers *against* the reinstatement of the tainted site of Gerizim, *not* in an effort to re-establish it. This is, in part, why we soon see some of his following change their minds and reject him.

I suggest that the very subtle reference back in John 4:45, i.e., to "the Galileans" having seen and heard Jesus at the festival and thereafter supporting his mission, might offer a clue as to why there is a second wave of followers and why the crowd is armed. What if the Galileans are the troublemakers in this scenario?

Judas the Galilean, along with a Pharisee called Zadok, founded the

Galilean sect, otherwise known as the Zealots, in c. 6 CE. They held that God alone was the ruler of Israel and incited the Jews to rebel against the payment of taxes to Rome; Josephus blames them for the destruction of the temple in Jerusalem. I suggest this group is certainly involved in the Samaritan tumult, and I propose this is why Luke later refers to them:

> At that very time there were some present who told him about the Galileans whose blood Pilate had mingled with their sacrifices. He asked them, "Do you think that because these Galileans suffered in this way they were worse sinners than all other Galileans?"
> Luke 13:1

Their blood was "mingled with their sacrifices" because the massacre occurred at the time of the Passover celebrations.

The question then becomes: Does Jesus *know* that these men are armed? (Compare the scene in John 18:10–11, where Peter wields a sword and yet Jesus doesn't seem in the least surprised). Is *Jesus* armed, as he was for the temple demonstration? Or is it possible Jesus is at Tirathaba (see below) and it is this second crowd, led by the Galileans, which makes the march up Mount Gerizim? This would suggest Jesus has lost control of the throng. He would be seen as the instigator, the ringleader, but the clash with the Romans could well be down to the zealous Galilieans who had heard him at the festival denouncing Jerusalem's elite and had latched onto his cause, only to usurp its momentum for their own agenda. It is a feasible interpretation of the evidence.

Musings on Josephus

Josephus' account of the Samaritan leader and the supposed whereabouts of the Ark is an oddity, for Moses never crossed the Jordan. This seems almost *too* blatant an error for the Jewish historian to make. Is he merely passing on a rumour he has *heard* and is thus having a sarcastic dig at the Samaritans' apparent gullibility, is he protecting something/someone, or can we really admit that he is so much in error?

Also, one small factor creates a most intriguing conundrum: Why does the village where the multitude meet (before attempting to ascend the mountain) have a Hindu name? Tirathaba is a composite of:

Tirath + *aba*

Hindu for "sacred place" + father
i.e., "sacred place of the father"

As you can imagine, several thoughts sprung to mind. I imagined Jesus on his travels, sitting with the holy men of India or some such place, learning the word they might have used for their own, personal retreats. Was *tirath* the word for his guru's sacred place? By extension, perhaps, when we see Jesus, in John 6 going up the mountain to sit and think, does he stop at his own 'sacred place' that subsequently becomes known as 'the sacred place of the father', i.e., *Jesus'* special retreat?

Or, on a much more profound and exciting level, could this be a place so named by Jesus himself because he knew it to be a sacred place already, that is, the sacred place of the Father (as used in the FG), God. Could this be something to do with the location of the Ark (as implied by Josephus)?

I also wondered if there might have been any confusion in Josephus' recording of that name. It appears nowhere else, so cross-referencing is impossible. However, there is a potential connection between Tirathaba and Timnath-serah, which, remember, means "portion/manifestation of the remnant." The latter name I deduced to be that of the burial place of Joseph, otherwise referred to as Sychar in the FG; this village lies north of Mount Gerizim. Could Joseph's bones be buried near or even *with* the Ark? The same Hebrew word *arown* is used to describe both his ossuary *and* the Ark of the Covenant. I have another theory about the site of the Ark that I present in "How Many Cubits?", so I am not claiming that I have the definitive answer to this conundrum; it simply shows how much more there is to seemingly superficial material and how much you can glean from titbits of information if you keep an open mind. I find such delving into new territory stimulating and enriching and if it helps others make new connections and new discoveries, then they are well worth the risk of derision.

We need to remember the Samaritan perspective; the Ark was, by divine edict, hidden beneath the mountain, awaiting the arrival of the Taheb. As the divine essence resided in the Ark, one might say anywhere the Ark is must be the 'sacred place of the Father'.

Another Version
Making this whole situation even more intriguing, is the strange but profoundly similar account in 2 Esdras, which is linked to a vision of a man walking on water (i.e., coming out of the sea):

> I looked and saw that an innumerable multitude of people were gathered together ... to make war against the man ... he carved out for himself a great mountain, and flew up on to it ... I tried to see the region or place from which the mountain was carved, but I could not ... I saw that all who gathered against him ... were filled with fear, and yet they dared to fight ... he sent forth from his mouth something like

> a stream of fire ... and burned up all of them ... I was amazed ... After this I saw the man come down from the mountain and call to himself another multitude that was peaceable ... many people came to him ... some of them were bound, and some were bringing others as offerings
> 2 Esd 13:5–13

This is uncanny. The 2 Esdras parallel further suggests that this man is called the "son of God" and the peaceable multitude represents the gathered northern tribes!

In each version of the Samaritan tumult, then, a man goes up a mountain and is set upon by hostile forces but in the FG and 2 Esdras, after he comes down (indicating the first mountain, i.e., Mount Gerizim, is *not* the site of his reign) there is peace. Shiloh, the 'peaceful' site of the new house of God, is the new centre of divine worship, e.g., the bringing of sacrifices ("bound") and converts ("others as offerings").[5]

In Josephus' telling of the event, the man who leads the Samaritans apparently claims that he can retrieve the Ark of the Covenant–and in 2 Esdras, the figure on the mountain breathes out fire ('a storm of sparks') that consumes the enemy: "And fire came out from the presence of the Lord and consumed them, and they died ... And Aaron was silent" (Lev 10:2–3).

This type of "fire" comes *only* from the Ark, i.e., the Shekinah. Possession of the Ark is implicit in all three accounts.

> *Rule in the midst of your foes. Your people will*
> *offer themselves willingly on the day*
> *you lead your forces on the holy mountains.*
> *... "You are a priest forever*
> *according to the order of Melchizedek."*
> Ps 110: 2–4

Cover up?

Now we have reason to question the motivations and accuracy of the FG author for the first time but there is nothing sinister in the fact that he has chosen to steer his readers away from the historical 'truth' and toward the

---

[5] In the Vatican archives is a document referred to as *Acti Pilati* (Pilate's report to Caesar), which, though of doubtful origin, and probably a Christian artefact, does offer a strange corroboration of the Shiloh link: "One day," Pilate supposedly writes, "in passing by the place of Siloe, where there was a great concourse of people, I observed in the midst of the group a young man who was leaning against a tree, calmly addressing the multitude." That the document goes on to say this man was golden-haired, celestial, and "about thirty years of age" really gives the game away, but one has to wonder why Siloe/Shiloh was mentioned, if there was not a valid and significant connection in *some* tradition or other.

spiritual lessons he is duty bound to disseminate. I suggest that John 6 was written as an *ideal*, symbolic account of Jesus' dynamic and precipitate 'sign'. The author shifts the Passover scenario to the evocative mountains of Bashan (thus he is able to exploit the significant scriptural precedents) and he makes Jesus' escape seem like a blessed 'miracle', but he retains enough veracity in the subtle details to make his account an honest one. For those 'with eyes to see', yet again, the truth is there: Jesus *does* go up a mountain, there *is* a huge crowd with him, Romans *do* arrive, there *is* a sense of matters spiralling out of control, and he and the disciples *do* flee.

I think the account of Jesus appearing to the disciples by standing on the sea, although a general allusion to the power of God to overcome the enemy, etc., is also to be understood as the moment Jesus lets his disciples know that he has not been captured or killed. That is their fear, which is why they react so when Jesus reveals himself, i.e., they think him one of those killed by the Romans. The sudden storm thus alludes to the arrival of the soldiers and the chaos that ensues.

If John 6 reveals evidence of the Samaritan tumult recorded by Josephus, paralleled in 2 Esdras, and hinted at in Luke and Mark, so many parts of the puzzle that make up the enigmatic Gospel of John fall into place. Similarly, the *augmented* Messiah ben Joseph tradition as a potentially post-Jesus phenomenon becomes more probable, and the glaring dichotomy between the FG and the Synoptics (e.g., the positioning of the storming of the temple scene within the narratives) is resolved.

Perhaps Lazarus could not justify describing the actual event, for the reality is so damaging to Jesus' supposed identity and mission. How could it be recorded that he failed to keep his 'sheep' safe, that he didn't foresee such an outcome, that he didn't manage to control the crowd—that he fled, alone. I think it is a case of damage limitation; the author takes the most important elements and reshapes the storyline.

I argue, therefore, that it is for this reason we are given two distinct 'years' in the FG, and several other calendrical clues throughout; we can deduce the timeline (historical context) of the gospel for ourselves if we wish to. The Romans and the Samaritans, at the very least, would chronicle the historical record of this highly turbulent year, 36 CE. Indeed, there is further corroboration of this date in Jesus' arrest scenes.

Here is a summary of the various accounts of the same (I claim) 'tumult':

2 Macc 2:4–7 (Jeremiah)
The prophet goes up the mountain where Moses is said to have viewed the Promised Land before dying. He takes with him the tabernacle, the ark, and the altar. These he places in a cave

dwelling and seals them in. A crowd who try to locate the hiding place follows him. He gets angry with them and tells them off, saying the sacred objects will remain hidden until the 'ingathering' is complete and 'mercy' is shown to Israel.

2 Esdras
The figure carves out a mountain for himself and ascends it. Many people pursue him; the mood is one of fear and anger. The exact location of the mountain is unknown ("unseen"). The man rebukes them. They are killed. He comes down the mountain and acquires a great following. He seems to inaugurate a new temple.

Messiah ben Joseph Tradition
He will be responsible for the downfall of the procurator (see "Josephus," below). His followers will rally to his defence and a force referred to as Armilus will kill many.

Gospel of John
Jesus has impressed the sect of the Galileans, a zealot group of revolutionaries. He goes up a mountain. He comments on the crowd following him. He performs a sign during a Passover celebration that excites the crowd so much they attempt to force him to be their 'king'. Romans come from Tiberias, e.g., to quell the commotion. Jesus flees and hides, avoiding capture. He speaks in the synagogue about his flesh and blood in a context of victory in battle. There is dissention within his following for the first time. At his arrest, Jesus refers to the bravery of his followers who would fight if they were there. There is clear evidence Pilate is concerned how Rome will perceive this situation.

Gospel of Luke
Pilate is said to mingle the blood of many Galileans with their sacrifices.

Gospel of Mark
Judas Barabbas is murdered during "the *insurrection.*"

Josephus
The man gathers a great multitude and tells them he will show them the sacred objects that Moses hid under Mount Gerizim.

They become excited and call even more together at a village nearby. They are armed. As they all ascend the mountain, the Romans intervene and a great slaughter of Samaritans results. Many escape, including the ringleader, but they are tagged for execution if caught. The incident is the primary cause of Pilate's extradition back to Rome, i.e., the 'man', *in effect*, 'slays' Pilate.

11
STUMBLING BLOCKS

Flesh and Blood
GETTING BACK TO THE FG'S SEQUENCE of events, Jesus, back in relatively safe Capernaum, is teaching in the synagogue, reiterating the concept of the previous 'sign' and referring to his "flesh and blood." This proves to be a difficult lesson. The pragmatists in the crowd hear in Jesus' words an apparent order to eat his body and drink his blood and they balk at this, for such an idea is anathema to a true Israelite. Not only would this constitute cannibalism of course, it flies in the face of the law, as expressed quite emphatically, in Lev 17:14, i.e., no one is to consume blood, on pain of excommunication. The blood of every living creature 'is its life' and this belongs to God; when an animal is slaughtered *for sacrifice*, its blood must be given to the priest so that he can then offer it up to God.[1]

It is important to link this passage to the previous two incidents, i.e., the feeding in Bashan *and* the boat on the Sea, which is why the author does not tell us right until the end that the synagogue scene is actually distinct. This, I suggest, is what *really* makes Jesus' analogy come to life:

> Assemble and come, gather from all around to the sacrificial feast that I am preparing for you, a great sacrificial feast on the mountains of Israel, and you shall eat flesh and drink blood. *You shall eat the flesh of the mighty, and drink the blood of the princes of the earth* —of rams, of lambs, and of goats, of bulls, all of them fatlings of Bashan. You shall eat fat until you are filled, and drink blood until you are drunk ... I will restore the fortunes of Jacob ... they shall know that I

---

[1] In Jesus' day, Passover sacrifices (for Jews) are to be made at the temple in Jerusalem, for the 'tent of meeting' no longer exists; if the crowd are to start slaughtering livestock up on the Golan Heights, even a Samaritan (who would normally insist that the blood be offered up to God on Mount Gerizim) would be disconcerted; but the FG gets around this by having (dried) fish and bread, rather than sheep (no blood is let).

am the Lord their God because I sent them into exile among the nations, and then gathered them to their own land. I will leave none of them behind.

Ezek 39:17–20, 25, 28

The sacrificial feast here, though intended for the birds and wild animals is, in effect, a feast for the celebration of God's return and his eradication of the oppressors and enemies of Israel; the house of Jacob will "live securely in their land" once more, having witnessed the downfall of the mighty. Of course, this is made contingent upon Israel's return to God, which is the focus of the Jesus' mission. Immediately after this declaration, the prophet is transported to a "very high mountain" "in the land of Israel" and is given the vision of the ideal temple where *all Israel* will worship and where only the pure in "heart and flesh" will administer. In Ezek 39:11 the location of this conquest and celebration is called the "Valley of the Travellers, east of the sea"; "travellers" is translated from the Hebrew verb *abar*, meaning "to pass over, through, or by, pass on" and the so the site is identified by many as the Abarim region—exactly where Jesus had been previously, offering Passover, and pertinent to the discussion of John 6:25–40 and the allusions to Moses.

The point is, this is *revolutionary* talk. When John affirms Jesus' bridegroom role in John 3, the insinuation is that rebellion is in the air; the same is being inferred here, and this has a bearing on Jesus' legal standing during his interrogation by Annas. He is saying all this *publicly* but in such a way that only those who 'read between the lines' can grasp his meaning; the rest, taking him literally, rather than perceiving the metaphor, simply think he is mad, but this is all part of the winnowing process, according to the FG author.

"Share in the sacrificial feast," Jesus is saying, "eat the flesh and the blood, for it is mine'. Jesus is not saying he is the physical sacrifice, for he never *actually* becomes (or *intends* to become) one. The context of Ezekiel 39 implies that the sacrifice is the *enemy* and this is a foreshadowing of what seems to happen in the FG. Taking Jesus literally simply does not work; it is nonsense without the context of the feeding, and the suppression-of-the-enemy themes. The flesh and blood is 'his' by possession, by spiritual conquest, not 'his' personally. Share in Jesus' victory, and you share in the kingdom of 'life', the kingdom of true worship and the will of God. Eat the flesh and drink the blood that belongs to the victor, and you assume the rights of the "son of man," i.e., you become one with the firstborn. The firstborn reinstated will live "forever." Jesus then asks, "what if you were to see the son of man ascending to where he was before?" The Remnant of Joseph, once the elect of God, has fallen into a desperate state but will soon "rise" to its rightful status again. This, at least, is the theological interpretation.

When you read these passages with the Samaritan tumult in mind, however, you get the sense that Jesus is referring to the near-miss he and his disciples have just had. Remember that there is a certain warlike nature to the Messiah ben Joseph, and the FG's Jesus is depicted in terms of aggression, either directly or indirectly, on more than one occasion (e.g., the temple scene, the fact that one of his disciples carries a weapon, and when arrested, he claims his followers would fight if present). Although "anointed for battle," perhaps Jesus simply doesn't have what it takes and the sheer overwhelming zeal of the crowd, ready to do *real* battle then and there, is too much for him. His strangely disturbing words echo the violence and confusion of the massacre on the mountain.

It is after the slaying of the Samaritans and Galileans on Mount Gerizim, which seems to be the *true* locale for the Passover of John 6 (remember, the *alluded to* setting of Bashan is the FG author's theological/symbolic construct, in an effort to detach Jesus from the debacle whilst being true to his duty to chronicle the movement), that many of Jesus' followers realise they have made an error in judgement and detach themselves from his following. With apparent hints of an impending bloody battle and sacrifice, so soon after the Samaritan tumult, those who walk away may simply decide they don't wish to sacrifice their own flesh and blood for someone who ran away at the first sign of trouble.

Peter

After Peter's introduction in John 1, the nature of his character established, nothing is said of him *directly*, until John 6:68. Perhaps he is now convinced that Jesus' revolution may be the way to secure a higher position, as he now seems to be a disciple; however, we will soon learn that he is merely hedging his bets.

Having been rejected by "many of his disciples," Jesus asks the "twelve" if any of *them* wish to leave and Peter, ever the apparently keen one, responds vehemently, claiming to "believe" Jesus is the chosen one of God. To this alleged confession Jesus responds by accusing one of them of being a "devil"; a strange response one may think but not so strange if we remember what "Cephas" implies, i.e., Peter is not trustworthy until he has proven himself contrite and humble. John 6:71 is probably an addendum because it draws attention away from the obvious suspect; it exonerates Peter by blaming Judas, illustrating a Christian perspective, not that of the FG. Besides, later in the gospel, Judas is said to be strongly influenced by the "devil," suggesting someone else holds this title within the narrative.

This caution regarding Peter is retained in Matt 16:23: "Get behind me, Satan! You are a stumbling block to me, for you are setting your mind not on divine things but on human things." Paul, too, has no high opinion of Peter, as is evidenced in Gal 2:11f, where Peter is rejected as a hypocrite who is too easily swayed by the circumstances in which he finds himself, rather than adhering to the path Jesus has, supposedly, set for him. As far as the FG is concerned, Peter is vying for a more superior position within the group but he is influenced by the machinations of someone in particular; just as in his depiction as the "lame man" unable to make progress of his own volition, he soon comes to rely on a stronger personality in his bid to rise in the ranks.

Jesus is, by now, fully aware that he is under scrutiny. According to the narrative, "emissaries" follow him wherever he goes; first at Bethany/Bethabara, then Aenon, now Tiberias. Is there someone amongst his disciples who is acting the mole? Could it be Peter?

Confusion
The pep talk Jesus seems to have given his disciples has fallen on a few deaf ears. He is hesitant to return to the south, where he is a wanted man. He feels pushed into things, claiming that his "time" has not "yet come"; determined, his closest allies try to coerce him into appearing again in public, i.e., "no one who wants to be widely known acts in secret. If you do these things, show yourself to the world" (John 7:4). "If you are who you say you are, prove it," in other words. *Who* would say such a thing? Jesus is in hiding; he had slipped away from the crowd on the mountain in secret, now he enters Judea in secret (John 7:10). For such a self-acclaimed authority he doesn't seem overly confident at this point.

The Festival of Tabernacles is the site of Jesus' next appearance in Jerusalem. The instructions for the celebration appear in Deuteronomy 26–7; there is an offering of first fruits, which is ritualized by the recital of the saving acts of God. A reminder of the pre-Egyptian heritage of Israel, including the 'signs and wonders' that freed the nation from oppression is given, and the need to "observe [the] statutes and ordinances" of God if the nation and the Promised Land are to be "holy" is emphasized.

The temple of Solomon was originally dedicated at this festival, emphasizing Jesus' intentions even more, perhaps. In his prayer of dedication for the new temple, Solomon makes the future of the religious institution, i.e., the "throne of Israel," contingent upon the nation's heartfelt adherence to the divine law (1 Kgs 8:25). In the subsequent response from God, this conditional arrangement is reiterated in terms of integrity and uprightness (9:4). So long as they deserve it, in other words, the line of David will sit on the throne; if they stray from the chosen path, they forfeit their right to rule. Such a concept is vital to understanding the FG's allusions to kingship; it is a very subtle threat that has potential ramifications for the entire establishment.

Jesus' reputation precedes him and the crowd talk of him amongst themselves, though secretly for fear of the Jews (confirming the distinction between the authorities, i.e., the Jews, and the general public). The FG says that *about* "the middle of the festival Jesus went up into the temple and began to teach" (John 7:14). As the celebrations last seven days (Deut 16:13–15), Jesus probably makes his appearance on the *third* day, a symbolically charged moment.

At the very beginning of the gospel Jesus had called Nicodemus the "teacher of Israel"; this title was originally attributed to the priests (Deut 33:10) but subsequently usurped by the Pharisees. Jesus is now assuming the function of teacher, taking *back* from the Pharisees what they had claimed illegitimately. Here he goes again! This is why the Jews are so "astonished"; Jesus is not a priest as far as they are concerned, neither is he a Pharisee, so how can he claim to teach Israel? He has not received the training they have received, so why is it he seems to know so much? The teaching Jesus offers, though, is not (according to the FG) some personal belief or agenda but the "word of God."

> *Whom will he teach knowledge*
> *...to whom will he explain the message?*
> Isa 28:9

Getting a little more daring, Jesus openly accuses the Jews of threatening him with death but it is the crowd, the general public, who answers: "You have a demon (i.e., must be mad), who is trying to kill you?" (John 7:20). Jesus is revealing the wicked intentions of the authorities, just in case anything happens; with everyone aware that he is in fear of his life, which of the Jews would be so rash as to try anything? Another riot is the last thing they want. Jesus adds the subtle warning: "I have not come on my own"; although on one level this could allude to the authority of "the Father" that is in him, as in John 16:32 (but that has a different context), it is also a statement of caution, in that he does still have followers who are willing to fight on his word.

Jesus' justification for 'healing' a "man's whole body" is phrased in terms of the circumcision of Moses (the significance of which the author of the subsequent addendum is obviously uncertain). This is not to say Moses *gave* Israel circumcision but that he, himself, was saved from death *by* circumcision (Exod 24:24–6). If the law permits this 'saving' ritual on the Sabbath, Jesus' 'saving' act should be just as permissible. Besides, there is a pliable, more practical and sympathetic interpretation of the Sabbath laws, an interpretation Jesus alludes to when he says, "Do not judge by appearances, but judge with right judgement" (John 7:24):

> If you refrain from trampling the Sabbath, from pursuing your own interests on my holy day; if you call the Sabbath a delight and the holy day of the Lord honourable; if you honour it, not going your own ways, serving your own interests, or pursuing your own affairs; then you shall take delight in the Lord.
>
> Isa 58:13–14

Jesus believes he is doing the work of God, honouring this holy day by bringing the lost souls back to the righteous path. How can any but the 'wicked' themselves say this is wrong?[2]

Once more, there is total confusion about who Jesus is. Is he the messiah after all? Are the authorities trying to keep it quiet? Some believe, some do not. Escaping arrest, Jesus' effect on the Jews is clear, for they are not simply querying what Jesus means when he says they will not find him where he is going, they are making a *promise*. That is, Jesus will *have* to go and teach to the "the Dispersion among the Greeks" (by this is meant the Israelites scattered beyond Palestine) if they are not to find him, for they have spies everywhere. Yet, is this not exactly what the FG is all about? The sending of a message to the scattered Israelites is *just* what Jesus *is* interested in, so this proves to be one of several instances where the truth (Jesus' truth) is placed on the lips of the unwitting antagonists of the gospel.

On the last day of the festival, the seventh day, again a day of special symbolic significance, and the day on which the Feast of Tabernacles includes the most number of priests, Jesus cries out, as if in desperation (the Greek verb *krazo* in John 7:37 implies a forceful exclamation and is used elsewhere, such as in Rev 21:4 and Heb 5:7, to denote a cry of lamentation, or a supplication): "Let anyone who is thirsty come to me."

Those who turn away from God, so we learn from Jeremiah, forsake the "living water" and perish, whilst those who "trust in the Lord" grow strong and prosper even in the wilderness, for they have set their "roots" in the saving "stream" (Jer 17:7–18). The passage goes on to recount the

---

[2] The Samaritans (and the Essenes) are known for being even more rigid in the definition and observance of Sabbath than the Pharisees, and right from the opening of the gospel we have seen that Jesus observes *some* form of Sabbath, i.e., the Day of Atonement he spends indoors, in John 1:39. The Samaritans have their own bi-annual calendar that is calculated from the meridian of Gerizim; the Talmud tells of the Samaritans vandalizing the Jewish beacon system that is meant to inform those in outlying areas of the time of the Sabbath. So, it *may* be that, as far as Jesus is concerned, he is not profaning the 'true' Sabbath at all.

conviction of the prophet, whose role as "shepherd" has led him into the snares of his persecutors but he refuses to give up in the face of adversity. The hope is that God will vindicate the prophet and turn his judgement upon the unbelievers.

Jesus is addressing a body of priests but note what he says next: "let the one who believes in me drink." Who is "the one"? Jesus has singled out one person in particular. He is searching for his new protégée, the boy promised to him up in Cana, i.e., Lazarus. He must now be a (trainee) priest and Jesus is ready to make the most of his promise to Nicodemus, especially since being disappointed with Philip's lack of understanding.[3]

> *I will surely gather ... the survivors of Israel;*
> *I will set them together like sheep in a fold.*
> *... The one who breaks out will go up before them;*
> *they will break through ... the gate, going out by it.*
> *Their king will pass on before them, the Lord at their head.*
> Mic 2:12–13

This passage from Micah anticipates Jesus' monologue concerning the gate and the sheep in John 10 but more significantly, it alludes to the formal arrival into the narrative of this special character. In John 11 we learn that Lazarus is the main reason many of the Jews convert, so in effect, he leads them out, i.e., they follow his example.

It is in these FG passages, however, that Jesus' Davidic heritage is so clearly questioned (John 7:42). The scriptures say that the messiah will be from the house of David but Jesus is "from Galilee," i.e., from the reviled northern tribes—how can this be?

Nicodemus 2

The gospel reintroduces Nicodemus in this, the second stage of his story. In a clever allusion to the words spoken by John back in 1:26 ("Among you stands one whom you do not know"), Nicodemus, presented as one amongst the chief priests and Pharisees ("one of them"), has truly become one whom they will soon not recognise, for his loyalties to the sect are failing. In their caustic response, "Has any of the authorities or of the Pharisees believed in him?" (7:48), the Pharisees once again reveal their ignorance, for of course there *are* converts and Nicodemus will be a prime example! They simply do

---

[3] Young priests were initiated into general duties when they reached physical maturity, i.e., at age thirteen or soon thereafter. Official serving duties were undertaken at the age of twenty (Talmud Bavli Hullin 24b).

not see.

Nicodemus uses his influence, while he still has some, to allow Jesus some leeway: "Our law does not judge people without first giving them a hearing to find out what they are doing, does it?" the Pharisees' retort is sarcastic but unwittingly correct, i.e., they infer that if Nicodemus can say such a thing he must be "from Galilee" too (i.e., a Jesus supporter). They tell him to "search" and "see" that no prophet is to come from Galilee. (Of course, the subsequent Messiah ben Joseph tradition stipulates that he shall begin his work in Galilee, but this part of the tradition arises *from* Jesus, it does not anticipate him, so I suggest). As self-acclaimed masters of Torah, they demonstrate their supposed knowledge of the scriptures but the FG author has the upper hand, for the *only* OT precedent for the saying "search and you will see" is in 2 Kgs 10:23. There, Jehu stands, disguised, amongst the Baal worshippers; his intention is to destroy their temple and to return Israel to the worship of the 'true' god. The Pharisees thus have the truth of Jesus' intention placed, yet again, upon their lips, i.e., he is to cleanse ("destroy") the defiled locus of worship through the destruction of the current cultus.

Nicodemus is, indeed, from Galilee, from Capernaum, as we now know from John 4. He is also a convert to Jesus' ministry. He is biding his time, using his status and position as an 'insider' to help the cause. However, his audacity here anticipates his next appearance, where he is threatened with punishment should he openly confess his allegiance to Jesus.

12
ADULTERESS

Mary's Trial

THE GOSPEL CONTINUES WITH THE depiction of the Samaritan woman, Mary; as the woman who is in an illicit union with her sixth and unsanctioned 'husband' she is committing adultery in the eyes of God. The footnote in the NRSV suggests that the most ancient authorities lack 7:53–8:11, or that it appears elsewhere in the narrative (which is intriguing given that the FG chronology can be questioned) but its conformity to the rest of the FG is so uniform, it would be an uncanny addendum. It fulfils the very next stage in Ezekiel 16's portrait of the divine bride, where she passes from infidelity to the public show of guilt: "I will judge you as women who commit adultery …. They shall bring up a mob against you and they shall stone you" (Ezek 16:38–40).

There can be little doubt that the story of John 7:53–8:11 echoes that of Susanna (in the Additions to the Book of Daniel, especially vv. 34–41). There is a similar element of catching a woman in the act of committing adultery; there are 'elders' present in both scenarios; there is a strong desire to put both women to death even before their trials; there is a reticence in each of the two leading male characters (Daniel and Jesus) to partake in the judgement; in each case the woman is acquitted; and in each the accusers are left with the guilt.

The Samaritan version of Susanna's story is known as "The Daughter of Amram." She is a Nazarite and two men falsely accuse her. It is worth noting that the name Amram comes from Exod 6:20, i.e., the father of Moses, Aaron and, in the Samaritan version of the LXX, Miriam. This is understood by current scholars to be a devised genealogy set down by the priestly sources of the text, in order to underscore the importance of Moses by giving him Israelite/priestly status. Thus, for the Susanna story, the woman is the daughter of a priest, where Amram is a representation of the priesthood (a commission name); although she is unnamed, the link to Miriam in Exodus makes it probable this name is inferred. She is the daughter not of any priest, but of the *high priest*.

According to the Qur'an, Amram is also the father of "Mary, Jesus' mother." If we allow for the Muslim interpretation of the Christian story to be influenced more by the dominant Synoptic version of events, we can ask with impunity: What if this Mary was actually the Magdalene? That would make Amram, Jesus, for by taking her under his wing, as the 'rod' of Ephraim, as the future wife of his 'adopted' son, or protégée, Lazarus, Jesus becomes, in effect, her father (in law). Unless Amram is truly Mary Magdalene's Samaritan father, a name not deemed important enough even for the FG to mention, let alone the Synoptics, it makes much more sense for this to be an epithet for Jesus, the man *assuming* high-priestly status.

A mediaeval Samaritan document, known as the "Chronicle of Abu'l Fath" contains a similar tale of a high priest who is *tested* for his impartiality as judge by certain men who falsely accuse his daughter, believing that he will use his authority to free her despite the charges. This daughter is named Maryam. The priest manages to reverse the focus of the accusations by openly challenging the credibility of the witnesses and accusers. Here too, the woman is not condemned.

According to Jewish law, a woman accused of infidelity, whether caught in the act or not, is to be presented before the *priest* for judgement (Num 5:13). If we accept this woman of the FG is Mary Magdalene, Jesus' apparently self-acclaimed priestly status is being *tested*, just as in the Samaritan documents.

In the account of adultery described in Deut 22:13–21, the focus on a woman's lack of virginity, her supposed 'prostitution' *and* her being potentially slandered by false accusations, emphasizes the *father's* role, not so much the husband's, which offers us another clue to Jesus' relationship with Mary, i.e., he is to be seen as a father, or father-in-law figure. However, in order for Mary to *be* accused (even falsely), she must already be married or betrothed (for as the woman is considered the legal property of the man, it is he who is considered wronged in such cases); the 'rods' of Ephraim and Judah were both *chosen* in John 4, but were they united (in the 'biblical' sense)?

This is where things start to get (even more) complicated. Unravelling the dual nature of the FG, with its intentional double meanings and apparently parallel stories, is something that has taken me many years, so it must be explained over several chapters. However, this story of the adulteress really brings home the confusion over whose wife she is meant to be. We have two ways of dealing with this situation:

✶ Mary is presumed by the accusing Jews to be *Jesus'* second wife and now the young Lazarus suddenly appears on the scene, more her own age. A man having sexual intercourse with another man's wife incurs the death penalty for *both* parties. The chances of something being misconstrued or intentionally fabricated are high, given the attitude of the Jews toward Jesus (and later Lazarus) throughout the gospel. If Jesus is the one cuckolded, then Lazarus and Mary must die (Deut 22:22–4).

★ If Mary is deemed Lazarus' legal 'property' as his betrothed (or wife) then the accusation is probably that Jesus is the miscreant. If a man lies with his daughter-in-law (Lazarus is effectively an adopted son) both are to be put to death (Lev 20:12).

The vicious rumours and spiteful accusations, just as in the Susanna precedent, bring Mary face to face with Jesus, her alleged partner in crime but also her supposed confessor, her 'father', the alleged high priest. In either scenario, Jesus' campaign is potentially nullified, for according to the law, *both* the man and the woman who commit adultery are to be stoned. Will Jesus place the blame on Lazarus, or will he take the blame himself? The Jews *anticipate* that the turbulent 'priest' can be dealt with swiftly using this potentially embarrassing and demeaning strategy.

The Retort
Beginning to perceive Jesus' ambition and goal, it may be that a sparring contest ensues between Jesus and the men who present Mary to him—a contest of legalities, to see who can be caught out first (in John 8:7 we learn that the men persist in questioning Jesus, so there is obviously more going on than is immediately made evident). The accusers, for instance may begin by citing: "Those born of an illicit union shall not be admitted to the assembly of the Lord" (Deut 23:2); or "… Judah was told, 'Your daughter-in-law Tamar has played the whore; moreover she is pregnant as a result of whoredom.' And Judah said, 'Bring her out, and let her be burned.'" (Gen 38:24). Either would infer that they realise why Mary is there, i.e., to bear Jesus' child. The first would suggest a priestly prohibition, the second, father-in-law status but these are merely potential citations. However, in the Talmud (Mas. Yevamoth 37a, note 42), it is claimed that "the Samaritans did not observe all the laws of betrothal, and any Samaritan might be the issue of an illicit union between his father and a woman who had been legally betrothed to another man." It may be that the Jews seek to prove the illegitimacy of any potential offspring.

Jesus might then reply with: "I will not punish your daughters when they play the whore, and your daughters-in-law when they commit adultery; for the men themselves go aside with whores, and sacrifice with temple prostitutes; thus a people without understanding comes to ruin" (Hos 4:14).

Some of the ancient versions of the FG include an additional phrase at John 4:8 not included in the text of the NRSV today; the addition implies that what Jesus inscribes in the soil *is* something to do with the "sins of each of them" (the accusers). Inflammatory and so fitting in the context of the corrupt priesthood, this scathing diatribe from Hosea seems a good candidate but there is an even better one:

> The sin of Judah is written ... By your own act you shall lose the heritage that I gave you ... those who turn away from you shall be recorded in the earth, for they have forsaken the fountain of living water, the LORD.
>
> Jer 17:1

According to Jeremiah 17, the prophet is instructed to stand by the gates of Jerusalem and warn the sinners of Judah that if they do not change their ways and return to the divine law given them when they left Egypt, they risk losing *everything*. The stubbornness and pride of those who are deemed leaders is emphasized, with the result being a conspiracy against Jeremiah and the plan to bring false charges against him. The subsequent passages tell of God the potter and the use of clay; the next major scene in the FG, after that of the adulteress, involves Jesus' use of clay to 'heal' the blind man.

Jesus' first inscription clearly isn't enough to do the job. What he continues to write in the dirt seems to take a while, for the amassed accusers leave "one by one" as he does so. Whatever precedent he chooses to illustrate his response to the allegations brought against Mary and/or him, they are powerful enough to make each and every one of the men turn tail.

There is another interesting precedent in Numbers. Here, we learn of the ritual of the "ordeal by the waters of bitterness" for the adulteress. The accused woman is brought before the *priest* and is subjected to a test whereby her innocence or guilt will be revealed. If she is proven guilty, her uterus will drop and she will never conceive. If innocent, she will be able to bear children. Again, the emphasis is on offspring:

> Then the priest shall bring her near, and set her before the LORD; the priest shall take holy water in an earthen vessel, and take *some of the dust that is on the floor of the tabernacle* and put it into the water ... 'If no man has lain with you, if you have not turned aside to uncleanness while under your husband's authority, be immune to this water of bitterness that brings the curse.... Then the priest shall put these curses in writing, and wash them off into the water of bitterness.
>
> Num 5:11–31

Interestingly, this is the ritual we see Mary, Jesus' "mother" being subjected to in the *Protevangelion*, a Christian document that tells an intriguing version of the pregnancy and marriage of Jesus' supposed mother, and Joseph. I shall come back to this.

Rabbinic interpretation of this law during the final years of the Second Temple Period all but annuls the ritual of the bitter waters by the gate but in Jesus' day it is still in use. However, the test is only applicable to those *not* "caught in the act" (Num 5:13) and thereby obliged to prove their innocence. Can the FG's usage of the identical phrase be a reference to this precedent, i.e., there *are no* witnesses and the accusations are thus false? This would also confirm, again, that Jesus is being tested as a priest. Indeed, in John 8:13, the Pharisees declare that Jesus cannot act as his own witness, which really does support the idea that he, too is 'on trial' here.

Mary is brought before Jesus by two accusers (two witnesses, as required by law, i.e., another detail that will be echoed John 8:13–18 and again in the arrest scenes of the FG). Either they have brought her to Jesus, her *husband*, who is then duty bound to take her to the priest for trial and condemnation, or they are taking her to Jesus to test his self-proclaimed role as priest. Either way, Jesus is potentially placed in an untenable position; he must lose his two special disciples (and thus his child) to stoning, or he must nullify his position as priest and risk failing in his theological mission.

Something bothers me, though; if this scene takes place in the temple, why is there *earth* and not stone beneath their feet? It is a small detail but one that should not be ignored, for it may be a direct invitation to the reader to recall Num 5:17 and the use of "dust," or earth, from the "floor" of the tabernacle which, of course, would have been the ground itself, not a constructed floor, as the tabernacle was a tent. The temple floor, on the other hand, was kept remarkably clean, as Bel and the Dragon reveals: Daniel has to cover the ground with ash from the altar, in order to discern the footprints of the priests who are entering the temple to eat the sacrificial foods. The keen reader who knew this would wonder why Jesus could make an inscription with his finger, unless, that is, he is outside, e.g., by the gate (see Deut 22:13–20), which would make the allusion complete. The emphasis in Deuteronomy 22 is on the proof of a woman's virginity; the focus of everyone's attention is the blood-stained bridal sheet spread out *on the ground* for all to see, in order to prove false witness against her. Is the FG hinting at a similar 'proof' here? Did Jesus convince the elders that she *was* a virgin when he went with her, and that she is, therefore, not an adulteress? There is no *biblical* law condemning mutually consented sex between a married man and a virgin, and if the priests themselves were philanderers (going with temple prostitutes, for instance), they would, indeed, be hypocrites by judging Jesus.

Such an allusion to Jesus' *apparent* polygamy would have been anathema to the early Christian Church, especially under the auspices of Paul, so I have no difficulty imagining that the incident was actually *stricken* from the record. Somewhere along the way, however, an original copy must have been found, or the passage was transferred orally until certain groups were independent enough to authorize its reinstatement. If, however, the tract is not original to the FG, which I find hard to believe, someone must have thought it necessary to include the adulteress' scene, and I think the only logical reason would be to combat later apocryphal texts that (also) hinted at a less than platonic relationship between their 'Christ' and this woman of (alleged) ill-repute! By showing Jesus as the judge, non-Jewish audiences would be under the impression that the woman and her crime had nothing whatever to do with Jesus, and that his mercy was unlimited and unquestionable, even by the authorities.

We can conclude, therefore, that Jesus is playing the role of priest (high priest) and that he is, in some way, intimately associated with the woman brought before him. The outcome of the scene suggests Jesus makes a wise on-the-spot decision. He chooses to defend the will of God over and above his duty as husband or father. Just as Susanna places her life in the hands of God and is rewarded by the intervention of Daniel, so Jesus surrenders Mary's fate to God's will (as he will also do with Lazarus', marking yet another parallel between these two young characters) and is inspired with a rejoinder the accusers cannot counter.

If God does not condemn the adulteress (i.e., Israel), neither can Jesus. Like the high priest in the "Chronicle of Abu'l Fath" (which is, I posit, *based* on Jesus and Mary Magdalene), Jesus reverses the focus of the accusations by openly challenging the credibility of the woman's accusers. We must remember, however, that although there is a mundane scenario taking place here, it has much more profound implications, i.e., it represents a specific stage of the harlot-bride allusion—her trial.

Note how Jesus tells Mary not to "sin again" but the threatening "unless something worse happens" is not added. Thus Mary, in her representational role as the sinning and rejected bride (Israel) is given her first step up the ladder to her ultimate elevation; she is forgiven.

What is vital to remember, however, is that there are *two* men in Mary's life, Jesus and Lazarus, and this is the way it continues, right to the very end. The pattern of the narrative should also be recognised from this point onward, e.g., the Samaritan woman's story is followed by that of the sick young man, then the adulteress is followed by the blind man. This is intentional and part of the symbolic, parallel rise of both Mary and Lazarus. Just as we are told about the first and second 'signs' in order that we can recognise the subsequent signs, we are given this pattern in order that we follow the pair's intertwining depiction.[1]

Polygamy and Protection
A number of the Mishnah tracts (the original codification of oral law, attributed to Judah the Prince, born c. 135 CE) address legal problems *directly* related to the practice of polygamy, suggesting it was very much a factor of everyday life in Jesus' time. There are laws pertaining to two wives, to three, four, and 'multiple' wives, up to a maximum of eighteen according to some, forty-eight according to others! The stipulation of Deut 17:17 is that any future *king of Israel* should not have too many wives, lest one of them turn against him. The distinction between what is allowed for the king and what is permitted for ordinary men is thus a matter of debate but the crux of the issue is not the *act* of polygamy itself but rather *how many* wives is considered proper.

It was not until the Middle Ages, when Rabbi Gershom ben Judah (960–1028 CE) convened a synod and urged Jews to give up the practice of polygamy, that having multiple wives became something one just 'didn't do', at least in public. Many have argued that this was due to the overwhelming influence of Christians who had by then rejected the practice. It would take until the 1950s to become more or less unanimous but there are still factions extant today who deem it their *right*, as the children of Israel, to be polygamous.

So, is Jesus a polygamist or does he have a sexual relationship with Mary outside of marriage? In both the Genesis well scenes emphasis is placed on finding a wife from amongst one's own kin, so again we are forced to consider both eventualities, i.e., Jesus must choose a woman from the northern tribes who will be 'raised' along with the 'rod of Judah' but she *must* bear the offspring of a Josephite. According to scripture, the high priest must marry from within his own tribe (kin) in order to preserve the bloodline of the priesthood.

Throughout my research the spectre of polygamy loomed. I knew it was an issue that needed to be dealt with but at the same time, my focus on the importance of Lazarus diluted any anxiety I may have felt about proposing that Jesus might be polygamous. I rationalized things by thinking of his relationship with Mary as a purely symbolic union. I had been working with the assumption that Lazarus and Mary were *actually* married, and Jesus

---

[1] There is a potential allusion linking this, a scene about the as yet unidentified Mary, to the as yet unidentified "blind man." The "dust" in this scene is the soil Jesus manipulates with his hand to make a 'sign', to prove a point; the "clay" of John 9 is, similarly, soil Jesus manipulates to reveal a 'sign' and prove a point.

and Mary only *figuratively* so. The entire Mary-Lazarus 'rods-united' symbolism permeates the gospel and is necessary to the understanding of Jesus' intentions but does this preclude Jesus marrying Mary first? There is such an air of ambiguity surrounding this issue. Why was it so necessary to make the two lead characters in the narrative so interchangeable, even down to their conjugal status? The answer has to do with succession and protection, which becomes clear as the FG continues.

Lazarus' position in the FG is made interchangeable with Jesus' on several occasions, with the reader uncertain who is actually being spoken about. Who is Mary calling *"Rabbouni"* at the tomb? Who is the father of the child? The ambiguity is cleverly contrived to protect the new dynasty. Confusion and hiding things in plain sight is the simplest yet most effective strategy to foil the plans of one's enemies to steal something important. In one of my humorous moments while researching (of which there were many!), I suddenly thought of the scene in the film *Spartacus* where everyone stands up and claims to be the man called Spartacus in a bid to protect the real Spartacus. This is what the FG does; it hides the child amongst multiple (well, two) fathers.

It also seems quite plausible now that in his duty as Jesus' official biographer, as the vindicator of the mission and Jesus' role in it, the FG's author has to find a way of removing all potential causes of complaint against his master. The primary issue, of course, is the Samaritan tumult; he works hard in his depiction of Jesus' mission to avoid placing him in the vicinity (physically or chronologically), yet being an honest chronicler, he does leave clues. An educated man, erudite and analytical, Lazarus uses his skill in both language and rhetoric to create an account that is so brilliantly dualistic and subversive, there is no way an accuser could point the finger and denounce Jesus as either king or high priest (isn't this exactly what happens in the adulteress' scene, where Jesus blurs the letters of the law so that neither Mary nor her paramour can be judged?).

For instance, wherever there is a moment in the FG where Jesus seems to be heading for trouble, for conflict that might suggest physical violence, something either miraculous or profound happens to draw attention away from the incident and toward the overall theological message. Wherever there are questions of ritual purity, there is a clever retort. Similarly, matters concerning Jesus' relationship with Mary, when viewed in the light of Torah, might create unease amongst potential converts and believers, so the dutiful author bends boundaries a little, confuses the issue, so that no one can impugn the King of Israel. As with any recorded history, the account is subjective and biased in favour of the perceived victors, so the FG maintains that no matter what happened during Jesus' revolt against the institution, he was above the law, untouchable until his work was complete, and blessed by

God in everything he felt compelled to do to meet his goal of resurrecting Shiloh.

In the discussion of the Samaritan woman I argued that Mary and Martha are presented in the FG as sisters in order to allude to the precedent of Rachel and Leah from Genesis, where both married the same man, the younger giving him the sons Joseph and Benjamin. I defy anyone with an open mind to re-read the FG with this possibility in mind and then reject the suggestion as implausible. There are just too many clues! To complete the picture, I offer this potential breakdown of the name Lazarus:

Laz + *zarah*

(from *levath/lavah*) "to unite" + "the rivals"

The Hebrew word *zarah* is used is 1 Sam 1:6, the story of the two wives of Elkanah, Samuel's father, to mean "rival." If the story were not so poignant, this could be construed as humour. There are several potential examples of wordplay when we deconstruct "Lazarus" and each has a profound relationship to the context within the narrative, thereby reaffirming the interpretation; these will be explained at the appropriate junctures.

By the end of the gospel we see Lazarus responsible for both Jesus' women. It is evident Martha is jealous of Mary's intimacy with Jesus; to have no choice but to watch her bear him the son he is yearning for must be heart-wrenching. One might see a similarity here to Sarah and Hagar's tale, also (Gen 16). Although Sarah brings Hagar into her home herself and thus differs from Martha in that respect, Hagar is clearly younger and able to conceive, she bears Abraham a son but falls out of favour with Sarah, who eventually ousts her from the family home, significantly, removing Ishmael (Hagar's son) from Abraham's inheritance. Under the cross Lazarus is officially made Martha's adopted son and thus the family ties are made fast; he must keep the women together, for the sake of the child. The fate of Ishmael *cannot* befall Jesus' young son.

13
ESCALATION

Not from God

JESUS DECLARES HIMSELF TO BE the "light of the world" and demands of the Jews (i.e., the "scribes and Pharisees" of John 8:3) that they reflect upon who the Father is. They do not *know* Jesus, they don't 'see' that he has come as God's representative; therefore, they do not truly *know* the Father. They see what they wish to see, believing and judging "by the flesh" rather than by the word of God.

Now this, the FG says, Jesus relates whilst "teaching in the treasury of the temple," the very heart of the trading establishment. Jesus is, yet again, denouncing the authority of the Jews and is flouting their self-acclaimed right to dictate the nature of the temple. "The slave does not have a permanent place in the household; the son has a place there for ever," Jesus reminds them. The rightful heir *will* return to claim his inheritance, i.e., stewardship over the *true* house of God.

So far, Jesus has disrupted the outer court of the moneychangers and merchants, he has attempted to convert priests at the Sheep Gate, he has taught inside the temple during a sacred festival, where there are many priests present, and now he has the audacity to stand at the very core of their corrupt little empire! That he is 'teaching', and this teaching is so obviously to do with the law, means that he is publicly taking on the role of priest, denouncing the Pharisees' monopoly on 'truth' yet again.

Scholars argue about where the treasury is in the temple; some say the reference alludes only to the donation boxes that were placed around the outer courts but this does not seem significant enough. Josephus, on the other hand, mentions several chambers that actually lined the walls of the inner court (*Wars.* 5.5.2), so one of these may be the treasury. This seems more plausible, for according to Ezra 8:24f, the money first granted by King Artaxerxes to rebuild the temple after the Babylonian exile was distributed amongst twelve leaders of the priestly families, to be guarded "within the chambers of the house of the Lord." The small collection boxes positioned around the temple are not the focus of Jesus' attentions. Rather, it is the allusion to the corrupt priesthood that has acquired great treasures from foreign 'investors' that makes Jesus' stance in the treasury a potent admonition. Jesus stands within the priestly court (a crime in its own right if he is not a priest, or if he is a Samaritan), castigating the very foundations of the establishment.

Again, we see Jesus under the threat of arrest but he is not actually seized; his 'hour' has not yet come. It is legitimate to question whether all these instances of Jesus evading arrest, escaping stoning, etc., aren't due to allies within both the upper echelons of the temple staff (e.g., the gatekeepers, the temple police, even the Roman guards?) lending a conveniently-timed hand. Or perhaps it is the FG author's invention, tempting us to anticipate an even greater escape!

Jesus becomes more openly hostile toward the Jews, claiming that he has "much to condemn" concerning them. Declaring his role as prophet, as one who speaks the word of God ("I have heard from him"), Jesus fully detaches himself from the 'world': "You are from below, I am from above," he says, reiterating the concept of 'rebirth from above', so clearly a stipulation for redemption in John 3. All who fail to believe in the "I AM" that is in Jesus, this authoritative blessing, this 'spirit', will be condemned to "die in [their] sins," Jesus warns. Still, they ask him *who* he is.

The NRSV reads, "Why do I speak to you at all?" (John 8:25) but the Greek infers that Jesus is what he has always claimed to be, i.e., "What I have told you from the beginning"— a man, a prophet, the Restorer, the representative (son) of God. "When you lift up the son of man," Jesus claims, "then you will know that I AM, and that I do nothing on my own"; the invocation of the divine "I AM" implies that this 'raising' will be God's will. Can it really be God's will that his 'son', his prophet, die such an ungracious and belittling death?

The Greek verb translated as 'lift up' is *hupsoó*, which is not a physical action; it denotes exaltation, magnification, a raising of status, etc. Christian tradition suggests this 'lifting up' refers to Jesus' crucifixion but I do not agree. Read as, "When you lift up the son of the man, then you will know 'I AM'" (which is a bit more sympathetic to the Greek), the scenario looks quite different. Jesus is actually saying: "When the Remnant is exalted, you will know God again." Of course, it *could* refer to Jesus' own anticipated elevation as the priestly King of Israel, the redeemed 'servant' who is to be 'lifted up' to his rightful position amongst the 'great' (Isa 52:13) but this seems too self-indulgent, egotistical, and unlikely; the "son of man" ideology, recall, is ambiguous, like many aspects of the FG, i.e., it can mean a person or a group (as in Isaiah 53, for instance). Jesus' words here are spoken as a conditional and optimistic future event (like 'seeing' Nathanael under the fig tree), by which the truth of Jesus' claim to authority will ultimately be proven. If this apparently pivotal sign is contingent upon *the Jews*, as Jesus implies, how will this ever come to be? It will soon become clear that this 'lifting up' has nothing to do with Jesus' earthly status or his crucifixion but with the 'raising' of Lazarus. Just as the "salvation" that comes from the Jews (John 4:22) turns out to be an action *by* the Jews that allows for the circumstances to suit Jesus' campaign (i.e., Hyrcanus' destruction of the temple on Mount Gerizim), so the Jews are to be participants in Jesus' plan for Lazarus; it simply won't work without them.

The escalation of Jesus' argument with the Jews reaches its zenith when he makes an even stronger claim to authority and primacy, a claim that clearly causes the Jews to attempt to stone him.

What Abraham Did

Jesus makes reference to Abraham, accusing the Jews of ignoring the example of the patriarch: "If you are Abraham's children you would be doing what Abraham did." What, though, did Abraham do? I suggest that the meaning of this strange statement lies in the meeting between Abraham and Melchizedek in Gen 14:18–23.

Abraham encounters Melchizedek, "the righteous king," the king of Salem and the high priest of El Elyon; Abraham immediately subjects himself to both king-priest and god. He offers tithes, receives a blessing, and swears himself to the divine entity. The Jews, Jesus is insinuating, are loyal to the *wrong* high priest and are thus misled in their devotion to their god *and* they fail to acknowledge the true king, the King of Israel. Jesus, the new Melchizedek, is the true high priest of the god of Abraham and should be treated accordingly but he is rejected and threatened with death. "You are a priest forever according to the order of Melchizedek" (Ps 110:4) implies the legitimacy of one who can, with the authority of God, command the priesthood *even without* the traditional hereditary criteria being met.[1] This is what Heb 7:11f is all about and what lies at the root of the Jews' rejection of Jesus; they claim to 'know' his lineage. He cannot be a priest according to *their* rules.

Once again, Jesus reminds his accusers that he is not acting alone.

The most abusive tirade from Jesus appears in John 8:44; the Jews are from their "father the devil," the "murderer," the "father of lies."[2]

---

[1] Josephus says of Melchizedek: 'he was without dispute ... made the priest of God' (*Ant.* 1.10.2).
[2] Such a title finds its origins, perhaps, in Jer. 16:19, where the Hebrew word '*ab* is used in the phrase translated in the NRSV as 'Our ancestors (i.e., 'fathers') have inherited nothing but lies'. The context is one involving God's rebuke of the propagation of deceit by leaders who have no business claiming divine authority.

> *As robbers lie in wait for someone, so the priests*
> *are banded together; they murder on the road to Shechem,*
> *they commit a monstrous crime.*
> Hos 5:9

Jesus has mentioned "the devil" once before, when speaking of his own disciples—one of them is a devil, he claims. His rebuke of the authorities who bear witness against the adulteress is now reflected here: "Which of you convicts me of sin?" The Jews do not understand 'sin' because they cannot comprehend the divine words of God. They are not "from God" in the first place, i.e., they are not sanctioned by heaven. This entire episode is a rephrasing of Isa 57:4–5: "Whom are you mocking? ...you offspring of an adulterer and a whore ... Are you not children of transgression, the offspring of deceit...."

This is the point at which Jesus is accused of being a Samaritan and, for the second time, of having "a demon," i.e., of being mad. His reaction reflects his skill in countering a challenge so obviously a factor of the adulteress' story; he is being provoked into an incriminating admission. As he had done earlier, though, Jesus manages to manipulate the situation so as not to give the Jews any success; he cannot deny that he is a Samaritan, as he *is* one, and if he denies it, his whole mission is meaningless.

Instead, he challenges only that he is mad but this evokes certain precedents. In 2 Kgs 9:11, the prophet who secretly anoints Jehu is considered mad, and in Jer 29:26 any "madman who plays the prophet" is subject to arrest by the "officers in the house of the Lord." In the latter scenario, a priest is granted the power to appoint officers of the temple to arrest anyone disturbing the *status quo* by claiming to be a prophet, and it is within this context, I think, Jesus is seen to come under the threat so often.

One must therefore query why the prophet in each instance manages to elude these officers for so long. The answer may lie in the fact that, at least in Jesus' case, he has allies amongst the authorities sent to arrest him, allies who will again prove helpful. On a more symbolic level, though, the identification of "false prophet" with "madman" may indicate once again Jesus' divine protection. That is, a true prophet cannot be mad because he has "the word of God" in his mouth (Deut 18:18–19).

> *I will put my words in the mouth of the prophet, who shall speak to them everything that I command. Anyone who does not heed the words that the prophet shall speak in my name, I myself will hold accountable.*
> Deut 18:18–19

> *"Do not touch my anointed ones; do my prophets no harm."*
> Ps 105:15

By claiming that he is honouring the Father, Jesus both rejects the Jews' claim and presents himself as a true prophet, without denying his theological/ideological affiliation with the Samaritans. By keeping silent, as he had done in the adulteress' case, Jesus would be failing to defend the *word of God* against false accusation ("if I would say that I do not know him, I would be a liar like you"); by calling his authority into question the Jews indeed dishonour the prophet but, more importantly, they dishonour the Father. This is already foreshadowed in v.47, and is supported by v.51, which compares the lack of the "word" with spiritual death. The Jews do reject Jesus, the 'word' and, therefore, God.

> *"The prophet is a fool, the man of the spirit is mad!"*
> *... Because of your great iniquity, your hostility is great.*
> *The prophet is a sentinel for my God over Ephraim, yet a fowler's*
> *snare is on all his ways, and hostility in the house of his God.*
> Hos 9:7–8

Hostility in the house of God indeed, and Ephraim's prophet must grapple with a 'snare' set for him time and time again. A further remark in John 8:56–8 criticizes the Jews' pride in claiming to be Abraham's "children." Back in 8:37, Jesus had admitted: "I know that you are descendants of Abraham" but this is a generic, non-committal way of saying, "you are Israelites by birth." Such a concept is far from saying "you are the *children* of Abraham."

Jesus says to the Jews: "Your father Abraham rejoiced to see my day and he saw it, and was glad." What does he mean? Gen 17:17f describes how Abraham is informed of his future son Isaac and the nation which will eventually arise from him (Israel); he falls to the ground, laughing. The word for "rejoiced" in the Greek FG is *agalliao* which, literally translated, implies that Abraham "jumped" with joy but this term can also be used in a figurative sense, to mean "gush, over-react," etc., which is more suitable to the scenario in Genesis. Falling on one's face with laughter is an equivalent depiction of overzealous rejoicing. So, when Jesus makes the claim that Abraham rejoiced that he might see Jesus' day (and notice that Jesus doesn't say "rejoiced to see *me*" but refers to his "day," i.e., his 'hour', his mission to reunify Israel), he symbolically replaces the *Remnant* as the true, anticipated 'child' of Abraham, therefore, as the 'true' Israel, ousting the Jews from their self-acclaimed primary position.

Now here is one of the most Samaritan-like references in the entire FG; the Jews take Jesus literally (never a good idea), mocking his allusion to Abraham "seeing" his day, when Jesus, himself, is "not yet fifty years old," to which Jesus responds: "before Abraham was, I AM." Jesus is not claiming that he, personally, was around when Abraham was but that the "light of heaven" was, i.e., the prophetic inspiration, or the divine distillation that imbued Moses and other prophets, and which is eternal. This is one of the basic tenets of Samaritan belief. This authority, this power comes from God, the "I AM," and it is to this belief Jesus again alludes when Pilate is questioning him.

> Joshua ... was the successor of Moses in the prophetic office.
> He became, as his name implies, a great saviour of God's elect...
> so that he might give Israel its inheritance.
> Sir 46:1

Not Yet Fifty

Because this reference to Jesus is so irreconcilable with the Synoptic tradition, where Luke, for instance, states that Jesus is "about thirty years old" when he begins his mission (Luke 3:23), many scholars have simply chosen to ignore it, or to rationalize "fifty" as a convenient round figure that is used in a generic sense. I am not convinced.

That Jesus is about thirty is likely to be an allusion to 2 Sam 5:4–5, where it is claimed that King David was this age when he began his reign. This is the *expected* understanding of Jesus' role, that is, as a messianic figure from the line of David, which we know is the foundation of the Synoptic gospels. Let's broaden our horizons for a moment and consider *alternative* potential precedents: "Joseph was thirty years old when he entered the service of Pharaoh, king of Egypt" (Gen 41:46); and, of course, in the 2 Esdras parallel, Salathiel is away from Palestine for "thirty years."

If Jesus is broadly considered to be in his early thirties, why would "fifty" be used in the FG as a rounding off or generic term, rather than "forty"? I have (again) a theory: Jesus, in the FG, is the same age as the *naos*, the sacred sanctuary of the temple in Jerusalem, which is why later scribes added the addendum of 2:21–2, suggesting that Jesus was referring to the temple as his own body, when he said he would offer the Jews a 'sign' to justify his actions in the courtyard (e.g., they, too make the connection between 2:20 and 8:57). If the temple is forty-six years old in April 36 CE, when Jesus makes his public demonstration (as previously discussed), so is Jesus. This means Jesus was born in c.10 BCE, just as the temple was inaugurated.

This is a typically FG method of presenting something very simple in a symbolic way that appears to the majority as something quite arcane and hopeless to interpret but it is quite straight forward, as long as we remember that no number or name in this gospel is without its purpose in the overall structure of the message. In other words, the gospel writer mentions both "forty-six" and "not yet fifty" for a *reason*.

The gospel has been written with a few key events transposed to a more convenient and theologically enlightening place in the chronology. If there were a precise age here, the author's intention of suppressing the truth about the Samaritan tumult would be dashed. By offering a vague "not yet fifty" in this *contemporaneous* scene, the average reader is not drawn into an unnecessary scrutiny of the phrasing. Those who have already surmised the timeline are given confirmation that their efforts have not been wasted.

14
THE BEGINNING OF THE END

Blind Man

JESUS HAS SHOWN THE WORLD certain signs that are meant to reveal his authority and intention but these are misinterpreted by the masses who are expecting a Davidic messiah. Jesus is assuming the status of a priest and his audacity has him on the run, a fugitive most of the time, wary and cautious all of the time. Under pressure to complete the 'works' given to him by the Father, Jesus must soon begin the formal procedure of inaugurating the new priesthood.

Jesus' confrontation with the Jews in John 7–8 takes place in October, during the Feast of Tabernacles. By John 10 the narrative has shifted to the Festival of Dedication (John 10:22), which is in December; the 'blind man's' story falls somewhere in between, with symbolic allusions to both events. We are about to witness Jesus performing the most controversial and overt conversion to date from within the temple priesthood itself.

In the FG, blindness is a metaphor for ignorance and misunderstanding. The opening of the eyes implies an opening of the mind, as in: "They do not know, nor do they comprehend; for their eyes are shut, so that they cannot see, and their minds as well, so they cannot understand (Isa 44:18); "Israel's sentinels are blind they are all without knowledge" (Isa 56:10); "a salve to anoint your eyes so that you may see" (Rev 3:18). The spiritual darkness, the persistent lack of vision, foresight, and even scriptural knowledge is a constant theme in the FG, and it almost always refers to the Pharisees (sometimes it includes the chief priests). In Matt 15:14 and Luke 6:39, the Pharisees are explicitly referred to in terms of the blind leading the blind.

Therefore it shall be night to you, without vision,
and darkness to you, without revelation.
Mic 3:6

From this point onward, the narrative becomes more intense; Jesus seems to be concentrating his efforts in Jerusalem now, without the intervening, frequent stays up north. He tells his disciples, in fact, that the 'works' he has been sent to do must be done "while it is day" for "night is coming when no one can work" (John 9:4). This anticipates a very important but short speech (11:9–10), and serves to emphasize the context of confrontation; 'night' is a euphemism for evil, danger. Jesus knows, at this point, that his time is limited. He cannot go on making bold declarations, intimidating the Jews with his signs and castigations. It is time to get the new priesthood started, before it is too late.

The young man of John 9, we are told, has been blind from birth and the disciples make the connection between the physical state and the concept of 'sin', something Jesus also does, in the scene with the lame man. In John 9, though, Jesus says the blindness has *nothing to do* with the sins of the man, nor of the father; it is another 'sign' for the revelation, or glorification, of God's will.

> *...you that are blind, look up and see!*
> *...to magnify his teaching and make it glorious.*
> Isa 42:18, 21

Some pertinent details suggest who the blind man is; Jesus seems to *know* that the father of the man is not sinful, *nor* the boy; he declares this in such a casual manner, suggesting he is already acquainted with them:

★ In John 7:38 Jesus had called out to the crowd of priests "let the one who believes in me drink." He is searching for his successor, his perfect protégée, the young Lazarus, son of Nicodemus.

★ The birth/rebirth theme links this scene with both Jesus' discussion with Nicodemus and the corresponding promised 'rebirth' of his young son into a better life.

★ The transfer of responsibility from the boy of John 4, whose future lay in the hands of his parents, to the young man who is now 'of age', links the two characters.

★ The inference that he was "about to die" meant, in effect, his childhood was about to end; he was about to become a man of legal age (and thus enter into the 'world' Jesus claims has no 'life' in it). If the boy was twelve then, he is thirteen now, legally a man.

★ The concept of 'begging' is familiar to both scenarios, first by the father, then, aptly, the son.

The blind man is Nicodemus' son, Lazarus.

Born into the blind world, Lazarus is as blind as anyone else not reborn from above, so this blindness is both metaphorical and inevitable. It does not have anything to do with the type of 'sin' the disciples imagine, which suggests a punishment for wrongdoing; rather, it relates to a general sense of ignorance and being led up the wrong path. Because of his father's foresight, however, the young man has been guaranteed this moment of insight; he has been promised 'life'.

Young Jewish men (at this time in Palestine) make a decision as to which sect, if any, they intend to be affiliated. Josephus, also of priestly stock, claims that he was a novice in each of the three sects, i.e., Pharisees, Essenes, and Sadducees, before making the choice, at the age of nineteen, to adhere to the Pharisees (*Life*, 1.2). The blind man's age is alluded to twice (vv. 21, 23), implying that he is 'of age' e.g., to make his *own* choice regarding sectarian membership; it is no longer a matter for his parents to influence. This emphasis is significant as it also implies the character's youthfulness, for why else would a parent have to state that he is 'of age' unless he was on the cusp of adulthood?

The son of a father who is both priest and Pharisee, this young man is seemingly destined to follow suit, which is why Nicodemus plans ahead and ensures that his son will follow in his footsteps as the 'servant of the king' (i.e., Jesus' servant) but *not* as a Pharisee.

> *...if this man has a son who sees all the sins that his father has done, considers, and does not do likewise ... he shall not die for his father's iniquity; he shall surely live.*
> Ezek 18:14–17

At the moment of truth, when the young man is due to make his entry into the Pharisaic sect, perhaps, Jesus steps in and steals more than just the scene. He spits on the ground in order to make a small amount of clay with which he anoints the blind man's eyes (to have someone else's spittle touch you would have meant dishonour, an uncleanliness to be ritually remedied. Any onlookers must have thought these two men completely mad). The Greek verb used for "anointing" here is *chrio*; nearly every instance of individuals being commissioned, chosen, delegated, etc., in the LXX, incorporates or specifies this verb. As the blind man is the only figure in the FG who is explicitly *touched* by Jesus, we must understand this application in terms of *election* (just as Jesus was elected by the symbolic resting of the hand of God—the dove—on his head).

The preparation for the new kingdom is, in a sense, an act of destruction *and* creation, as Jesus infers when he storms the temple. The lame man's tale reveals the infirmity at the heart of Israel and demonstrates the relative ease with which spiritual bondage can be rejected and the oppressors destroyed. In the story of the blind man we see more of the creation aspect (a renewal) for in the production of clay, and in its application, Jesus is understood to be performing a symbolic act of creation as part of the works of God.

Provocative imagery echoes Gen 2:7, where the inspiration of the "dust of the ground" is the pinnacle of God's work. Having moulded Adam from the earth, God witnesses the increasing degradation and profanity of his creation. Israel anticipates the day when God, as the divine potter will remould the "spoilt" Israel making it "good to him" once more, as it was in the beginning (Jer 18:6). With Adam began the kingdom of men, with Jesus, the FG suggests, begins the kingdom of God.

In the parallel of 2 Esdras, both dust and spittle are mentioned; Adam's foundation of dust is contrasted with the "growing" mind (7:62). The main gist of the passage is that the mind is free to transcend the flesh, so there is no real excuse for being unfaithful to the commandments (and this is echoed in John 16). The spittle is compared to "the other nations that have descended from Adam," i.e., the non-Israelites who domineer and oppress God's elect (2 Esd 6:56).

Putting these together, in the context of the anointing or election of the man who is 'blind', we get this: Jesus uses the spittle and the dust to make a clay, which he places over the eyes of the young man to represent the corrupt, impure world that closes his eyes to the 'truth' and to God. He is then sent to the Pool of Siloam to wash away the clay, i.e., to wash away the 'world' and all its iniquities.

In Hebrew, the word for Siloam is Shiloah (i.e., Shiloh), which appears in Isa 8:5–8; the context is one of a warning. The Samaritans have, it seems, threatened to take Jerusalem but God responds by claiming they do not deserve it because they have refused "the waters of Shiloah that flow gently." For this they must endure the torrent from the north (i.e., Assyria, under the guise of the River Euphrates), which will act as a sweeping judgement. It must be assumed, then, that those who *do* accept the waters of Shiloah—*those who accept Shiloh—will* be allowed to 'take' Jerusalem. This bodes well, then, for Jesus.

The young man, Lazarus, obediently takes himself to the pool and washes away the filth of the 'world' that has made him, figuratively, blind. He accepts the "living water" of this, the holiest mikvah: it is from the Pool of Siloam that the priests gather pitchers of water for the temple libations on the first day of the Feast of Tabernacles. The pool is thus inextricably linked to the priesthood and ritual cleansing but it also marks a vital turning point in Jesus' campaign, for it is at this juncture the young Lazarus comprehends and accepts what is expected of him.

This scene, wonderfully succinct yet packed with information, tells us that Jesus has found his protégée, his confidant, for he trusts this young man with his most profound secrets. Interestingly, the theological concept of the mikvah entails a spiritual rebirth, a rise in spiritual status, or a transformation. It is used when consecrating a new priest, when initiating a 'coming-of-age' (*mitzvah*), and when converting a proselyte.

Unlike the lame man (Peter), the young Lazarus comes back seeing. The connection becomes clearer in John 9:11, when he tells the crowd that Jesus had said to him, "Go to Siloam and wash" making the command, in effect, "Accept Shiloh and wash away your past life." The crux of the matter is that Nicodemus' son, the son of a man of high repute, great authority, and priestly heritage, has openly and unabashedly made a *choice*—yet another long-running theme throughout the FG. He has made a choice to serve Jesus, *not* the institution.

The immediate reaction of the "neighbours" and those who recognise this 'blind man' is to query whether he is truly the "beggar" they had seen on the streets. Elsewhere in the NT, the term "begging" (or "beggar") is used in a very illuminating context; in Gal 4:8–9, for instance, the life before conversion (to the 'way' of Jesus) is seen as an enslavement, with the old laws (i.e., Pharisaic law) imposing a "begging" spirit upon men, which they must overcome. In Eccl 40:28–30, however, "begging" is a worse fate than death, i.e., "one who is intelligent and well instructed guards against" it. The one for whom a father had begged, once destined to grow up to be a "beggar" himself, is now transformed into something unrecognisable (cf. Luke's Lazarus [16:19f] who is also depicted as a "beggar" yet rises to the right hand of Abraham. Luke's gospel is the closest to the FG in date and substance, I suggest).

> *He raises up the poor from the dust...*
> *to make them sit with princes*
> *And inherit a seat of honour.*
> 1 Sam 2:8

The blind man is taken not to a temple priest, which is the accepted procedure for the final assurance of cleanliness after an ailment or disease (Lev 12ff) but to the Pharisees, whose first reaction is to deny, or refuse to believe that the man was blind *in the first place*, demonstrating, yet again, their inability to *see* and *understand*. Ironically, however, by taking the 'blindness' literally, as a physical condition, they imply Lazarus *is* sighted and thus confirm this blindness *symbolic* within the narrative.

The Pharisees have a warrant out for Jesus' arrest yet here he is *again*, performing such deeds on the Sabbath. This is apparently all they are interested in, just as in the case with the lame man. The young Lazarus, who is keen to tell everyone that "the man called Jesus" put clay on his eyes and made him see, is asked where the so-called 'healer' is but, instead of betraying Jesus' whereabouts, as Peter had done, he says he does not know (this is the first attempt to get the young man to incriminate Jesus). He has already proven more trustworthy than Peter. Asked what he "says" about Jesus, the blind man replies: "He is a prophet" (John 9:17; the second attempt). He does not say, "He is the messiah." A third time, the young convert is pressed into incriminating Jesus (John 9:24f) but, just as in Jesus' discussion with Nicodemus, the emphasis is shifted and those who seem to be seeking insight expose their own ignorance. Like Jesus with the adulteress, Nicodemus' son manages to turn the tables, making the Pharisees seem ignorant and desperate.

"You are his disciple," they accuse him, meaning it to be a derogatory remark but the comment simply confirms what has been going on in the scene, i.e., a conversion. Claiming to be the "disciples of Moses," the Pharisees think they maintain their loyalty to the law but they expose their fundamental ignorance of who Jesus is. They know that God spoke to Moses, they say, but "this man" is an unknown quantity; they do not know where he comes from. Have they not admitted to knowing his mother and father, and to his coming from Galilee? It is his self-acclaimed authority, his 'power' that is a mystery to them because, as Jesus himself has told them to their faces, *they* are not 'from God' and thus cannot recognise it. No wonder they can have such a man "amongst" them and not know him. In Jesus' symbolic affiliation with the secret realm of Arzareth, this apparent confusion, contradiction even, is justified.

> *There are those who rebel against the light...*
> *and do not stay in its paths...*
> *they are friends with the terrors of deep darkness.*
> Job 24:13, 16

There is another clue, here, to the link between Nicodemus and the blind man. In John 3:2, Nicodemus declares: "we know that you are a teacher who has come from God; for no one can do these signs that you do apart from the presence of God." In 9:33, we hear his son say with confidence to the Pharisees: "If this man were not from God, he could do nothing." Lazarus, the boy left in Capernaum while his father seeks out for him a place in the new order, now echoes his father's conviction.

So, three times this once 'blind' man is in a predicament and must choose to betray, or be loyal to, Jesus. Three times he proves his conversion is complete. This intentional forerunner to Peter's three denials serves to illustrate a rivalry that will increase in intensity throughout the gospel—a rather one-sided rivalry, perhaps, between Jesus' chosen successor and the aging priest whose ambition gets the better of him.

Having been taught by his father everything Jesus had explained, Nicodemus' son becomes Jesus' elected 'son' who will eventually be his successor. Rather than becoming one of those who steal the rights of the firstborn (e.g., the Pharisees), he is given the sanction and status *of* the firstborn. Lazarus now represents the ideal Israel, the Israel Jesus anticipates will be 'risen'—and the Pool of Siloam sits silently in anticipation of its most significant role.

Baptism of the Soul
Compare what has just taken place in John 9 to these excerpts from Ps 51:

- **blot out my transgressions;** "clay on my eyes"
- **Wash me thoroughly from my iniquity and cleanse me from my sin;** "wash in the Pool of Siloam"
- **Indeed, I was born guilty, a sinner when my mother conceived me;** born blind / concept of "who sinned?"
- **You desire truth in the inward being; therefore teach me wisdom in my secret heart;** a personal conversion / hidden wisdom
- **put a new and right spirit within me'** the 'spirit' is inherited
- **Then I will teach transgressors your ways;** teacher of Israel (and *parakletos*)
- **and sinners will return to you;** other conversions

This is the sort of initiation John performs when we first encounter him, in John 1. It is a cleansing ritual that demands "truth in the inward being" (the sort of baptism Josephus describes in his apparent reference to John). Only Jesus, it is said, can baptise with the Holy Spirit (the inspirational, or authoritative 'spirit' from God), and this implies something beyond the basic spiritual cleansing, i.e., it implies election and transference of knowledge and authority:

> He shall ... impart true knowledge and righteous knowledge to those who have chosen the Way. ... (He) will instruct them in the mysteries of marvellous truth....
>
> Manuel of Discipline, DSS

Not only does this provide a precedent for the conversion scene itself, it also anticipates the future role of the successor, e.g., to be a teacher, so that others may also find the 'way'.

Perturbed Pharisees
The reaction of the parents in John 9:22 is: "…he is of age; ask him." They are justifiably afraid of the wrath of the Jews. The focus of the Pharisees' anger is upon the *choice* the son has made and the apparent affirmation of Jesus' authority, so they threaten excommunication if there is any further rebellion from the family. The Pharisees are taking this particular action very seriously indeed, one may even say, personally. Already assuming his (father's) role as teacher, Lazarus infuriates the Pharisees and he is driven out. Jesus had warned that this rebirth would be a painful one, and things have only just got started! Some scholars see problems in the historicity of the alleged threats of excommunication (John 9:22) against those who confessed Jesus to be the messiah, for it was not a crime to support a messianic contender. Jesus, in the FG however, is *not* a messianic contender in the traditional, or common, sense; it is, rather, because his followers are seen to be adopting an alternative religious *identity* that they are dismissed from the synagogue. They are rejecting authority and familiar tradition.

The only other time a synagogue has been mentioned is when Jesus is teaching there, in John 6, where the confusion over his 'flesh and blood' sends some away thinking him to be mad. This synagogue is in Capernaum, the town in which the 'blind man', as a youth, had been living; the town in which his father, Nicodemus is an elder and, perhaps, a chief of the synagogue and lesser Sanhedrin. Obliged to carry out the will of the greater council in Jerusalem, Nicodemus would be subject to their ruling. The Sanhedrin has a tiered excommunication practise, called *herem*, ranging from a very mild slap on the wrist and 'don't come to the synagogue for a week' to 'you are dead to Israel'. Although the degree of excommunication we are seeing in John 9 seems to be relatively mild, in effect, it would, if the parents confess allegiance to Jesus, remove Nicodemus from his life-long role as a public teacher. It is a preventative measure intended to thwart any attempt to spread the word about Jesus, or to allow Jesus access to the synagogue for recruiting purposes.

The Pharisees have taken all this as such a personal offence because Jesus is openly commissioning one of their own for his cause; one can even suggest that the entire episode has been fabricated, planned, for why else would the young boy go through with the charade of pretending to join the Pharisees (when his father has already promised him to Jesus), if not to help Jesus in his plan to create a 'sign'? Jesus, with the help of the young man is, in effect, publicly humiliating the Pharisees. It was one thing to see him making a fool of the pathetic ordinary priests in and around the temple but it is preposterous to think that any of their *own* people should follow him (cf. John 7)! When the young man is finally driven out of the synagogue the Pharisees, in their ignorance, believe they have gained the advantage but there is an ironic twist here, for this detachment is *just* what Jesus intends for his convert.

Echoing the scene with the 'lame man' once more, Jesus "finds" the one 'healed' and tests him; "Do you want to be made well?" is now "Do you believe in the son of man?" This acts as another clue in linking Nicodemus with the official's son, for it was *only* to Nicodemus that Jesus mentioned the 'son of man' in a context of belief and knowledge; now he is asking Lazarus, who has just washed the 'world' from his eyes, if *he* believes as his father does. When the lad answers, he does so with the question, 'Who is he?' (i.e., he requests knowledge) and Jesus answers in exactly the same words as he responded to Mary's (the Samaritan woman's) declaration that she knew the Restorer, was coming: "you are speaking with him," thereby once again linking the two young but pivotal characters.

Jesus declares that he has come to make the blind see, and to blind those who do see. What does this mean? The whole idea of blindness, remember, is metaphorical; it is equated to spiritual darkness, ignorance, a lack of mental, not physical vision. In Isaiah's long and passionate account of God's plea for the return of his people, the deaf and the blind are described as those who are deaf and blind to the god of their ancestor, Abraham. Abraham's 'offspring' Israel (the commission name of Jacob) is described as God's friend, his servant. We already know, though, that Israel is divided, with the loyal Remnant and the iniquitous majority distanced by religious argument and legal superficialities. Jesus has also, symbolically, replaced himself (and "those given" to him, i.e., the Remnant, represented by Nathanael) as the 'offspring' of Abraham, the "servant," so making the sighted blind, must have another meaning: "Who is blind but my servant .... Who is blind like my dedicated one, or blind like the servant of the Lord? (Isa 42:19). The "dedicated one," the Remnant, and the "servant" Jesus, are blind not to the one true god but to the 'world' and its temptations—the false worship, the oppressing laws, the "lies." To make the sighted blind, Jesus implies, is to open their eyes to the truth, the truth that will set them free from the darkness of an ignorant world (John 8:32).

The Pharisees, their ears against the wall yet again, overhear Jesus' comments and, as usual, reveal their own ignorance in an ironic response: "Surely we are not blind, are we?" By saying they 'see' the Pharisees admit their sin (and here, the sin is parallel to that attributed to the 'lame man'); they *cannot* see the 'truth' and so they *are* blind.

> *Ah, you who are wise in your own eyes, and shrewd in your own sight...*
> *have rejected the instruction of the Lord ... and have*
> *despised the word of the Holy One of Israel.*
> Isa 5:21, 24

For now I am bringing you to judgement for saying "I have not sinned."
Jer 2:35

Just as Nicodemus' portrayal revealed the need to release one's mind from long held presumptions and inhibitions, so the father's son follows suit, teaching us not to see with the eyes but with the mind. In other words, 'see' what the gospel is saying by understanding what *isn't* obvious, rather than be like the Pharisees, who reckon they know the scriptures inside out because they have memorized them but who fail to comprehend them. This is the key to the kingdom—the key to "Siloam" (Shiloh)!

Bad Shepherds

Jesus reiterates his rejection of the children of the "liar" (those who follow the "father of lies" Caiaphas, i.e., the incumbent priesthood) and also his insistence that he and his chosen ones are the means to Israel's redemption. The priesthood consists of "thieves and bandits"; they have not entered through the "gate." Although many interpreters have difficulty with the juxtaposition of 'shepherd' and 'gate' in the same analogy, suggesting, even, a corruption of the original text, there is really no problem.

The gate, metaphorically, has two distinct meanings; it is a place of legal authentication (because it is at the gates of the city that elders and judges sit, e.g., Gen 23:10; 2 Sam 15:2; Ruth 3:11–4:1), and a place of union with the divine (as in Gen 28:17, where Jacob has his dream of the ladder). The one who enters 'by the gate' has authority and is in contact with God, while those who "climb in by another way" are illegitimate "shepherds" who do not know God, e.g., the "thieves and robbers" who make the house of God an illicit "market place," a "den of robbers" (Jer 7:11). The "sheep" are the elect, the Remnant, the converted (as in Mic 2:12–13). Their "fold," *aulen* in the Greek ("court/yard"), is actually the *locus* of worship, i.e., in this context, the temple.

The followers of the true shepherd, the righteous high priest, are called by name (as demonstrated first in the early scenes of the FG narrative, where the disciples, each representing a tribe, are called by name) and "he leads them out" (literally, in due course, out of the temple!) through the gate that he, himself, represents (John 10:9). Those who are converted have 'life' (are reborn) and those who are not are 'destroyed' not by God but by the ineptitude and iniquity of the "thieves and robbers" and their "father of lies." There is none so blind as one who *will not* see. The analogy is lost on the Jews.

Jesus persists, with a clear allusion to Ezekiel 34 (and several chapters of Jeremiah, especially 23:1–4), where God chastises the bad shepherds who have been "feeding [them]selves" on the fat of the sheep, using their wool, leaving them to get sick and die, scattering them and making them vulnerable to attack by wild animals (Ezek 34:2–6). God continues: "I am against the shepherds ... I will rescue my sheep from their mouths" (34:10).

> *Strangers shall stand and feed your flocks*
> *... But you shall be called priests*
> *of the Lord, you shall be named ministers of our God.*
> Isa 61:5–6

One of the most talked about passages of the FG is Jesus' comment: "I have other sheep that do not belong to this fold. I must bring them also, and they will listen to my voice" (John 10:16). Interpretations abound, including that he meant the Greeks (which the FG Jesus would have cringed at). I suggest it simply means the scattered Remnant. Some are in Samaria, many off in Arzareth somewhere, but they must be gathered so that there will 'be one flock' with one 'shepherd'.

God, according to Jesus, loves him because he "lay[s] down [his] life in order to take it up again" (John 10:17). In the Greek text of the FG, the word translated as "life" is *psyche*, which actually means "soul," whereas *bios*, or *zoe*, better imply 'life'. Jesus does *not* lay down his 'life' he lays down his 'soul'. This, once again, connects him to the "suffering servant" of Isaiah 53, who is said to have "poured out [his soul] to death," meaning he made himself *vulnerable* to death by doing the works of God (cf. Joel 2:28), and for this he is to receive "a portion with the great." This is, perhaps, one of the earliest clues pertaining to Jesus' ultimate crucifixion and the subsequent events. Division amongst the Jews again reveals that some of the priests, Pharisees, Levites, etc., follow Jesus, while others presume him insane.

The Festival of Dedication is an apt arena in which to play out Jesus' final public stand against his opponents; it is a commemoration of the recovery and purification of the temple by Judas Maccabee (164 BCE), after the abomination of illegitimate (Syrian) occupants (1 Macc 4:52f). So too is the reference to his standing within the portico of Solomon significant, for it is Solomon's dedication (1 Kgs 8:65) that makes the site of the temple in Jerusalem a *fait accompli* (recall that in John 7 Jesus is at the Feast of Tabernacles, the festival at which Solomon performs this original dedication).

Standing in the footsteps of Solomon, Jesus' authority and intent are reaffirmed, i.e., as Solomon was granted the authority to establish a new house, so Jesus claims a similar authority. With the ritualistic election of Nicodemus' son, he demonstrates that the new priesthood is underway; the new house of God is being created. Just as in the rebuilding of original temple described in Nehemiah/Ezra, the process begins with the Sheep Gate, which is where we see Jesus' first symbolically 'rebuilding' act, i.e., the attempted liberation of the ordinary priests through Peter.

It is one thing to claim authority but quite another to claim, or prove, legitimacy. The 'name' of God dwells wherever the Ark is, and only for as long as the people heed the commandments (see 1 Kgs 8:6f). The Ark is *no* longer in the temple; the people *no* longer heed the word of God, so God is *no* longer in the temple. Jesus wants to reinstate the seat of God at Shiloh, so it seems to me that he either *does* know or he *thinks* he knows, where the missing Ark is. It is really the *only* thing that will legitimize his new house of God. Did he, one may wonder, 'come across' it or discern its whereabouts whilst on his travels (as Salathiel)? Was this discovery what instigated this campaign?

In response to the demand for Jesus to reveal himself as the messiah (John 10:24), Jesus repeats his claim that he has already shown the people *who* he is and by *what* authority he performs his works, but that it is *they* who have failed to believe and so identification with the Davidic messiah is again rejected in the FG. "The Father and I are one," he says, not implying that he is a divine being, as the Jews interpret it, but simply that he is God's representative (his 'son' in the manner explained). Or could it imply that he and the Father are 'one' because of the Ark (with Jesus' holiness being directly contingent on his connection to the Shekinah, the divine force contained within the Ark)? It should be noted that in both Heb 9:4 and Rev 11:19, in the description of the *ideal* temple, the Ark has pride of place once again, suggesting the return of Israel to the commandments of God and the consequent return of the Holy Spirit to dwell there.

The Jews do not believe, therefore they do not "belong to [Jesus'] sheep." They have no place in the new "house." Alluding to the passage in Deut 14:1, where God declares, "You are the children of the Lord your God," Jesus defends his intimacy with the Father. He relies on the law of the scribes and Pharisees, something with which they can actually identify, to get the idea across. If those who had been given the word of God at Sinai are reckoned the 'children' of God, does that not make them 'gods' also (not deities but in some way imbued with the divine, i.e., they have 'holiness' within them because God chooses them)? Why then, Jesus asks, should he not be able to call himself a 'son' of God, as he, too (so he claims) has received the word of God (and this is a good time to recall the 2 Esdras account of Salathiel's calling)?

Escaping a stoning and an arrest, *yet again*, Jesus returns to Bethabara, on the northern tip of the Dead Sea, on the Jordan salt flats, where John had been baptising earlier. It seems Jesus has a strong following here and this is doubly significant, for Josephus tells us that there is a general amalgamation of dissenters, renegades, and revolutionists who live in this area, just across the Jordan (*Ant.* 17.10.2), adding fuel to the fire regarding the level of militancy in Jesus' mission. On the other hand, we should take note that John is *not* here, and he is spoken of in the *past* tense and in a way that, once again, subjugates him to Jesus. A parting of the ways has happened and/or John is now dead.

There is no way of knowing precisely how long Jesus stays in Bethabara but the subsequent calendar clue suggests he remains across the Jordan for about a year. It is during this period, I suggest, that Jesus has further contact with the Galileans, who, according to John 4, have an interest in his campaign. Recall that the scenario of the feeding in Bashan (John 6) is a theological manipulation of the Samaritan tumult, which I claim occurs (chronologically) just before the 'raising of Lazarus' account, and which potentially includes the Galileans as the troublemakers. The sequence of Jesus going to a site of known rebels for a prolonged stay, leading what turns out to be a politically charged and ultimately violent demonstration on Mount Gerizim, then having the necessary 'forces' on hand to stage the event to come (the Lazarus situation, below), and then later referring to supporters who would "fight" for him, suggests Jesus *does* invite the "revolutionists" to join his mission. It is another error of judgement, however.

It is also during this retreat that Mary Magdalene becomes pregnant.

15
LAZARUS

Conversion and Election

THERE IS AN APPARENTLY COMMON theory that the raising of Lazarus story is nothing more than an amalgamation of Synoptic themes plus some as yet unverified but unique source. Some have suggested that although the episode seems to have a theological purpose, it is all but hopeless to imagine that the original intention and/or source of the story can be found! As a result, they claim the historical significance of the work has also been lost. Others argue that the entire episode causes problems with any attempted harmonization with the Synoptic sequence and would benefit the FG only by its removal! In our attempt to comprehend this seemingly problematic episode in the FG, we must not lose sight of the duality inherent in the gospel; there are two distinct levels to the story, i.e., one theological, one historical. Far from being more beneficial to the gospel if it were removed, the raising of Lazarus turns out to be the penultimate victory of Jesus' entire mission, succeeded only by the 'resurrection' itself!

First, we must review a few things that have led us up to this moment in the story: the character Nicodemus firsts meets Jesus in secret, apparently uncertain of his allegiances; he is the first character of the gospel narrative to be revealed in any lengthy discussion with Jesus and this discussion is extremely profound, centring around the concept of spiritual rebirth; he offers up his own son as Jesus protégée, who appears next under the guise of the blind man.

The open and antagonizing conversion is enough to warrant the young man's excommunication from the synagogue and the Pharisaic sect itself; confirming his loyalty to Jesus three times, he is the only figure, apart from Peter, who is declared a 'disciple' of Jesus by anyone outside Jesus' own circle of followers; and he is the only character Jesus purposefully touches. Nicodemus' son, the blind man, is about to *become* the character Lazarus within the narrative and thus receive a new commission name that means "God is helper"; he has been helped from the darkness of his previous life, he is elected, cleansed, and made Jesus' right-hand man.

There are other clues to support this identification of the blind man with Lazarus. Observe, for example, the connection between the act of "worship" undertaken by the blind man in 9:38, and the reciprocal act of "love" bestowed upon the disciple Lazarus after his raising. This reciprocity of worship and love is reiterated in John 15:9–10: "If you keep my commandments, you will abide in my love, just as I have kept my Father's commandments and abide in his love."

As the "friend" of the group, Lazarus is *already* familiar to the others, yet he is supposedly a new character in the narrative; the FG author, as I maintain, does not introduce new disciples throughout the story; he is using this ambiguity as a means of expressing a transition between commission names, and this is done more than once.

In addition, there is in John 11:4 an echo, in structure and in content, of Jesus' claim concerning the blindness of the man in 9:3: "This illness does not lead to death; rather, it is for God's glory, so that the Son of God may be glorified through it (11:4); "Neither this man nor his parents sinned; he was born blind so that God's works might be revealed in him (9:3). Both excerpts show a remarkable similarity in presentation, with the blindness/illness being introduced through the misunderstanding of the disciples and the women. In both, Jesus clarifies the situation, effectively disassociating 'blindness' from 'sin' and 'illness' from 'death'. The blindness will lead to the revelation of God's works, the illness to the glorification of both God and the Son of God.

The bridge between the blind man and Lazarus is further emphasized in John 11:37, where the people assume that because Jesus has "cured" the former, he should have the power to save the latter from "dying." Similarly, in both instances, Jesus makes a curious statement regarding the necessity to perform his 'works' while it is still daylight, for "night" is coming (John 9:4; 11:9–10), i.e., an obvious allusion to the inevitable (subsequent) interference of the Pharisees, which occurs in both stories.

Lazarus, through his conversion, is Jesus' elected, ritualistically adopted 'son'. This intimate filiation is made explicit at the very start of the chapter, with the specification, "he whom you love" (11:3). Precedents for the use of such a saying in the OT are few and each is quite specific: in Song 3:1f, the phrase pertains to the lover-husband relationship; in Eccl 9:9, the one who is loved is a wife; but in Gen 22:2, the relationship is one of father and son. Although the first two are possible contenders (i.e., in the context of the divine 'bride' theme), the latter is the most appropriate for the two men, Jesus and Lazarus, and is fully supported by subsequent actions and themes in the FG narrative. This father/son perception of the "beloved" (Gen 22) progresses from God, to Abraham, to Isaac, and this is repeated in the FG, i.e., from God, to Jesus, to Lazarus. As Abraham must sacrifice his son

Isaac, so too must Jesus allow Lazarus, *his* beloved, to "die" (e.g., by remaining at a distance). Redemption and glorification, however, are essential to each scenario; the sacrifice of Isaac secures the Israelite nation, the sacrifice of Lazarus will secure the glorification of Jesus and the *new* Israel.

As the adopted son who reflects the traits and beliefs, etc., of his father, Lazarus must now follow in *Jesus'* (rather than Nicodemus') footsteps. The first indication we get that there is going to be some sort of father-son relationship, with Jesus as the father figure, is right back in John 1, when Philip is "found" by Jesus; we cannot afford to forget Philip, despite his low profile in the narrative after John 6, for he is Jesus' first choice, his firstborn, and the verb *phileo* ('to love' with brotherly affection), recall, forms part of his name. In John 11:3, the word for love, with respect to Lazarus, is also *phileo* (as the "friend" he is the *philos*) but this changes after the raising scene, to the stronger *agapao*, 'to love' with devotion. This will distinguish the priority of the rivals in the FG epilogue.

It is prudent to note also that the name Lazarus is akin to "Eleazar," the name given to the 'son' and heir of the high priest in Exod 6:23ff.[1] Jesus' life is in jeopardy; if the motivation behind his mission is to create a purified priestly kingdom through which the repentant Israel can return to God, it is perfectly understandable that he will have to plan ahead, should he be unable to lead them into the new Promised Land. Just as the priesthood of Aaron had been passed on to Eleazar (Num 20:25–6), and as Moses had handed over the 'spirit' to Joshua (Deut 34:9), so Jesus will eventually pass his authority over to his chosen successor, his heir-elect, Lazarus.

Illness

Lazarus is, in the Greek text, declared an *asthenon* (John 11:1), a "sick one," making him akin to the "sick" boy of John 4 and the "infirm" (e.g., priests) who anticipate a 'healing' at the Pool of Beth-zatha, in John 5. If this character is the converted son of Nicodemus, why is he again "ill"? The concept of infirmity in the FG is symbolic, representative, not actual; it may, for instance, depict emotional crises, or times of deep distress, as in the OT: "Hope deferred makes the heart sick (Prov 13:12); "So I, Daniel, was overcome and lay sick for some days; ... I was dismayed by the vision and did not understand it" (Dan 8:27). Daniel's situation is echoed in 2 Esd 10:29–33, where Ezra is "lying there like a corpse" because a vision has confounded him; he seeks understanding and is subsequently 'raised'.

---

[1] In Josephus' *Wars.* 2.20.4, a certain 'Jesus' (the high priest), 'Eleazar' (the son), and 'John the Essene,' are mentioned together (66 CE). Intriguing?

Illness is also used as a literary tool, in a precedent very similar in structure to John 11, to shift concern for the possible death of an individual, to the potential, spiritual death of Israel. In 1 Kings 14, Abijah, the son of Jeroboam falls sick and his mother is sent as a messenger to find the prophet Ahijah who, it is said, will "tell [her] what shall happen to the child." Rather than receiving words of comfort, she is told that by the time she returns her son will have died; his death will be a punishment for the wickedness of his father and for the failure of his father to promote worship of the one true god. Many will grieve for him, though, the prophet assures Abijah's mother, because in him alone is found "something pleasing to the Lord." God will then 'raise up' a king over Israel who will bring an end to the corruption.

In the tale of Lazarus, the "sisters," Mary and Martha, send a messenger to the prophet Jesus. Like Ahijah, Jesus does not respond with any expected haste or optimism; like the prophet in 1 Kings 14, Jesus seizes the opportunity to make this eventuality a 'sign'. Ahijah's 'sign' is to the iniquitous rulers of Israel (represented by the "father"), so too is Jesus'. The boy, Abijah, "dies," as does Lazarus, and both are mourned by the people. There is "something pleasing to the Lord" in Lazarus, the one whom "God helps" and, indeed, there is a subsequent 'raising', a dual one, in fact—the raising of Lazarus *and* the 'lifting up' of the new, ideal Israel. This raising is also fully *intended* to bring an end to the corruption of Jerusalem (whether or not it works is yet to be seen), and to bring glory to Jesus, the orchestrator of the 'sign' in God's name.

Such infirmities as do not actually result in physical death (John 11:4) are, nonetheless, mourned as vehemently as death itself: "Job's three friends heard of all these troubles that had come upon him ... they raised their voices and wept aloud; they tore their robes and threw dust in the air upon their heads (Job 2:11–12). Job was as good as dead but he was *not* dead.

Understanding this pivotal scene thus requires an understanding of the metaphorical exploitation of sickness. Lazarus is not physically sick, just as the blind man was not physically blind. Like Job, he is undergoing a traumatic experience, but why?

Not Guilty

Under the same roof in Bethany live Martha, Mary, Lazarus and, at times, Jesus. We know that Mary and Lazarus represent the 'rods' of Ephraim and Judah that are to be united before the kingdom of God can be inaugurated. We know that Mary was the Samaritan virgin at the well, whose symbolic role is to be the unfaithful divine bride, and that somewhere along the way she is brought before Jesus with accusations of adultery against her.

Lazarus is the young son of Nicodemus, offered to Jesus up in Cana, sought out at the Festival of Dedication, and formally elected as Jesus' new right-hand-man. The name Lazarus, recall, has several potential meanings, the first of which being "unite the rivals," discussed in the context of Martha as Jesus' wife. Hints of a homophonic pun implying betrothal can also be found, i.e., a betrothal to the woman a certain "father's servant" (Jesus as God's servant) was sent to find at the well in Samaria:

laz + *'aras*

(from *levath/lavah*) + "to engage for
"to unite" matrimony/to betroth"

It is said that Mary and Martha are sisters (in order to extend the allusion to Rachel and Leah) and that they live together in Bethany. Then there is a statement that clarifies *who* this Mary is, i.e., "the one who anointed Jesus" (John 11:2). This is another awkward passage, for it seems like an addendum, as it is mentioned in the past tense, yet her anointing scene follows in the *next* major scene; why would the author feel the need to offer this premature interjection of Mary's identity? The addendum attempts to disassociate this Mary from the Mary under the cross; it is an enforced segregation of the alleged 'harlot' from the sanctified moment of Jesus' death by Christians swayed by the Synoptic version of Mary.

Although they are depicted as brother and sister, it would not be without precedent for the relationship between Lazarus and Mary to be more than it appears. The sister can also be the bride (Gen 20:12; Song 4:12; Tob 7:11). In the diatribe against the "whoring" Israel (the northern tribes, represented by the "rod of Ephraim," Mary; in Jer 3:6f, the harlot-bride is referred to as the "sister" of Judah; Lazarus is the representative of the southern tribes, i.e. the "rod of Judah." Lazarus is the 'son' for whom Mary was chosen at Jacob's Well (in accordance with Gen 24) but she is still in the probation (betrothal) period (prescribed in the Book of Hosea) and is unready to marry, i.e., *no sexual intimacy between the young couple has taken place.*

Betrothal is equivalent to marriage in the eyes of the law (e.g., Deut 22:23–4) and sexual consummation of the contract can occur at any time from a few days after the betrothal to a year or even two (especially in the case of virgins). There are three recognised methods of contracting a betrothal, i.e., the man presents the woman with a coin (or ring) and pronounces before two witnesses, 'You are consecrated to me'; there is a mutual contract; or the two parties cohabit. The latter option is the least preferred by the rabbis. Generally, the betrothed woman moves out of her family home and lives with other friends or relatives until the marriage ceremony takes place but I think the uniqueness of this situation (where safety is a concern) allows for Mary and Lazarus to be resident in the same household, with Martha as chaperone. They are, indeed, living *as* 'brother and sister'.

According to Deut 24:5, when a man is first married or betrothed, he must undertake no obligations pertaining to work, or official duties, and must remain "free at home for one year, to be happy with the wife whom he has married." This is why Lazarus is not with Jesus and why there has been a period of almost a year between the blind man's scene and this one.

Partly because the two characters are so uniformly paralleled and partly because of the implications of the adulteress' scene, it is clear that Lazarus is *not* dead in John 11, just as he was not dying in John 9. I am going to suggest that Lazarus has, like Mary, been hauled before judges, accused of some wrongdoing. To fit the narrative thus far the accusation would have to be the same adultery charge we see enacted in John 7–8, for, by law, both parties are subject to the charges, so for both Mary and Lazarus to undergo similar 'trials' is apt and justifiable.

The point is Jesus *has* chosen Mary as a major part of his plan, i.e., to bear a suitable heir to the new kingdom. Although an understanding has been entered into between Lazarus and Mary, an understanding that the initiation of John 9 probably formalized (in theory, i.e., Lazarus 'sees', comprehends, and agrees to the plan), the heir to the new priestly kingdom *must* be legitimately Josephite. In another potential play on words, the name Lazarus *can* be interpreted to mean "*not* the one to conceive":

$$la' \; + \; z\bar{a}ra'$$

"not"/negation + "to conceive"

If Mary were to become pregnant during the time Jesus is *supposed* to be away from the family home (in Bethabara), to the 'blind' observer, Lazarus would be the one responsible. In fact, the surreptitious conception would suit the overall plan to keep the future kingdom safe until all was completed; by allowing people to think the child is illegitimate and Lazarus', Jesus' heir remains incognito and out of harm's way. Still the clever duality persists, i.e., Jesus and Lazarus are interchangeable. Some of the evidence points to Jesus and Mary being married, while some infers she and Lazarus are husband and wife.

One further interpretation of the name Lazarus involves the word *zuwr*, meaning "stranger" and this can suggest a "harlot" or "loose woman"; in Prov 6, a young man is warned that if he makes a pledge to such a stranger (*laz·zār*), to such a woman, he is "bound" by that pledge as if in a "snare."

Only strict adherence to the Commandments can save him "from the wife of another." *Strong's* also offers the translation of *zuwr* as "to commit adultery"; with the negation of *la'*, however, one could read: "one who did *not* commit adultery." The fascination with wordplay in the Hebrew language is profound; there is no knowing how many other possibilities for hidden meaning in the name are exploited by the author of the FG, i.e. "Lazarus" himself!

Bethany or Jerusalem?
One vital piece of information which is often overlooked here is the fact that John 11:1 suggests Lazarus is 'from/of' the town of Bethany, not that he is 'in' Bethany when the story opens (and this is further supported by the fact that in John 12:1 we are told specifically that *this* subsequent scene takes place in the home at Bethany, a superfluous statement if we are already there).

"Bethany" is another of those names that is not attested outside the NT and so it cannot be identified with any OT or historical precedent. The name has received many interpretations including "house of figs," which really has no bearing in the FG context, other than a slight link to the fig-tree scene with Nathanael; "house of obedience," which Origen suggests as an apt name for the house of Mary (I would argue that the name "Mary" actually means "rebellious"); and "house of the poor," which may suit the 'beggar' allusion in John 9 but this is tenuous, as the poverty is metaphorical not actual. I believe the symbolism of a commission name must be more profound than this.

There is, for instance, a play on:

beth + *'aniy*

"house" + "mine"

Thus, it associates the FG *author* with the site, i.e., "my house." The closely related phrase *beth 'aniyah* means "house of mourning" is also a perfectly fitting commission name for the home in which both Jesus and Lazarus are mourned. If the author *is* hinting at his own identity here, we must deduce that he is none other than Lazarus, and this actually has further corroboration in subsequent passages, particularly pertaining to the *parakletos* and the FG's epilogue.

The very first similarity drawn between 2 Esdras and the NT, recall, is: "The word of the Lord that came to Ezra son of Chusi" and the reference in Luke 8:3, where Chuza is a steward of the king. The author of 2 Esdras, then, or at least of part of it, is the son of a 'servant of a king', i.e., just as Lazarus is the son of the Nicodemus, the king's official (where the king is Jesus) in John 4:46, and whose name *also* means "help." Yet *another* 'coincidence'?

The house at Bethany becomes Jesus' base in Judea; he has moved in order to be closer to Jerusalem for the imminent day of reckoning. This is why the Messiah ben Joseph tradition claims that although he is a Josephite, this messiah will live in Jerusalem. Although he has gone into Perea, on the other side of the Jordan, there is no reason to suggest Jesus never comes back to Bethany on occasion but, a year after his first departure to proselytise beyond the river (to recruit support?), we find him away from the family residence.

Mary and Martha are at home but Lazarus is not. He has gone missing. The women discover that something is wrong and send for Jesus who is now in Bethabara (John 10:40). The fact that he remains there two days before leaving, yet finds Lazarus has been "in the tomb" for four days, implies a two-day journey, which corresponds to the sixty-kilometre hike from one place to the other.

However, Jesus does not enter Bethany when he eventually returns to see Lazarus; he is stopped on the road by Martha and is taken to where Lazarus *is*, the position of which is, actually, undisclosed. The disciples fear for Jesus' safety, referring to the fact that the Jews had just tried to stone him and this, we know, occurred in the temple at Jerusalem. Yet, in John 12, when all are *in* Bethany again, there is a sense of relative safety, so it seems to be the case that Jesus is *headed* for Jerusalem, not Bethany. Lazarus, then, is probably in Jerusalem itself. He has, I suggest, been detained by the Sanhedrin, ostensibly for adultery but also in revenge for his insubordination and his humiliation of the Pharisees, *and* because he is the perfect bait for flushing out Jesus. If he is the turbulent priest's new right-hand-man, what a boon for the Jews to have him under lock and key! Forced to speak for himself without Jesus to protect or influence him, young Lazarus is basically on trial. Can Jesus turn the tables as he did with the adulteress? The triple intimation that had Jesus been at hand Lazarus would not have "died" (i.e., 11:21, 32, 37) suggests that Jesus' influence at the critical moment might have averted Lazarus' capture.

Recalling the Abraham/Isaac parallel, though, *we* know that Jesus has no choice but to allow these events to unfold. The glorification of God depends upon the victory of Jesus over the 'world'; what better show of strength than to draw from the clutches of apparent death, new life? In the discussion between Ezra and Uriel, in 2 Esdras, the righteous, the new Israel, will be reborn from the womb of Hades.

Raising the Son

Before he leaves for Jerusalem, Jesus is found to be at crossed purposes with his disciples; is Lazarus merely "asleep," or is he "dead"? We must remember that this story has both a mundane and a theological level of interpretation and the one cannot be separated from the other, which is why Jesus *seems* to be contradicting himself by initially saying that Lazarus' illness will *not* "lead to death," then saying he *is* dead.

Lazarus, in the clutches of the Sanhedrin, removed from the safety of the Bethany retreat, is in despair, he is metaphorically 'ill'. His death sentence is probably a very real possibility, now that such a charge is apparent (e.g., he may be stoned if proven guilty of adultery) but once again we are faced with contradictory evidence, for it is only *after* his 'raising' induces others to leave the priesthood (John 12:10–11) that a warrant for Lazarus' execution is made formal. This would suggest, once again, that the charges are known to be unfounded, or improvable. It is, nonetheless, a risky business but Jesus seems to be determined that his plan is worth it. Interestingly, an audience before the Sanhedrin *is* considered a kind of 'death' so Josephus tells us (*Ant.* 14.9.4), a symbolic death that is preceded by trepidation and despair ('illness'): "... everyone, whosoever he be, that comes to be tried by this Sanhedrin, presents himself in a submissive manner, and like one that is in fear of himself ... with his hair dishevelled, and in a black and mourning garment."

Apart from the pragmatic implications, for the blind man/Lazarus character this is also a time of symbolic rebirth and in order to be reborn, he *must* first die. This death is a 'cutting off' from the 'world' he has been so much a part of; he accepted this inevitability when he went to the Pool of Siloam to wash the clay from his eyes. Now he must leave that world behind completely.

> *Give light to my eyes, or I will sleep the sleep of death,*
> *and my enemy will say, "I have prevailed."*
> Ps 13:3–4

The general format of Lazarus' raising stems from the vision of Ezek 37:1–14, where the prophet is brought to a place of death, a valley of bones where there is a divine commission to reveal the glory, or knowledge, of God; there follows a 'miraculous' resurrection of the dead instigated by spoken commands. What makes this vision so significant is its interpretation in vv. 11–14; the 'dead', so the prophet is told, are Israel—"Our bones are dried up, and our hope is lost; we are cut off completely." Lazarus, here in the "tomb," symbolises the Israel that is devoid of hope, which has no 'life'. He is about to become the new Israel (of 2 Esdras), plucked from Hades:

> And you shall know that I am the Lord, when I open your graves, and bring you up from your graves ... I will put my spirit within you, and you shall live, and I will place you on your own soil.
>
> Ezek 37:13–14

Through this vision in Ezekiel the nation is assured salvation, even from (what may seem to be) the very grave itself. We can imagine that Jesus has a similar 'sign' in mind: "I am glad I was not there, so that you may believe" (John 11:15). If Jesus can manage to pull Lazarus back from 'death's door', the new priesthood will be assured; if the priesthood is created, it must be the will of God; and if it is the will of God, the new kingdom will be ushered in, the worship of the one true god can be reinstated in the land promised to the "children of Abraham," and the messiah can come!

Everything, then, rests on this ultimate proof of Jesus' prophetic and priestly calling. He must refrain from being too hasty, for his own obedience to the will of God must parallel Abraham's; Jesus *must* sacrifice Lazarus so Israel can be saved but redemption is close at hand, Jesus believes. "All who are in their graves will hear his voice and will come out—those who have done good, to the resurrection of life" (John 5:28–9).

The raising of the metaphorically dead from one life to another, as a sign of God's intention to restore the tainted relationship between him and his people, to show mercy and exalt the righteous, is strong in the Israelite tradition. The visual imagery of a 'dead' Israel, lying in its tomb, awaiting the divine gift of the 'spirit' in order to bring it back to 'life' would not have been a new concept for the early readers of the FG.

> *I have chosen you ... I will raise up the dead from their places,*
> *and bring them out from their tombs,*
> *because I recognise my name in them.*
>
> 2 Esd 2:15–16

The idea of a confrontation between Jesus and the Jews, first related in terms of 'day' and 'night' in the election of the blind man, now culminates in the raising of Lazarus, where Jesus answers the disciples' concern for his safety in Jerusalem with the cryptic assurance: "Are there not twelve hours of daylight?" There are *twelve* divisions of light; there is a divinely elected circle of twelve disciples. Those who walk in the light do not stumble because God is in that light; those who walk at night stumble because the "light is not in them," i.e., God is not in them; they walk in darkness (are 'blind').[2]

---

[2] This is another possible connection between Jesus and the Essenes, who write of

There is a parallel to this concept *also* in 2 Esdras (14:10f), where the "age is divided into twelve parts, and nine of its parts have already passed" (an allusion to the scattered tribes): Ezra is told that now is the time to "renounce the life that is corruptible" and to "set [his] house in order."

God, of course, is on the side of righteousness and Jesus has full confidence in the success of his army of light. The ideology behind this battle context has a precedent in the challenge of Elijah to the worshippers of Baal, in 1 Kgs 18:17f. Elijah, called the "troubler of Israel," claims that *he* has not troubled Israel but they who "have forsaken the commandments of the Lord" have troubled Israel and so, too, their "father's house." Determined to prove his god greater than Baal, Elijah sets up a contest which, naturally, he wins; before the moment of truth, however, Elijah takes the time to say a prayer (18:36–7) that sets the form and context of Jesus' own prayer in John 11:41–2. In other words, 'God, make this work, or they will never believe I am who I say I am, and everything will be for nought'.

Initially, though, Jesus apparently delays his response for *two* days and this has long been a matter of contention. Some have proposed that the delay represents Jesus' determination to prove that Lazarus is truly (physically) dead, thereby making the 'miracle' all the more profound. Others suggest that Lazarus is *already* (physically) dead when Jesus gets the message and that Jesus withholds this information from his disciples until he is ready to leave (why, I do not know). I will offer an alternative suggestion (no surprise).

When Jesus arrives at the crossroads, where Martha meets him, Lazarus has apparently been 'dead' for *four* days. The Greek text actually supports a 'prisoner' interpretation, here, for it reads, "four days already *being held*." There is no earthly reason why the women should not send out a message to Jesus immediately, so I suggest they do so, but because it would take a messenger just as long to get to Jesus, as it takes him to get to Bethany, the round trip would, indeed, be about four days. To say that Lazarus has been *detained* for two days before word is even sent to Jesus is not feasible. In fact, the timing is fully acceptable when the rules about trials by the Sanhedrin are taken into consideration. For instance, if a man is accused of adultery, and a death sentence is possible (yes, they *do* have law to put a man to death), the trial takes place on one day but the sentencing must wait until the following day, after further deliberations (Mishnah Sanhedrin 4.1); so, perhaps Jesus is awaiting the formal sentencing, in order to make the sign truly unmistakable (he knows Lazarus will be found guilty, as he knows this is a set up). The Sanhedrin, however, are not allowed to hold capital trials

---

the Battle between the Sons of Light and the Sons of Darkness. 'Sons of Light' is also a Samaritan concept.

on the eve of a Sabbath or a festival (Mishnah Sanhedrin 4:2), so although it may seem a risk, Jesus is calculating the timing very carefully, for this is, very likely, a festival week, with the arrest and trial of Lazarus occurring before the limitations of pre-Sabbath preparations; he would simply be kept prisoner in the meantime, especially if the Jews *are* using the trial as bait to lure Jesus into Jerusalem.

Remember the emphasis on numbers in the 'sign' on the mountains of Bashan? There, we were forced to take note of the pattern of:

$$\mathbf{2} \text{ (thousand)} + \mathbf{5} \text{ (thousand)} = \mathbf{7} \text{ (thousand)}$$

... here we have it again.

$$\mathbf{2} \text{ (days)} + \mathbf{5th\ day} \text{ (in tomb for 4 days, } \textit{already}\text{)} = \mathbf{7} \text{ (days)}$$

(Another way of calculating this symbolic number is to add the two-day journey of the message reaching Jesus to the two-day delay, then add the two-day journey of Jesus to Jerusalem, so the day of the 'raising' can land on the ritually important seventh day.)

The sign of the 'coming-of-age boy' (Lazarus) was the "second" sign; *this* is now the seventh (again giving us 2+5=7). When Jesus *first* calls Lazarus (to "come forward"), as "the one" amongst the priests at the Feast of Tabernacles, the two symbolic timeframes are alluded to, i.e., the "third day" and the seventh. The stay of two days at Bethabara also allows for the symbolic implication of Jesus' timely arrival: "After two days he will revive us; on the third day he will raise us up, that we may live before him" (Hos 6:2). Thus, this scene continues with the identification of Lazarus with the young boy, Nicodemus' son.

The third and seventh days echo the day of the Sinai covenant *and* the period prescribed for the sequestration and ordination of priests, respectively:

> On the morning of the third day ... Moses brought the people out of the camp to meet God.
>
> Exod 19:16–17

> You shall not go outside the entrance of the tent of meeting for seven days, until the day when your period of ordination is completed. For it will take seven days to ordain you.
>
> Lev 8:33

This suggests a Passover timing for this event, which makes sense, given the "Let my people go!" theme that will permeate Lazarus' story.

In the Secret Gospel of Mark, this same *seven-day* period is employed in the context of an initiation rite; *after* six days, i.e., on the seventh, Jesus gives orders to a resurrected youth, who then comes to him *later that evening* (by Jewish timekeeping, the eighth day, as stipulated in Lev 9:1), dressed in linen (i.e., the under-tunic of a priest is of a fine, white linen). He undergoes some sort of indoctrination, where he receives the "knowledge" of God. The FG's 'raising' scenario, then, clearly suggests a day of union with the divine, i.e., a priestly ordination ritual.

Martha goes out to meet Jesus, who is heading straight for Jerusalem. She chastises him for staying away, as only a wife could, perhaps; if he had been around when he was needed, none of this would have happened. Reassuring her that Lazarus "will rise *again*" Jesus affirms that Lazarus has 'risen' once before and this, we now know, refers to his election in John 9; that is, Lazarus was raised up to be Jesus' son, his elected heir, and he will be raised up not at the *eschaton* (i.e., the end days), as Martha predicts, but *now* and in a different sense. He *will* be raised up as a fully initiated priest of the new order but in his representative role as the new, ideal Israel, he will be "lifted up" to the status of firstborn and (figuratively) sit at the right hand of God.

According to the Samaritans, because of the "light of holiness" that is said to imbue them, the ancestral saints can intercede with God on behalf of the righteous. These saints are "with God" but Jesus is still living in the 'world'. Martha seems to acknowledge the basic premise but her whole attitude in this scene suggests she is not fully convinced her husband can take on the Sanhedrin.

Jesus reiterates that *he* (or rather his mission) is the path to "everlasting life" (for Israel), the resurrection from the darkness of a spiritual (not physical) death. Martha's subsequent affirmation sounds almost like a feigned surrender, though, for what has Jesus done in these few moments, other than to tell her what she should have known all along, that makes her suddenly seem so confident? It is almost as if she is saying, 'Yes, alright, so you're the Son of God, now can we get going, please!' It just doesn't ring true. We are reminded of the adage that a prophet has no honour in his own home (and this is where the addendum of John 4:44 would have been more aptly applied).

Then, to confirm the intimate relationship between Mary and Lazarus, Martha is sent to *fetch* Mary for *she* is the other half of this vital union, the representational "rod of Joseph" to be united with the "rod of Judah" so she *must* be there to be by Lazarus' side when he 'rises'.

According to (ancient) Jewish tradition, for a woman to outlive her husband (and if betrothed, Lazarus would be legally Mary's husband) is deemed a "disgrace" (Isa 54:4), especially if the husband is young when he dies; his premature death is seen as a punishment for a sinful life and the reproach is extended to the widow. To remain indoors is thus a matter of protection also, for, although the moral code stipulates that one be generous to widows and orphans, the reality of everyday life makes it a difficult transition. Often widows are ejected from the family home, left destitute but, significantly, the *daughter of a priest* is allowed to return to her father's house, so long as she has no children (Lev 22:13), so Mary, still only pregnant at this point, has been staying indoors. It would also make sense for Mary to be housebound during her pregnancy, her time of confinement, especially if accusations and rumours abound.

Martha's position, or role, as 'mother' in this scenario, is further supported by the precedent of 1 Kgs 17:17, where the son of the "mistress of the house" becomes ill and dies, only to be raised again by the prophet Elijah (a 'sign' of the legitimacy of the prophet). Lazarus, as Jesus' adopted son, becomes Martha's, too (and this is made official by the end of the gospel).

The phrase "disturbed in spirit" illustrates Jesus' reaction when he perceives that Mary has accepted the "mourning" of the Jews and is weeping with them; even *she* has her doubts now? Such a scenario echoes Saul's reaction (in 1 Sam 11:4f), when he discovers that the Israelites have all but surrendered to their enemy: "And the spirit of God came upon Saul in power when he heard these words, and his anger was greatly kindled." Saul subsequently sends out the message that any who do not follow God's chosen leaders are destined for destruction. It is very similar, too, to Jer 4:19f, where God speaks of his broken heart and his anguish because his people are so foolish and fail to understand. In Jesus, as in Saul, anger arises in the 'spirit' (the God-given aspect of their being) because *God* is angry; he has sent his 'helper' but the people are still weeping for themselves! In 2 Esdras, however, Ezra sees a woman mourning the death of her son and he becomes "embittered in spirit and deeply distressed" because she is mourning for the loss of one human, when God is mourning for the loss of *his* 'son', the whole of Israel. This, perhaps, is the most significant precedent.

In Jesus' own weeping is observed not the personal grief the Jews see (remember, the Jews always get it wrong in the FG ... what they 'see' is not what *is*) but an allusion to Jesus' lamentation for the situation at hand, i.e., the captivity of God's chosen: "...my soul will weep in secret for your pride; my eyes will weep bitterly and run down with tears, because the Lord's flock has been taken captive" (Jer 13:17). The pride and the iniquity of the attendant Jews make their mourning both ironic and hypocritical: "return to me with all your heart, with fasting, with weeping and with mourning; rend your hearts and not your clothing" (Joel 2:12–13).

Some of the onlookers ask: "Could not he who opened the eyes of the blind man have kept this man from dying?" illustrating the link between the two characters (why didn't they say '…he who made the lame man walk,' for instance?).

Jesus' question, in the Greek text is "Where have you put him?"; it is rephrased in the NRSV to imply, more emphatically, a *burial*, using "laid" instead of "put" but this is misleading, and as his question is so generally addressed, it may just as easily be directed to the Jews who are there and who subtly mock him, as to Martha. That Jesus does not seem to know *where* Lazarus is being "held" is significant, for if Lazarus is truly dead, his body would be in the family tomb but Jesus doesn't even hint at this. There are clues, however, that can potentially identify precisely where the young man is held captive.

A Clever Play on Words

What of the "stone" that is said to be blocking Lazarus' exit from the cave? My first instinct was to link *lithos* with the rock of the Chamber of Hewn Stone, which is the highest court of the Sanhedrin, where, capital cases (such as adultery) are tried; the problem is, the Chamber of Hewn Stone is not a prison. Also, if the "stone" is to be a physical object that someone removes, it doesn't really make sense, unless this court of the Sanhedrin has a stone door, which would be unlikely. However, when we look a little closer at the language of this scene, we learn that the stone is said to be "resting upon," i.e., using the preposition *epi*, meaning "on or upon." In the NT, *epi* is used to mean "over" more often than it to suggest "against"; I submit this is the translation that is heavily influenced by subsequent ideas about a burial chamber, i.e., by those who did not understand the symbolism of the FG. This implies the cavern where Lazarus lies is *vertical* rather than horizontal. In addition, the verb used to denote "remove" is *airo*, to "lift *up*" but why would a huge stone against a tomb entrance be lifted? It would be *rolled* away. This suggests not only a vertical removal but one that is somehow different, for *airo* alludes more to a figurative lifting, a raising, or a suspension, e.g., the lifting and swinging out of a stone on some sort of pivot/pulley perhaps?

This little clue eventually led me to:

> The chamber of the captivity: a well was there which they of the captivity had digged, *and a wheel was placed upon it*, and thence they provided water for the whole court.
>
> Middoth Perek V.4

Under the same roof as the Chamber of Hewn Stone are the Chamber of Wood and the Chamber of the Captivity. The latter name ignites the imagination with Lazarus, the ideal/new Israel in bondage, having been exiled (from the Pharisees) in John 9:34. Haven't we just seen Jesus 'weeping' for the captive Israel (Lazarus)? Just as Joseph is hurled down a well by jealous brothers (Genesis 37), is it possible that Lazarus is "being held" in the cistern within the Chamber of Captivity? (Both men are also unjustly accused of adultery.)

It is said that those of the captivity (Babylonian exiles) built a cistern with a large 'wheel' atop it,[3] to channel waters from the Gihon Spring into the temple; it is called the Chamber of the Well. The play on "captivity" is loud and clear. Thus, the physical layout of the temple chambers allows for Lazarus to have been incarcerated immediately upon leaving the chamber of the Sanhedrin, and this serves to set the greatest trap for Jesus, for he must, literally, enter the heart of enemy territory if he is to attempt to free his right-hand-man. The allusion to the temple chambers also foreshadows Jesus' own arrest scene, as we shall see.

Yet, there is more symbolism in the imagery of a stone being removed before Lazarus can be set free. Consider this series of potential clues:

✯ In the discussion of Mary at Jacob's Well (John 4:7f), the allusion to Genesis 29 was mentioned, i.e., the stone that must be removed from the well before the sheep can drink.

✯ In the story of the 'lame man' Peter (John 5), the aging priest is told to "get up" and shake off the bonds that keep him fettered to an illegitimate cultus.

✯ Peter's nickname is Cephas, meaning "a hollowed-out rock" and insinuates a need to be humbled/disciplined.

✯ The stone mentioned in John 11:38 is depicted by the Greek word *lithos*, which can also imply a "stumbling stone" (e.g., as in 1 Pet 2:8, one of the letters I later claim is very Johannine in style and content).

In order for the new Israel to emerge (represented by Lazarus), the "stumbling stone" must be removed. Whether the action of the crowds is to be taken as a physical removal of an obstacle (e.g., the 'wheel' atop the well/cistern), or purely a metaphorical one, I am not certain but there is a possibility that it is both, as is the case throughout the narrative.

---

[3] The Hebrew for "wheel(s)" in Jer 18:13 is *al haabnayim*, i.e., "the stones."

I am going to suggest that it is Peter who stands in the way, who acts as the barrier between Lazarus and freedom. Peter was so keen to tell the authorities what Jesus had done at the Sheep Gate, he might well have been involved in informing on the young Lazarus back in John 9, which resulted in the latter being hauled before the Pharisees, i.e., Peter is behind this incarceration of Lazarus. I can just imagine him feeling superior, having assisted in rigging some accusation or other, regarding Mary, to get the young man arrested and out of his way. As we shall see, Peter is intensely jealous of Lazarus' honoured position by Jesus' side; the whole idea of the 'lame man' always being left behind by others who get ahead before him, was to illustrate the rivalry between Peter and Lazarus. Just as Joseph's jealous brothers cast their sibling down a well, so too, perhaps, Peter's jealousy overrides his sense and his incriminations get Lazarus incarcerated, i.e., Peter is the 'brother' (fellow disciple) who resents the rights of the firstborn being invested on the youngest. This would be in keeping with the FG's less than flattering depiction of Peter and would provide a rationale for Jesus' declaration (at the meal) concerning the one who would betray him, i.e., this could mean Peter rather than Judas, for Jesus knows Peter is determined to rise in the ranks at any cost. Jesus is constantly on guard where he is concerned. Removing the stone may, therefore, imply getting rid of the troublemaker, Peter (who, of course, represents the established, corrupt and impotent priesthood).[4] The scene, alluding to the Joseph precedent, also serves to foreshadow a future commission name of Lazarus: Joseph of Arimathea.

> *Then they said, "Come, let us make plots against Jeremiah—for instruction shall not perish from the priest, nor counsel from the wise, nor the word from the prophet. Come, let us bring charges against him, and let us not heed any of his words."*
> *... For they have dug a pit to catch me, and laid snares for my feet. Yet you, O Lord, know all their plotting to kill me.*
> Jer 18:18; 22–3

So, Lazarus is about to exit his 'tomb' on an implied 'third day', after a symbolic seven days' confinement. There is a "stench," Martha warns Jesus (even though the tomb is still apparently sealed), reflecting again her rather mundane understanding of what is going on, and Jesus picks up on this in his response; if she believed, she would 'see'. Part of both the

---

[4] The scene with Mary at the well, alluding to the 'thirsty' sheep of Gen 29 and promising the "living water" demonstrates Jesus' vision for the necessary 'removal' of the established cultus—in both Jerusalem *and* Samaria—before those who thirst can 'drink'.

Samaritan and Jewish belief systems is the notion that the *righteous* who die remain sweetly scented, while those who die in sin release a foul stench. The stench of death is thus equated with guilt, so Jesus' response implies that Martha should realise that Lazarus *has* no guilt, just as the 'blind man' had not sinned. The misapprehension arises because Lazarus has been found guilty by the Sanhedrin and has been ejected from the temple priesthood. Martha assumes this guilt must be justified. She sees with the eyes not with the mind!

In Zechariah's description of the raising of the future ideal priest, the order given to the observers to "Take off his filthy clothes" (3:4), not only reflects Jesus' own order to unbind Lazarus but also symbolises a disassociation from the concept of guilt: "See, I have taken your guilt away from you." Thus, the "stench" in John 11 signifies the inevitable, inherited guilt which is exuviated so that Lazarus can fulfil his role as a holy and pure priest of God. Any stench is the stench of the 'world' and all its iniquities, the 'world' he is to disassociate from (just as Jesus has done) and fully cast off, i.e., the fulfilment of the ritual cutting-off that began with the washing away of the clay in the Pool of Siloam.

In the ordination ritual of the Sinai priesthood (Lev 8:34), the new priests must separate themselves from the rest of the community for seven days so that atonement can be made. This is Lazarus' period of segregation and, in fact, the other disciples go through a similar process but theirs is much more subtle.

Break Out

If this is an attempt to flush Jesus out from his retreat, it has worked but if it is an attempt to thwart his plans and to publicly reclaim what the Pharisees perceive as their own, it has not, for the FG's account of the incident makes the entire scene one of complete victory for Jesus. If the authorities can catch Jesus in the act of trying to free their prisoner, they will have him; this seems to be their plan.

Jesus, however, has allies within the temple's echelons (how many times does he escape arrest?) and these are the people, I suggest, who free the access point on his command and pull Lazarus from the 'well'. All Jesus has to do is *call* Lazarus from 'death' to 'life' and this calling echoes Jesus' cry at the Feast of Tabernacles, for "the one" who believes to come forward (Lazarus). Calling out to someone does not incriminate Jesus; legally, he has done nothing wrong.

The order to "unbind" Lazarus acts as a profound allusion to Exod 5:1, i.e., "Let my people go," i.e., so that they may celebrate the true god; the first emancipation had been from oppressed religious worship and this one is no different. The bindings are described as *kerias,* the linen strips used to wrap the bodies of the dead but also, significantly, the newly *born* (as swaddling). However, and this is important, the FG stipulates *only* that Lazarus' hands and feet are bound, *not* that his entire body is wrapped—the imagery alludes to a forceful bondage, just like that of the Israelites in Egypt, and serves to confirm that the man is not physically dead at all but a prisoner.

In the subtleties of language there are many clues and here again we find that the choice of words used to describe this raising scene tell of a more down to earth event. In the original Greek, the phrase "Unbind him, and let him go" (John 11:44), are two words that help support the prisoner/escape scenario. One is *lusate,* from the verb *luo,* "to loosen," which has the connotation of setting someone or something 'free'. If merely removing smelly bandages or burial cloths is implied, why not use the verb *paraphero,* which means "to remove, take away"? I think the intention is to indicate Lazarus' *escape,* both literally and metaphorically. The second word is *hupagein,* from the verb *hupago,* "to depart, go." This word, however, is usually translated as "to lead under," and understood to indicate a *silent, stealthy* departure; it means "quietly leaving," i.e., *escaping.* Had Jesus simply ordered Lazarus be allowed to "go his own way," as many early interpreters suggest, another choice of verb would had proven more apt, e.g., *exerchomai* ("to come out /go forth"), or *poreuo* ("to go on one's way"). There can be little doubt that Jesus, with help, is breaking Lazarus out of his enforced confinement.

Remember that there is also a sacrificial element to this episode, one that reflects the Abraham/Isaac, father/son concept. In Gen 22:9 Isaac is, indeed, "bound"; in an arcane passage from Ps 118:27 is another reference to the 'binding' of the sacrifice. Once Abraham has proven himself to God, a covenant is made which grants Abraham multiple descendants and to them is promised prosperity and possession of the "gate of their enemies." Jesus is expecting a similar outcome.

> *Shake yourself from the dust, rise up, O captive Jerusalem;*
> *loose the bonds from your neck.*
> Isa 52:2

The imagery of the young Lazarus, the 'son of the man', the representation of the new Israel, being *lifted* out of the cistern/well must not be overlooked. This is the precise moment, symbolically, the "lifting up," or raising, of the "son of man" takes place. *This* is Jesus' ultimate demonstration that the new kingdom *will* be a reality.

The cloth that is said to cover Lazarus' face, the *soudarion,* signifies not the cloth placed over the facial area during the burial wrapping process, for none has taken place; I suggest it alludes to something far more significant. This is *not*, as has been suggested by others, the *turban* of a priest; it does not tally with Jesus' apparent order for all the burial cloths to be *removed*. In Ezek 24:17 there is a commandment for the priest to "bind *on* [his] turban" in times of mourning and distress. Josephus describes the priestly turban as being wound about the *top* of the head like a crown, not as being bound about the face like a veil (*Ant*. 3.7.3). Lazarus is not the *high* priest ... yet. Jesus is. The transference of the priestly turban comes, as we shall see, later in the narrative.

I think the entire raising-of-Lazarus scene is based on his purity and fitness as a *priest* both in terms of his position within the temple cultus *and* his role in Jesus' campaign. The adultery charges may well be fabricated by the mischievous Peter, in a bid to render Lazarus unworthy for the role Jesus has planned for him. In the overall pattern of the FG narrative, the duality of the Jesus-Lazarus depictions, and the consistency of the character of Peter, it would be fitting for Peter to attempt to disqualify Lazarus *three* times, just as he denies Jesus three times. First perhaps, he informs on the young man who goes to the Pool of Siloam, then he attempts to prove Lazarus an adulterer (or worse), and then during Jesus' arrest scene, he does something that is shocking, in an effort to rid himself of this tiresome rival.

> (In the Chamber of Hewn Stone) the great Sanhedrin of Israel sat, and judged the priesthood. And the priest in whom was found disqualification was clothed in black, and veiled in black, and went out, and had to go. And if there was not found in him disqualification, he was dressed in white, and veiled in white; he went in and served with his brethren the priests. And they made a feast-day, because there was not found disqualification in the seed of Aaron the priest ....
>
> Middoth Perek 5.4

Lazarus is found guilty by the Sanhedrin and is thus disqualified from his duties as a priest of the *temple*. His 'smelly' burial cloths might represent the black garments of rejection (as above). Note how the very next scene in the gospel is a festive meal; although modern interpretation implies the meal is for Jesus, what if it is a celebratory meal for Lazarus? Just as the 'blind man' was ousted from the Pharisees and that was to suit Jesus' plan, so Lazarus is ejected from the "den of thieves" and is thereby released from his certain 'grave' to live the 'life' promised by Jesus.

The veil might represent, on a more theological but not unrelated level, the 'veil' of Moses. According to Exod 34:29–35, when Moses "went in before the Lord," his face shone and when he left the presence of God he would put a veil on his face. Being in such proximity to the divine is something to fear, something to dread, not because it is a bad thing but because it is so awesome (Gen 16:13; Judg 6:22, 13:22; 2 Esd 10:25, etc.).

In his confinement Lazarus is undergoing a priestly ordination ritual (a tough one), and this is for the glorification of God but it is also the symbolic 'third day', recall, *the* day of union with the divine, so we can deduce, theologically and symbolically, that God is there *with* Lazarus, breathing the spirit of life into him (see Job 33:4).[5] The veil thus functions as a symbol of Lazarus' rise to glory: "Many of those who sleep in the dust of the earth shall wake ... those who are wise shall shine like the brightness of the sky" (Dan 12:2–3).

Unlike Moses, however, who dons the face covering when he exits the tent of meeting, Lazarus' veil is *removed* when he emerges from his tomb (which has served as his own, private, 'tent of meeting'). Such an act echoes the ritual disrobing of the priests after they exit the sanctuary, lest they "communicate holiness to the people" (Ezek 44:19). In Zech 3:5, the placing of a "clean turban" on the head of the new priest comes *after* the order to "Take off his filthy clothes," implying that the ritualistic *removal* of garments affected (either positively or negatively) by one's contact with 'a greater force' (either good or evil) must be observed.

The idea that the FG's Jesus would use this latter-day ideal of priestly diligence, rather than the Mosaic precedent, reiterates the northern influence of the gospel, and the consistent theme of a superior purity and legitimacy of the new order (i.e., the rejection of the Aaronite institution). Not prescribed until the Book of Joshua (3:5), the assigned distance to be maintained between the Ark (and the priests who carry it) and the congregation is 2000 cubits; it makes sense for the priests to change their clothes before approaching the community, for the clothes have been imbued with the Shekinah. Joshua is one of the biblical books most closely cherished by those of northern sentiments, so 'our' Jesus is justified in his allegiance to *its* more definitive ruling.

In Paul's letter to the Corinthians (2 Cor 3:12–18), the veil of Moses is seen as a barrier to the peoples' understanding of the scriptures. The very concept of a *facial* veil being 'set aside' by Jesus is all but unique in the NT, the only other instance being here, in the FG, which begs the question, did Paul feel the need to denounce the concept of the veil because he understood that it was a sign of rebellion against Mosaic law? Could it be because it is alluded to only in the FG's 'raising of Lazarus' scene, and this is the gospel Paul will later admonish? All other references to a 'veil' being removed or destroyed (e.g., in Matthew, Mark, Luke, and Hebrews) pertain to the veil of the temple, which is analogous to the curtain that surrounded the Ark in the days of the tabernacle (Exod 40:3).

---

[5] In the Gospel of Nicodemus, Joseph of Arimathea is incarcerated, and before he is rescued, he sees a 'lightening flash' (the arrival of Jesus, who saves him).

A Deed More Profitable

As usual, there is a division of the crowd; some believe in Jesus, others want him stopped. The Pharisees are again informed of Jesus' actions (they probably know already but this consistent theme of 'telling' or 'betraying Jesus to his enemies' is significant to the narrative). A meeting of the council, the great Sanhedrin, is convened to discuss the options open to them.

The irony and the ignorance of the "Jews" culminate in the bold statement of Joseph Caiaphas, the high priest: "You know nothing at all! You do not understand that it is better for you to have one man die for the people than to have the whole nation destroyed" (John 11:49–50). This is the NRSV translation. The Greek reads: "… it is profitable for us that one man dies, and not the whole nation." There is quite a difference.

I am not certain about the authenticity of John 11:51–3; though the gathering of the "dispersed children of God" does seem to fit, the overall effect is one of Christian clarification. It grates a little with Caiaphas' inference that it would be better for *them* (he is talking to the Sanhedrin members, i.e., the "Jews") if Jesus dies; his words are words of self-preservation, not altruism. Take a look at Caiaphas' statement: "What are we to do? This man is performing many signs. If we let him go on like this, everyone will believe in him, and the Romans will come and destroy both our holy place and our nation" (John 11:47–8). Just as in John 6, where the eagerness to see Rome vanquished blinded the masses to Jesus' promise of a spiritual conquest, Caiaphas' concern is more for the Romans' ability to thwart the Sanhedrin's power. This an apt juncture to recall that at some point in the FG narrative (between the lines) the Samaritan tumult takes place; Jesus is stirring up a *lot* of support and is causing too much unrest. If the Jews are seen to be lacking the power to control these outbursts of zeal, the Romans will put their foot down even harder on the neck of Judea.

There is an interesting parallel to this in Josephus, where a fight breaks out between the Galileans and the Samaritans just as the Jews are heading toward Jerusalem to celebrate the Feast of Tabernacles. A Galilean is killed and a group of enraged men head out to Samaria to seek their revenge. The "rulers of Jerusalem" prepare themselves as if for mourning and try to persuade the men not to cause another disturbance …

> …lest by their attempt to revenge themselves upon the Samaritans, they should provoke the Romans to come against Jerusalem; to have compassion upon their country and temple [and not] bring the utmost dangers of destruction upon them, in order to avenge themselves upon one Galilean only.
>
> *Wars.* 2.12.5

This confrontation, notably involving Samaritans and a violent backlash from the Romans, occurred under the procurator Cumanus, who presided from 48–52 CE. Is this the (more public and therefore on record) origin of the speech placed, retrospectively, on Caiaphas' lips (hence the mention of "prophecy," which I believe to be a later insertion)? As it is, Caiaphas' comment not only sets in motion the plan to have Jesus killed off, it sets the context in which the execution will take place, i.e., the Romans will have to *fear* him. They will have to see that Jesus' actions are a threat to *them* and that the rest of the 'nation' rejects him, so only *he* can be punished. From this moment on, Jesus becomes the high priest's scapegoat but this is where the irony of Caiaphas' intentions lies, for Caiaphas uses the imagery of the temple being destroyed and he envisions Jesus being the cause of this destruction. By killing Jesus he thinks he will save the temple but, in fact, the opposite proves to be the case (eventually).

So, the Samaritan tumult on Mount Gerizim (alluded to in John 6) takes place *just before* the 'raising of Lazarus' episode. It would prove the perfect time for Peter to exploit the chaotic situation and lay his hands on the young Lazarus while Jesus is in hiding. It is for this reason the FG author inserts a historically verifiable and pertinent quotation regarding the Samaritans and the Romans. The speech might never have been an aspect of the original events surrounding Jesus' arrest but it provides the reader with yet another clue to the history that must be suppressed for the sake of the 'good news'.

I suggest that the Synoptic writers chose to put the storming of the temple scene as the precipitous event that leads to Jesus' arrest based on their understanding of Lazarus' testament, i.e., they (Luke and Mark) *did* know of the Samaritan tumult debacle but chose not to even hint at a connection to their Christ; it was all just too messy and too linked to the (by then) rejected right-hand-man, "Lazarus."

On a more theological level, there is further significance to Caiaphas' speech and the raising of Lazarus. Another interpretation of the commission name "Lazarus" helps this connection formulate in the mind of the (Jewish, or Hebrew-speaking) gospel reader of the day, i.e., the Hebrew term for Temple Court (comprised of the Court of Israel and the Court of the Priests, not the outer courts) is '*azara*. By raising Lazarus on the third day, Jesus raises the new "temple," the new priestly sanctuary, as promised. The Jews had asked for a 'sign' by which Jesus' violence in the temple could be justified; now they have received one!

Lazarus, then—the 'son of the man', the son of Nicodemus, and Jesus' adopted 'son'—is lifted up as the representation of the new, spiritual temple, the new divinely-sanctioned Israel. By this 'sign' the house of Joseph will regain its position as the firstborn of God. The vision of the mourning woman in 2 Esdras, mentioned earlier, concludes with *her* face shining brightly, she screams, then she disappears, and in her place a city is built. This is interpreted by the "angel" to mean "no work of human construction could endure in a place where the city of the Most High was to be revealed" (2 Esd 10:54). Not only does this tie in with the veil Lazarus wears but it reflects the very sentiment Jesus had expressed to the Samaritan woman, in that the true locus of worship will be where *God* is, not where someone decides to construct a building!

The young Lazarus, who had already been accepted as Jesus' protégée, was nevertheless allowed to enter the priesthood and become a (novice?) Pharisee; this was so Jesus could openly demonstrate his ability to pluck the 'chosen' from the jaws of spiritual death. It also foreshadowed Lazarus' final test and elevation, as the embodiment of the new Israel plucked from the edge of Hades, completing the symbolic inclusio.

Jesus and his disciples make a tactical retreat to Ephraim, the land of Jesus and Mary's forefathers, the inheritance of Joseph and Joshua. They return to the very place tradition holds is the seat of the Messiah ben Joseph, i.e., *the home of the firstborn*. Having fled the bloody debacle atop the mountain, probably just a matter of days, or perhaps a couple of weeks earlier, the Samaritan rebel Jesus is the nation's most wanted criminal. He is in hiding, under a death sentence. It is here, I propose, Mary gives birth to her son, the firstborn of the new Israel, the firstborn king/high priest of the new dynasty (further clues help support this claim).

While they are in Ephraim, the Passover draws nearer, i.e., the Passover of 36 CE.

16
MEAL 1: SIX DAYS BEFORE PASSOVER

Celebrations
FROM HIS FATHER'S EARLY INTEREST in Jesus' discussion on spiritual rebirth and his rejection of worldly relationships (e.g., with the Pharisees), to his tortuous rebirth from his prison in Jerusalem—from his election, through cleansing and elevation, a parallel to the harlot-bride pattern is being revealed through the character Lazarus.

The FG states that Jesus returns to Bethany (the site already noted as implying Lazarus' own house) exactly "six days" before the Passover, so again, an important action will take place on the *seventh* day. The following scenes, though specified as being in Jesus' honour, *are* somehow connected with Lazarus, who is mentioned *three* times during the course of the first seventeen verses, a strange and unprecedented concentration, demanding a direct focus of our attention. It is yet another instance of the FG's duality, where the delineation between Jesus and Lazarus is intentionally obscured. Is the meal a celebration after the symbolic extraction and elevation of Lazarus from the jaws of death, or a wedding celebration for Mary and Lazarus? They have been chosen for marriage, from the beginning.

Meals are a significant part of several important ceremonies in the Jewish tradition and the most obvious one, of course, is the Passover Seder, which is consumed on the eve of 15 Nisan, the final day of a week of celebrations, to remember the emancipation from captivity in Egypt. As Jesus arrives in Bethany six days *before* Passover, this cannot be a Seder.

Given the redemptive context of Lazarus' raising in John 11, we can see in Isa 25:6–10 the redeemed of Israel receiving a "feast" in celebration of the conquest of God over the (figurative) "death" of the people (perhaps enough of a similarity to the Passover remembrance). In the case of Aaron and his sons, however, both before (Lev 9:31f) and after (Lev 10:12f) a week of preparation, the new priests engage in a number of symbolic sacrifices and share in specific *ordination meals*. The rite serves to establish them as the elite of Israel. In Saul's case, the meal takes place during *his* election and elevation (1 Sam 9:15ff): "for today you shall eat with me," Samuel says

(9:19). This is why there are *two* distinct meal scenes in the FG, set a week apart.

In both 1 Samuel and the FG, emphasis is on *serving* the meal, the special attention to the two guests of honour, and the *sharing* of the food with the guests. Saul is then anointed, and appointed "ruler over [God's] heritage" (1 Sam 10:1; Heb 10:21.). Lazarus joined the inner circle as the only other fully functioning priest, besides Jesus. His year's rest, as is tradition, i.e., to focus on his marriage, is over (from the 'blind man' scene to the 'raising') and now he must assume his responsibilities.

There is, however, another, perhaps more significant election of a leader that occurs before an important religious day, i.e., the appointing of the high priest's official deputy, precisely one week before the Day of Atonement, in case he is prevented from carrying out his duties for some reason, e.g., loss of purity. Josephus describes such an eventuality (*Ant.* 17.6.4), when a certain high priest, Matthias, supposedly has a "dream" the night before the Day of Atonement in which he enjoys intimate relations with his wife; he is disqualified from officiating and his deputy steps in for him at the last moment.[1] The link to the Day of Atonement is made clear in due course.

There are, then, several potential purposes for this first meal:

★ Lazarus' first initiation meal to celebrate his 'rebirth' from the clutches of the institution as a priest of the new order.

★ His election as Jesus' deputy high priest.

★ A wedding feast, with Lazarus as the groom (marriage feasts last for seven days).

★ A wedding feast with Jesus as the "bridegroom"; allusions made to this role early in the narrative and the obvious divine bride representation of Mary throughout would seem to make *this* couple's union almost inevitable, though the FG intentionally keeps us guessing (i.e., in order to maintain the mystery and protect the child).

★ A *bris*, (*Brit Milah*), i.e., the circumcision of the young son (eight days after his birth). The baby's mother is central to the ceremony and in ancient Samaria, some have suggested, it is *she* who performs the act itself, so it is fitting that Mary is *not* also in a 'serving' role at the feast. The father is treated as the guest of honour, as is Jesus. A collection of money is made for

---

[1] Only the anointed high priest or the priest "consecrated as priest in his father's place can make atonement" (Lev 16:32). The concept of a second priest is also found in 2 Kgs 25:18.

the child; in the second meal scene Judas, recall, is responsible for the group's "purse."

In this timely portrayal of the celebratory meal, then, we find Lazarus' apparent acceptance of his new status, echoing Jesus' open acceptance of his mission in John 2. Martha, the dutiful mistress of the house, serves her guests, but what of Mary?

Mary and Marriage
The Hebrew name Miryam and its Greek equivalent Maria stem from *meriy*, meaning "bitterness/rebellion" and, ultimately, from *marah*, "to disobey, to rebel." This is apt for the only known Miryam in the OT, i.e., the sister of Moses who rebels against him and is chastised by God for her behaviour (Num 12:1–15); it is a good example of a commission name. It is also an apt name for Ezekiel's Bride of God, who is also the focus of divine remonstration, i.e., for her (spiritual) unfaithfulness.

The depiction of Mary in the Synoptics (Mark 16:9; Luke 8:2), whom Jesus apparently cures of "evil spirits and infirmities," corresponds with this perception; perhaps this suggests a slightly skewed inheritance from the Johannine tradition. In the FG, of course, Mary represents the harlot-bride ascending; as the Samaritan woman she is the unfaithful "wife," as the adulteress she is tried and forgiven. As the representative "rod of Ephraim" she is elected to rise alongside Lazarus, at the celebratory meal we assume she makes a covenant of marriage, and now she will be both cleansed and anointed, fulfilling the cycle set out in Ezekiel 16.

Some scholars have argued that the significance of Mary's anointing action lies in the *metaphorical* use of the oil, where it is understood to represent, for example, a prayer, as in Ps 141:2. In the first three verses alone, however, are echoed at least four phrases from the beginning verse of the Song of Solomon: "smell/odour" (*osme*, Song 1:3, 4, 12), "ointment" (*muron*, 1:3, 4), "to recline at table" (*anaklithesomai*, 1:12), and "spikenard" (*nardos*, 1:12). Such an obvious reference to the Shulammite woman, is not coincidental.

Until this juncture in the echo of the bride-of-God pattern, Mary has been depicted in derogatory and humbling terms; she is the harlot, the accused. It is fitting, therefore, that Jesus' *feet* be the primary object of Mary's attention, for in Ps 141:5 is the adjuration, "Never let the oil of the wicked anoint my head"; Jesus *must* pay attention to ritual (despite the modern belief that he tries to eliminate it), if he is aiming for a pure and legitimate priesthood, certain precautions *have* to be taken (and this comes up several times in the narrative). Only now is it time for Mary, as the divine bride, to *begin* her symbolic elevation.

There are two instances in the OT where the themes of 'marriage/bride' and 'feet' are intertwined, namely 1 Sam 25:41–42, and Ruth 2:10–13; 3:7f. In the first case, Abigail offers herself as a servant, stooping down to wash the men's feet; she is seen as submitting herself to David and is taken as his wife. Ruth prostrates herself at the feet of Boaz, an action explicitly connected with the ritual of betrothal; she, too, is taken as wife, for she has demonstrated the ideal qualities of the Israelite bride.

Here we have that ambiguity again; if Mary is betrothed to Lazarus, why is she performing this prenuptial act, in a very obviously sexual context, for Jesus? A marriage to Lazarus would seem the right thing to do to keep tongues from wagging, and to ensure Mary and the child a safe future but a marriage to Jesus *is* so clearly alluded to here.

Anointing

Mary anoints Jesus' feet with the expensive oil, the spikenard, and about this oil I have more to say at the right time. What scholars mostly argue about, though, is the fact that she uses her *hair* to wipe away the excess oil; no one has really come up with a satisfactory explanation as to *why*.[2] I suggest that there is a dual anointing taking place in John 12.

The first anointing is Jesus'. The Greek verb used to reflect Mary's action of anointing is *aleipho*, which is also used in Gen 31:13 (LXX), where Jacob's pillar (erected by Jacob after his dream at Bethel [Gen 28], the site of a sacred vow) is anointed. The same word appears in Exod 40:15 and Num 3:3, in the description of the ordination of priests. Jesus explains that Mary has the oil in anticipation of his burial and this can only be fully explained in light of what happens *during* the burial scene, so I shall hold off on that for now. Her action, however, becomes one of *premature* but intentional sanctification and, because of the sweet-smelling oil, there is an allusion to the belief that the righteous will give off a pleasing odour after death (something that is also related to Lazarus' 'burial', recall).[3]

---

[2] Josephus states that to the Essenes 'oil is a defilement' and that if 'one of them be anointed without his own approbation, it is wiped off his body' (*Wars*. 2.8.3). Loose hair is also a sign of mourning (Lev 10:6). Oil is a requirement when a sacrifice is made (Josephus, *Ant*. 3.9.4) and the underlying theme of the entire passion narrative is of sacrifice. Deut 33:24 employs the analogy of an oil-covered foot to symbolise prosperity and success; it is used in Moses' parting song to the Israelites, in the context of a final victory of God's chosen over their oppressors. This would also fit well into the FG scenario, for the farewell discourse is soon to follow, which focuses on a similar theme.

[3] Lev 14:18 stipulates that the ritual for one who is to be cleansed of guilt involves just such an anointing: "The rest of the oil that is in the priest's hand he shall put on

The second anointing is Mary's and this exhibits the basic characteristics of the Nazarite consecration in Numbers 6.[4] The Nazarite vow is one of devotion to God; it is a sign of piety and humility. The three main stipulations recorded in Numbers 6 are: 1) the Nazarite must avoid strong drink; Mary, as the Samaritan Woman, lives in Sychar, which, recall, could be a play on *shekar* (noun) / *shakar* (verb), meaning "strong drink / drunkard; "to be intoxicated." 2) The Nazarite must not cut their hair; the only identifying feature of Mary is her long hair. 3) The Nazarite must not come into contact with the dead; Mary resists entering Jesus' tomb, and later, Jesus warns her not to touch him. The purging, or cleansing of the Nazarite symbolises a *separation* from one way of life and a 'cleaving unto' another. The FG, then, surreptitiously depicts Mary as receiving the same oil that has just sanctified the feet of the high priest, Jesus; the *hair,* deemed the most sacred area of the Nazarite's body, represents the holy vow itself, imbued, as it is, with the oil of consecration. (The daughter in the Samaritan version of the tale of Susanna, mentioned earlier, is also a Nazarite.)

Why, though, would Mary be taking the vow *now*? What came to mind initially was the example of Samson's mother, who was sworn to the Nazarite restrictions for the length of her *pregnancy* (Judg 13:14) because the son she was to bear was also to be a Nazarite, one consecrated to God for his entire life, from his mother's womb. If Mary has already given birth, however, this does not have quite the same effect, though I think the taking of the vow is so apt for this character and the delay until the sex of the child is known so logical, that the precedent can still be seen as one of motherhood, male offspring, and devotion to the cause. It seems a fitting moment perhaps, if this is a *bris,* to have Mary anointed and thus purified for her task but more significantly, this is the penultimate stage of the symbolic harlot-bride before her rise to glory. We can say that the cleansing and anointing aspects of the Bride of God ascension are combined here.

We should also take note of the fact that this act of anointing provides for a parallel with Lazarus' anointing in John 9 (as the 'blind man'), for these two characters, Lazarus and Mary, are the only two disciples to have physical contact with Jesus, both employing a liquid substance.

Judas' Disdain
The name Judas stems from the tribal name Judah, which later becomes the Hellenistic Judea, the seat of Jewish power and assumed identity. It is a

---

the head of the one to be cleansed."

[4] Josephus (*Wars.* 2.15.1) remarks on Bernice, a woman of repute who undertakes a similar Nazarite vow.

fitting name for this character. In John 13:29, Judas is described as holding the "common purse" (12:6 is an addendum). He is the only other disciple to receive a 'son of' name, apart from Peter, which links the two characters thematically. He is referred to as the "son of Simon Iscariot"; as a "son of Simon" he has a precedent in Simon, the Captain of the Temple in 2 Maccabees 3.

Finding fault with the "administration of the city market," Simon instigates a dispute that culminates in the betrayal of the temple treasury to the governor. The takeover of the temple bank is planned covertly and the governor's envoy, Heliodorus, gains access to the treasury. In 2 Maccabees 4:1f, we learn that Simon's crime is doubly bad because he has betrayed his own country and that his malice has been intensified by the influence of those who have a vested interest. Thus, Judas and Simon, Captain of the Temple, both exhibit an interest in financial matters, both contest the use of community assets (Judas argues concerning the cost and use of the oil), both are under the influence of a greater authority whose vested interest compels them to perform acts of betrayal.

As the 'son of Simon', Judas inherits the characteristics of his namesake and not only perpetuates the idea of betrayal but affirms his affiliation to the "market place" and the "traders" of the temple cultus. Judas, we will soon realise, is a "Jew," i.e., a chief priest, in fact! Obviously, there is more to say on this character at the right juncture.

The Fish Gate

In John 12:9, curious people now come to see Lazarus *as well as* Jesus, perhaps suggesting that both have just returned after being in Ephraim since the former's escape, for they would have come to see him before, surely, had he been in Bethany all along. By now, the chief priests have realised Lazarus' true significance. He is not just Jesus' sidekick, nor just a rebellious youth; *he* is seen as the cause of other Jews leaving their posts, i.e., deserting the establishment. The FG term, "Jews," recall, implies priests, Levites, Pharisees, etc., not the general public. *They* are the ones leaving, hoping to find a place in the new order, just as Nicodemus, had done. That it *is* the chief priests who find this influence unacceptable, not merely the Pharisees as before, emphasizes Lazarus' *priestly* heritage yet again.

Lazarus is now also on the top of the chief priests' hit list, which is why he probably flees to Ephraim with Jesus and Mary; he is mentioned no more in the FG but he has *not* disappeared!

The mood of the passage from John 12:23–13:1 is one of resolution, i.e., Jesus begins to speak of the "seed" dying so that its fruit can prosper, and of his 'hour' of glorification but this is in direct response to Andrew and

Philip who come with the message that some Greeks desire to see Jesus. It seems an odd response, almost out of context but in 12:15 is a reference to Zech 9:9, which helps clarify the entry-into-Jerusalem scene, and which serves as a rationale for Jesus' response to Philip's request.

The Oracle of Zechariah 9 speaks of the "triumphant and victorious" king who comes on a humble donkey's colt, to save Israel. This is where most interpreters end the parallel. It continues though, with the declaration that he will stop the fighting between the northern and southern tribes and in their united effort they will defeat their enemy; the scattered "house of Joseph" will be gathered and 'redeemed', and they shall "rear their children and return." No wonder orthodox interpreters omit this part! This is one of the most powerful attestations of Jesus' entire mission, as expressed in the FG, yet it is all but ignored because it challenges the traditional conception of Jesus as the Davidic messiah.

Jesus rides into Jerusalem in triumph because his mission has, at least according to his own expectations, been so successful (by now, perhaps, this seems either arrogant or naive). His route into the city is thought by many to be down the Kidron Valley and through one of the eastern gates that would lead him to the old City of David, thus emphasizing his alleged Davidic descent. I suggest, however, that he comes in through the northern most Gate of Ephraim, from whence he has just come, to indicate his Josephite heritage. This gate is also called the Fish Gate.

Perhaps it is from *this* very public declaration of his bloodline and intention that Jesus is identified, very soon after his disappearance form the 'world' and maybe even before, with the fish (usurped by the Christians as their own symbol for "Jesus Christ Son of God," i.e., the *icthyus*). Remember, the feeding sign of John 6 used two *fish* to represent the two sons of Joseph and thus the northern tribes. The allusion is consistent.

Gate of Ephraim = Fish Gate
Fish = Sons of Joseph
Fish = Symbol for Jesus

Mary and Lazarus are safe, the child is born; Jesus enters the city as bold as brass, as if thumbing his nose at all the Jews who had doubted, or tried to thwart, him. Further, by alluding to Ps 118:25–6 through the use of "Hosanna! Blessed is the one who comes in the name of the Lord" ("Hosanna" in the psalm, is more literally expressed as "save us"), the text of the FG makes it clear that Jesus, the King of Israel, is in a defiant mood: "What can mortals do to me?" the psalmist writes; "*I shall look in triumph on those who hate me ... **I shall not die, but I shall live**.*" This is a very subtle but vital clue in the FG, hinting at Jesus' now finalised 'plan' for the culmination of his mission (which must have been formulated during the stay in Ephraim, with his right-hand-man, Lazarus), i.e., he has no intention of dying at the hands of the "Jews" who hate him.

Jesus apparently sits on the donkey colt to further illustrate the *manifestation* of the will of God. The disciples are, just as in the telling of the 'sign' in John 6, unaware of Jesus' meaning until later, suggesting that his actions are not intended to promote *common* preconceptions about the Davidic messiah. He is using a more obscure scriptural precedent to illustrate his firm belief in his own vindication and the *eventual* cessation of occupation and oppression *if* the nation unites and returns to God—the same message he has been declaring all along.

Moses himself makes a decisive re-entry into Egypt on a donkey, with his wife and sons. Though the precedent there implies that all enemies are now dead, which is obviously not the case for Jesus, the parallel image of a 'holy family' riding on lowly beasts is not to be ignored.

The palm boughs, however, are *not* mentioned in the oracle of Zechariah 9 but they *do* appear in this parallel:

> These are they who have put off mortal clothing and have put on the immortal, and have confessed the name of God. Now they are being crowned, and receive palms ... "Who is that young man who is placing crowns on them and putting palms in their hands?"... "He is the Son of God, whom they confessed in the world."
>
> 2 Esd 2:45–7

Making this palm-bearing even more unique is the Greek word *baion*, which signifies palm "*branches.*" The *only* biblical precedent is in 1 Macc 13:51, which describes the entry of the Simon Maccabeus into Jerusalem and the subsequent rededication of the temple. In the FG such an act is anticipated in Jesus' appearance at the Feast of Tabernacles, which alluded to Solomon's dedication of the first temple, and in his subsequent appearance at the Festival of Dedication, where he stood on Solomon's portico; it is now *symbolically* fulfilled, here, in John 12:13. (Samaritans do not celebrate the Jewish Festival of Dedication for they reject the Jerusalem temple itself, which is why Jesus is not seen to be partaking of the celebration in John 10 but is *exploiting* it). The dedication, as far as Jesus is concerned, is for the *new* temple he said would be 'raised' on the third day, i.e., Lazarus and the new priestly kingdom at Shiloh.

To the Romans, the bearing of palm branches indicates a victory in battle; considering the tumult on Mount Gerizim is still very fresh in the minds of the soldiers, the procurator, and the Jews, the entry through the Ephraim Gate with supporters waving, in effect, flags of victory, would be more than enough to order Jesus' immediate arrest.

If Jesus is a wanted man, with the entire nation on the lookout for him and probably a healthy price on his head, one can imagine him wanting to make his final appearance one to remember! Jesus returns in a show of defiance that is profoundly symbolic but very dangerous; he knows perfectly well the consequences of this action.

The passages of Zechariah 9 also speak of a confrontation between the 'sons' of Zion and the 'sons' of Greece (9:13), that is, between the Israelites and the Gentiles. Divine conquest and glorification are inevitable and imminent, so it is into this matrix the anticipated meeting between Jesus and the Greeks is placed, and from this understanding that Jesus knows his "hour has come" and the end is near. Just as John had stated, "He must increase, but I must decrease," so Jesus must now 'decrease' so that the "fruit" of his labours can increase. This notion of the "fruit" is one of issue, progeny, the ultimate result of all his 'work' in the 'world', the reaped rewards. The "fruit" is both the new divinely-sanctioned priestly kingdom at Shiloh *and* his own offspring, the progeny of the union between him and Mary, i.e., a truly Josephite future high priest and the dawning of a new age for the Remnant.

Jesus' farewell speech reiterates the concept of a death that brings life and speaks of the pain of a woman in childbirth. The scenario of a woman in childbirth is often linked with oppression and the anticipation of redemption, as in Isa 13:8; 21:3; Jer 4:31; Mic 4:10, etc., and the subsequent overriding sensation of joy once the child is born (John 16:20) is clearly an allusion to Jesus' anticipation for a successful end to his mission. Jesus has, metaphorically, struggled through a difficult 'birth' and his 'child', the new kingdom, is to be the cause of joy that will override the loss of his presence. The disciples, Jesus makes clear however, *will* see Jesus again.

An Ideal Israel
Getting back to the Greeks, what they have requested, significantly, is to "see Jesus" but Jesus himself declares that one who sees him sees the Father (John 14:9). The Greeks are Gentiles; they have no affinity for the religion of the Israelites. Theirs is a request based on curiosity and sensation, not upon faith. Had they requested to "see the Father" Jesus might well have obliged. As it is, the actual meeting is never mentioned; Jesus' cryptic response is directed only to Andrew and Philip, the two disciples who bear Greek names, suggesting that there is an exclusion zone here. Jesus' message

is *not* for the Gentiles but with his "glorification" the process will be set in motion that will return Israel to its original role as the righteous and exemplary leader of the rest of the world. There is no place for the Greeks in Jesus' concept of the new Israel. Andrew and Philip are simply oblivious to this distinction. Jesus is once again "troubled" in his spirit, as he was when he found Mary weeping; Philip, Jesus' firstborn and original potential protégée, and Andrew, the hopeful representative of the first to enter the new Promised Land, just don't get it.

It is the time for the 'son of man' to be glorified, the time for the 'house of Joseph' to be raised, the time for Jesus to earn his glory. When Jesus calls on God for further proof of his credentials (just as he prayed in order that the mourners at Lazarus' 'tomb' be convinced) a voice comes from heaven: "I have glorified it, and will glorify it again." If Jesus' fulfilment of his 'works' (in the raising of Lazarus) was to the glorification of God, what is meant by "I will glorify it again"?

The voice from heaven comes in the form of thunder because at Sinai, God says: "I am going to come to you in a dense cloud, in order that the people may hear (i.e., the thunder) when I speak with you and so trust you ever after" (Exod 19:9). That only some of Jesus' observers recognise the sound as a voice reiterates the schism between believers and non-believers throughout the gospel and, indeed, the exodus story. Yet, there is more in this short passage than meets the eye. We need to think about what has just happened: Jesus has been in Samaria with Lazarus and Mary, and the child—to all the world a child of either Lazarus *or* Jesus. They have ridden into Jerusalem in a provocative and symbolic show of victory, and have aroused the interest of some Greeks. Such a confirmation of Zechariah's oracle becomes a 'sign' that Jesus' time is almost up, but what of Shiloh?

Jesus prays that he will not be denied the final act of inaugurating the new gate of heaven, the new house of God at Shiloh, where the divine name will be present (i.e., the Ark will return) and the commandments will be followed. This implies but one thing: Jesus hopes to, in fact, *intends* to survive his impending capture and probable execution. Just as Lazarus' rescue from a symbolic death constituted the first glorification, so Jesus' future escape from real death will act as the second glorification. Yes, he will 'give his soul up to death' but I suggest Jesus *expects* God to intervene and save him, just as Isaac was reprieved, for instance.

If you will walk in my ways and keep my requirements,
then you shall rule my house and have charge of my courts,
and I will give you the right of access among
those who are standing here.
Zech 3:7

The interjection of Isaiah's declaration at John 12:38–40 serves to echo the sentiment of John 9 and the figurative theme of the 'blindness' of the 'servant' versus the 'blindness' of those who *will* not 'see'. It is not for Jesus to judge them; he has simply shown them the way to Shiloh. With several allusions to the 'light' of his truth and his mission, Jesus retreats yet again and we hear in his final cry a similar tension to that exhibited in John 7:37, when he called out in earnest to the gathering of priests on the last day of the Feast of Tabernacles. He is, effectively, telling those wavering Jews that this is their last chance to make their break. If they choose not to believe that Jesus is the one who will lead them into a new covenant with God, they will be left out.

17
MEAL 2: THE DAY OF PREPARATION

Preparation
THIS IS MORE LIKELY TO BE the Seder, the meal consumed on the eve of Passover, as several elements in the depiction correspond to the traditional meal rituals, such as the washing, the reclining position, etc., but Jesus adapts the situation to meet his own needs. It is also the second of Lazarus' ordination meals.

Prepare to meet your God, O Israel!
Amos 4:12

    The manifestation of Peter's rivalry can be seen in clearly this scenario and the surfacing of his true colours is aptly timed, for this is a turning point for Jesus' disciples. Peter, at first, reacts with astonishment to the apparent subservience of Jesus, who is washing the men's feet. When Jesus declares that without this cleansing ritual, there can be no share in the new kingdom, Peter over-reacts, desiring to have his hands bathed also, as if twice the deed could procure twice the share, i.e., the *traditional inheritance of the firstborn* (Deut. 21:17). At a Seder, the hands are ritually washed, suggesting yet again that Peter represents the 'old school', the priests who adhere to the letter of the law, not its spirit. In his request to receive additional cleansing, Peter unwittingly reveals his own dubious allegiance and ambition, and provides the opportunity for Jesus to remark on "the one" who is wholly clean, fully converted (i.e., "bathed"), Lazarus.
    The priestly aspect of this ritual is supported by Lev 16:4, which stipulates the ritualistic cleansing of the high priest before the Day of Atonement (and Jesus' personal Day of Atonement is fast approaching, as we will see); and, more pertinent in this immediate context, by Exod 30:18–21, where the high priest and his ministers are required to wash their hands and feet in a basin of water before approaching or entering the house of God (this again confirms Peter's institutionalised version of priesthood, as the dual washing is what he expects—it's what he is used to!).

Jesus refers to his elected body of disciples as his *huperetai*, or "ministers," reflecting their role as servants/ministers of the new high priest and they receive their foot-washing in preparation for the glorious entry into the new spiritual kingdom, Shiloh, i.e., sacred ground.

Jesus makes a point of the fact that he is called "Teacher" and the true teachers, so the OT states, are the legitimate priests; he accepts this honour.[1] He claims that the foot-washing is an example the twelve must follow; his "twelve" represent the twelve tribes of Israel, *united*, as on the high priest's breast piece). Jesus intends for all his ministers to be equal; there is no room for rivalries, no excuse for condemning those who are younger, or those who represent the northern factions, for example. All twelve must work together, as they represent the reunited "children of God." There is, however, a high priest, a master, a teacher, and this Jesus makes clear; he has already chosen his successor, so any rivalry is futile (John 13:10). Peter, however, is proving to be ambitious and untrustworthy.

The identity of the disciple the addendum (in John 13:23) refers to as "the one whom Jesus loved," has been a matter of debate amongst scholars for centuries. If we have followed all the clues thus far, however, we do not need the addendum, for we already know that Lazarus is Jesus' "beloved" disciple, by virtue of the father-son relationship. At the previous meal, Lazarus was the only disciple directly mentioned in terms of dining with Jesus, so the parallel here is fitting. Besides, the Greek text gives us a stronger idea of the closeness of the disciple, i.e., "reclining at the bosom of Jesus." Traditionally, the closer one sits to the host, the more respected or esteemed one is deemed, and even in today's political language, proximity implies power.

By now Lazarus is under a death threat also and after the triumphal entry into Jerusalem he is mentioned no more. The commission name Lazarus has served its function; now that the character has moved on, his name must change. It does so after this scenario, in which Judas and Peter play the key roles.

Reclining at Table?

For centuries, the western imposition of its own customs has obscured the true nature of this very simple meal, and only recently have a few interpreters begun to argue that Jesus and his group are not sitting upright at a long dining

---

[1] Verse 14 acknowledges the title but there is an addendum after the hyphen, in v.13; it so obviously attempts to confirm Jesus' divinity. However, the Greek word for Lord here implies only a master or one of higher status, such as 'sir'. The Christian scribe wants to emphasize Lord as in 'God'.

table (as traditionally depicted) but are reclining on couches, eating off three tables arranged in a 'U' formation known as a *triclinium*. This, they explain, is why the beloved disciple is said to be so close as to be able to 'recline' with his head near Jesus' chest. I have a problem with this, though.

Not only is this method of eating a Gentile method, it is usually restricted to the *upper classes* of Gentiles, such as the nobility. The Romans and the Greeks (and the wealthy Jews) who hold themselves in their own high opinion are the people who eat this way.[2] Can we really see the Jesus we now see in the FG emulating the very people he rejects as inconsequential? Why would he act like a Gentile, given how determined he seems to be to bring back the old Hebrew ways? Indeed, he seems to perceive himself as 'nobility' of a sort, but not *this* sort.

Jesus says "It is the one to whom I give this piece of bread when I have dipped it in the dish" (John 13:26); the word translated as "bread," however, is *psómion*, which means "bit/morsel." In the Seder, after the hand-washing, a vegetable (or 'greens', to represent new beginnings) is dipped into a bowl/cup of bitter liquid.

In the first instance of "reclining" in John 12:2, the word used to describe all the disciples 'at table' with Jesus is *sunanakeimai*, which is made up of three basic components: *sun-* "together/union"; *ana-* "each/several"; *keimai-* "to lie outstretched." The first component suggests a fairly intimate, friendly gathering, with the guests forming a close group. The second, used not as a prefix but within the body of the word, seems to suggest each man in the group. The third, which is what probably led translators to deduce that the men are propped up in this Gentile fashion, actually suggests *utter* prostration (as a corpse lies on the ground), which would be incongruent with dining (but could suggest resting afterwards). According to the Mishnah (Pesachim 10:1) all must recline when eating on the first night of Passover.

On the other hand, the latter portion of *sunanakeimai*, i.e., *keimai*, can also mean "to appoint, to set," etc. Thus, in the first meal scene, we see 'each man' in the group appointed, or set up as a minister, as a potential priest-to-be, which corresponds to the contemporaneous, symbolic foot-washing. In the meal of John 13, however, Lazarus, the beloved disciple, is singled out and the *sun-* prefix is removed. When *ana-* is used as a prefix, it means "again," implying repetition; Lazarus is thus *appointed*, or set up *again*, just as Jesus had promised Martha. Now Jesus' right-hand-man, his high-priestly deputy, Lazarus is entrusted with the place of honour at Jesus' 'bosom'.

---

[2] In Gen 37:25 we see diners sitting. In 1 Kgs 13:20 chairs and tables are used. By the time of Amos 6:4, reclining at table was fashionable for the elite but was clearly considered ostentatious and was held in contempt.

It is in this context of intimacy, of joining in a *communal* meal, in a *circle* on the floor, that Jesus assures his ministers that in the Father's house there are many "dwelling places." Again, this is a favourite passage in the Christian tradition, as it is said to imply that Jesus is offering Christianity to the entire world but the FG is not interested in the 'world'; it is interested in Israel, and the *ideal* Israel at that. Once Israel is redeemed, the rest of the world, theoretically, will follow.

In Ezekiel 45, there is a description of the *ideal* abode of God, the divine temple of the *eschaton* (end days), where there will be a place for *all* Israel: "it shall belong to the whole of the house of Israel ... And my princes shall no longer oppress my people; but they shall let the house of Israel have the land according to their tribes (Ezek 45:6, 8). The oppression, notice, is the oppression of the tribal representatives in the temple, the oppression Jesus has come to eradicate, *not* the Roman oppression.

Jesus' statement in John 13:16, then, with respect to the exemplary foot-washing, is underscored by the symbolism of the united circle of disciples, each representing a tribe, and emphasizes this necessity for equality, sincerity, and tolerance in the new order; 'love one another' he warns—he gives the first commandment of the new covenant. It comes as no surprise that in one of Ezra's visions (2 Esd 12:13–16) the new kingdom will be ruled by twelve "kings," each of *equal* duration (see the list of comparisons between the FG and the legends of King Arthur in "Excursus").

Peter

Peter's spiritual impotence, so obviously a factor of his representation in the lame man's story, reveals itself once more. Unable to speak to Jesus directly, Peter must employ Lazarus as mediator in his request to learn who is to be the one to betray Jesus. That he has to do this implies Peter is *not* in a position of high rank or favour, for he is not seated near Jesus. Consistent with his characterization in John 1, Peter does not 'hear' or 'understand' even at this late stage.

When Jesus tells his disciples that he will soon be leaving them, Peter has to ask, "Where?" Echoing the keenness he had exhibited during the washing, to show a desire for more responsibility and a greater status within the group, he is the first to offer to follow Jesus then and there; he will lay down his life for Jesus, he claims. Peter is afraid Jesus has guessed his underhandedness, perhaps, and worries he will be accused openly, so he becomes obsequious, feigning loyalty. Back in John 6:64, the author claims Jesus knew from the beginning who would not believe and who would betray him; this, of course, refers to the scene with Peter as the 'lame man' in John 5, i.e., Jesus knows the moment he meets Peter what a weak man he is. Peter is told in no uncertain terms, however, that *he* will deny Jesus three times before the "cock crows." The three denials, then, both parallel the three attempts at belittling Lazarus and contrast with the blind man's three affirmations of Jesus. Lazarus (the blind man) proves his loyalty; Peter proves he is not worthy of responsibility and this will be repeated in the FG's epilogue.

What many interpreters tend to overlook or underplay here is the connection between Judas' going out into the night to betray Jesus, and Peter's triple denial during the *same night*, before dawn. The parallel 'darkness' motif at this stage is significant, for it anticipates the arrest scene to come and the treacherous alliance between these two characters. Judas and Peter are symbolically linked in a partnership of subterfuge, a pairing which is anticipated in their respective relation to the name Simon, their tribal affinities (i.e., Peter is of Simeon and Judas of Judah, which become amalgamated), and their parallel connection to the "devil" theme, in John 6:67–70 (and this will become even clearer when we discuss the arrest). Peter has a vested interest in everything Judas does, for he seems to see Judas as the path to personal advancement so obviously unattainable in Jesus' clique.

The Iscariot

The precise interpretation of "Iscariot" is difficult and there have been various suggestions, including a "man of Kerioth" (a place in Moab mentioned in Jer 48:24, 41 and Amos 2:2), and 'nothing more than a surname'. It has also been suggested that the name relates to the Sicarii, the "dagger bearers" who were supposedly known rebels at the time but there are problems with this. Although the overall impression of Judas might suit such identification, according to Josephus (*Wars.* 2.13.3) the Sicarii did not fully arise until the era of Nero, after Herod's death. A ragtag group of armed rebels must have formed the basis of an organized group, so individuals with more militant ideals would probably have been drifting around before then. The Sicarii have also been identified with the Zealots, the "fourth sect" mentioned by Josephus (*Ant.* 18.1.6), whose violence and "immovable resolution" seemed mystifying to him, yet even these are said to arise during the time of Gessius Florus, which was in 64–6 CE. This does not really help to explain Judas, some thirty years prior to this, who is not *explicitly* mentioned as having a weapon, nor why it is that *Peter* is the one with a dagger during the arrest scene (unless Judas gives it to him, but this is not supported by the text).

Personally, I think there is a synthesis of the "Kerioth" aspect and the Hebrew (Aramaic) root for "falsehood" or "lie," *shaqar*, which suits the character well. In Psalms 41 and 53, for instance, the term is used to portray the "enemy"; Judas would thus become a 'liar', an 'enemy'. In almost every instance where *shaqar* is used in the OT there is a context of castigation, false pride, or conceit. Take Jer 13:25 for example, which exposes the falsehood of the priests and prophets and the folly of those who believe in them, and compare this to Jesus' accusation that the Jews follow the "father of lies." There is also Isaiah's attack on the "sentinels" of Israel (Isa 56:10) who have "turned to their own way," and on the "children of transgression" (57:4) whose mockery is turned against themselves. Micah claims that a false preacher represents a false people, and only those who 'break out' can follow the true 'king' the 'Lord' (2:11–13).

A city bearing the name Kerioth exists in the territory of Judah, making the tribal link complete (Josh 15:25) but it is Jeremiah's invective against Moab (Jeremiah 48) that offers us important clues as to Judas' nature and fate. The rebuke comes in the form of a prophecy of doom, an *inevitable* punishment for Moab's pride and arrogance. It is said that Moab has made Israel a "laughingstock" and has boasted falsely about deeds that were themselves false. In Jer 48:41, Kerioth (the proper name, curiously, is relegated to a footnote) is used as the representation of all the towns of Moab *chosen for destruction*. This is supported by Amos 2:2, which describes Kerioth as the "stronghold" of Moab, which will be devoured by fire.

Judas, in the Greek FG, is called the "son of destruction" (John 17:12, which the NRSV translates as the "one destined to be lost") and so this allusion to Kerioth is apt. As for making Israel a laughingstock and boasting proudly about false actions, all these become keen reflections of Judas' role in the FG as the narrative progresses. For instance, Jesus is ridiculed and humiliated in direct consequence of Judas' actions but, as Jer 48:26 predicts, Kerioth (Moab) will have the tables turned against it and will become the laughingstock in Israel's stead. That is, Judas is eventually destined to an ignominious demise and infamy, whilst Jesus, the one originally fated to be humiliated, is exalted—but there is another level to this that must await discussion!

Judas, then, is to be understood in terms of his relation to the 'stronghold' of a proud and arrogant people, to a people whose falsehood others foolishly accept and whose 'haughtiness' will eventually return to haunt them. He is symbolically associated with inevitable destruction simply by virtue of his commission name. The portrait of Judas in the FG falls neatly into the depiction of the extant priestly institution. His authority is likened to that of Simon, Captain of the Temple, who could challenge the administration of revenues, etc., and he is related by association (as a "son of destruction") to the "thieves and robbers" who do nothing but "destroy" (John 10:10). He is *linked with* the *diabolos* of 6:70 (i.e., as discussed, I

The Testament of Lazarus

argue this is a pro-Peter, Christian addendum and that Peter is the *diabolos* within Jesus' circle) and 13:2 ("The devil had already put it into the heart of Judas son of Simon Iscariot to betray him," i.e., Peter is linked to Caiaphas via their respective identifications as the *diabolos*, suggesting again that Peter is a priest); as a "liar" Judas is, almost certainly, under the influence of the deceitful "father of lies," Caiaphas, who is also referred to as a *diabolos* (8:44). Like the temple high priest, Judas is an 'enemy'. Now compare Judas with the "unnamed disciple" of John 1 and 18:

⋆ In John 1, the unnamed disciple's anonymity suggests potential for deception; Judas conducts his dealings with the opponents of Jesus under the cover of darkness.

⋆ In John 18:16 the unnamed disciple is "known" to the high priest; in John 18:3, Judas is seen to be in league with chief priests, who are acting on Caiaphas' 'orders'.

⋆ The unnamed disciple is present at the arrest of Jesus (John 18:15); Judas is present at the arrest.

⋆ There is an apparently consistent association between Peter and the unnamed disciple that is ultimately in conflict with Jesus' mission; Judas and Peter are linked throughout the FG and, as we shall see, their combined efforts hail potential disaster for Jesus.

It would seem that Judas and the unnamed disciple of John 1 and 18 are one and the same. It would also make sense if Judas is the mole who keeps the Jews informed regarding Jesus' whereabouts and actions. No wonder the 'spies' or emissaries keep turning up all over the place! They have a vested interest in Jesus and his mission and Judas is their means of keeping tabs on what he is doing and we *know* this to be the case in the arrest scene. Originally sent out to spy on John, Judas, highly ranked within the temple cultus (this gradually becomes clearer), is an infiltrator, an informer, a plant. It is Peter's influence, however, that tips the balance and makes him a reluctant traitor.

Philip's Fall
In John 14:9–10 Philip's weak facility for faith and understanding reaches a critical point. Back in John 6 he had failed miserably the simple test Jesus had set before him and in 12:20f he had attempted to introduce the Greeks, with much the same degree of success. Philip behaves just as the Greeks had, in that he fails to see the Father in Jesus (even more ironic if Jesus *is* his biological father). His initial optimistic election by Jesus (which I suspect

would have been encouraged by Martha, perhaps once she realised Jesus had chosen Mary to bear his child) and his potentially symbolic role in John 6 have come to nothing. "Have I been with you all this time, Philip, and you still do not know me?" Jesus asks, and we perceive a degree of frustration, or annoyance: 'If you are not going to believe *who* I am, believe in *what* I am doing', his words imply. Herein lays the crux of the FG and its account of Jesus: believe in the 'word' (i.e., the will) of *God* and the results will justify the messenger. If Jesus' credentials are false, his deeds will come to nothing but if his message is true, he will be vindicated and glorified (John 8:13–14).

Although Philip misses out on his chance to succeed Jesus and fades into the background of the narrative, he maintains his status as a 'loved' disciple and is there at the end of the gospel.

The Other Judas

There is a subsequent reference to "Judas" which is (aptly) deceptive. The addendum in John 14:22 insists that the Judas of this particular scene is *not* the Iscariot, implying the sudden interjection of a name already employed but now wholly unconnected with the narrative in any other sense! This is not the way the FG works. The addendum is partially correct; this is, indeed, *another* Judas but *not* a new disciple!

Recall that Peter and Judas are linked by their tribal affiliations, where Simeon is strongly influenced by Judah and is all but assimilated. They are also linked in their mutual nocturnal duties. It is in this context we must interpret this second Judas but before we do, in order to understand the subtleties of the naming here, we must look at the disciple "Thomas, who [is] called Didymus."

"Thomas" is a Hebrew name, translated to mean "twin" but the Greek "Didymus" *also* means "twin." There is, then, in keeping with the consistently ambiguous, dual representation of people and places in the gospel, a *double* emphasis placed upon the 'twin' aspect of this character, causing the reader to take note and investigate. We need to ask ourselves the following questions: Who, in the FG, is the only disciple who explicitly receives an alternative nickname? Who is it that has *both* Hebrew and Greek names? Which two disciples have a name in common (i.e., Simon)? Which disciple is associated with another, so much so as to imply his shadow, or twin? Of *whom* is Thomas a twin? There is no other answer than Peter, the effective 'twin' of Judas. Peter and Andrew are merely 'brothers' by profession and they have no ongoing relationship in the FG, so this is not an option.

The primary and fundamental characteristic of any twin in the Bible is that of rivalry. Esau and Jacob (Gen 25:22ff) vie for the position of firstborn; Perez and Zerah (Gen 38:27–30) struggle even during delivery for the rights of succession; Ephraim and Manasseh (Gen 41:50ff) are fated to compete for supremacy. If Thomas is identified with Peter, this rivalry theme would be consistent with his desire to obtain the rights of the firstborn.

First appearing in John 11:16 as the disciple overtly keen to accompany Jesus into Judea despite the danger, Thomas reveals his reflection of Peter both in his ignorance and in his keen enthusiasm. His words are ambiguously phrased and can relate either to Jesus or Lazarus. For instance, Jesus has just explained in the parable of the 'twelve hours' (11:9–10) that righteousness is the light by which God's chosen can walk without stumbling; he fully expects to be protected until his works are complete. For Thomas to suggest that *Jesus* will die is to deny faith in Jesus (and therefore the will of God). If this is, however, an allusion to the symbolic 'death' *Lazarus* is undergoing, then Thomas must have an idea of what is going on and, echoing Peter's overzealous enthusiasm, he presumptuously suggests that the rest of the disciples do likewise. If he does not understand the subtleties of the event and truly believes Lazarus has died, then Thomas' apparent bravery serves to foreshadow Peter's declaration, "*I will lay down my life for you*" (John 13:37). Both are vacuous statements. Whichever way you look at it, Thomas and Peter speak with the same voice.

Similarly, in John 14:5, Thomas reveals his apparent ignorance by claiming that he does not really understand "where" Jesus is going, nor how to follow him (he does not understand the significance of Shiloh). Jesus responds by reiterating the idea that only those who aspire to the kingdom of God through *him* can know the Father. Jesus emphasizes that Thomas *does* know and *has* seen the Father, i.e., in Jesus himself. Peter's denial is thus implicitly foreshadowed.

In this supper scene, the other Judas becomes involved in a dialogue with Jesus concerning the apparently subversive nature of the mission: "how is it that you will reveal yourself to us, and not to the world?" he inquires, in a taunting manner, paralleling the urging statement in John 7:4, where Jesus is advised to make himself known in Judea, despite the dangers there. It is at *this moment*, the moment during which the Iscariot is off betraying Jesus to the authorities (something the lame man had also done, recall), that Peter/Thomas 'becomes' a Judas (i.e., the tribe of Simeon becomes assimilated into Judah) and is inextricably linked to Jesus' imminent capture and execution.

Early Christian tradition actually *identified* Thomas as "Judas Thomas," inadvertently, or perhaps intentionally, *making* him "Judas' Twin." It is also worth pointing out that Peter's derogatory name, Cephas, is phonetically very similar to the Hebrew word *chephes*, or *chaphas,* which means "covert," "disguised," etc.)

Jesus responds directly to this disciple, by making the distinction between those who love him and keep his commandments (and therefore the 'word' of God) and those who do not. He intimates that *this* Judas falls into the latter category, i.e., those who do not 'love' him. What the English translation loses, however, is the fact that John 14:23–4 contains the very key to the testing of Peter in John 21, i.e., a threefold expression of 'love', each based on the verb *agapao* – to love with *devotion*. The disciple who 'loves' Jesus will be 'loved' by the Father but whoever does not 'love' him will not keep his 'words'.

Peter, until this moment, has just been Judas' 'twin' but now he is the very essence of Judas himself.[3]

The *parakletos*

Unlike the Latin term *advocatus* ("advocate," as the NRSV reads), which has legal connotations, the Greek *parakletos*, simply indicates a person called to the aid of one in need of assistance, i.e., a 'helper'. The commission name Lazarus, recall, means (in one of its many facets) "God is helper," and we know that he has been preparing as Jesus' successor, so let us just see if the role of *parakletos* fits the character of Nicodemus' son, the blind man, Lazarus:

✶ The *parakletos* is evidently a man in whom the 'spirit of truth' resides, for Jesus claims the disciples already know him and that he will be 'amongst' them (John 14:17); Lazarus receives the 'spirit' at the Pool of Siloam and during his 'raising', and he is amongst the disciples.

✶ He was not known to the disciples at the outset (John 15:27); Lazarus first appears as the young boy in John 4:46f but is kept at a distance, not being "of age" until formally appearing as the blind man.

---

[3] In Josephus (*Ant.* 17.10.5-6), a certain Simon, a "slave of the king" (see "Mutilating Malchus" below), attempts to set himself up as a king, apparently thinking "himself more worthy ... than anyone else." Immediately prior to this, a "robber" called Judas did a similar thing, but with more violence. These characters were well known rebels; so again, local history might have served to add verisimilitude to the FG. I did have a passing consideration that Judas might be related to Peter, e.g., his son, hence the emphasis on "son of Simon" in the Greek. The only Simon we are introduced to is Peter.

⋆ The *parakletos* will be sent from the Father after Jesus negotiates his appointment (John 14:16, 15:26); Lazarus stays with Jesus, in 21:22, preparing for and confirming his new position as Jesus' successor.

⋆ He will be sent in Jesus' name (John 14:26); Lazarus adopts Jesus' family name later in the FG.

⋆ The *parakletos* will testify on Jesus' behalf (John 15:26) and this testimony will vindicate Jesus' mission and confirm the conquest of his adversaries (16:8–11); Lazarus is the author of the FG (e.g., 21:24), which vindicates Jesus' mission in terms of the creation of the new priesthood and kingdom, and his battle against the forces of 'darkness'.

⋆ His arrival is contingent upon the glorification of Jesus (John 16:7); Lazarus' position is dependent upon Jesus' 'exaltation' as King of Israel, and on the elevation of the ideal Israel at Shiloh, i.e., Jesus' work must be justified.

⋆ The *parakletos* will convey "whatever he hears" (John 16:13); as the blind man, Lazarus affirms Jesus' role to any who will listen, as Lazarus he conveys Peter's request for knowledge, and as Jesus' successor, he will convey what he 'hears' from his master and from God.

⋆ He will be the cause of Jesus' glorification (John 16:14); the raising of Lazarus is the act that will glorify Jesus.

⋆ The *parakletos* will "take what is [Jesus'] and will declare it'" (John 16:15); Lazarus inherits both Jesus' status and family, and the child he will take as his own and 'declare' as King when he is 'of age'.

⋆ He will have a similar relationship with Jesus as Jesus has with the Father (John 16:15); Lazarus is Jesus' adoptive/representative 'son' as Jesus is (symbolically) the Father's son.

> *When the father dies he will not seem to be dead,*
> *for he has left behind him one like himself.*
> Eccl 30:4

It is rather an uncanny coincidence if these similarities in depiction are unintentional; it is far more likely the case that the *parakletos* is, or *is to be found within*, the disciple Lazarus, who is elevated to a unique position within the community after Jesus' departure from the 'world'.

It is also just after Peter's apparent vie for supremacy during the foot-washing that Jesus says: "Whoever receives *one whom I send* receives me; and whoever receives me receives him who sent me" (John 13:20), meaning only those who accept Jesus' successor will see the Father and will enter the kingdom of God (at Shiloh). The 'sending' aspect clearly echoes the 'sending' of the blind man to the Pool of Siloam (a name the addendum actually translates as "sent"). The term *parakletos* is a commission name but of a different sort; as with a prophet, it is the 'spirit' *within* that is significant, not the vehicle in which it is conveyed, i.e., the man. As the *new* kingly high priest in Jesus' stead, Lazarus *will* fulfil the anticipated role of the 'helper' (i.e., to assist the new ministers in their responsibilities in the absence of Jesus) but in the interim he will take on two *more* commission names!

18
LAW AND ORDER

The Arrest

THE SITE OF JESUS' ARREST is, at least traditionally, the "garden of Gethsemane" at the foot of the Mount of Olives but let us look at the evidence from the FG perspective. To start with, the 'garden' in which Jesus is arrested is not given a name. The Mount of Olives is an ancient site of worship and the link in the Synoptics to Jesus going there to pray as he agonizes over his fate and the outcome of his mission, is based on the incident with King David in 2 Samuel 15.

David's throne is under threat of usurpation by his ambitious son, Absalom, who conspires against the king in secret, gaining support of the masses who are, apparently 'innocent' of the treachery. David decides to flee, taking the Ark of the Covenant and his entire household with him but when a certain Ittai (which means "God is with me"), who is new to David's house, is offered his freedom (lest he also be put into danger), Ittai says, "As the Lord lives, and as my lord the king lives, wherever my lord the king may be, whether for death or for life, there also your servant will be" (2 Sam 15:21); this parallels John 12:26 and may reflect Lazarus' role. David agonizes over the fate of Jerusalem and his decision to remove the Ark from the temple and decides to send the priests back into the city; if he is truly God's chosen one, he will be vindicated and will return in triumph. At one stage, David goes up onto the Mount of Olives to pray "where God [is] worshipped." A messenger arrives and prostrates himself before the king, pressing his face to the ground as a sign of respect but also as an act of praise for David's vindication; he truly *is* in God's 'favour'. Absalom, the traitor, eventually receives his just reward and is found 'hanging' in a tree, where he is put to death (sounds like Judas?).

The name *Kidron* means "a dark place' and by extension "a place of mourning"; this area is the site of an ancient burial ground, so the connotation is apt.

The Missing Torrent
The significant aspect of David's escape in 2 Samuel, as far as locating Jesus' 'garden' is concerned, is *where* David goes to flee the traitor. He leaves the City of David, *crosses over* the "torrent Kidron" and moves toward the wilderness, which is to the north. *Then* he reaches the Mount of Olives, and ascends it; the Mount is some distance from the city and the "torrent Kidron."

In the description of John 18:1, according to the NRSV, Jesus goes with his disciples *"across the Kidron* to a place where there was a garden." Tradition holds that this must mean the "garden" is on the Mount of Olives. In the original Greek, the wording is: Jesus went out "across the *torrent* of Kidron," just as in the precedent with David. *Flowing water* is implied by the name but in Jesus' day, so it is thought, the area of Kidron is devoid of water. Is this an obvious error by the FG author or another of his clever clues?

Some early Christian scholars tried to justify this discrepancy by suggesting that there once ran through the Mount of Olives area (where they assumed the 'garden' was located, thanks to the Synoptics) a seasonal brook; they called it the "winter-torrent" but there is scant (if any) evidence for this. To increase its flow to anything more than a trickle heavy winter rains would be needed but, come April (Nisan, the month of Passover), such torrential downpours would be unlikely. The "torrent (wadi) Kidron" of David's day was probably the original flow of the Gihon spring before it was diverted into the city. This was to the *south* of the Mount of Olives, immediately opposite the old City, in the low conflux of the valleys of Hinnom and Kidron. The FG author is apparently providing us with an oxymoron, a deliberately erroneous juxtaposition; this usually means we are to find a deeper meaning from a precedent in the Jewish scriptures and to apply it to the situation at hand.

Intriguingly, there are only six passages in the OT where the two words "torrent" and "Kidron" appear together, which makes our detective work a little easier, and only one proves germane to the FG, i.e., 1 Kgs 2:37, which reads: "For on the day you go out, and cross the torrent Kidron, know for certain that you shall die; your blood shall be on your own head."[1] The context of both 1 Kgs 2:37 and the 2 Sam 15:23 precedents (see footnote below) is one of *disassociation* from Jerusalem, that is, the crossing of the

---

[1] The others are 2 Sam 15:23 (King David leaves Jerusalem and heads into the wilderness); 2 Kgs 23:6 (the Asherah is burned and its ashes spread over the graves nearby); 2 Kgs 23:12 (ashes of burnt altars are thrown in); 2 Chr 30:14 (illicit altars broken and thrown into it, suggesting some depth); Jer 31:40 (mentioned as a boundary only).

Kidron waters symbolises one's removal from or rejection of the city and thus the nation.

Jesus is in Bethany in John 13. His *alleged* final words, "Rise, let us be on our way," have never been satisfactorily explained but they would make sense if the group is now to make their way *back* into Jerusalem for Jesus' expected capture. Only, Jesus supposedly carries on talking; he offers his final advice and warnings whilst enroute *to* Jerusalem, it would seem. When he reaches the Valley of Kidron, his words spent, the city of Jerusalem immediately before him, he steels himself for the point of no return, i.e., the crossing of the 'torrent', his own Rubicon, one could say. Thus, Jesus and the disciples cross the valley at the same point David had crossed but are heading in the *opposite* direction, i.e., not away from the city but toward it.

Thus, if 1 Kgs 2:37 is in any way a clue or precedent, we can deduce that in *reversing* the direction, the opposite outcome can be expected, i.e., 'you shall live'! Remember, too, that Jesus, as the Samaritan Taheb, is destined to unite the kingdom, to take the throne of Judah as half of the new Israel. Thus, Jesus must not be seen crossing the Kidron *away* from the city, rejecting what he believes he has conquered; he must enter Jerusalem and reassert his victory. There is, however, another precedent that provides us with not only the crossing of water into a new kingdom but also, the focus on priests, bare feet, following, and the Ark. Take a look at Joshua 3.

Joshua and the tribes who have followed him are instructed by God to cross the Jordan in a manner not unlike the crossing of the Red Sea by Moses. After three days of camping by the overflowing river (i.e., a torrent) the people are told to sanctify themselves because the *next day* is going to be a day of divine signs and wonders. The priests, of whom twelve are selected to carry the Ark, are told that when the soles of their feet enter the water the river will be parted and a passage across made clear for them. The people are told that when they see the priests carrying the Ark, they "will know the way" and must follow at a respectable distance (of 2000 cubits). So, we have the allusions to a priestly context; the possession of the Ark and the duty to follow it; and the purification of those who will cross over into the new world. Is Jesus emulating his namesake again here? Joshua leads his people across the Jordan and into the new kingdom.

Joshua 3	**FG**
Torrent (Jordan)	Torrent (Kidron)
Encampment	Holed up in Bethany

Sanctification the day before	Disciples made 'clean' day before arrest
12 priests, one per tribe	12 'ministers', one per tribe
People told how to know the way (how to follow)	Peter/Thomas suggest they don't know the way (how to follow)
Priests feet in water a sign	Ministers' feet washed (sign)
Cross together	Cross together
Take the city of Jericho	'Conquest' over Judah

Garden Fit for a King

John 18:1–2 suggests that Jesus and his disciples enter the "garden" on several occasions. Judas, we are told, "knows" of this meeting place. Considering the Synoptic idea of the site being the Mount of Olives, it must be remembered that the Mount of Olives, a mile-long ridge to the east of the city, has *several* 'peaks', each given a name; the original Mount of Olives was the northernmost peak, near which are an ancient burial ground and the Fullers Field, suggesting potential purity issues. It would not have been a secluded site for clandestine meetings, which is what John 18:2 suggests, i.e., Judas "knew the place" (didn't everyone?). Both issues have a bearing on the FG's location of the "garden."

The Hebrew word for garden, *gan*, derives from *ganan,* meaning "protect/defend" and most gardens, especially those involving (expensive) irrigation, or unusual plants, etc., are either walled, or hedged (e.g., Prov 24:13, Isa 5:5). There is often a watchtower, or hut, in which resides the gardener (Job 27:18). I think *this* is the type of 'garden' Jesus and his disciples retreat 'into' when they want to be alone and away from prying eyes; there is much secrecy and 'planning' that needs to take place; there are members of the temple cultus and/or the even the army who need to converse with Jesus concerning his demonstrations and how they can help him, etc. The Mount of Olives would be too exposed and frequented to be a safe rendezvous point. There is an enclosed, protected garden, however, just across the Wadi ('torrent') Kidron" (as one approaches the city, as Jesus is doing), i.e., the King's Garden, which backs onto the city wall. Jesus is the

King of Israel, supposedly, so the site would be fitting for this reason alone but as we shall see, there is much more to it than that.

Faint Soldiers
When Jesus declares himself, using the now familiar "I AM" phrase, the reaction of the arresting officers is to step back and fall to the ground as if overcome by the strength of his words. The men say they seek "Jesus the Nazorean (of Nazareth)," the symbolic title *we* already comprehend. Jesus acknowledges this title by linking it with the divine "I AM." In a similar context to that presented in the story of David (2 Samuel 15), falling to the ground is an act that depicts the recognition of divine will. Similarly, in 2 Maccabees 3:14f, those who storm the holy temple are made "faint with terror" by the "power of God":

> And see that you who have been flogged by heaven, report to all people the majestic power of God .... For he who has his dwelling in heaven watches over that place himself and brings it aid, and he strikes and destroys those who come to do it injury.
> 2 Macc 3:34, 39

The imagery is undoubtedly symbolic, meant to convey the ease with which God can smite the foe; just the utterance of the "I AM" is enough to (figuratively) knock the soldiers off their feet! The reader must keep in mind, though, that Jesus is but a conduit through which the 'will' of God is revealed. He has yet to fully inaugurate the new kingdom, so he must be protected until then; Jesus does, indeed, have supporters among the temple 'security staff'—he would have to. It may well be that this little scene confirms that, i.e., though some soldiers simply follow orders and attempt to arrest Jesus, others step in and try to stop them. This could very well be a sign of an escalation in the violence of the situation Peter misinterprets, or sees as a distraction so he can take control (see below). The FG author exploits it as a scene of God intervening, as Jesus always expected.

There is also an apparent echo of the emissaries' failure to 'see' the one who comes to save Israel, for now Judas stands amongst his compatriots, unable to recognise 'Jesus the Nazorean' *or* the power/authority of the 'I AM'. Revealing yet again his alienation from the new order, Judas sees only the troublemaker, the priestly pretender, the threat. As a priest of the current institution, he does not recognise "I AM" because he does not have "I AM" (God) within him.

The Mutilation of Malchus
One of the most obscure figures of the FG is this man named Malchus (John

18:10f), a name that is derived from the Hebrew, *melek*, which means "king" or "royalty." Ultimately, it stems from *malak* which means "to ascend, set up, reign" and is linked to *mal'ak*, which means "to dispatch as a deputy," i.e., to be a priest, teacher, or messenger.

Malchus is said to be the servant of the "high priest" but, just as in the portrayal of the contrasting unnamed disciples, i.e., one who is Judas and the other who is Lazarus, so the FG author exploits this ambiguous characterization to emphasize the context of confrontation and the dual claim to supremacy, for there are now apparently *two* high priests, i.e., the "father of lies" (the high priest of the temple, Caiaphas) and Jesus. Who have we encountered in the narrative, thus far, who can possibly be connected to both the 'kingly' interpretation of the name *and* the high priest? Lazarus! As the son of the "royal official" in John 4, Lazarus inherits the role as servant to the king (Jesus); as Jesus' heir-elect he acts as deputy and, as the future *parakletos*, a 'messenger'. The Greek term for "servant/slave" is *doulos*, which stems from *deo*, meaning "to bind" and thus reminds us of the imagery of Lazarus 'bound' in his 'tomb'. Back in the foot-washing scene of John 13, Jesus calls his new priestly ministers "servants," which provides an internal precedent.

Adding to the priestly nature of Malchus, the name is a possible reflection of the Greek term *malakos*, which indicates something "soft or fine"; the priestly vestments and the tabernacle curtains, etc., are all referred to 'soft' or 'fine' materials. As Jesus' new priesthood is symbolic of the cleansed, purified ministry of the new kingdom of God, the allusion to the 'soft robes' echoes the symbolic exchange of "filthy" clothes for new ones (Zechariah 3) that is also alluded to in John 11.

The most obvious precedent of a name derived from *malak*, however, is in Gen 14:18f: Melchizedek ("King of Righteousness") is *both king and high priest*. The connection to Melchizedek has already proven significant in the FG and we know that Jesus (and by extension, his heir) is considered a kingly high priest. There is also the king's servant in Jer 38:7f, called Ebed-Melech, who saves Jeremiah from certain death and who is assured that he will not fall by the 'sword' because he has believed in God and in the prophet. Malchus, we will soon see, is attacked with a sword but escapes with his life.

Most significantly, in 1 Samuel 22:14f there is Ahimelech, the priest of Nob, who protects David when Saul is on the warpath. Because of their loyalty to David, Ahimelech and his fellow priests are sentenced to death but "the servants of the king" refuse to "raise their hand against the priests of the Lord." In order to get into Saul's good books, Doeg the Edomite takes it upon himself to attack the priests and he kills eighty-five of them ... but one of Ahimelech's sons, Abiathar, escapes to perpetuate the priestly line. Oddly enough, this is the priestly line of Eli, *High Priest of Shiloh*!

The mysterious figure of Malchus, then, is Lazarus, Jesus' successor, under a new commission name; circumstances have changed, making the deputy the *acting* high priest.

Recalling the discussion of John 8:39f, where Jesus alludes to the 'children' of Abraham and the failure of the Jews to defer to Jesus' higher authority, the introduction of Malchus into the narrative allows for another interesting pattern similar to that involving Andrew and the unnamed disciple, and the early settlers of Canaan:

Abraham honours Melchizedek
Abraham's children honour Jesus (the new Melchizedek)
Children of the kingdom of God honour Lazarus (Malchus)

There have already been hints of the rather one-sided rivalry between Peter and Lazarus, e.g., the desire on Peter's part to receive the share of the firstborn (symbolically), the opposing depictions of the two characters in terms of their loyalty to Jesus, and the potential for Peter's involvement in Lazarus' arrest. All this was just the tip of the iceberg. Because of Peter's outrageous behaviour toward Malchus, and the significance attributed to this new character, we can safely assume that what we are witnessing here is another attempt to remove Lazarus from his elevated position. This is one of those scenes that forces us to reconsider the degree of violence Jesus tolerates amongst his group. We have seen how Peter, as the lame man, was (apparently) verbally threatened by Jesus himself, and how certain other instances might warrant or even require a little force (e.g., the freeing of Lazarus, the warning that Jesus is not 'alone', etc.). What interests me in this scene is the fact that Jesus does not seem at all *surprised* that one of his men is carrying a weapon. In fact, the subject crops up again, when we deal with Pilate. It only really makes sense in light of the violent tumult on Mount Gerizim.

The word for "sword" in the Greek text is *machaira*, which actually represents a large knife or dagger, rather than a true sword (i.e., *xiphos*), implying the possibility of concealment (hence the possible connection to the Sicarii), and there is a biblical precedent for such a weapon, in Judg 3:16–22. That Jesus simply tells Peter to put his dagger back into its sheath and that he does not say something like, 'Peter, who told you to come armed?' or 'I told you never to use a weapon', makes me think he has known all along that Peter is armed—perhaps that *all* his disciples are armed (as the Samaritans were on Mount Gerizim).

On the other hand, the biblical definition of a soldier is simply "one who draws a sword" (2 Kgs 3:26) and Josephus (*Wars*. 18.3.2) describes an incident where a body of *Roman soldiers* intent on surprising a group of rebellious Jews (i.e., those petitioning against Pilate's intended usurpation of temple funds) are concealing daggers under *their* clothes. Jesus' rebellious group is considered an equal threat, e.g., as armed soldiers. In addition, this is a clue to Peter's allegiances. Luke's version of this scene reads: "Have you come out with swords and clubs as if I were a bandit?" (Luke 22:52). This is an understandable, historically sound and congruous perception, considering the fact that Jesus is, by every definition, a rebel. Luke, realising the provocative nature of the situation, however, exonerates Jesus of any overtly violent tendencies.

The term *machaira* is also used to describe the opposite state to 'peace', implying *intended* confrontation, not simply self-defence (cf. Matt 10:34), for it ultimately stems from *machomi*, "to war, quarrel, dispute," etc. What, though, is Peter disputing? How does he know what is about to take place in the garden (and thus the need to be armed) if he, like the other disciples at the dining table in John 13 simply thought that Judas had left the room, momentarily, on business pertaining to the group?

It is only when Jesus demands that his disciples be set free (notice, they do not 'abandon' him) that Peter strikes, as if he sees some opportunity slipping away. He lashes out, not in defence of an attack on Jesus, for none is mentioned (the guards supposedly fall, remember) but in an offensive attack against *Malchus*, the young Lazarus, heir to the highest position in the new order. Recall that Peter had waited thirty-eight years for a chance of promotion since Eleazar was made high priest; now he is witnessing another Eleazar (Lazarus) advance to the highest status "before him." It is more than Peter can bear. Echoing Doeg the Edomite, Peter is revealing his allegiance to Judas, and thereby to the (temple) high priest; he is willing to do what the guards are not.

By striking off the *right ear*, Peter re-enacts the disqualification of Hyrcanus II, whose right lobe was severed by Antigonus in a bid to render him unfit for the office of high priest (Josephus, *Wars.* 1.13. 9). According to Exod 29:20, in addition to the anointing of the head, the new priest is to be anointed on the right ear lobe, right toe, and right thumb; imposing a blemish, especially to one of these sacred parts, would normally prohibit the priest's functional duties (Lev 21:17f, etc., cf. Lev 8:23).[2]

In the FG, however, we have already witnessed the manner in which Peter is excluded from the intimacy that Jesus and his beloved, Lazarus, enjoy. At the meal in John 13, his question is never really answered; only Lazarus is privy to Jesus' response. Peter's actions here, in the garden, are made not only superfluous but pitiful, for nothing he does to Lazarus now

---

[2] In Luke 22:51 the ear is miraculously reattached, i.e., Jesus nullifies the action.

can alter the fact that a new, *hereditary* priestly kingdom is established (cf. John 12:16).

There is another sense in which Peter's hasty actions result in an unwitting confirmation of Lazarus' (Malchus') position; in Exod 21:2–6, there is a law pertaining to the release of male Hebrew slaves (Malchus is Hebrew, a male, and a slave/servant of the high priest). After a period of six years, "in the seventh" (there is that special number again), he shall be 'set free' but if he should declare his 'love' for his wife, children, and master, and choose to stay, his ear is to be pierced, signifying his life-long devotion.

Peter, still carrying the weapon he (probably) brought with him to Mount Gerizim, lashes out at the newly appointed deputy high priest, Lazarus. Hoping to disqualify him from serving as Jesus' second, Peter reveals his desperation and limited understanding of Jesus' mission. When we recall that Lazarus was made Jesus' deputy at the meal in John 12, six days before Passover, the seventh day, i.e., Passover, is the day Malchus the 'slave' will be granted the honour of having his ear pierced (metaphorically speaking). Thus, although Peter attempts to thwart Lazarus' ascension, ultimately, he reinforces the concept of election and honour by unwittingly imposing the 'piercing' himself!

Peter's personal ambition simply gets the better of him. He has created for himself two possible courses of action. If he can get Lazarus off the scene, he may be able to usurp the position of the firstborn and thus put an end to 'others getting' promotion before him, or, he can side with Judas and the cohort and secure a good position as a reward for helping to thwart Jesus. Whichever side wins, he seems to think, he can exploit the situation. That he is *known* as the one who is easily swayed, that Jesus constantly refers to him in the shadow of Judas' influence, and that he seems so keen to show that he is not one of Jesus' trusted men, suggests that Peter and Judas *are,* indeed, co-conspirators.

It is to this intended coup, then, that Jesus responds by asking, 'Am I not to drink the cup the Father has given me?' Jesus has worked hard to establish this new priestly line—is Peter really going to deny Jesus his long-awaited moment of glory by getting them *all* killed? Jesus calms the situation, as if recalling what had happened on Mount Gerizim; there has been enough bloodshed.

Cockcrow

Soldiers, officers, and the Jewish police are involved in Jesus' arrest but when the action shifts to the site of the inquest, 'servants' are again mentioned and in *direct* relation to Peter's anticipated denial. The first person to query Peter's involvement is said to be a female "gatekeeper" but there is problem—women do not perform this function.

According to 1 Chr 9:17–27, the gatekeepers (guardians of entrances) are all *sons* of Levites, i.e., men. There is a context in which women *are* seen to "serve at the entrance of the tent of meeting" (Exod 38:8) but according to 1 Sam 2:22, this seems to be one of prostitution (indeed, the idea of the priests cavorting with prostitutes has already surfaced in the FG). They are not there as 'guards'. So why would the FG author say a female gatekeeper is there at the arrest, and *why* would she bother speaking to Peter? The function of door/gatekeeper, therefore, must be metaphorical and used as a play on Jesus' own analogy of the "door/gate."

In the NRSV, the term translated as "woman" here (which would normally be the Greek word *gune*) is *paidiske*, i.e., "maidservant" or "female servant." Jesus' disciples are his 'servants'; which female follower would be a fitting character to receive the added attribute of 'gatekeeper' (and who has been depicted in a context of illicit sexuality)? Mary Magdalene, of course. The new 'gate', the *son* of Jesus (i.e., Jesus is the gate, so his son follows suit), is what Mary, the mother, guards.[3]

Judas says something to her; we do not know what—maybe a threat, maybe a warning to keep away? We already know his attitude toward her since his flagrant disdain when she anointed Jesus' feet. If she has approached the Cheil, the boundary between sanctified and profane (or less sanctified) areas of the precinct, she may be receiving a scolding, for she has recently given birth and there are strict stipulations prohibiting such women from entering this area.

Mary speaks up, aware that she is risking arrest, urging Peter to remember his allegiance to Jesus. The NRSV alters the emphasis of the question by phrasing it: "You are not also one of this man's disciples, are you?" In the Greek, however, it is: "Are you not also of the disciples of this man?" This original phrasing more strongly suggests that the woman *knows* Peter is a disciple, and is trying to get him to admit it, whereas the English version intimates that the woman can scarcely believe Peter would be involved with this 'criminal'. That makes for a very different interpretation of what is going on.

This instigates Peter's first denial.

---

[3] Recall the emphasis placed on 'gates' throughout the FG narrative: the Sheep [Gate], the allusion to the Gate of Ephraim (Fish Gate), the illicit rulers who enter not by the gate, the allusion to Jacob's vision of the 'gate of heaven' which was in Samaria, etc.

The Testament of Lazarus

Denial

We are told that the servants and the temple police have made a coal fire to warm themselves and that Peter is with them. This is an odd little detail to throw into such a significant scene, so there must be more to it than mere narrative embellishment (which is all but lacking throughout). The fire itself offers the clue and it is symbolically linked to the imagery of a 'gate'.

Fire, in the OT, is a very common theme, ranging from the burning of sacrifices, to the presence of God himself (e.g., as in the "pillar of fire" in the exodus story). We have also encountered the single burning coal pressed against the lips of the prophet, in order to cleanse his mouth so that nothing but the 'truth' can be spoken. The coal fire is a refining fire and is used as a divine tool for *testing and separating* the righteous from the wicked (e.g., Ezek 22:17–22, Mal 3:2–4):

> They are all stubbornly rebellious, going about with slanders; they are bronze and iron, all of them act corruptly. The bellows blow fiercely, the lead is consumed by the fire; in vain the refining goes on, for the wicked are not removed. They are called 'rejected silver,' for the Lord has rejected them.
>
> Jer 6:28–30

What an apt moment to allude to the fire of judgement. We know Peter is the one who must be disciplined and humbled, and the fire scene reminds us that he is *not* the one chosen by Jesus to be his successor; this is the moment of *his* 'rejection' (and it will be repeated in John 21). The fire in this scene is seldom mentioned by scholars as being anything more than an aspect of the setting, or maybe a sign that Peter is trying to pretend he is just one of the crowd, warming himself. It proves to be quite significant not only in this chapter of the FG but also in John 21. It also provides an important clue as to the location of this pivotal scenario, which will be discussed in a moment.

Peter is mentioned as being around the fire again in v.25, suggesting either that the three denials come one after the other and *before* he enters the high priest's chambers with Judas, or, that he enters and returns. Nothing is preserved concerning *why* Peter has an audience with the high priest (John 18:16) but I suggest that he is called as a (legal) witness, and I will have more to say on this.

The "servants," Jesus' other disciples who are also huddled around the fire, try to coerce Peter into speaking up but he denies his involvement a second time. Finally, a "relative" of Malchus attempts to make Peter admit his association. The term used in the Greek text is masculine, and signifies a blood relative, i.e.., a kinsman. The only blood relative of Malchus/Lazarus the FG has provided us is his father, Nicodemus.

Mary has already tried to convince Peter, and the other disciples (who have *not* fled except, perhaps, for Lazarus, who must be protected[4]) have also tried. Now Nicodemus, who was probably witnessed the attack on his son and the arrest of Jesus, speaks up. I can imagine him getting very close, facing away from the police, and looking Peter right in the eye: "You were *in the garden* with him," he reminds him. I can even imagine him hinting he will not stand a chance of Jesus' favour now, if he does not speak up. Peter, like the lame man who is weak and unable to do anything on his own, has not the guts to 'stand up' for Jesus.

As Cephas, Peter must live with his error of judgement and must pay the consequences of his hubris. The cock crows, indicating that it is morning. As no hour, day, or festival is mentioned in the Greek text, this does not fall into the Table of Hours discussed previously; it merely indicates that the events described have gone on for hours, during the night.

Annas
Meanwhile, Jesus is before Annas, who asks him questions to which we are not privy but the scene seems to be implying that there is an attempt to find some legal loophole through which the priests can incriminate Jesus (which is also what Matthew says in Matt 26:59); I want to talk about this in more detail in a moment. One of the accepted roles, or functions, of the high priest is to act as a mediator between the Roman governor and the local people; it is thus his duty to attempt to deal with any local insurgence before Pilate is called on to get involved. This is what Annas tries to do, though without success.

If Jesus was taken first to Caiaphas, perhaps the outcome would have been different; *he* might well have had Jesus surreptitiously extinguished in some dark alley but Annas takes the trouble to follow the rules, trying not to back the Sanhedrin into any legally-ambiguous corner.

Temple Business
The NRSV describes Jesus being brought into the "courtyard of the high priest" (John 18:15). The Greek word translated as "courtyard" is *aulen* and

---

[4] In Mark 14:51 a "young man" is said to be following Jesus even after the other disciples apparently flee. He is dressed in a (white) linen garment, which he leaves behind when an attempt is made to capture him. If this young man is the figure Lazarus, it would make sense for the soldiers to try to arrest him, for there has been a warrant on him since the 'raising' event back in John 11–12. He has yet to receive his high priestly vestments; cf. my discussion on Peter's depiction in the FG epilogue. Recall, too, the devoted Ittai, from 2 Samuel 15!

this same word is used in Rev 11:2 to define a certain area just outside the *naos*, the sanctuary. The courts outside the *naos* are the priests' and the Israelites' courts. In John 10, recall, Jesus had used the phrase to describe the illicit entry of the "thieves and robbers," the unholy priesthood, into the once sanctified realm of worship, the temple. Originally, however, the word *aulen* implied a farmyard or "sheepfold"; it would seem to be an apt allusion to the 'sheepfold' already defined in the FG (John 10).

It is known that the priests *do* enter the temple by night but only on very special occasions, such as the evening before a major festival (which this *is*, of course), when complex preparations have to be made (e.g., 1 Chr 9:33, 2 Chr 35:14 and Ps 134:1, which reads, "all you servants of the Lord, who stand by night in the house of the Lord"). So there is often activity in and around the temple at night, despite some interpreters' denials.

To get a better understanding of the scene in hand, consider the following:

★ I talked earlier about the 'fire' being a strange little detail to include in the story and that it has symbolic meaning pertaining to Peter. The FG suggests the men who have arrested Jesus stand around this fire.

★ On the northern wall of the temple are various gates and chambers, including one called the Place of the Fire (Place of the Hearth). This is a vast, domed room containing a huge, constantly lit fire to warm the priests after they have conducted their ritual ablutions. It also heats the dormitory where the officiating priests sleep the night before their duties begin. In one corner of this area is a sanctified chamber called the Chamber of Approved Offerings; this is where lambs are brought in preparation for sacrifice. A wholly apt setting for this scene, with Jesus, the lamb being led to slaughter (i.e., the more sinister side of Christianity's 'cute, innocent lamb' metaphor).

★ The Greek terms used for the men standing by the fire are *doulos* (servants) and *huperetai* (officers). The former, as mentioned earlier, refer to Jesus' followers, while the latter represent the 'police' sent by the priests and the Pharisees to arrest Jesus. These would have been from the (lower/ordinary) priestly ranks.

★ The assembly of men, the posse if you will, is referred to (John 18:12) as *speira*, i.e., a band of men at arms. Josephus translates *speira* into the Latin *manipulus* ("something wound tight/together"), which originates from the practice of winding straw around a pole to use as a makeshift standard in the field of battle. Hence, *manipulus* became known as the number of men who could see and follow such a standard, i.e., about 200 to 300 men. This is a large, military gathering.

★ Only the FG uses the word *chiliarchos* in the context of Jesus' arrest (18:12). Translated literally, it refers to a commander of 1000 soldiers (from *chilios*, "a thousand" and *arch*, "to rule"). It is, however, the recognised term for a Roman military tribune, the commander of a cohort, or 600 men. The Synoptic accounts of the arrest implicate only the Jews, whereas the FG implies that a powerful leader of the Roman forces was also involved. The question then becomes: Why send a tribune with so many armed soldiers to arrest what we are otherwise led to believe is a fairly harmless but annoying thorn in the side of the Jewish authorities? We may argue that the Romans' tight hold on the Jews at the time of the Passover means that any such disturbance is hastily quashed but this doesn't explain why the great number of armed guards should be deemed necessary to arrest one middle-aged man sitting in a garden after dinner! This cohort is under the authority of a senior officer who must have the authority of the procurator, i.e., Pilate, to assemble such a troupe. If Jesus' arrest is based solely on religious grounds (e.g., blasphemy), or even royal ambition, the Romans would probably oversee proceedings to thwart anything getting out of hand but they wouldn't bring such a show of strength. It simply wouldn't be worth their time and effort. There has to be more to it. Now, of course, the reader can interpret the scene in light of Jesus' notoriety as the Samaritan mountaintop rebel. Suddenly it makes sense.

★ The fact that the *chiliarchos* must first discuss the situation with his commanding officer (Pilate) is the key to understanding subsequent events, so I shall come back to that in the next chapter.

★ According to the Mishnah (Middoth 1.2), the Captain of the Temple visited each guard of the temple at night, his presence heralded by a group of Levites bearing torches before him. Might the reference to torches in John 18:3 be another allusion to Judas as Simon, Captain of the Temple?

★ The gate at which Peter is standing, the gate associated with the Place of the Fire, is called the Gate of the Offering, i.e., the gate of the sacrifice, through which the offerings of the highest sanctity were brought to slaughter. Jesus is the supreme sacrifice, if Caiaphas has his way, so the location is symbolically apt.

★ A female 'gatekeeper' is mentioned; an anomalistic clue to Mary Magdalene's presence, as discussed, but there *is* a Gate of Women located between the Gate of the Song (a gate potentially associated with Lazarus' incarceration; see below) and the Gate of the Sacrifice (associated with Jesus'), making the FG's consistent ambiguity concerning Mary's relationship with these two men a noticeable factor even in this scene.

The Testamet of Lazarus

★ What is more, the chamber associated with the Gate of Women is none other than the Chamber of the Well; Mary's initial depiction is, recall, that of a woman at Jacob's Well.

★ She is standing at the Gate of Women, where those who have given birth come to present their sacrifice. Mary is Samaritan and the primary follower of Jesus' northern mission, so although this isn't the reason for her being here (and who would bring a sacrifice at night?), we can't ignore the allusion, yet again, to her just having had a child). If nothing else, this apparent coincidence simply supports the northern-temple setting.

★ The Chamber of Hewn Stone is high in the northern wall of the temple, above a gate called the Gate of the Song. Through this gate the Levites and the musicians would enter to reach the platform above the Court of Israel on which they would assemble to sing Hallel, a song of praise that is commanded to be sung at each of the festivals and eighteen other days of the year. It is a verbatim recital of Psalms 113–118. These Psalms speak of the raising of the "poor from the dust…to make them sit with kings"; they imply a rejection of an imposed 'death' and the choice of 'life'; they mention the "loosening of bonds" and the opening of gates; and they emphasize a public show of thanks, a request for "success," and the act of God listening to his "servants." The Hallel song is, for all intents and purposes, contained within the context and phrasing of Jesus' short prayer in preparation for the release of Lazarus (John 11:41–2).

★ The high priest's 'courtyard' is a court of the inner temple complex. Next door to the Chamber of Hewn Stone is the Chamber of Wood, otherwise known as the Chamber of the Parhedrin or Chamber of the Official. Here, the high priest segregates himself from the community seven days before the Day of Atonement. It is referred to as the Chamber of the Official because during this (Second Temple) Period high priests are appointed on an almost annual basis, i.e., as an 'official' duty. So, the FG mentioning the fact that Caiaphas is the high priest this 'year' (John 18:13) suggests the 'courtyard' in question is immediately in front of the Chamber of the Official, between the Chamber of Hewn Stone and the Gate of Women.

★ Jesus is first taken to Annas, not the officiating high priest. The reason for this becomes clear in due course.

★ The meeting doesn't take place within the high priest's chamber but just outside. The FG's dualistic approach to everything including the significance of the festivals at this time is important to remember. Although the historical events take place at Passover, the *symbolic* context is one of Jesus' personal Day of Atonement (yet to be fully explained). During this latter festival the high priest chooses his deputy, is incarcerated in the Chamber of Wood (the Official), and conducts the scapegoat ceremony.

✶ Annas then hands Jesus over to the 'official' Caiaphas, who is probably receiving his guest in the Chamber of Hewn Stone, the only legitimate site for matters of this sort.

✶ The Letter to the Hebrews suggests that although Jesus' body is dealt with unceremoniously, like the bodies of sacrificed animals that are disposed of outside the city gates, his blood is "brought into the sanctuary by the high priest as a sacrifice" (Heb 13:11). Is this purely metaphor or is there more to this comment than meets the eye?

So, we are certainly dealing with the northern chambers of the temple. I have tried to find a suitable symbolic link to the gate through which Jesus would be taken from the temple to Pilate. I considered the ritual of walking to the right around the temple and left in times of mourning. I considered the southern locale of the palace, relative to the northern chambers where the action occurs, and I speculated about the Gate of the Firstborn, on the southern wall. This would be an interesting choice, given the FG's emphasis on the 'firstborn' theme but the evidence wasn't clear to me.

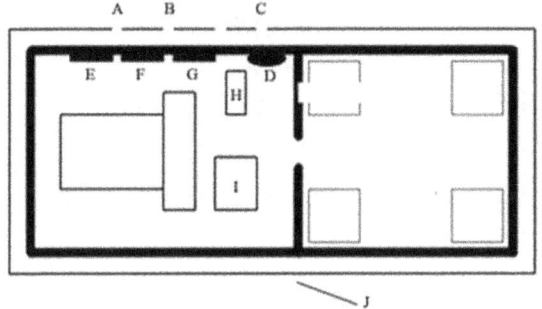

Temple Chambers

A. Gate of the Sacrifice; **B.** Gate of the Women; **C.** Gate of the Song; **D.** Chamber of Hewn Stone; **E.** Place of the Fire; **F.** Chamber of the Well; **G.** Chamber of the Wood; **H.** Slaughterhouse; **I.** Altar; **J.** Scapegoat Gate

Completing the symbolic reflection of Jesus' fate, however, and following the clues regarding the chambers and gates of the temple, we can consider another option. Situated between the Place of the Fire and the Chamber of Hewn Stone is the Chamber of the Vestments (we will discuss Jesus' vestments soon), the slaughterhouse, and the altar (in that sequence), past which Jesus *might* be led through and out of the temple to Pilate. One is forced to recall again John's reference to the innocent 'lamb' and the 'suffering servant' being led to 'slaughter'. Beyond, to the southeast, is the

Gate of the Scapegoat (the southern gate on the eastern wall) through which the sin-laden animal is released on the Day of Atonement. The only argument against this being the actual *physical* route taken after the arrest, is the fact that Jesus would be considered by the authorities to be ritually impure and thus not (normally) allowed into the court of the Israelites. It may be a case of 'needs must', or it may be the FG author's symbolic invention intended to emphasize Jesus' *raison d'etre*.

Also, there is known to be an occult passage built by Herod leading from the Fortress Antonia to the inner temple, "that he might have the opportunity of a subterraneous ascent to the temple, in order to guard against any sedition which might be made by the people against their kings" (Josephus *Ant.* 15.11.7). Latter day archaeology has revealed a veritable labyrinth of subterranean passages beneath the Temple Mount, so could it be possible that in order to protect themselves from a potential riot, the authorities clandestinely transport Jesus to Pilate through these tunnels? Thus the purity question is dealt with (so too might be the issue of the long walk 'round the houses' from the temple to where Pilate is domiciled farther to the west, in the old palace), while maintaining the symbolic ritual passage of the scapegoat/high priest on the Day of Atonement.

19
TRUTH AND CONSEQUENCE

Pilate
LOOKING AT THE INQUISITION SCENE from a realistic perspective, we are faced with the problem of the procurator's *apparent* willingness to defer to Jewish pressure. Perhaps though, this is just what we have been led to believe all these years[1]; when I shook off my orthodox upbringing, I began to see a very different Pilate, a very cunning, *slightly* anxious but entirely manipulative procurator. If Jesus *is* this Samaritan troublemaker, the alleged ringleader of an armed march up Mount Gerizim, there is no deferring to justify for he is already a marked man and Pilate *wants* him 'slain'.

Pilate hates the Jews under his authority; his aim is to "abolish the Jewish laws" by any means (Josephus, *Ant.* 18.3.1). He places effigies of Caesar and Roman ensigns inside the temple, which is an outright desecration; he ambushes and murders dissenters of his plan to redirect a river into Jerusalem using money from the temple treasury. Now, he has murdered many Samaritans (i.e., 'they all look the same to him'). Pilate's apparent insistence that the Jews take responsibility for Jesus' sentence is a case of passing the buck. He *knows* he is going to be in trouble for failing to keep the peace in his territory and for acting so recklessly, so he tries to limit his chastisement by getting the Jews, who also want this troublemaker out of the way, to take responsibility for the execution.[2] If Pilate can get the Jews to condemn Jesus to death, the Samaritans will have to redirect their protestations.

That the Jews are "not permitted to put anyone to death" (John 18:31) is a concept that needs attention; have not the Jews sought to kill Jesus ever since his healing 'sign' at the Sheep Gate, back in John 5? Have they not attempted to stone him? Did they not put a death sentence on Lazarus, when

---

[1] Pilate was canonized by the Ethiopian Church in the sixth century!
[2] Philo quotes a letter from Agrippa I, in which Pilate is described as an obstinate man, violent, cruel, and often at odds with not only local authorities but the judgement of Rome itself. One can almost imagine Tiberius shaking his head and saying 'what's he done now?'

others of the Jews began to convert? Since when do they not have the death sentence? Why have the *right* of sentencing, if the court is unable to carry it through (albeit with the aid of Roman soldiers)?

The Talmud (fourth and fifth centuries CE) suggests that "about forty years" before the War of 70 CE, i.e., about 30 CE, the Sanhedrin shifted its place of meeting to a "bazaar" (or "Halls of Commerce"; echoes of the "traders" Jesus rails against?) and was deprived of its authority to impose the death sentence; there is nothing in Josephus to corroborate this, and I think it would have been a big enough change for him to mention it. Besides, the Upper City was colloquially called the Upper Market-place, and four-hundred years is a long time for such colloquialisms to become vague.

We must also understand that number 'forty' is a very common and generic term to indicate a substantial but unspecified period, e.g., the rain that created the first flood lasted forty days and nights; the Israelites wandered in the wilderness for forty years; Jesus spent forty days in the desert, etc. The period leading up to the 'wars' of 66–73 CE is recorded in history as being one of profound 'signs and wonders' and retains an air of punishment and purging about it. The loss of the Sanhedrin's powers is just one of the casualties of that period but the exact nature of when and why is lost in the rubble of the razed temple. What if the removal of the Council's authority actually *stemmed* from this messy incident with Jesus? There is no concrete evidence to suggest a precise date for any changes to the site, authority, or policies of the Sanhedrin but if Jesus' public mission *began* in c. 33 CE (with the meetings at Qumran), this might be close enough to make "about forty" a comfortable fit for posterity, some half-a-millennia later.

Likewise, there is no historical evidence to suggest that the Sanhedrin was not *entitled* to carry out executions. The only ruling that is known to pertain to the passing of death sentences is dated after c.150 CE, and suggests that capital punishment could only be voted on by an assembly *within the temple chamber* (which is why Jesus is taken there after his arrest); of course, the temple had been destroyed by then, so it is a moot point. There are several instances subsequent to Jesus' arrest, in which the Sanhedrin passes and carries out death sentences, related in both the New Testament and Josephus, so I do not see why Jesus' case would have been any different.[3] According to Josephus (*Ant.* 14.9.3), the great council of the

---

[3] There is a law that allows them to hang the executed one on a tree (Deut 21:22–3) but this seems to suggest a post-execution warning-sign, like placing heads on spikes (and Josephus supports this idea; cf. Josh 10:26). This law implies they must first have the right of execution. Compare the description of Jesus' *execution*, in Acts 10:39, and potentially in 2 Esd 1:32 (note 'n'). According to the Talmud, the hanging of a criminal usually took place *after stoning*, and the bodies were hung up by the hands, "as butchers do an ox or a sheep." When people passing would ask why this

Sanhedrin was the only authority within the Jewish legal system that *did* have the authority to sentence a prisoner to death but only after a full and lengthy trial. This is the point. Jesus has to die before the crowd catches wind of the situation and as the Jews can do nothing over the Sabbath, the Romans can prove to be useful on this occasion. As for not being allowed to *carry out* an imposed death sentence, in John 19:6 Pilate actually tells the Jews to do the job *themselves*, i.e., he *grants* them permission, whether it is formally required or not. The volleying between Pilate and the Jews is actually a display of legal manipulation and a degree of trickery on both parts.

For the Jews, then, the problem lies *not* in their right or ability to confer a death sentence but in the complicated legal implications of Jesus' actions; they simply are unable to *convict* him by their own laws. They want him dealt with but not at the cost of the judicial system itself.

Let me just explain a few things about a trial before the Sanhedrin, as described in the Talmud. There were civil cases and criminal cases, tried by one of two councils, depending on the case. Most capital offences were tried by a group of twenty-three ordained judges, the lesser Sanhedrin,[4] whose aim, in fact, was to *avoid* pronouncing death sentences whenever possible; a court which passed such a sentence more than once in seven years risked "killing the court." There were stringent rules governing the testimony of witnesses, the biases of judges, and the quality of evidence. Two witnesses had to be found (see John 8:17), neither of whom could be incriminated in any way for any offence, nor could they be related to the accused or the judges. The testimony of the two witnesses had to concur, or the case was dismissed. These stipulations are vital to our analysis.

The crime had to have been witnessed with the accuser's own eyes, so accusations of non-action crimes, such as hatred or, as in Jesus' case, subversion, were notoriously difficult to try. Also, the one accused had to have received a formal warning immediately *before* performing the deed, i.e., that his actions would result in arrest and possibly a death sentence— *and* he had to acknowledge the warning verbally! Obviously, this was not possible in most cases, which is one of the reasons death sentences were so rare.

A majority vote of one was needed to acquit a man but a majority of (two or) three was needed to condemn him. The vote was cast after the testimony of the witnesses; no counsel was employed on either side, and the judge had the final say, arguing for or against as he saw fit. It was his

---

person had been hanged, the apparently all-encompassing response was: "He blasphemed."

[4] The term *sanhedrin* simply means 'assembly' or 'council' and is just as valid when describing an *ad hoc* assembly of a few members, as a formal meeting.

responsibility, however, to seek evidence in *favour* of the defendant. In some instances, the defendant was allowed to have someone enter the court and speak on his/her behalf.[5] The court was under caution never to prolong a sentence, or to keep a person in suspense as to his/her fate; acquittals were granted the same day but the death sentence was often postponed until the following day, which is why capital offences could not be tried on the eve of a Sabbath or feast day, such as in Jesus' case. This is why we see Jesus delaying for two days in John 11, i.e., he must be certain Lazarus is fully judged and sentenced.

Only the great Sanhedrin, which, legend told, had its roots in the council of seventy sages Moses had inaugurated, could try cases dealing with false prophets, subversion against the law, and grave offences against the high priest or the monarchy. The council was headed by a pair of sages called the *zugot*, one of whom acted as president, the other as the head of the law court. Its range of punishments included life imprisonment (which was not in the Mosaic Law) and flogging (which was the most common) but it *was* capable of passing the death sentence.

Also, a word or two about the charge of blasphemy (John 10:33f): notice how the accusation is *not* repeated during the trial scenes. Why not? It is simply because it has no bearing on the legal context of the arrest. That is, Jesus has never perpetrated blasphemy and the Jews know it. His more public show of disdain in John 10 demanded an instant reaction to demonstrate to the onlookers that Jesus was not going to get the upper hand but just as in the scene with the adulterous woman, the focus of the accusation is shifted to the accusers and no stoning occurs. There is no substance to the aspersion. Blasphemy would entail a contempt of God, the use of abusive language directed *toward* God or associated 'sacred' phenomena; the only aspect in which Jesus *could* be accused of such an atrocity would be his apparent disregard for the temple in John 2:13f. If there is no charge of blasphemy at that time, the Jews coming under Jesus' fire realise (resentfully of course) that what he is saying is true. That is, they know the *truly sacred* aspects of the temple are missing, so he cannot be condemning what is holy. They dare not expose themselves to public scrutiny, so they channel what would be an unfounded blasphemy charge in this context (an offence easily understood and probably unchallenged by the general population), into Jesus' *supposed* deification, something they fail, however, to 'rely on in court'!

Jesus' situation, then, is proving to be a bit of a dilemma. His inevitable arrest and trial are foreshadowed in Nicodemus' statement in John

---

[5] The importance, and the consequences, of not performing a *just* hearing is clearly reiterated in Josephus, *Ant.* 4.8.14.

7:51, where the Jews are reminded that no one can be condemned before being given the chance to explain himself, yet Jesus keeps insisting that his whole mission has been an explanation of who he is and what his intentions are. If they do not understand, there is nothing he can do about it. This gets the Jews angry.

The Jews have a duty to perform the trial according to their own rules but how can they win? Jesus is not officially warned of his conduct before he does something supposedly illegal because in most instances there is no one about *to* warn him; in the case of the lame man and even the blind man, the Jews learn of the deed after it is done. In the case of the Samaritan tumult on Mount Gerizim, we cannot be certain Jesus is the acting ringleader or if his own agenda has been hijacked by the more zealot Galileans; he certainly becomes the scapegoat for the debacle but the incident takes place beyond the jurisdiction of the Sanhedrin.

There are also no *objective* eyewitnesses. This makes the apparent threat to the lame man even more plausible, e.g., 'do not bear witness against me, or something worse will happen to you' and this foreshadows Peter's position during the inquisition scene.

Jesus insists he has said nothing in secret, that he has "spoken openly to the world" and this is true, for he has taught in the synagogues and the temple. He *has* openly incited revolution (what *is* secret he has *kept* secret and that which is ambiguous cannot be claimed as secretive, just difficult to understand).

> *I did not speak in secret, in a land of darkness;*
> *I did not say to the offspring of Jacob, "Seek me in chaos."*
> *I ... speak the truth, I declare what is right.*
> Isa 45:19

Jesus invites the high priest Annas to go and *find* testimony *in his favour* (John 18:21; part of the legal process, recall) from those who actually *listened* to him, the *true* offspring of Jacob—a cheeky demonstration of Jesus' own familiarity with the law that gets him punished on the spot. This is why Jesus appears so hesitant to fully expose his intentions and identity; he *knows* the law, he *knows* the 'darkness' that will try to prevent him. The illegitimate "tenants" *will* seek to kill the rightful 'son', the firstborn, given half a chance.

His offences *are* toward the high priest, they *are* subversive, and they *imply* prophesy, therefore, Jesus *must* be tried before the great Sanhedrin, which is why he is first taken to Annas *and* Caiaphas, the *zugot*. Annas, the father-in-law of the high priest, so the FG author insists on telling us (clue!), is an ex-high priest himself and takes on the role of 'advisor' just as Moses' father-in-law Jethro did, in the legal deliberations of Exodus 18 (especially).

He is the 'president' figure, while Caiaphas, the ruling high priest, is effectively the head of the law court. The Jews want *advice*: Does Annas think there is enough evidence for a death sentence? Can they *risk* putting it to a vote? They *really* want Jesus out of the way.

Furthermore, when Jesus is brought in to see Annas, Peter remains outside, only to be called in when Judas (the unnamed disciple) sends for him; no one who has spoken favourably for a prisoner can then be used as a witness against him, and no witness can bear testimony if he is incriminated in any way. Peter's denial is thus doubly damning, for by denouncing any involvement with Jesus, he makes himself available as the elusive *objective* eyewitness. At this point, we should recall that Jesus' castigation of the *diabolos* within his group of twelve has been translated, traditionally, as "devil" and I have chosen to maintain that concept until now, but here in the *legal* context of both Judas' and Peter's apparent roles as witnesses against Jesus, the actual translation of the term is most fitting: "accuser" (see 1 Tim 3:11; 2 Tim 3:3).

In the end, Jesus proves too difficult a problem and the Jews choose to defer to Rome, handing the troublemaker, in effect, *back* to Pilate. He is left with the job, after all. Playing on what they perceive to be Pilate's ignorance of Jewish religious customs, the chief priests and the Pharisees quickly drop Jesus off at the procurator's headquarters, refusing to go in because of some rule about ritual cleanliness and the Passover. Eating the Passover is an absolute *must* for all God-fearing Jews and because of this provision is made in the law for *any* Israelite (*even* those defiled by the dead, or on a journey) to keep the Passover (Num 9:1–14). The Jews have no *real* excuse not to go in; they just do not want to debate the issue. They want to leave Jesus and go! 'Of course he's a criminal' they assure Pilate (as they head for the exit). The point is, the Jews leave with the parting comment that they are not "permitted to put anyone to death" (John 18:31); they are either declaring that the Sanhedrin has not successfully arrived at a death sentence, or that they are not permitted to impose a death sentence on the eve of the Sabbath. Either way, there is nothing in the narrative to suggest the Sanhedrin is powerless, at least not at this stage; they assume Pilate is utterly ignorant of these details and they seem to be correct . . . but are they?

The volleying now begins between Jesus and Pilate, two very intelligent, sophisticated men, each with a personal agendum: "Are you the King of the Jews?" Pilate begins, but what has given him this idea? Although he harbours no sympathy for, nor has any interest in the Jewish religion, he does, no doubt, have a very good intelligence committee keeping him informed about everything untoward. How could any procurator be ignorant of the general expectation of the (Davidic) messiah, for example? Every Passover, troops near the temple are increased precisely because of the threat of messianic fervour but the subtleties of *Jesus*' messianic identity would, indeed, be lost on Pilate. Given Pilate's well-known nature and his anti-Jewish, anti-Samaritan tendencies, it is perfectly plausible to suggest he is, at first, unaware that this is the Samaritan rebel he has at the top of his 'Most Wanted' list! Because Jesus is astute, well educated, and a quick thinker, he plays with Pilate's apparent ignorance in a profoundly ironic game of cat and mouse, in which the roles are briefly reversed.

Jesus replies: "Do you ask this on your own, or did others tell you about me?" This is so teasingly ambiguous; he answers with a question, not committing himself. The "others" of course are the FG's "Jews." Have they truly *mistaken* Jesus' identity and told Pilate he is their Davidic king—why then have him killed? Have they known all along who Jesus is claiming to be, i.e., "can the authorities really know?" (John 7:26)?

As always, Jesus never speaks outright, just in case.

"I'm not a Jew, am I?" Pilate responds (in other words, 'you can trust me'); "Your own nation and the chief priests have handed you over to me. What *have* you done?" Given the length of time Jesus and Pilate share an audience, we cannot possibly be given the entire dialogue between these men. It must be that sometime during the proceedings Pilate becomes aware of *who* Jesus is, i.e., the ringleader of the Samaritan rebels. There is an edge to his words now, reflecting his devious and calculating nature; it is almost as if Pilate cannot understand why the *Jews* should be so concerned about this Samaritan. Maybe, Pilate seems to think, this can work to his advantage, so he begins a long, drawn out interrogation, in an effort to exonerate himself and vilify the Jews.[6]

Jesus' "own nation" however, is not that of the Jews, a theological subtlety that is lost on Pilate. "My kingdom is not from *this* world. If my kingdom were from this world, my followers would be fighting to keep me from being handed over to the Jews"; Jesus' 'kingdom' is somewhere else, i.e., the kingdom of Israel at Shiloh, in Samaria.

"So you *are* a king?"

"*You* say that I am a king" (again, note the truth on the lips of the antagonist); "For this reason I was born, and for this reason I came into the world, to testify to the truth." Jesus is again ambiguous in his response but the truth of which he speaks is that pertaining to the divinely prophesied return of the firstborn, i.e., of the reestablishment of the house of Joseph and

---

[6] Jesus and Pilate spend many hours together yet we are given just a snippet of what was apparently said. Who would be privy to such information, to record it for posterity? Was a guard present who later converted to Christianity (as some undoubtedly did) and told the tale? Did Pilate relate the information unwittingly to someone who then passed the words on? Or did Jesus himself recount his audience with Pilate (e.g., to Lazarus) before he died?

the King of Israel.

Pilate, anticipating his own subsequent actions, replies: "What *is* [the?] truth"? In other words, 'who are they going to believe—you, who are about to die like a criminal, already rejected, or me, the one who holds all the power here?' The ambiguity of truth, as implied by Pilate, has become a familiar biblical allusion today but in the context of the FG it is a poignant and profound statement. Jesus' truth is *not* the same as the Jews' nor Pilate's; their 'truth' seems to be whatever works to their benefit.

This is a signal to the gospel readers to be aware that what they see on the surface may not be what is true. It is a warning for us to be on our guard as we continue to read these final but profoundly significant passages. The truth of the FG is that the Remnant is returning to claim its inheritance and it is to *this* Jesus must testify, for *this* reason he must 'pour out his soul to death'.

Paschal Pardon

In an attempt to clarify the meaning of the Barabbas story, some scholars propose that it was originally a Marcan interpolation of an actual prisoner-release custom intended to incriminate the Jewish population for Jesus' death, rather than the Romans, in an effort to further disassociate the Christians from the Jews. Some insist that the character of Barabbas is to be identified with Jesus, based on the interpretation of "Barabbas" as "son of the father" or "son of the teacher" but as we shall see, these identifications can apply to *another* father-figure.

In the NRSV, Barabbas is described as a "bandit" and, although there is obviously an element of violent behaviour in Jesus' campaign, I wonder at the *FG author's* use of the description for *Jesus*—it simply does not fit. Such a derogatory term would not be applied to him *within* the gospel, unless it was on the lips of a Pharisee or priest. The Greek word here, however, is *lestes*, a "robber," and back in John 10:1 the term was used in conjunction with *kleptai*, "thieves," in Jesus' own diatribe against the illegitimate, corrupt priesthood of the temple.

The 'father/teacher' inferred in "Barabbas" I suggest, reflects *not* Jesus but the "father of lies," the leader of the corrupt institution, i.e., the high priest Caiaphas. "Barabbas" then becomes synonymous with 'son of the father of lies'. As a 'son' he is a representative, so Barabbas is also the *representative* of the temple's high priest. This provides for some very interesting historical not biblical evidence.

The idea of the paschal pardon, of which Barabbas is supposed to be an example, has long remained a mystery, with the majority of scholars supporting the view that there is not enough evidence in external sources to imply that any such custom ever existed in Roman-occupied Judea. In the Bible, some argue, there is an ancient record of the release of the King of Judah from Babylonian custody (e.g., 2 Kgs 25:27–30; Jer 52:31–4), and similar customs of releasing prisoners during certain festivals were known to have existed in Greece; but the link to a penal tradition *specifically* Roman/Jewish is tenuous. Perhaps the answer to this paradox lies elsewhere. It may be that what is transpiring in the FG is *not* the release of a human 'prisoner' per se, for the word is *never used* by Pilate in John 18:39 but something analogous (i.e., he says the equivalent of 'someone').

Josephus reveals what happens when Vitellius, once consul at Rome and now the president of Syria, arrives in Judea after Pilate has left for Rome but he explains the context into which the event must be understood. Up until this time there has been a tradition whereby *the vestments* of the high priest, always under *lock and key* (effectively, held 'prisoner') in the tower of Antonia since Herod the Great's day, are ritually handed over to the priests seven days before a festival (so they will have time to purify them). *This* is the 'custom' the FG author has Pilate refer to. The 'someone' Pilate emancipates is the temple's high priest, *represented* by the vestments. So, Josephus explains:

> Vitellius came into Judea, and went up to Jerusalem; it was at the time of that festival which is called the Passover. Vitellius ... gave them leave to have the care of the high priest's vestments, with all their ornaments, and to have them under the custody of the priests in the temple ... this he did as an act of kindness, to oblige the nation to him.
> *Ant.* 18.4.3

The Jews have already sent a written (formal) request to Tiberius for the return of the vestments to the custody of the priesthood; Tiberius dies on 16 March 37 CE but it is thought by historians that permission must have already been granted, for Vitellius to award such a transfer. This is how he knows of 'the custom' and why he makes such a grand gesture of it. The final handing-over of the vestments into the authority of the cultus at the temple takes place at Passover, making it a truly paschal 'release'. This particular event occurs in early 37 CE, the year after Jesus' crucifixion (Vitellius was consul in Rome in 34 CE and was engaged in battles for the next two years); it is, almost undoubtedly, the symbolic basis of the Barabbas story (which I claim takes place in 36 CE).

Having been in Ephraim between the raising of Lazarus and the Passover, Jesus is in the right place at the right time to fit the description of the Samaritan leader in Josephus' history of the tumult on Mount Gerizim. Because Josephus does not name this rebel and because he does mention, often, that this period was rife with 'tumults' and rebellions, etc., it is certainly *possible* that this is an obscure figure other than Jesus but the coincidental parallels would be amazing, especially in light of the Messiah ben Joseph tradition. The alleged ringleader of the tumult is said to escape alive but is under Pilate's sentence of death; when Jesus returns to Jerusalem from Ephraim, he already knows that his time is up (John 13:1) and it is only a matter of days before Jesus is finally caught and executed. Exploiting the political events only a year after Jesus' crucifixion emphasizes the 'choice' that is made on a theological level, i.e., Barabbas (the representative of the temple high priest) and Jesus (the leader of the rebellion against the current cultus) are, in the narrative, both 'captives' of the Roman procurator.

This is the moment of truth, for Jesus. Will the people choose Barabbas, the way of 'destruction' and 'darkness', or will they choose Jesus and the path to 'life' and 'light'? In John 3:19 it is claimed in the *past* tense that "men loved the darkness more than the light," a retrospective claim to the persistent division between those who choose to follow Jesus and those who do not, i.e., the choice to preserve the extant cultus, or to accept Jesus' offer of revolution.

> *I have set before you life and death...*
> *Choose life so that you ... may live.*
> Deut 30:19

Joshua, on the eve of *his* death, also gave the people a choice: "choose this day whom you will serve," i.e., the gods of Egypt and Canaan, or Yahweh (Josh 24:15). Elijah, faced with the Baal worshippers, cries out: "How long will you go limping with two different opinions? If the Lord is God, follow him, but if Baal, then follow him" (1 Kgs 18:21). The choice is one of *religious worship*, bringing the entire narrative of the FG back to its beginning and its symbolic representation of the ideal Remnant that rejected the supremacy of the priesthood who worshipped the sun in Jerusalem (and to the original context of the supposed exodus from Egypt).

Follow Jesus and there will be eternal 'life'; follow the "father of lies" and there is only spiritual 'death'. Making the irony of this choice all the more profound is the fact that although the Romans are seen to release the vestments of the Jewish priesthood into the custody of the temple, the emancipation is superficial, for those who don them are *themselves* corrupt and their iniquity has been, or will be, the *destruction* of the temple. Jerusalem will never be free, nor the new kingdom of God fully manifested until the true representative of God, the true 'priestly kingdom', is chosen over and against Barabbas and what he represents.

Christianity perpetuates the notion of Jesus as the scapegoat sacrificed for our sins but seldom is there offered any justification for this concept, considering the rite is exclusive to the Day of Atonement and not Passover, when Jesus is crucified. I believe the very early Christians knew full well what this implied but, thanks to Paul, the entire FG-based theology in which this scapegoat idea makes complete sense, was suppressed. What remained was just an echo of the intended and profound symbolism, conveniently linked to Caiaphas' supposed prediction.

The representation of the scapegoat in the FG, however, involves not just one man (Jesus) but two: Jesus and Barabbas, reinforcing the echo of Leviticus 16 and the ritual of the two goats on the Day of Atonement where one is released and one killed. The goat with the 'sins' symbolically laid upon its head is led out into the desert and lives, which is what the original word ('scapegoat') meant, i.e., 'the one who escapes'.[7] The other, the one that *is* sacrificed is intended as a sin offering to atone for the people's transgressions (Lev 18:16). This is just a little too obvious an inference for the complex and profoundly cryptic FG. There is reason to suggest an alternative understanding of this parallel to the ritual of the two goats, as I shall attempt to explain.

Although the actual day of Jesus' meeting with Pilate is that of the "day of preparation for Passover," we are given another cryptic calendar clue. It is about the "sixth hour," making it between the hours of 9 A.M. and 12 noon *and* between the 9th and 12th day, according to the calculation of "Hours," discussed previously. The Passover lamb, although *selected* on the tenth of Nisan (Exod 12:3), is not actually *killed* (and eaten) until the evening of the fourteenth, but the Day of Atonement falls on the *tenth* day, i.e., of Tishri (Lev 16:29).

The FG narrative concerning Jesus' actual (historical) mission begins with the Day of Atonement (the meeting between John and Jesus); the celebratory meal and the election of Lazarus as the deputy high priest takes place the prescribed 'week' before this final, symbolic Day of Atonement, i.e., the 'hour' for which Jesus has been preparing all along. The reference to the "sixth hour" also provides a general time of day, i.e., mid-to-late morning, while the explicit references to the Passover give us the *actual* timing of the event. Thus, the allusion to the scapegoat ritual is wholly intentional and compels us to see the dual nature of the scene, so common a tactic of the FG author. In the historical timeline we are witnessing the build up to Passover, in Jesus' theological and symbolic world, it is fast approaching his Day of Atonement. The two are inextricable.

In John 18:36, Jesus explains to Pilate that this is the way things must

---

[7] In the Talmud, the Azazel goat, the one let out into the desert, is forced over a cliff in a ritual to appease the Devil and so *does* die but this was never the biblical understanding.

go; if his has been an earthly ambition, as the crowd on the mountain had expected, his followers would be ready to 'fight' for him, suggesting that if Jesus had given the word, they would, indeed, come armed to break him out, as they had Lazarus.

Jesus has now been with Pilate for anywhere between six and nine hours (if he was taken to Pilate at about 3 A.M., after cockcrow); that is a long time. Would any run-of-the-mill troublemaker have received so long an audience with such a busy man?

The Other Scapegoat

The death of Judas is not mentioned in the FG. It does seem rather odd that someone so significant should just disappear from the narrative but then again, in Lev 27:29 it is explicitly stated that those who are "devoted to destruction" cannot be "ransomed" but are "put to death"; as the "son of destruction" Judas is *destined* to die, destined to be the one 'lost', and no one really has any qualms about this.

Back in John 10:8, Jesus rebukes the "thieves and robbers" who lead the "sheep" away from safety and into danger, and by this we understand that Jesus implies the current incumbents of the temple—the traders of the market place, the illegitimate priesthood. The character of Judas, too, has connections with the temple cultus, both as one "known" to the high priest, and in his echo of Simon, Captain of the Temple. The addendum of John 12:6 was disregarded at that juncture because I was trying to understand what appears to be the original text, without subsequent clarifications, so the description of Judas as a 'thief' had to be postponed, despite the fact that it would have served my purpose well at that time. Only by connecting the character of Barabbas to Judas, and thus Judas to the extant priesthood, however, could an early Christian scribe deduce that Judas is a "thief." I suggest that Judas is the embodiment of the temple cultus, i.e., Judas is Barabbas.

As far as the FG author is concerned, Judas' fate is not so much insignificant, as *inevitable* and, therefore, implicit in his entire depiction. His role in the narrative is as a tool of 'destruction', a reflection of the corrupt priesthood. Once he has been 'chosen' by the nation (echoing the ritualistic casting of lots for the two goats), there is no need to waste time discussing his fate; what happens to Jesus, Lazarus, and Mary is far more important in this testimony. Again, comparing the ideology of the FG to that of 2 Esdras, when Ezra seeks enlightenment about the fate of those who follow 'evil' he is told:

> [D]o not ask any more questions about the great number of those who

perish. For when they had opportunity to choose, they despised the Most High, and were contemptuous of his law, and abandoned his ways. Moreover, they have even trampled on his righteous ones, and said in their hearts that there is no God—though they knew well that they must die.

2 Esd 8:55-8

To conjecture about Judas' *personal* fate is to go beyond the FG but I think there is enough intriguing evidence elsewhere to warrant such an excursion into what may be the ramifications of this character's actions. In Mark 15.7, for example, we learn that Barabbas "was in prison with the rebels who had committed murder during the insurrection," yet nothing is offered in way of explanation for this 'insurrection'. Who were the rebels? If the author of Mark's gospel considered the event a matter of general knowledge, it must have been a significant one, e.g., the Samaritan tumult.

Note how Barabbas is not portrayed as one of the rebels, but as being in prison *with* them. Barabbas, Judas seems to get away with his crime, and a crime it would have been; the Jewish law came down severely on anyone who informed on an Israelite to an alien authority, i.e., they were *usually* considered an outcast (and recall, Judas goes first to the Romans, the soldiers who come to arrest Jesus). He would be beyond the protection of the law and susceptible to an immediate death sentence, which the *community* itself was allowed to carry out.

This is what I think might have happened:

The Jews have used Judas as an infiltrator and are now about to sacrifice him to spare themselves, perhaps unwittingly, perhaps intentionally, but just as Caiaphas had predicted, concerning Jesus (i.e., one to die to save the many). Maybe Judas has begun to feel uncertain of his actions and has become a bit of a liability. Or maybe, feeling that they have been just a little too manipulative in this matter and not intending for one moment to be out-manoeuvred, Pilate, at the last moment, orders one of the Jews to be killed, too—a parting gesture he would have found quite satisfying, I am sure. In an ironic twist of fate, it is *Judas* who ultimately becomes the paschal *sacrifice*, the 'goat' who is *killed*. This suggests just one thing; Jesus must be the *other* scapegoat, the one sent out into the desert *alive*, the 'sin' of the nation upon him!

In the Synoptics the character of Simon the Cyrene (Matt 27:32; Mark 15:21; Luke 23:26) may well be the "son of Simon," *our* Judas of the FG, for each account involves the sudden appearance of a Simon immediately after the so-called 'release' of Barabbas, and employs a verb which implies *coercion* or force (i.e., *aggareuo*). He is *forced* to take a cross up to Golgotha; forced, perhaps, by the community who see this act of justice (for his betrayal of a fellow Israelite) their *own* right? Mark 15:21 states that this

Simon is the father of Alexander; I argue later that Alexander *is* the son of Judas). The Gnostic belief was that this Simon died on the cross. Amazingly, the Quran holds not only that Jesus did not die on the cross, but that *Judas* was crucified in his stead! I did not know this until I had finished writing this book!

Concerning the tradition of Judas being a *sicarius,* a murderer/assassin, as discussed earlier, after the Jewish Revolt (66–73 CE) many of the Sicarii fled to Cyrene. Yet another coincidence, or perhaps the later dating of the Synoptics allowed for this hindsight characterization of Judas?

Remembering the reversed fate of Kerioth; it is possible that Judas is also preserved in the Lucan account of the 'good' thief who realises that his treachery against a man of God has led him to the very fate assigned to the man he betrayed. 'We are getting what we deserve for our deeds', this thief is reported to have confessed.[8]

> *As you have done, it shall be done to you;*
> *Your deeds shall return on your own head.*
> Obad 15

Judas, it would seem, dies on a cross next to Jesus. Thus, by Jewish law, he is seen to receive his just reward and by Pilate's reckoning, he has paid the price for the Jews' audacity.

Matthew's account of the death of Judas reveals that it is the *chief priests* who tend the body. It seems strange that these men should even bother to acknowledge Judas after this messy episode *unless* he is considered one of their own, and remember, the burial preparations, etc., are the responsibility of the deceased's *family*. Once again, Judas and Barabbas are united in their intimate association with the highly ranking priests. There is one other pertinent footnote to Judas and the priests contained in the writings of Paul, which I'll mention in due course.

An interesting 'sidebar': In 1990 two rusted crucifixion nails were found in a tomb in Jerusalem, purportedly to be that of the high priest, Caiaphas. However, there is controversy surrounding their discovery, as a) they immediately 'disappeared' for several years and b) another archaeological source claimed they were found in a different tomb twenty years before, in the 1970s. Popular intrigue led to a documentary that claimed the nails were from Jesus' crucifixion (of course) and that Caiaphas

---

[8] According to the Talmud, thieves were not given any sort of physical punishment, let alone capital punishment. Their penalty was to offer reimbursement to the victim and pay a fine. Even Herod's 'new law' of extradition, which was deemed abominable, spared them the cross (Josephus, *Ant.* 16.1.1).

must have had a pang of conscience and kept them "as a memento." Clearly, there is a problem with this. If the FG faithfully describes Jesus' body being handed over to *his* family, surely it would be they who would have access to these nails, not the priests who *wanted* him executed. Would the manipulative Caiaphas really have had such a drastic change of heart so soon after the crucifixion? Lazarus and Nicodemus retrieve the body hastily, recall; Caiaphas would have had to intervene within hours, but there is no hint of this in any of the gospels.[9] *If* these nails are genuine, and not a hoax, and *if*, indeed, they were found with Caiaphas' ossuary, wouldn't it be more fitting for them to have been the nails used on Judas? Caiaphas would have had direct access to these, having secured Judas' body after his death, i.e., as part of the "family" of priests who took his body for burial. The nails would have been a sober reminder not of the high priest's decision to 'sacrifice' Jesus but of his misguided cunning and hubris in dealing with Pilate and the unexpected loss of *his* own 'son' (biological or cultic).

Another consideration: Is Judas deliberately silenced (sacrificed) by the chief priests who see him as a liability? Is the story of the 'blood money' (which isn't mentioned at all in the FG) a reference to the "thirty shekels of silver" granted to the "shepherd of the doomed flock" as "wages" in Zechariah 11? Judas casts the money into the 'treasury' and at that moment the "family ties between Judah and Israel" are broken (Zech 11:14). That is, Judas is cut off from Jesus' new Israel; there is no salvation for him at this point. The money attributed to Judas is wages earned from spying and informing. It is not a sudden aberration but a drawn out, methodical, and calculated term of employment for which he is now getting paid. Such a sum, according to Zech 11:13, is a "lordly" fee for a job well done but the moment it is accepted Judas' fate is sealed. I wonder if this aspect of Judas' story, if genuine, became known only later in history, hence appearing only in the Gospel of Matthew and Acts. Despite its strong symbolism it does have a ring of truth about it.

Furthermore, Matthew 27 preserves a possible link between Judas and the 'treasury'. Was the 'blood money' given to Judas (as wages) simply a larger portion of the tithes apparently routinely fleeced by the

---

[9] In 1968 the heal bone of a crucified Jerusalem man called Yehohanan ben Hagkol was found in an ossuary with the nail still insitu, suggesting the deposition of a crucified body was not as simple as pulling the nails out and carrying it away. These were substantial iron nails, bent at the rear to prevent slippage; Jesus, with perhaps only his wrists pierced, is probably removed with the nails insitu, too, to prevent massive blood loss until he is secured in the Pool and 'medical' assistance is at hand. Caiaphas would have had to order some menial or other to retrieve the nails (even if left in the wood), which would have been an open declaration that he had been wrong. I can't imagine this would happen.

priest/treasurers, used as an incentive? That the money is quietly relocated by the priests after Judas' death (Matt 27:6–7) is suspiciously like a plan to cover their own tracks, e.g., rather than have the extra money resurface in the banks and lead to questions concerning its whereabouts. If Judas was a temple treasurer, this would explain his unique interest in the group's "purse" and his reflection of Simon, the Captain of the Temple.

Judas' fate, as far as the FG is concerned, is that of all the others who choose 'darkness': "Cursed be anyone who takes a bribe to shed innocent blood" (Deut 27:25).

"We have a law"
Pilate's insistence that he can find no 'crime' in Jesus sounds more like fishing the crowd than any leniency toward the accused; he keeps asking for evidence of a crime so that, maybe, someone can be found to accuse Jesus of something Rome cannot tolerate and would *itself* stamp out. The incident up on Mount Gerizim was a fiasco and the whole affair has got out of hand; Pilate has to find support for his actions, at least as far as his superiors are concerned; neither justice for, nor the sentiments of, the Jewish people are in his mind. He needs to find a 'crime' to justify his previous violent and obviously disruptive outburst.

The Jews respond with a bit of a riddle; they declare that they have a law that requires Jesus must die because he has claimed to be the "Son of God." Part of the tradition of Torah, however, is that Israel *is* God's son, that the Jewish people *are* the children of God; Solomon was called a "son of God" when he was divinely elected to build the temple. It *is not* a capital offence to affirm such a title. Pilate is afraid, we are told, but why is he? It comes down to a clever play on words. Remember that "son of man" was made into a proper noun because Christian interpreters saw this as an alternative name for Jesus, their 'Christ', and that the Greek really only says "son of the man"; this simplicity actually allows for a very profound, multi-layered meaning. This is another case in point, for the Greek of "son of God" actually reads, more precisely, "son of the god." Just as in the Mosaic precedent described at the beginning of this investigation, we are confronted with the question: "*Which* god?"

Did the Jews *mean* son of Yahweh? We already know that this is not a crime, so why risk resting their entire case against Jesus on something so easily gainsaid? Why would Pilate, of all people, be concerned with this? He does not care a fig for Yahweh. If, however, they simply say "son of the god," Pilate's Roman nature kicks in; if this man (Jesus) is claiming to be a descendent of a god, perhaps he really *has* made a mistake in taking him on. Things really will go against Pilate at Rome if he angers the gods! Fearing for his own position, he resolves to find a way to calm the situation down and release Jesus, if possible.

Meanwhile, though, unwilling to play this futile game, Jesus refuses to offer Pilate any way out. Once more we are reminded of Jesus' mysterious origins: "Where *are* you from?" asks Pilate. Holding Jesus' life in his hands, he simply cannot understand why this man is so obstinate—maybe he is not divine at all; 'don't you know the power *I* have?' he adds, as if challenging this supposed but seemingly pathetic demigod. Jesus, though, sees Pilate in terms of the divine plan, a tool in the hand of God, as Assyria and the Greeks had been to the nation, i.e., a tool to humiliate and suppress Israel while 'she' lives in her state of adultery. *Pilate* is the "puppet" here (with gratitude to Andrew Lloyd Webber), with no real power at all.

Pilate, then, is simply trying to avert *more* trouble. The Jews, on the other hand, realising that the prefect has not comprehended their meaning, push on and spell it out for him: "You are no friend of the emperor ... Everyone who claims to be king sets himself against the emperor"; so, *that* is it! The reference to the emperor does the trick, for not only are the Jews emphasizing their right to convey complaints about the incumbent governor directly to Rome, underscoring Pilate's tenuous situation and his desire to tip the scales in his own favour, they make the accusation against Jesus more directly threatening to *Rome*. Jesus is denounced as one who is setting himself up against the Roman emperor! So, they *do* know Jesus is claiming to be a king (the King of Israel); they fear the return of the firstborn, the true 'son' of God, and need Jesus extinguished!

The point is, so Pilate finally grasps, Emperor Tiberius is the *only* "son of the god," the official Filio Dei[10] and *no one* dare challenge this title. Although Jesus, personally, could hardly be taken seriously as a threat to the Roman Empire, if word reached Tiberius that a man who was openly going around calling himself by this designation, especially after the massacre in Samaria, had been freed, Pilate would be finished. He has a *duty* to put such a pretender to death; he *has* his 'crime'![11]

'Look,' the Jews seem to be saying to Pilate, 'the man has just tried to lead a crowd of armed followers up a mountain! You killed most of them, but since his escape he's even had the nerve to show up right outside the temple. You should have seen the reception he got! We can't risk him trying to take the temple, and you can't risk him gaining enough of a foothold to

---

[10] This is from Roman texts; the mediaeval Latin New Testament uses the form: *filium dei*. The Roman title was first introduced with Augustus, the adopted son of the deified Julius Caesar.

[11] The Romans used crucifixion as a last resort; it was the most drastic of punishments (e.g., they also used beheading, drowning, and burning); it was used, for the most part, for those accused of sedition, i.e., political rebels, revolutionists.

push you out of power ... we both need him out of the way'; Pilate, apparently, agrees.

There is, perhaps not surprisingly, a historical parallel to this scenario in Josephus (*Wars.* 2.10.4–5), where Petronius (the president of Syria under Caligula) is forced to deal with the anger of the Jews after Caligula orders that a statue of himself be placed within the temple. The Jews threaten that they will all kill themselves, rather than allow this atrocity, and they remark on how they dutifully honour the emperor with sacrifices. Petronius gets restless because word might get back to Rome that he is not doing his job properly, and he starts having private deliberations with certain members of the community (the 'men of power'), in a bid to convince them to drop their complaint. At times he uses "persuasions," at others "advice," and, ultimately, he succumbs to "threatenings" but finally he makes a statement that suggests he is under pressure to save his own skin, and that if they can all come to some agreement, *both* parties will be saved the anger of Rome.

Caligula ruled from 37 to 41 CE. Another coincidence or contemporaneous inspiration for the FG narrative?

Judas or Peter?

In John 19:11 Jesus says: "The one who handed me over to you is guilty of greater sin." To most readers of the FG this implies Judas, the one who told the authorities where to find Jesus. However, the Greek for "handed me over" uses the verb *paradidómi*, which can mean to "deliver, betray, abandon." I think this is one of several instances where the author of the FG is pointing the finger at Peter's disloyalty. Jesus is not laying the blame on Pilate (he is doing his duty and playing his role in the greater scheme of things, as preordained by God); he is not blaming Judas (who was hired to do a job and was never *truly* one of Jesus' disciples); he is putting the blame on Peter, the one whom he had warned not to sin any more, the one who had been so zealous in his outward support of Jesus, the one who then made a conscious *choice* to betray him, to abandon him.

Gabbatha

At this stage, the FG provides us with another mysterious name, i.e., Gabbatha, the site to which Pilate takes Jesus for the last appeal to the Jews—are they certain this is what they want?

The site of Gabbatha is given both its Chaldean and Greek names, which echoes the FG's emphasis on the duality of the 'truly Israelite' (those given, who bear Hebrew names, for instance) and the 'too Hellenised" (those with Greek names, who are deemed lost). The Greek name is Stone

Pavement (*lithostraton*) and there are two levels of understanding here, as usual. Firstly, the only precedent in the OT that pertains to a stony pavement is in the Book of Jeremiah; the prophet is trying to warn the people of Judah that they are making a great mistake in deciding to go to Egypt to flee the famine that is ravishing them. "Be well aware," he says, "that I have warned you today that you have made a fatal mistake" (Jer 42:19–20). He is told by God to collect some large stones and to place them in the "clay pavement" that is situated at the entrance to the Pharaoh's palace, then God adds: "I am going to send my servant ... and I/he will set his throne above these stones that I have buried, and he will spread his royal canopy over them" (43:10). The site functions as a place of judgement, where all are resigned to their destiny, after which the servant-king is given credit for destroying the temples and false practices of the Egyptians, only to *escape* "safely."

In the FG passage, I propose, it is *Jesus* who is seated on the "judges' bench," not Pilate (and the Greek *can* be read this way, i.e., "Pilate led Jesus out. And he sat down on the judgement seat"). Jesus is robed *as a king*, being mocked *as a king*, so the prefect stresses the ridicule by seating the accused on the tribunal, a seat symbolising Roman authority (Josephus, *Wars*. 2.14.8; 18.3.1); "Behold the king!" Pilate announces, sarcastically (John 18:14). The point is, Jesus *is* a king, as far as he (and the FG) is concerned, i.e., the King of Israel. He is God's 'servant', he has been campaigning for the overthrow of the rule of Judah; he has symbolically 'destroyed' the temple. The Jews are, indeed, making a "fatal mistake" but fatal to *them*, not to Jesus, for Jesus *will* escape with his life. How much closer does it have to be?

Secondly, just to make the parallel even more *profound*, the place in which Jeremiah's 'king' (commonly interpreted to imply Nebuchadnezzar) is to concentrate his attentions is Heliopolis, that is, the city of On; it is the daughter of a priest of On, recall, whom Joseph (son of Jacob) marries, and it is Joshua who, on returning Joseph's bones to his native land, declares that all contact with the Israelites' Egyptian heritage must be rejected. Now Jesus, son of Joseph, the new King of Israel, fulfils the cycle by symbolically coming to sit over the 'pavement', the *final sign of victory* over everything that has held Israel back. We should also make note of the fact that "mercy seat" is the term used for the cover of the Ark of the Covenant in Exod 25:17–22, inferring once more that Jesus and this sacred object are to be linked somehow.

The position of the original 'pavement' at the entrance of the Pharaoh's palace provides another clue as to where Jesus and Pilate are standing, i.e., both the 'pavement' and the name Gabbatha hint at a royal palace context but there are two to choose from, and here Josephus is not very helpful, as he simply refers to "the palace" (*Wars*. 2.14.8). It is a fair guess, however, that the Roman leader would opt to stay in the more luxurious and isolated Palace of Herod, on the western fringe of the city, than the older and smaller Hasmonean Palace, which was really in the thick of the town. For a military *tribunal*, however, the Hasmonean Palace seems perfect; it is located much closer to the temple, and the public square below provides for an elevated position overlooking the crowd, which seems to justify the common understanding of "Gabbatha" as "a raised place, or elevation." Indeed, early Christian tradition maintained that the Hasmonean Palace *was* the site of Jesus' open humiliation by Pilate, though many scholars today opt for Herod's Palace.

Regarding the name "Gabbatha," what makes Jesus' kingship legitimate is that the Father has sent him, so the FG has been telling us; his is a divinely sanctioned office, right? The passage from Jeremiah suggests that whoever sits over these stones is God's 'servant' and the rightful leader; in the Additions to Esther 12:1, the personal name Gabatha (given to a *servant* of the *palace)* is generally translated as "given by God" or "given of the Father." This interpretation has never been applied to the seat of judgement simply because it is incongruous with the traditional, Christian interpretation of the scene. With the force of the evidence *now* available to us, we can see how this becomes the FG's final statement of Jesus' inevitable victory.

The Final Word
Pilate *hands* Jesus "over to them to be crucified," i.e., he hands Jesus over *to* the Jews (again insinuating that they *are* allowed to execute him). As far as Pilate is concerned, the Jewish authorities want the rebel dead, so *they* can go away and kill him, while he sits back, 'washes his hands' of the whole affair (which isn't so much a sign that he wants nothing to do with it but rather, that the entire debacle is over), and returns to Rome with his tale of defending the realm. As far as the Jews are concerned, Pilate has sanctioned the death of a man they, by their own judicial system, could not *justly* execute. The wrath of Rome is kept at bay (for the Jews) and Pilate's soldiers perform the deed, leaving the Jews free to prepare for the Passover. It all seems quite neat and tidy.

However, Pilate makes certain everyone in the land knows of the consequences of trying to manipulate the representative of Rome, by wording the inscription on the *titulus*, the sign above Jesus' head: "Jesus the Nazorean, King of the Jews" and not "This man said: 'I am King of the Jews'," as the Jews have requested. This final insult to the people Pilate so vehemently dislikes is so in keeping with his nature, yet the joke is on Pilate *and* the Jews, for Jesus *is* the Nazorean, the consecrated one, etc. He is very soon to become the Jews' king, symbolically, by virtue of taking up the "ruler's sceptre" at Shiloh, the final 'sign' that will affirm the fall of the 'ruler' of Judah. As ever, in the FG, the truth is revealed in the words and actions of those who are ignorant of it!

Jesus the High Priest
According to Lev 8:6–9, the investiture of the high priest includes: tunic, sash, robe, ephod (an apron-like tabard said to be used for divine communications or divination), breast piece, turban, and crown. There is also a trouser-like undergarment mentioned in Exod 28:42 and Lev 16:14 (a precaution against a priest accidentally exposing himself), so there are eight items of significance.

On the Day of Atonement, however, only four garments are worn: the undergarments, tunic, sash, and turban (these constitute the vestments of the ordinary priest, indicating that the high priest is humbled when he enters the Holy of Holies). These four items are called the "white garments" because they are made from pure linen.

> *He shall put on the holy linen tunic, and shall have*
> *the linen undergarments next to his body,*
> *fasten the linen sash, and wear the linen turban;*
> *these are the holy vestments.*
> Lev 16:4

The FG supplies us with no fewer than eight items of clothing for Jesus, if you are attentive. Some are explicitly mentioned, others symbolic or inferred, but they are all there:

★ The disciples represent the twelve tribes; the breast piece of the high priest symbolises the union of the twelve tribes, so whether or not Jesus actually walks about with a decorative pendant of twelve stones about his neck doesn't really matter. It is there symbolically.

★ Before the foot washing of John 13, Jesus is described (in the NRSV) as removing an "outer robe." In the Greek the passage reads: "lays aside the garments" (*himatia*) —in other words, he puts *at least* two garments aside. This ambiguity is intentional to get the reader to question *why* he would need to take off more than one piece of clothing to wash his disciples' feet.

I suggest we are to understand that Jesus puts aside: **ephod / crown / robe**. He is left, symbolically, with: **sash / tunic / turban / undergarment.** That is, the four "white garments" of the high priest on the Day of Atonement. The **breast piece** is represented by the twelve disciples themselves, and the **ephod**, perhaps the strangest of all, might be said to represent Jesus' own 'communications' with the Father.

* He wraps around himself a *lention* or linen cloth. Compare this to Josephus' description of the priestly tunic and the doing of physical (ritualistic) labour:

  > [The tunic (*kethoneth*)] is girded to the breast a little above the elbows, by a girdle often going round, four fingers broad ... the warp was nothing but fine linen ... when it had gone often round, it is there tied, and hangs loosely there down to the ankles: I mean this all the time the priest is not about any laborious service ... that he may not be hindered in his operation by its motion, he throws it to his left and bears it on his shoulder.
  >
  > *Ant.* 3.7.2

  The *lention* thus acts as the "girdle" wrapped around the tunic but note that Jesus' 'girdle' is of the lowly, ordinary priest design, not hanging down like that of the high priest. This is to reiterate Jesus' humility in preparation for his Day of Atonement, a humility he uses as an example to his disciples (John 13:14–15).

* The Roman soldiers place upon Jesus' head a "wreath" (*stephanos*), i.e., a "crown," and they place about him a "purple" garment in their bid to ridicule him as a self-imposed king. Again, the irony of the situation rests on the actions of the antagonists, for not only is purple a royal colour, it is also the colour of the altar cloth, as described in Num 4:13, emphasizing the symbolic *sacrificial* theme of the event. Further, in the NRSV version of Job 29:14 "righteousness" and "justice" are worn like a 'robe' and a 'turban', and in Bar 5:2 the "robe" represents righteousness and the crown/diadem, glory, making Jesus' *apparent* demise an utterly honourable one.[12] These two articles, however, serve a dual purpose: they are both *priestly* and *regal* symbols.

  The *chiton,* or "tunic," is purposefully described in terms that relate to the high priest's robe, i.e., "this vesture was not composed of two pieces, nor was it sewed together upon the shoulders and the sides, but it was one long vestment" (Josephus, *Ant.* 3.7.4). According to Exod 28:32, the 'robe' of the high priest is to have a "woven binding around the [neck] opening ... so that it may not be torn." Scholars searching for a 'priestly' Jesus often cite this as evidence but hasten to point out that it is the *himation*, the outer

---

[12] The use of *stéphanos*, according to *Strong's Concordance*, suggests "properly, a wreath (garland), awarded to a victor in the ancient athletic games (like the Greek Olympics); the crown of victory ...." So, this is a positive allusion, a sign that Jesus is the victor in this scene, not the victim.

robe, not the *chiton*, or under-tunic, of the high priest that is made in such a way. Jesus has just been ridiculed as a supposedly fake-king; he is wearing an outer 'robe' already, the purple one.

★ In the narrative of John 20 is an allusion to the turban of the high priest. I will discuss this at the appropriate juncture.

We cannot ignore the clear parallel to the violent stripping of Aaron of his priestly garments before he is killed; in both instances the incumbent high priest is rejected. Neither can we overlook the fact that the high-priestly vestments are themselves sacred objects and can atone for various sins. Most interestingly, the tunic atones for killing.

One also has to question why Roman soldiers would be interested in a (traditionally poor) Semite's clothes, especially if they are ripped and bloody. It may be conjectured that they want them as trophies but this would be a salacious little comment to include, bearing in mind the profundity of the FG message thus far. I think the FG author has cleverly developed this scene to reiterate the Barabbas tale about the choice the people make; but what is more, he makes it *certain* that we see Jesus as a humbled high priest, preparing for his entry into the (symbolic) Holy of Holies on his own Day of Atonement.

The soldiers' division of the clothes into four parts reiterates Jesus' four sacred "white garments." The casting of lots for Jesus' clothes is a certain reference to the same act performed by priests when the high priest's garments are removed. When they become stained with blood (from sacrificial rituals), or are too threadbare, etc., the priests cast lots to decide who will remove them and store them away. Taken symbolically, we have already seen how the vestments of the temple's high priest have been released, depicted by the choosing of Barabbas. Now we see Jesus' vestments removed in a mocking and humiliating manner, underscoring the utter rejection of his high-priestly claims by the Jews. Thus, the Roman soldiers in this scene merely serve as actors in the FG author's tale of Jesus' final denunciation by the Jews.

20
CULMINATION

Esteemed One
AT THE FOOT OF THE cross stands Mary, now the Magdalene. The name Magdalene is often translated to mean "tower" but often nothing more is said of this epithet. In fact, it stems from the Hebrew word *migdalah*, the root word of which is *gadal*, which means "to make large," i.e., "to magnify, increase, become great." It is used in Song 4:4; 7:4; 8:10; as we saw in John 12, Mary's anointing scene is introduced with *four* allusions to the Song of Solomon and to that woman's ascent from a more fundamental status.

According to Eccl 26:22, a "married woman" is equated to a "tower," so we can again assume that Mary is, indeed, married. A tower is usually associated with the defence of a gate and Mary has already been described as the guardian of a 'gate' (both metaphorically, as the mother of the child and within the storyline, as the "gatekeeper"). Having completed her rise to glory from the harlot-bride, the adulteress, the Nazarite, Mary is now honoured; she becomes the 'tower' of God, the beloved and rejoiced-in bride who has turned away from her 'wicked' past.

"Magdalene," which indicates Mary's symbolic elevation in status, also incorporates the Hebrew term *magdiy'el*, which means "preciousness of God":

meged + *'el*

"to be eminent, valuable" + "God"
(also another meaning of *gadal*)

As the consecrated tower, the new Bride of God, Mary *is* the 'eminent' one. If she is now the guardian of the first *conceived* heir to the high-priesthood of Shiloh, she *is* 'valuable'.

Wife of Clopas
The name Clopas appears in John 19:25 in association with a Mary often presumed to be a character *distinct* from the Magdalene. We have not come

across a "Mary the wife of Clopas" but "Mary the wife of Clopas, the Magdalene" would make perfect sense. There is a duality to the FG remember, that is consistent and permeates almost every scene; characters are purposefully linked or renamed, in an effort to urge the reader to make a connection. The clue to deciphering this name is the fact that this is the *only* instance in which a woman in the FG is mentioned by *direct* reference to her husband. Mary, our Mary Magdalene, is the only woman to be similarly depicted, i.e., as the Samaritan woman who has many husbands, as the adulteress, and as the woman offering herself at the feet of Jesus.

There are two schools of thought regarding the name Clopas. One is based on Luke's gospel, in which a similar name occurs (and remember, Luke also has a Lazarus), i.e., Cleopas (Luke 24:18). A contraction of Cleopater (or Cleopatros), this is a Greek name and refers to a disciple who meets Jesus on the road after the supposed resurrection. Its translation is "of a renowned father." Is this "father" the divine Father, making Jesus "Clopas," or is Jesus the father-figure, making his 'son-figure', Lazarus, "Clopas"? Again, the clues are ambiguous, pointing to either Jesus or Lazarus! The other side of the issue is the fact that some scholars claim Clopas is not a true derivation of Cleopas, that it is an Aramaic name the same as "Alphaeus," which appears in the Synoptics to indicate the father of James the Less; Alphaeus means, of all things, "changing," and this, also, suits both Jesus *and* Lazarus, who are about to undergo 'changes' in the upcoming scenes. In any case, Clopas cannot be reduced to the same Hebrew root as Alphaeus, so the two cannot be identical even if they both have potential significance to an FG character.

Retaining the FG's 'Clopas' then, what can we discover? Well, phonetically, the k-l-o-p elements of the FG's Aramaic-based name, in Greek, i.e., *Klopas,* form the basis of *kalopoieo,* which means, "to do well, or to live virtuously," an apt description of both Mary *and* Lazarus, who have undergone a moral/spiritual conversion. It may also be a play on *chalowph,* the Hebrew term for "surviving," derived from *chalaph* ("to spring up, pass on, renew," etc.). Such a term is used in Ps 102:28, where it is stated that the "children of [God's] servants shall live secure; *their offspring shall be established in [his] presence.*" It also appears in the passage concerning the purification of the nation in Zech 3:4, and in the Isaiah passage (Isa 40:31) echoed in John 12:38–40: "wait, for the Lord shall renew their strength." There is one other possible phonetic play on words:

kallah + *paz*

"son's bride" + "who is pure"
(i.e., "daughter-in-law")

245

So, whatever its original form, and whatever its linguistic roots, I think the name in John 19:25 is a created name, i.e., a commission name, intended a) to combine the various elements common to both Mary and her husband, to give them both a new, exalted status, and/or b) to reiterate the dual nature of the marital arrangement between Mary and the two men.

Last Will
Jesus is reaching his hour of glory when his suffering will come to an end; once he has 'poured his soul out to death' he will be redeemed and glorified by the Father. This is the plan, anyway. Jesus *intends* to be a scapegoat for the sake of Lazarus, Mary, and the child but he does *not* intend to die. Besides, only false prophets die an ignominious death (Deut 13:5f); in his role as the "servant" Jesus has been promised a "portion with the great"—a "future."

The first clues we really have to suggest this might be the case come in the form of the patterns within the narrative of the FG, i.e., they are consistent and always reveal something new within the context of the ongoing theme of reunification and resurrection (of Shiloh). We have seen how the author uses duality, triple repetition, the placing of truths upon an adversary's lips, the use of OT passages to allude to something happening in the 'present'. In the passages of the FG that are overtly calling on OT precedents, e.g., by paraphrasing or quoting directly, you will find that most instances reflect the sentiments found in the Psalms. The rest echo the books of Isaiah, Jeremiah, and the Pentateuch in that order of frequency.

In John 19 we see three allusions to Psalms in quick succession. Each one of these psalms depicts the dire situation of its author, held captive, at death's door, tormented, injured, seemingly without any hope. At the last moment, however, God intervenes and *rescues* his loyal servant from certain death.

John 19:24 & Ps 34:20: "He keeps all their bones; not one of them will be broken."
John 19:28 & Ps 69:21: "They gave me poison for food, and for my thirst they gave me vinegar to drink."
John 19:36 & Ps 22:18: "They divide my clothes among themselves, and for my clothing they cast lots."

There is no doubt in my mind that Jesus, though preparing for the worst case scenario, has every intention of securing for himself the future he has been preparing for and the Promised Land he has been promising his followers. As part of his duty to have every contingency prepared for (e.g., such as having his deputy ready to stand in for him), Jesus is seen to hand his 'beloved' Lazarus over *not* to his "mother" but to his wife, Martha. The important theme of this scenario is inheritance, i.e., a formal adoption is taking place.

According to the inheritance laws of Deut 21:15–17, a man with two wives is not permitted to favour the sons of the preferred wife over and above those of the first wife. The greater portion is the absolute right of the firstborn; Lazarus became Jesus' symbolic 'son' long before Mary conceived and the duties and responsibilities expected of the eldest cannot be expected of the child, so it is Lazarus who is formally and legally *granted* the status of firstborn, so he can inherit Jesus' worldly goods, his title, his responsibilities, and his affiliation to the Josephite tradition.[1] To make such an inheritance legal, Jesus must hand over his estate while he is *alive* and must do so in front of witnesses (in the Jewish tradition a person on the brink of death is called a *goses* and his verbal Last Will and Testament is binding). This is just what he is doing.

What of Philip? Is he not Jesus' firstborn? Technically, yes, but remember that much of Lazarus' story parallels that of Joseph, son of Jacob, who inherited the rights of the firstborn over and above his less competent older brothers; Lazarus now accepts the duties and responsibilities of the eldest son. Lazarus thus takes on the name Joseph, and this will act as his final commission name, i.e., Joseph of Arimathea. He also takes on the role of protector of Martha, who is, *legally* at this point, Jesus' widow, but is Mary also? This is another clue to a marriage having taken place between her and *Lazarus*, for no provision is made for this all so important figure; she must already be secured a future with her young husband, the new Joseph. The "Clopas" designation hinting at the 'pure daughter-in-law' thus becomes more meaningful.

Whether Mary and Jesus are united in a purely symbolic marriage, or a real one, I do not know but it does seem that once the ritualistic significance of the relationship and the conception of the son is assured, the mundane responsibility of her charge falls to Lazarus, who will act as regent until the child is 'of age'.

Thus, the strange but well-attested and long-since celebrated legend of Martha fleeing to safety in Avignon with Lazarus and Mary, where she becomes the famous dragon slayer, sounds just a little less spurious, at least in terms of who went with whom. Someone else, it would seem, realised that Lazarus and Joseph of Arimathea (the male companion in most other legends) were one and the same, and that it was Martha, not Jesus' 'mother'

---

[1] Num 27:5–11 explains the order of legal inheritance as being first son, then daughter, brothers, father's brothers, and finally, nearest kinsman.

beneath the cross.

One should always pay heed to even the strangest of myths!

Potion and Piercing

Jesus declares that he is "thirsty" and an addendum points out that this must refer to some fulfilment of scripture, but how? The only precedents that would fit this context are Ps 69:29 and Ps 107:5, which tell of the hunger and thirst of those who cry out to be "delivered ... from their distress" *and their subsequent rescue*; and Isa 21:14, which orders water be brought to those who have *"fled from ... the stress of battle."*

Some interpreters suggest that the original word, *hussos*, in John 19:29 for the stick or lance that is used to raise the liquid to Jesus' lips, means "javelin," copied and transmitted erroneously as "hyssop." The gospel actually implies that it is Jesus' *own* disciples at the foot of the cross who give him the vinegary drink, i.e., "they" have just completed the transfer of inheritance, and then "they" give him the 'sour wine'; Jesus' disciples would not have a Roman javelin/spear. I argue that "hyssop" is, indeed, correct, as we shall see in a moment.

There are two types of vinegar-wine, one inherently Jewish, the other, Roman. The former is a strong wine that has been allowed to turn sour, or an intentionally fermentable mixture of barley and cheap wine; it is notoriously unpleasant to drink (Ps 69:21; Prov 10:26) and is used as a liquid for the 'dipping of the sop' when labourers are to be fed (Ruth 2:14). The latter, the Roman *acetum*, is a thin, sour liquid, again, used to fortify soldiers (who, presumably, will drink anything!). As the disciples bring it, we can assume it to be the former.

Admittedly, one of the first symptoms of dying by crucifixion seems to be thirst but why not bring water? Why give Jesus a drink that will probably make him sick into the bargain? Unless, of course, the foul taste of the wine is intended to disguise the bitter taste, or perhaps strong smell of a concoction placed within it, just in case someone else should notice? A concoction, that is, intended to knock Jesus out. Water would not hide anything and the fermentation of the 'sour wine' may well speed up the effect; in fact, the Greek term used to describe the liquid is *oxos*, which stems from *oxus*, meaning "keen/sharp/swift." Some scholars have questioned whether this mixture could have contained hyoscine, a powerful muscle relaxant and sedative used even today as a pre-med before surgery, which is extracted from the mandrake root, something of which early physicians and/or herbalists would certainly have been aware.

In fact, Josephus offers quite a lengthy discourse (*Wars.* 7.6.3) on the mandrake root (called Barras, after the area in which it was found), in which it is claimed that only the urine or menstrual blood of women could subdue its powers as it was plucked from the earth. This would have been common folklore. This may seem a bit of a tangent but when you consider the only people the FG states are under the cross are the *women* (John 19:25), perhaps there is an intended clue here; if only women can handle the toxin 'safely', perhaps it is they who administer it. True in the pragmatic sense or not, it is yet another 'coincidence' that serves to affirm it is the family who give Jesus the potion, not the Roman soldiers.

By comparison, in Luke 23:36, the 'sour wine' becomes an aspect of the soldiers' mockery (Ps 69:21); nothing is mentioned of Jesus taking or rejecting it. In Mark 15:23, Jesus refuses the drink containing myrrh, a known stimulant; he wants to be unconscious not have his senses heightened, at least, not at this stage, which could be another indication of Mark's lack of understanding; as myrrh figures in the FG's 'resuscitation' scene, it may be that Mark simply gets his wires crossed (thereby suggesting a post-FG Gospel of Mark?). Only in Matt 27:34 is there a more detailed description of the concoction; it contains gall (in Hebrew, *rosh)*, which is intensely bitter. "Gall" seems to refer to a poisonous plant (Deut 29:18; Lam 3:19; Hos 10:4) and some botanists have suggested it could be a poppy-like weed which, if it bears any resemblance to the source of opium, would certainly act in the opposite way to myrrh, i.e., it would be a sedative. Jesus apparently takes a sip, though he does not drink the lot.

In the FG, Jesus appears to be signalling to (his 'beloved') Lazarus below him that *now* is the moment to give him the drink previously prepared. There is an echo, here, of Jesus' words in the garden during the arrest scene: "Am I not to drink the cup my Father has given me?" If Peter's actions had led to everyone getting killed by the soldiers, Jesus' anticipated rise to glory would be impossible; he would simply be another Roman statistic, killed by the sword for causing a disruption.

So, Jesus is given this 'sour' wine to drink, perhaps on a sponge balanced on a hyssop branch. During the original Passover in Egypt, when the "Lord [passed] through" killing the firstborn, the blood of the lamb was spread over the lintels of the Israelites' houses—*with a hyssop branch*—so that Death could not enter (Exod 12:22). This symbolic act is thus alluded to in the FG, insinuating yet again that Jesus will *not* die on the cross; at *this* Passover; Death *will* 'pass him over'. One apparent inference to Jesus' survival may be coincidental or even imagined but there are repeated hints within the text of the FG that point to this very conclusion.

In Num 19:14–20, the hyssop is used to sprinkle the water of purification onto one who has come in *contact* with the dead; the ritual is to be repeated on the third and seventh days, i.e., the FG's sacred days. It is used as a purging or cleansing agent in Ps 51:7, in a context of atonement and sacrifice. Jesus is hanging between two dead prisoners and is thus rendered unclean; if this action with the hyssop is intended to symbolise an attempt to carry out the purification process, Jesus' reaction to Mary on the *third* day (i.e., he warns her not to touch him because he is *preparing* to go to the Father) is even more understandable. He has been defiled and cannot risk nullifying his purification ritual. When Jesus is met again, later, wounds still fresh, he invites Thomas to 'touch' them, so the final ritual on the *seventh* day must also take place, in order for him to accept contact.

No sooner does he drink, than Jesus is rendered unconscious and so deeply that the Roman guards do not even bother to break his legs. The breaking of the legs, requested by the Jews in John 19:31, is done to hasten death. Although it would normally be a merciful act, where the condemned has hung on the cross for several days and is near death anyway, the situation here is different; it is Passover, and the Jews simply want to be away in time to prepare. No work can be done the next day, as it is the Sabbath, and no one can venture out to 'check' on the crucified. To ensure Jesus' speedy demise, the Jews request this violent act be performed with haste. By the time the other two prisoners are thus 'broken', Jesus is out cold. Many interpreters suggest this serves to further emphasize Jesus' role as the Passover lamb because this animal is not allowed to have its bones broken (Exod 12:46) but, as I explained earlier, the lamb does not bear away any 'sin'.

Jesus' legs are not broken for the sole reason that he *appears* to be dead. The plan is to rescue him, which is why the drink is provided so quickly; his escape will be hindered, perhaps even foiled, if he is injured so severely. Nail wounds, even the wounds from the flogging, though painful, are not necessarily life-threatening. Men *have* survived worse. However, I wonder if such a turn of events took Jesus and his entourage by surprise and if the piercing wound (not a superficial scratch to test response but a faster plunging, potentially fatal alternative to the breaking of the legs) that ultimately causes Jesus' death not too long later.

"It is finished" (John 19:30), Jesus declares. Theologically, he refers to his mission "in the world" and he "delivers up his spirit" i.e., the 'spirit' he has had conferred upon him as a prophet, as God's chosen 'son' or representative. It is his divine authority that Jesus surrenders; he is no longer the instrument of God's will on earth. Lazarus must now take over, having prepared for this moment the week before, when he was formally made deputy high priest. Perhaps, though, we should hear the uncertainty in Jesus' voice that we can see in his handling of the Mount Gerizim disaster, hence the Synoptics' emphasis on Jesus questioning why he has been abandoned by God at such a critical hour. Clearly, the FG author could not suggest this, so he turns what might be deemed ill fate into a holy sign by claiming water, rather than blood, spouts from the unexpected wound.

This has become a matter of some debate amongst historians, biologists, doctors and theologians. Such a question, though, reflects the various levels of comprehension demonstrated in John 12:20f, where the Greeks had asked to 'see Jesus' and not to 'see the Father': it is a question asked at the very basic, empirical level, rather than at the interpretive. If we understand what Jesus has been trying to do throughout the narrative of the FG, we must anticipate a deeper significance for the 'water' that leaves his body as he hangs upon the cross. Again, we must recognise what is historical and what is theological.

Consider what has just happened. Jesus has been sent to die a terrible death; he has been handed over by fellow Israelites, and he has been subjected to the humility of having Barabbas chosen over him by the very people he had invited to follow him. He has offered himself as the source of 'life' in the Father: "Let anyone who is thirsty come to me" he calls out at the Festival of Tabernacles (John 7:37).

The NRSV translates the subsequent verse as, "Out of the believer's heart shall flow rivers of living water" but in the Greek, it reads, "Out of *his belly* shall flow rivers of living water," making the imagery of the crucifixion scene all the more profound. Now reflect on the following passage:

> Be appalled, O heavens, at this, be shocked, be utterly desolate says the Lord, for my people have committed two evils: They have forsaken me, the fountain of living water, and dug out cisterns for themselves, cracked cisterns that can hold no water.
>
> Jer 2:12–13

The excerpt was referred to in the context of the waters of purification at the wedding feast in John 2 but it suits this context even better; when Jesus' body is opened by the lance, out flows the "river of living water" he had *promised* would be there for those who sought it. The choosing of Barabbas (and thus the extant priesthood) only reveals the ignorance and susceptibility of the people; they think they are safe and wise in their choice. They do not see that they are digging for themselves a 'cistern' which will not hold the water to quench their spiritual 'thirst'. This symbolism has nothing whatever to do with Jesus' physical body. It should not be taken literally, and the gospel's earliest intended audience, i.e., devout Israelites, would not have taken it thus (see 1 John 5:6).[2]

To the Samaritans recall, the "rivers of living water" would flow from Mount Gerizim in the end days, as a sign that all is 'restored'; the FG shifts the location, but not the concept!

---

[2] I see John 19:35–7 as a post-FG (Christian) addendum.

Joseph

Josephus explains that when someone dies, the "nearest relations should perform their obsequies" (*A. A.* 2.27). The Roman governor would generally allow a member of the family to receive the body of the crucified relative if petition were made. Lazarus, now "Joseph" and legally (not just symbolically) Jesus' 'son', receives the body.

Joseph's action echoes that of his ancient namesake, Joseph, son of Jacob, in Gen 50:4f, for both approach a foreign leader with a request to remove the body of one who is much loved, i.e., a father, and both are granted their request. Also, the fate of both characters runs parallel; each endures a type of bondage, a leader releases both, and both are elevated to an important position at the leader's right hand. The Josephite tradition in the FG provides a sort of cyclical fulfilment to the history of Israel and here, below the cross, the pattern is complete, for Joseph of Arimathea becomes the King of Israel's beloved son, just as the original Joseph had been the beloved son of Israel (Jacob). There is about to be a *return* to the land of Joseph, to the religion of Joseph's ancestors.

Some researchers have queried the description of Joseph going "boldly" to Pilate in Mark 15:43, i.e., why should there be any element of fear or trepidation, if the accepted procedure is to hand bodies over to the relatives, anyway? If that 'relative' is *already* in fear of his life, as Lazarus is, trepidation seems justifiable. Lazarus, under a death sentence (John 12:10), has been incognito (reflected in his temporary lack of a commission name). His secret alliance to Jesus is mentioned explicitly in John 19:38, where the word *krypto* is used, which implies hiding, or concealing. In the full commission name of Joseph *of Arimathea* is also a subtle verification of this disciple's dangerous situation: Arimathea (Gk), from *Ramathayim* (Hb), from *ramah* ("to delude/deceive"). Although this may seem an isolated incident, actually, it is not, for we soon enter into another situation where Lazarus is *expected* to be in disguise—on the day of Jesus' release from the 'tomb'.

This is a good time to mention the Gospel of Nicodemus, for, although it is a much later document, it concentrates very much on the supposed fate of Joseph of Arimathea; he tends to Jesus in the tomb but he is *also* incarcerated by the Jews in a "building without a window," is sentenced to death, 'miraculously' emancipated, referred to as 'Father' as a sign of status (i.e., Clopas, above), anointed, and found in the company of the 'risen' Jesus. Sounds very much like the Lazarus/Joseph of the FG, allegedly written by (or attributed to) the character we now know to be the boy's father, Nicodemus.

21
SECRETS AND SURVIVAL

Myrrh and Aloes

BACK IN JOHN 12, MARY had used but a handful of the oil Jesus had assigned for the time of his 'burial'. There is, however, no mention of the Synoptics' now famous "alabaster jar"; spikenard was a very expensive spicy oil from India and Tibet and its strong perfume was protected on export by thick-walled alabaster jars, small jars, which would normally be sold individually because of the cost. How she procures and handles the oil is a clue we should not overlook and the mere presence of such luxuries does suggest a wealth that Joseph of Arimathea is supposedly renowned for (e.g., in the Synoptics).

Mary, we are told, takes a 'pound' (*litra*) of the nard. Where does she take it from and how much is there in *total*? This is not just a small dollop in the palm of the hand; this is a substantial amount of something apparently very valuable. It is, it seems, being stored in *larger* amounts somewhere in the house at Bethany, Lazarus' (Joseph's) house.

Nicodemus' "myrrh and aloes," it must be noted, have seldom been connected to Mary's action, other than to remark that both are mentioned in terms of a burial. Many scholars suggest Jesus' body is merely *anointed* with this "mixture" but why would so *much* be needed, i.e., "almost a hundred pounds"? Embalming has also been a potential explanation but the procedure is extremely rare in Jesus' day, and would need extraordinary skill, effort, time (traditionally seventy days), and facilities; there is nothing in the FG to suggest this is what is going on, besides, Jesus *is not* dead, remember!

The substances Mary and Nicodemus use come, I suggest, from the same source, i.e., the secretly stored oils of the new priesthood; some would be for incense, some for anointing. Some, though, double as medicines. Spikenard is used in the ancient world to treat joint pain and chest ailments—handy for someone just crucified! Myrrh is a known *antiseptic* and has been used as such for centuries even by this time; in large amounts it can also accelerate the heartbeat and acts as a purgative. The aloes, perhaps a blend of several curative plants, including *aloe vera*, are specifically renowned for their wound-healing capabilities; they soothe, generate tissue repair, and reduce the risk of infection. Aloe may *also* be used as an extremely potent purgative. If Jesus is dead, why bring healing gels and purging potions? If he has been given a strong sedative, however, and his heart has slowed down, such stimulants would revive him, albeit rather drastically. He has to flush out his system and tend his wounds, in order to be up and ready for what is to come. It makes the whole scene very realistic, down to earth, and un-miraculous I know, but in the *real* world of first century religious zeal and medical know-how, it makes sense.

The manner in which Jesus' hasty 'burial' is described suggests that the lengths of linen called *kerias* (as in the binding of Lazarus' hands and feet) are *not* used but that larger 'sheets' of linen, called *othonioa* are used. Why? Because they are more suited to the job in hand, i.e., the rapid concealment of a still-breathing body and the poultices on still bleeding, widespread wounds. The term used to describe Jesus being "wrapped" in these linens is actually a derivative of *deo*, "to bind" but his *entire* body is bound, unlike Lazarus' (indicating, yet again, that the two supposed 'burials' are far from similar); the process, we are assured, follows the "burial custom of the Jews" (John 19:40). Why, *if* this phrase is original to the text, should the FG author make such a statement, given the alienation from the Jews throughout? The whole point is to *act* as though Jesus is dead. They have not yet brought him to the makeshift 'tomb', so the wrapping must take place somewhere between the cross and the site of burial, where anyone can see. The disciples must feign burial procedures, so the Jews suspect nothing. They bind Jesus with some of the 'spices' just as they would a dead body but the ointment is intended as a salve for his wounds.

> *[B]ruises and sores and bleeding wounds ... drained*
> *... bound up ... softened with oil.*
> Isa 1:6

> *And when the physicians once thought it fit to have [Herod] bathed in a vessel full of oil, it was supposed that he was just dying: but upon the lamentable cries of his domestics, he revived*
> Ant. 17.6.5

Jesus has been whipped, pierced by nails, and (unexpectedly) stabbed, so the oils bound closely to his sores act as a poultice, a cleansing agent, and even a local anaesthetic.[1] I am not of the opinion that Jesus was nailed to the cross by his hands *and* feet. None of the gospels make inference to this, so

---

[1] The notion that someone could be rescued from, and survive crucifixion is supported by an entry in Josephus (*Life.* 75), where he describes his own visit to Titus to plea for the retrieval of three of his crucified friends. They are taken down, tended, and one survives.

it is difficult to imagine how the stereotypical image came about; the FG mentions only the nail wounds in the hands (in John 20:25, however, the Greek term *cheir* is said to apply to anything from the elbow to the fingertips, so the wrist may also be inferred here, to tally with modern biological investigations).

Oils of Consecration

The large amount of oils, of "myrrhs and aloes,", may be required to 'immerse' Jesus' entire body in order to revive and soothe it, in the manner described by Josephus but taking into consideration the profundity and imminence of the situation at hand, i.e., Jesus' Day of Atonement and his rise to glory as the new King of Israel, I think we need to interpret this substance on a much deeper level. The following is just one possible take on the issue—I maintain that all numbers on the FG are significant to the consistent symbolism and themes, and the answer has to be accessible using the Hebrew scriptures and the known units of measure:

> Take the finest spices: of liquid myrrh five hundred shekels, and of sweet-smelling cinnamon half as much, that is, two hundred and fifty, and two hundred and fifty of aromatic cane, and five hundred of cassia–measured by the sanctuary shekel–and a hin of olive oil; and you shall make of these a sacred anointing-oil blended as by the perfumer; it shall be a holy anointing-oil.
>
> Exod 30:23–5

Being 'blended as by the perfumer' suggests the skilful act of *distillation*, which means the mass of the dry matter becomes inconsequential to any investigation into the final amount of the original anointing oil. As the base oil is a *hin* of olive oil, we may safely deduce that the holy oil was produced in batches of about one *hin*, to a semi-liquid consistency. There is a lack of consensus about the modern equivalent of the *hin*, and even early Jewish sources are uncertain as to the exact volume. Most conversion tables today, however, suggest 3.6 L, or 124 fl oz, so let's use that in our reckoning. Also, we need to take into consideration the *specified* vagueness, i.e., "about" in John 19:39, i.e., even the FG author can muster only a relatively accurate measurement. The Roman pound, or *litra* equates to about 12 oz. So without becoming pedantic about the odd few ounces this way or that, and bearing in mind that the intended audience had to make sense of this too, a simplified comparison offers us this: 3.6 L = 124.0 fl oz = 10.3 *litrae* (Roman pounds). So, the original anointing oil had a mass of *about* 10 *litrae* (plus or minus a few ounces).

The amount of 'mixture' Nicodemus brings to the tomb is said to be "*about* one hundred pounds (*litrae*)," so:

100 − 1 *litra* (previously used by Mary) = 99 *litrae*

99 *litrae* ÷ 10 *litrae* (original oil) = (9.9) 10 batches

Nicodemus could be transporting ten times the quantity of the original anointing oil but why would he? For many years I was convinced Jesus had arranged for the oils of consecration to be premixed and packed up awaiting transportation to Shiloh but as with everything else in the FG, the oils, spices, aloes, etc., in this scene offer *two* insights, one physical, one symbolic. It wouldn't make sense, when you think about it, for Jesus to expect his small group to haul that amount of liquid in heavy jars at night, when time will be of the essence and the element of risk high. Therefore, I suggest that in this brilliantly devised scenario we see Nicodemus arriving with enough salve to tend to Jesus' wounds and treat his condition but the mentioning of the amount, especially as it echoes the term *litra* used in Mary's scene and thus urges us to make a connection (more on this in a moment), is *intended* as a clue. We are led back to the only other "mixture" ("blended") of such ingredients, also with their amounts described, i.e., the sacred oils of Exod 30:23–5.

The original anointing oil (or rather the precise recipe) was supposedly 'lost' in the days of Josiah and, along with the Ark, marks the most fundamental deficit in the claim to the temple priesthood's supremacy. Jesus, it seems, is declaring he has both.

One may suggest that Jesus intends to have each of his disciples take one batch of the oil with them when they set out to gather the 'lost' out in Arzareth but why only ten portions? This may be the only hint in the FG of Judas' demise; he is not deemed fit to mention again but somehow between the meal at Bethany and the post-crucifixion scene he has been written off. Another possible affirmation that he died alongside Jesus that very day? Of course, the other missing portion is that belonging to Peter, for he does not receive ordination with the others, as will be discussed shortly.

According to Num 4:16, Eleazar, the 'son' of the Sinai high priest, Aaron, had *sole charge of the sacred oils used in all the priestly rituals*, and in 1 Chr 9:30, the "sons of the priests prepared the mixing of the spices," so it *does* make sense that Lazarus, 'son' of the *new* high priest, would keep any oils and spices pertaining to the priesthood at *his* house. Nicodemus carries the unguent to the site of Jesus' crucifixion (and it would not seem strange to see the grieving family arrive on the scene of execution with a bag full of cloths, jars, sponges, etc., for preparing the 'dead' body), allowing the younger and stronger Lazarus the freedom to deal with Jesus.

It is to the use of this supposedly *sacred oil*, not just any oil, that Judas reacts in John 12. An anointed priest outranks one merely invested, so perhaps he sees this blatant act of assumed superiority on Jesus' part as the final straw and cannot help but reveal his consternation (it does seem to be from the episode of the premature anointing by Mary that Judas' betrayal becomes inevitable), thus revealing his loyalty to the temple institution. Besides, the specifications of Exod 30:32–3 explicitly prohibit the use of the sacred recipe for personal use, on pain of excommunication. One could suggest, then, that Judas' apprehension is due to the apparent use of a holy oil for 'personal use'.

There are only three instances in the OT in which 'myrrh and aloes' are directly linked; two have to do with sexual intimacy, which does not suit the situation *here*. The remaining instance is this:

> In your majesty ride on victoriously for the cause of truth and to defend the right ... Your throne is a throne of God, it endures for ever and ever. Your royal sceptre is a sceptre of equity; you love righteousness and hate wickedness. Therefore, God ... has anointed you with the oil of gladness beyond your companions; your robes are all fragrant with myrrh and aloes and cassia ... In the place of ancestors you ...Shall have sons; you will make them princes in all the earth. I will cause your name to be celebrated in all generations; therefore the peoples will praise you for ever and ever.
>
> Ps 45

This combination of priestly and kingly anointing brings us back to Jesus' identification with Melchizedek and there is further evidence to suggest such an anointing, when we uncover the *site* of Jesus' hasty burial. That such oils have been kept for Jesus' burial implies a dual usage, both medicinal and ritual.

It is also worth noting that in Gen 37:25 and 43:11 of the KJV, the word "myrrh" is used to translate the Hebrew *lot*; in the NRSV the term is rendered as "resin." This substance is known for its stickiness and this property seems to be what has led to an assumed connection between '*lot*' and *luwt*, meaning, 'to wrap up, cover'. It is also phonetically similar to *lowt*, signifying a 'veil'. These two Genesis precedents, we need hardly be surprised, pertain to Joseph, son of Jacob, who is thrown into a cistern/well and is subsequently taken away to Egypt, where he rises in status and glory.

Whither Golgotha?

"Golgotha," the FG tells us, is Hebrew (*gulgolet*) or Aramaic (*gulgulta*) for "the place of the skull" (*kranion topon* in John 19:17), where Pilate has Jesus crucified. The first claim to its whereabouts wasn't until the fourth century (326 CE), when Empress Helena founded the Church of the Holy Sepulchre in Jerusalem. Over the centuries, this location was questioned by some, revered by others, but in the nineteenth century, Scottish doctor R. F. Hutchinson (1870) proposed Golgotha lay on the slopes of the Mount of Olives. Twenty years later, General Gordon made an expedition to Jerusalem and suggested an area below a rocky outcrop just beyond Old Jerusalem's northern wall, near the Damascus Gate. Legend had it this was the site of "Jeremiah's grotto" and that it was a place of stoning. It was said the rocks bore a passing resemblance to a face or skull and became known as Gordon's Calvary. So there have been at least three suggested sites. It will come as no surprise that I shall offer a fourth alternative, based on what we find in the FG.

The *traditional* site of Golgotha lies at the loose juncture of three main roads, i.e., one leading to Bethlehem, one to Galilee, and the other to Jericho. This is, admittedly, an apt place for a *Roman* site of execution, being in a prominent place for all to see and be warned by the executions. The name Golgotha however, is not Roman (Latin) but Hebrew, the FG makes this clear, implying a pre-occupation, Jewish site. After all, we know that the Jews did 'hang' people on trees, to show their disdain for executed blasphemers, etc., so they must have had a suitable, regular place for such occasions. The Romans, known for adapting local customs to suit their own needs, would surely have taken over an existing site, just as they seemed to have taken over the main roads, cisterns, and the like. Had Golgotha been in this central location, anyone entering or leaving the city by the main gates there would be contaminated by the constant presence of death, and as neither Josephus nor any contemporary historian suggests this was a problem for Jerusalem, it cannot have been the case. It would seem more practical to place such an ignominious but obviously necessary site as far *away* as possible from the more distinguished Upper City area, which housed the royal palaces, the high priests' houses, etc.

According to 2 Kgs 23:6 (see Jer. 26:23) there is a burial site beyond the walls, near the south-eastern corner of Temple Mount, for the "common people"; this would be a more likely situation for the burial of criminals than in the upper quarters, where the wealthy choose to carve out their tombs. Also, on the Mount of Olives, which I mentioned earlier, with respect to the "garden" Jesus is arrested in, is the site of the burning of the red heifer, the ashes of which, alone, could be used to purify oneself after contamination with the dead. If we accept the traditional sites for Golgotha northwest of the city, we must ask why a supposedly constantly-used site of execution be on the *other* side of town to the means of purification. Yes, it could be carried in small quantities elsewhere but why not have all such things together, in the same place? The Fullers Field that is mentioned in 2 Kgs 18:17 and Isa 7:3 (36:2) seems to lie in this very region, or at least to the east rather than the west of the city walls. The scene depicted in these passages, intriguingly, is one of secrecy, strategy, and the rights of kingship. The first (2 Kgs 18:17) involves King Hezekiah (who will figure again in a moment) and the attack of the Assyrians on Jerusalem; the place of meeting between the *three* representatives of the Israelites and the Assyrians is "by the conduit of the upper pool, which is on the highway to the Fullers Field."

The attack of the Assyrians progresses not from the north as one would generally assume but from the south, as they take Gaza first, then Lacish (which is south-west of Jerusalem), *then* they head up toward Jerusalem. The "conduit" is in the general area of the main entrance to the old City of David, that is, to the southeast of Jerusalem, where the Gihon spring feeds the Pool of Siloam. When one considers what a fuller does, there is a satisfying continuity with other aspects of this side of the city; a fuller cleanses and whitens clothing, and makes the whitewash for warning signs at places of burial. It is a messy, smelly job, involving urine and chalk, and no doubt would have been relegated to the generally degraded east side of town. Thus the Fullers Field must be on the eastern side of the city, between the Gihon and the Mount of Olives. So, to suggest that the site of continual death, i.e., thousands upon thousands of crucified men, should lie quite a distance away from the graves, the fuller's yard, and the preparation of the ashes of purification, seems erroneous.[2]

Another reference, almost unnoticed, is provided in John 19:20: "Many of the Jews read [the] inscription because the place where Jesus was crucified was near the city." Could this suggest that the site lies closer to the city than 'normal' crucifixions? Could it be that due to the surreptitious nature of the arrest and trial, with everything done at night and in secret, the last thing the authorities want is to suddenly reveal their plans to the masses? In the account of the choosing of Barabbas, it is the "Jews", not the 'crowd' who are baying for Jesus' blood. Wouldn't it be prudent for the crucifixion itself to be carried out quietly? If there are only three to be executed (19:32), and the affair is clandestine, perhaps there is an alternative site. Why

---

[2] There is a suggestion from certain archaeologists that a fuller's quarter existed in the Essene community near Mt. Zion, to the south west of the city, and that one of the many cisterns found there was probably used as a bleaching bath for their white robes. The exact location of Mt. Zion, however, has not been verified, nor have the Essene dwellings within the city walls. Even if the suggestion is valid, it would make sense for the restrictive Essenes to provide their own fuller, in order to meet their own exacting standards. Such a small operation would not have been sufficient for an entire city. Josephus also lists the "Monument to the Fuller" at the north-eastern edge of the city (*Wars.* 5.4.2).

mention that many people notice the *titulus* above Jesus' head? Again, if the traditional site is on a public thoroughfare, wouldn't *everyone* see it? If, however, the normal site for executions is well away from the city (which to me makes more sense), then fewer citizens would venture out (apart from soldiers and the families retrieving the dead), so the fact that 'many' did see it suggests a closer location than *usual*.

The Kidron area has four hills, the most northerly being the Mount of Olives, while the most southerly, at the juncture of the Hinnom and Kidron valleys, is commonly referred to as the Mount of Offence. Solomon supposedly erected sites of worship there for his foreign wives (1 Kgs 11:7) and when Josiah later demolished these, the hill was referred to as the Mount of Destruction (2 Kgs 23:13), a fitting epitaph that will again prove significant. Then, in Jer 19:1f, the area was labelled the Valley of Slaughter. This is sounding more and more like a suitable place for crucifixions.

We know that a soldiers' barracks existed just inside the eastern wall of the city. Taking into consideration the process normally involved in arresting, sentencing, and executing prisoners, and the frequency with which such Roman sentencing obviously occurred, it makes sense for the soldiers and the execution site to be in close proximity. The reference in Neh 3:16, to the "graves" and "the house of the warriors" would seem to point to this same area and although this clearly predates any Roman invasion, it is another example of the occupying forces taking over established sites that suited their own purpose, i.e., in this case, a place for troops.

The Hebrew *gulgolet* is translated as "skull" with an emphasis on the roundness aspect; it appears in only two places in the OT, i.e., Judg 9:53 and 2 Kgs 9:35, neither of which offer any insight into the FG's usage. *Gulgolet*, however, stems from *gālal*, meaning "to roll/roll down, or away" and can also suggest "to commit, to remove." At the point of the Kidron Valley *southeast* of the city, the walls of the valley soften into rolling mounds, rather than steep hills; and one can take "commit, remove" to imply burial, or rejection. Either way, it suggests something to be kept at a distance. This brings us to an alternative root of *gulgolet* i.e., *gālāl,* used to indicate (a ball of) dung, i.e., it is a pejorative term inferring ritual uncleanliness and is thus apt for a place of death. Just to add verisimilitude, there *is* a city gate in the southeast *called* the Dung Gate[3] (*Sha'ar Ha'ashpot*) in Neh 2:13–14: "I went out by night by the Valley Gate past the Dragon's Spring and to the Dung Gate .... Then I went on to the Fountain Gate and to the King's Pool."[4]

---

[3] Also referred to as the Potsherd Gate, indicating a place of refuse, e.g., a midden; etymologically, both terms have the same root. Some translate this as Gate of the Ravine, suggesting a slope down which rubbish could be thrown.

[4] The Valley Gate overlooked the Tyropoeon Valley, the Dragon Spring was

There is more. Just in this southern corner of the Temple Mount, where the structural extensions were built by Solomon (referred to as Solomon's Stables), there is a small Muslim site known today as Jesus' Cradle. It is a simple chamber with a stone alcove where, it is said, Mary laid Jesus before presenting him to the temple, when he was forty days old (other sources suggest he was born there). Whether legitimate or not, the point is that this specific corner of the city, adjacent to the Dung Gate, is inextricably linked to the Jesus of history. It isn't hard to imagine why such a link would be downplayed or even swept under the carpet by Christian interpreters but when the FG's secret story is decoded, the link becomes even more provocative, as we shall see.

Just to complete the picture, this southerly spot is also where the King's Garden" is, i.e., the garden in which Jesus is arrested. Nehemiah's journey from the Valley Gate culminates here, in the area of the King's Garden, at the King's Pool. Neh 3:15 tells of the construction of the walls of the "Pool of Shelah of the King's Garden, as far as the stairs that go down from the City of David" and of the repairs done in the general area "opposite the graves" (previously mentioned). The King's Pool, the Pool of Shelah, is understood to be the Pool of Siloam, i.e., the site of the election of Lazarus ('blind man') as Jesus' right-hand-man.

So, my suggestion for the site of Golgotha is somewhere on the southern end of the Mount of Olives ridge, i.e., on the lower side of the hill that is known as the Mount of Offense/Destruction. Though 'near the city', if the crucifixions took place down in the Ravine, say, there would be less of a chance of the proceedings being spied from the city itself, which is why "many" and not "everyone" saw the *titulus*. It is both symbolically and physically apt in every respect; and for Judas, the 'son of destruction', to die on the hill of Golgotha, the Mount of Destruction, is so poetically just.

There is absolutely no reference to Golgotha in Talmudic literature. Surely, if this was a well-known, commonly used place for the people of Jerusalem and/or the Romans, there would be some mention of it somewhere! Even Josephus fails to include it in his descriptions of the city. "Golgotha" seems to be a commission name.

---

probably the 'torrent' of the Gihon (the Hebrew name suggests "sea monster," i.e., a raging watery monster?). There was once a Serpent Pool to the south-west of the Mount, according to Josephus (*Wars*. 4.3.2). The Fountain Gate was adjacent to the Dung Gate.

The Testament of Lazarus

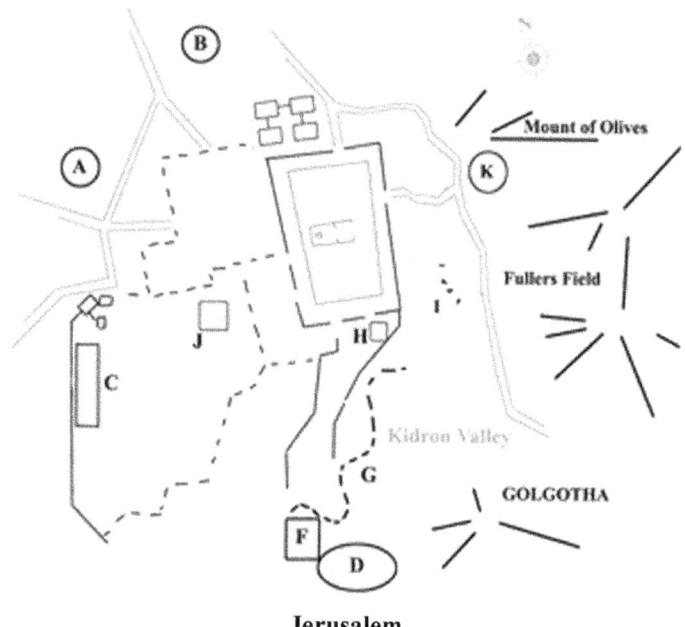

Jerusalem

A. Traditional site of Golgotha; **B.** Traditional site of 'garden tomb'; **C.** Herodian Palace; **D.** Dung Gate; **E.** King's Garden / Jesus' Cradle; **F.** Pool of Siloam; **G.** Spring Gihon and Hezekiah's Tunnel; **H.** Small Barracks; **I.** Tombs; **J.** Hasmonean Palace; **K.** Traditional site of the "garden" (Gethsemane)

You can see how simple and yet practical the layout is, compared to the traditional sites of the garden, Golgotha, and the tomb, i.e., a lot of unnecessary and unwanted exposure for the authorities, a lot of wandering about with a 'body' for the disciples. Jesus has planned for this eventuality; the proposed site of Golgotha must already be known as a site for the execution of rebels (criminals).

Lazarus' Little Jibe
By stating "which in the Hebrew (Aramaic)" in John 19:17, the FG author forms a direct link with 5:2 and the 'lame man's' scene ("called in Hebrew" [Aramaic]), just as the two scenes involving the oils of consecration are linked by the repetition of *litra/litrae*; we are invited to investigate. In John 5 the name Beth-zatha is a play on Hebrew words pertaining to "separating, or winnowing," but more significantly, to a "house of the wicked, or adulterers." This is in the context of Peter, the ineffectual priest who blames others for his lack of advancement. Peter, re-named Cephas, is the one who must be humbled, he must "bow down," as his commission name implies;

he proves himself untrustworthy, all too keen to land others in trouble, and he questions Jesus' tactics. When we come to discuss the FG epilogue, Peter is once again the centre of attention and not in a positive way. It is generally understood that Chapter 21 is written by a different person and I agree but although that will have to await the proper juncture, it seems as if the original author has encoded a similar but perhaps more scathing and personal invective within the FG-proper.

If Golgotha is not the recognised name of Jerusalem's commonly used site of execution, it must be included to emphasize the south-easterly aspect of the scene, which will prove vital if the reader is to understand the subsequent scenes. So, what of the Greek alternative, the Place of the Skull? The Greek term for "skull" is *kranion*, which stems from *kara*, or "head." Most interpreters leave it there. Once again, however, there is a play on words, for the Hebrew verb *karah*, indicating the act of "digging," can suggest a "boring out" or, in one significant instance, "piercing": "My God, my God, why have you forsaken me? ... I am poured out like water ... my mouth is dried up ... a company of evildoers surrounds me, my hands and feet have *shrivelled*" (Ps 22:1, 14–16). The NRSV suggests "shrivelled" but the Hebrew is *karah*, i.e., hands and feet "bored out, or pierced." Obviously, Matt 27:45–6 refers to this precedent but, for me, it is just too simple. The FG author's technique is more sophisticated than that, as each example of allusion or wordplay thus far has proven very specific and more insightful. It's almost as if Matthew suspected the significance of the play on *karah* but jumped on the most obvious precedent.

There is another verb, however, very similar, phonetically, to *karah*, i.e., *kara*; this means "to bend the knee/to bow down or cause to bow (subdue), to prostrate." There are thirty-six instances in the Bible pertaining to bending down physically or subduing an enemy but there is one example which stands alone in its profundity. In the Book of Esther the word *kara* relates to the character Mordecai, who refuses to "bend down" to Haman. As a result, Haman convinces the king to issue a decree that the entire Jewish nation, although scattered, is to be slaughtered on one day! He advises the king that it wouldn't be expedient for him to let them live. The decree is issued in multiple languages and the day is chosen by the drawing of lots. Haman offers to put "ten thousand talents of silver into the king's treasury" if this is done but the king tells him to keep it. In the end, Haman hangs on the gallows built for Mordecai.

This is how it seems to me (this includes some references to the Synoptic tradition but I have no problem admitting that these authors were privy to some details of Jesus' movement that were not recorded in the FG, e.g., the fate of Judas, as discussed):

★ The author of the FG-proper is Lazarus.

★ Peter is jealous of Lazarus' intimate relationship with Jesus and his election as successor; he tries to maim the young man and is probably instrumental in his arrest by the Sanhedrin (and probably the false accusation against Mary).

★ He is given the commission name Cephas to allude to his haughty nature, i.e., he must "bow down" to Jesus to prove himself one of the inner circle.

★ From the very start Peter proves a thorn in Jesus' side; he reports him to the authorities, he questions Jesus' plans, he risks everything when he attacks Lazarus (Malchus), and ultimately, he bears witness against Jesus before the high priest.

★ "Golgotha" tells us where Jesus is taken, while "the Place of the Skull," another literary creation perhaps, reminds the reader of the Esther parallel, i.e., because of one man's refusal to "bow down" the Israelites are threatened with elimination.

★ The priests convince Pilate that to let Jesus live would not be expedient—better *he* die than the nation; "pieces of silver" are given and the refusal to have it put into the 'treasury' (Synoptics); the casting of 'lots'; a decree in several languages; and even the execution of the antagonist in place of the protagonist (Judas is the slain scapegoat)—all these should tell us that the FG author is intending a direct allusion to the Book of Esther.

★ The outcome of Esther is that the Jewish nation is redeemed and given the right to defend themselves against their oppressors.

★ What did Jesus say when Peter attacked Lazarus (Malchus)? "Am I not to drink the cup that the Father has given me?" If we see this 'cup' as indicating Jesus' anticipated conquest over the 'world' and his 'glorification' as the anointed priest-king, yet another interesting idea comes from the use of "Golgotha"; the Hebrew term *gōl* means "cup" and is used to suggest a 'cup for oil'.

What this all suggests is that Lazarus, has used this opportunity to record his feelings about Peter, without compromising his account of the arrest and crucifixion of Jesus. It would seem that after years of dealing with Peter's jealousy and betrayal, Lazarus holds quite a grudge and blames him for Jesus' predicament. In truth, the entire situation does lean more toward Peter's fault than Judas' (controversial, I know). It is because of this, and because Lazarus and his testament are later outlawed by Paul, while Peter goes on, in effect, to usurp the position and inheritance of the firstborn, that the FG epilogue is written. How frustrating and infuriating to see him take what Jesus never deemed him worthy to take.

The Secret Tomb

The FG states that no body has ever been placed in the tomb before; it is a "new tomb" not newly made, necessarily, just functioning as a 'tomb' for the first time. We then discover that it is used because it is close at hand; the Sabbath is approaching and everything must be prepared quickly. Now, taking into consideration all the previous hints and insinuations that Jesus fully expects to survive his ordeal, is there any structure in the immediate area that could function as a stand-in tomb? Actually, there is, i.e., the Pool of Siloam. Lazarus, of course, *knows* this site will function perfectly for a hasty concealment of the unconscious Jesus but it also has profound symbolic significance for the mission in hand.

The Pool of Siloam is adjacent to the "King's Garden" and its overflow waters the terraces there, allowing for the lushest area in the vicinity. According to Josephus, the Pool lay *outside* the walls of Jerusalem itself in the first century (*Wars.* 5.4.2, i.e., the city wall "went southward, having its bending above the fountain of Siloam") and it wasn't until the mid-fifth century CE that the southern wall was extended (by Christian convert, Empress Eudocia) to include the Pool. In Jesus' day, then, it lay *beyond* the walls of the city and thus was accessible (for purification rituals) to those already in the area attending crucifixions (yet another reason to suggest a south-easterly site for executions). One can easily imagine Jesus and Lazarus sneaking into the garden, perhaps under cover of darkness several days earlier, making final arrangements.

The waters of Spring Gihon are directed to the Pool of Siloam through a tunnel called Hezekiah's Tunnel, i.e., the aforementioned 'conduit'. It is a tunnel large enough for people to walk through. To preserve the precious water during times of war or siege, a masonry enclosure was built to contain the Pool, so that it and the tunnel itself could be sealed up with stones. Inside the Pool's enclosure are a rock-hewn bench and some niches; a perfect place for a makeshift tomb (and should anyone accidentally witness the men there, they could simply claim to be purifying themselves).

Hezekiah, the king of Judah who redirected the water to Jerusalem (2 Chr 32:30), lived in the seventh or eighth century BCE but his story is very interesting; he too was a proponent of religious reform, he also 'cleansed' the temple (2 Chr 29), was interested in reuniting the tribes at the Festival of Passover (2 Chr 30) and, more significantly, he was apparently rescued from death! In 2 Kings 20, Hezekiah becomes sick and is at the point of dying; he is warned by Isaiah that he is to die but at the last minute he is told that "on the third day" he must "go up to the house of the Lord," and there he shall be granted another fifteen years of life. According to the "suffering servant" passages in Isaiah, when the *oppressors* offer the 'servant' up as an "offering for sin" (e.g., Caiaphas offers up Jesus in a bid to redeem the nation from Roman persecution), "he shall *see* his offspring, and shall *prolong* his days" (Isa 53:10). The 'suffering servant' offers himself up to death but, in fact, he *survives*! Jesus expects nothing less.

Seeing is Believing
When Mary first arrives, so the NRSV says, it is the "first day of the week" which, to the modern western reader, suggests she arrives on the third day after Jesus' traditional Friday crucifixion (hence Easter Monday). The Greek actually says she arrives "on the first of the Sabbaths." This is much debated amongst scholars, for it is not a phrase that can be easily verified by direct precedents. Consensus seems to suggest that the Christian tradition of Jesus being crucified on a Friday is so strong and entrenched in even the earliest of records that it is probably one of the few 'facts' of the entire story. Also, the Jewish phrase "day of preparation" applied to every Friday, not necessarily the day before a festival. Similarly, it is proposed by some scholars that the "first day of the week" implies not a Monday but a Sunday, for the weekdays were referred to by *reference to* the Sabbath so the "first of the Sabbaths" is the first day after Saturday, i.e., Sunday.

Then there is the enigmatic statement in John 19:31: "Since it was the day of Preparation, the Jews did not want the bodies left on the cross during the Sabbath, *especially because that Sabbath was a day of great solemnity.*" Most interpreters suggest that the Passover Sabbath fell on a Saturday that year, which is assumed to be 33 CE, and this is what the FG author is implying by the 'great solemnity' of the day (for it was a double Sabbath, so to speak, the first day of Passover constituting a Sabbath also). This proves interesting, for there are *two* potential dates for this occurrence, i.e., 33 CE (equating to 3 April) *and* 36 CE (30 March). Christian tradition chooses the former, while I argue for the latter.

Consider, however, the day in hand. This is Jesus' own symbolic Day of Atonement, i.e., *the* most solemn day of the Jewish calendar, referred to as the Sabbath of Sabbaths. We have been led by the FG's clues to this symbolic day so we would be foolish to disregard it now. I think the mentioning of "solemnity" is a clear allusion to this *symbolic* Day of Atonement.

The special 'third day' motif is *not* overtly employed in Jesus' burial/'resurrection' story but why not? Perhaps it's because no such event takes place on the third (sunset to sunset) day after the crucifixion (i.e., Monday). The FG's 'third day' implies not only the sacred day of union with the divine but also the third day of the week, i.e., Tuesday, the day deemed most propitious for marriage ceremonies, the day inferred by the wedding at Cana. Tuesday would be the most significant day for Jesus' own role as the symbolic 'bridegroom' but this can only come about when the new sanctuary at Shiloh is inaugurated.

So, Mary comes to the Pool of Siloam in the early hours of Sunday morning, while it is still dark. No one is about. Jesus has been safe down in the rocky recess of the pool over the Sabbath but now Mary has come to check on him. She comes here secretively, not in full view as a mourner, as she had in the scene with Lazarus; she is impatient and is breaking the Sabbath, for it is not yet dawn. Her very enthusiasm reveals there is no entombed corpse here. She *knows* Jesus is still alive! Mary has not come to mourn but to help "take [Jesus] away" (John 20:15). Martha, on the other hand, Jesus' wife, must be *seen* to be mourning, e.g., by staying indoors.

On finding someone has already been there and disturbed the scene, Mary presumes Jesus has been moved but she doesn't actually *enter* the tomb (which suggests to me that she is maintaining her Nazarite vow and is under strict instruction not to risk defilement; there is more to this, as I will explain in a moment). Hers is a gut reaction, not a reasoned one (just like her previous mourning over Lazarus); have things gone ahead of schedule without her knowledge? She immediately runs to Peter and the "other disciple" to tell them what has happened (echoing her actions as the Samaritan woman).

The NRSV translates John 20:2 as "the other disciple, the one whom Jesus loved," seemingly identifying this character with the disciple at the meal in John 13 and the one in John 19:26 but this is misleading. The Greek suggests that this character with Peter is *another* disciple whom Jesus *also* loves (i.e., "the other disciple whom Jesus loved") and we know that there is, indeed, another 'loved' disciple, i.e., Philip. The term here for "loved" is *phileo*; Lazarus is now defined by *agapao* (explained further below).

In John 20:4, the two disciples are running together; they are, effectively, racing. This is not so much historical detail as metaphor, for this is the moment of truth for Peter, the disciple who has been vying for the position of firstborn, of favourite, all along. Echoing his portrayal as the lame man, who complained because others always reached the 'waters' before him (note the echo of the pool, too), the 'other disciple' arrives ahead of him. We are about to witness the transfer of the high priest's vestments to his successor, according to the stipulation of Exod 29:29. The two disciples, Peter and Philip, arrive at the mouth of the pool but Philip waits at the entrance, having seen the linen "wrappings" lying on the stone bench in the alcove to the side. Peter, ever the zealous one, catches up and goes straight in. I think Philip sees more than is let on explicitly, for implicit in the narrative there is a transition from "the wrappings" to "the wrappings *and* the cloth"; the action inside the 'tomb' is *still taking place* when Philip peeks in, which is why he waits outside. A few seconds later there is apparently nobody there (Jesus, Nicodemus, and Lazarus have slipped away) but this second piece of clothing has been placed in full view.

Jesus' head-dressing is said to be "rolled up," for which the Greek verb *tulisso* is used, which means "to entwine/wind up" and it is on, or around the *head* rather than around the face, as in Lazarus' case. *This* object, put aside "in a place by itself" for Peter to see (e.g., probably to the right of the other cloths, indicating transference to his right-hand-man, Lazarus) is the priestly turban. This 'twisted' appearance reflects the intertwined description of the wreath in 19:2 (e.g., *pleko*), making the irony of the Romans' action all the more apparent. The *rolling up* of a vestment of office is also described in 2 Kgs 2:8,13, where Elijah rolls up his "mantle" before being taken up in a "chariot of fire"; his successor, Elisha, picks up the mantle and is recognised as having the 'spirit' of his master come to rest on him. This is precisely what is intended in this scene in the 'tomb'. Lazarus is about to become the official high priest in Jesus' stead.

We should also note that in the Samaritan tradition priests wear the white turban on the Sabbath only, *taking it off* and wearing a coloured one (red or blue) for the subsequent six days, reaffirming that the previous day in the 'tomb' *was* a Sabbath day. Even more significantly, the high priest, recall, wears his four white garments on the Day of Atonement (and these we saw alluded to during Jesus' crucifixion); these are ritually removed within the Holy of Holies, remaining where they lay while he attends to his ablutions. Jesus' most important moment occurs here, in the Pool of Siloam's darkened recesses. It is, for all intents and purposes, *his* Holy of Holies, the sanctuary where he makes atonement for his people, communes with the divine, and prepares for the final stages of his mission to create the new kingdom.

This simple evidence instigates "belief" but belief in what?[5] John 20:9 ("for as yet they did not understand the scripture, that he must rise from the dead") may or may not be an addendum; the concept of resurrection is

---

[5] Back in John 16:29–33, the disciples apparently declare their unified 'belief' in Jesus as God's emissary but then Jesus says: "The hour is coming ... when you will be scattered, each one to his home, and you will leave me alone." It is only in John 20:10 that the disciples are said to return "to their own homes," i.e., long after the arrest and crucifixion. This passage may be the foundation for the Synoptic tradition that the disciples flee when Jesus is *arrested* (which they do not do in the FG), and evidence that the 'belief' in John 20 pertains to something *other* than Jesus' own divine authority (if 'belief' is so unanimous at this stage, why mentioned it again in John 20?). John 16:29–33 is considered a post-FG addendum.

relatively scarce in the OT and really becomes evident only in the Psalms and the Prophets and this usually has to do with the *nation* (which had a bearing on Lazarus' raising), or the resurrection *at the end of days* (as Martha understood it). The FG author, however, is simply saying, 'these two disciples were not in on the secret'; there is, after all, an intimacy between Jesus and Lazarus that is unique, so for others not to grasp the subtleties of the plan would be understandable but perhaps there is something else going on here that will make this statement more meaningful.

Notice that only the 'other' disciple, Philip, believes as a consequence of seeing this 'sign'. Peter's response is not recorded; this is very important, as it suggests that Peter is again in denial. This is the *official* handing over of the vestments from Jesus to Lazarus; what more will it take for Peter to 'believe' in the 'one' chosen? This is the moment Jesus *proves* that the Father and he *are* one, for he *has* survived, just as he implied he would, to complete his Father's work. *This* is the subject of the new 'belief'.

"*Rhabbouni*!"

When they see what has happened inside the 'tomb' the disciples leave Mary alone and weeping—why? Were they instructed to do this, just as Martha was instructed to fetch Mary so that she would be with Lazarus when he came out of the cistern? Lazarus is undergoing *his* final elevation in this scene also, so it is fitting that Mary is there again. Martha, as stated, must be seen to be in mourning by staying indoors. Widowhood was anathema at the best of times, let alone if the husband died a criminal's death. Martha does not risk attending the tomb.

Now 'weeping' because she thinks Jesus has been moved and she will not, perhaps, see him again (another allusion to her weeping at the raising of Lazarus, indicating that despite her profound symbolic representation, she is still an emotional young woman), Mary finally decides to *look down* into the pool for herself (another emphasis on her *not entering*). There she sees "angels in white, sitting where the body of Jesus had been lying, one at the head and the other at the feet" (John 20:12).

Because Josephus describes the Essenes as wearing "white garments" (*Wars*. 2.8.3), those interpreters who want to make the connection between Jesus and Qumran suggest that these two are members of the Qumran sect, come to tend Jesus' wounds (as they were also well known for their interest in medicinal remedies, though this argument also presumes Jesus is still alive) but I have reason to suggest this is *not* the case and this is explained in the section called "The Qumran Quandary" in the Epilogue.

Recall that Jesus has planned this whole affair so that his chosen deputy will be officially sanctioned to take over for him on this, Jesus' self-made Day of Atonement; this is just what is happening. The high priest, when performing this function *is* dressed in white to symbolise his purity and humility. Similarly, in 2 Esdras, those who "have departed from the shadow of this age" receive "glorious garments" and those who have "fulfilled the law" and have been "made holy" are "clothed in white" (2 Esd 2:40).

The Greek word for "angel" is *angelos* and really just means "messenger," which is why all the angels in the Bible seem to come with something to tell a human; they are mediators between the world of the divine and the world of the mundane (as in Jacob's dream). We have come across this concept before; the name 'Malchus' was linked to the term *mal'ak* and this meant "messenger, teacher," etc. It also becomes a factor in the description of the *parakletos*, the helper who will relay everything "he has heard." We know that Nicodemus and Joseph of Arimathea (Lazarus) are father and son, so what Mary is 'seeing' is neither two Essenes, nor two spiritual beings but the acting high priest and his assistant. The one "angel" (Lazarus) sits at the head (at the 'right hand' just as at the supper) where Jesus once lay, to symbolise the rank he now possesses (i.e., the rolled up turban on the bench near him). The other remains at the feet, to indicate he is still a 'servant' (and Nicodemus had been the "servant of the king" earlier, recall).

The 'angels' ask Mary why she is weeping. When she answers them, explaining that she doesn't know where Jesus is, she *turns around*, only to see a man standing there, whom she presumes to be the "gardener." In describing the Palestinian garden I mentioned that it was usually walled and had a resident keeper, or warden. It is no surprise, then that Mary thinks she is being interrupted by such a man but, remember the FG author's skill in providing a double meaning; there is a play on words that is *very* subtle.

The Greek word for "gardener" is *kepouros*; *kepos* ("garden") plus *ouros* ("warden/keeper"), i.e., "protector of the garden." Where have we come across a similar word? The "protector of the gate" or "gatekeeper" (*thyroros*) during the arrest scene was Mary. In the OT, the ideal Israel is often compared to a well-tended garden (e.g., Isa 58:11; Jer 31:12), so if Mary is the guardian of the 'gate', who is the one who protects the garden? Who cares for, nurtures, and defends the new Israel? Once again, we have a scene where both Jesus and Lazarus can be identified with the same alter ego.

Lazarus had been disguised when he received Jesus' body (because he was under a death threat), so Mary *expects* him to be disguised again, now. What better disguise than the 'gardener'? No one would question *his* being there so early in the morning, even on the Sabbath (he lives there and is allowed to venture within a certain distance from his abode on such a day).

She assumes that, for some reason, Lazarus has left Jesus somewhere and has returned. The plan had been, so she thought, to leave and never come back; there must have been a change in strategy. When she ran to tell the others, she said: *"They* have [already] taken the Lord out of the tomb," meaning Lazarus and Nicodemus, the two who had 'buried' him and had remained with him during the Sabbath. Obviously, she had presumed the disciples would know who she meant without further explanation.

She calls the gardener "lord" (*kyrie*), the name given to the head of a household; she is married now, so her husband, Lazarus (whom she *assumes* this to be), fits this role. Then again, she refers to Jesus using the *same* word, "they took away my lord." There *are* two 'lords' in her household, so both receive the honour. (This echoes Jesus' dual use of the word *gune* in John 2:4 and 20:15, indicating that both Martha and Mary are considered equal, for the term means 'woman' but *suggests* 'wife'.)

Mary's presumption that Lazarus and Nicodemus have taken Jesus is echoed in 20:15, where she says to the 'gardener': "if *you* have carried him away." Why would the real gardener have touched a *supposedly* dead body on the Sabbath? Thinking this to be Lazarus, she begs him to tell her where Jesus has been "*put*" (again, the NRSV stresses "laid" in order to strengthen the burial imagery) so that *she*, though on her own, can go and "take him away." How would she manage a body all on her own? Why, if Jesus is truly dead, does she not say something to the effect of 'where have you buried him so that I can mourn him?'

Jesus is *not* dead, nor even unconscious by this time, as Mary expects him to be able to travel. Afraid, perhaps, that daylight will soon hinder their journey, Mary offers to slip away with Jesus while it is still dark (and remember, it *is* dark, so if we really need to rationalise her apparent failure to recognise Lazarus, Nicodemus, and Jesus, consider just how limited visibility would be down in a walled well, and how white clothing would detract attention from the face by reflecting any penetrating light. Jesus, on the other hand, does not wish to be noticed, so he carries no lantern, is wearing unfamiliar clothing, and probably has his face concealed by a hat, etc.).

Jesus then calls Mary by name (just as he had called Lazarus from his tomb, to tell his 'son' that he was there and that all would be well) and this is the strange part, i.e., she *turns around again*. The first turn faced her *toward* the 'gardener', who is Jesus of course, and *away* from the 'angels' but this second turn faces her back *toward* them. *Then* she exclaims "Rhabbouni!" which is often described as being the emphatic form of Rabbi, or "Teacher" (*didaskalos* in the Greek). The Aramaic term, historically, was almost always applied to the president of the Sanhedrin; in the time of Jesus, this meant *one of two high priests* (one retired, one acting)!

So, to *whom* is Mary saying this? Although she is facing Lazarus at the time, the intentional ambivalence serves to strengthen the idea that there are *two high priests* present at the 'tomb'; *both* deserve the title, though one is ritually impure and cannot function as such. Thus, the simple act of turning her head as she speaks this one enigmatic word provides affirmation that Jesus and Lazarus share the role of Mary's 'lord and master' but also, that they are indistinguishable in their mutual high-priestly status.

Another little detail that requires more attention than is generally given it is Jesus' order to Mary not to 'touch' him. Remember the allusion to the third-day and seventh-day purification ritual inferred by the hyssop: *Jesus* is still unclean. This is only the first day after his internment; he cannot afford to risk defilement (recall that in the Messiah ben Joseph tradition the figurehead would be 'slain' but would be 'revived' so long as nothing 'unclean' had touched him; this can hardly be coincidence).

Mary is under a ritualistic vow with purification issues of its own; that she has not helped to tend Jesus, nor entered the tomb, suggests she is dutifully attempting to retain her vow. According to the Talmud, a female Nazarite who comes in contact with the dead (and remember there were others crucified at the same time as Jesus who did die) must undergo a punishment of "forty stripes."[6] It is also a source of extreme uncleanliness to touch the scapegoat, which Jesus represents. Mary is excited, however, and must be reminded of what is at stake.

If we look at the wording in the NRSV, Jesus says, "Do not hold onto me" (John 19:17) and many have taken this to imply a desire to 'hold on' to Jesus, the 'master' even though they know he must go to the Father. The Greek, however, says, "Do not touch me, *not yet*," with the word "touch" originally utilizing the verb *haptomai*. This verb does not suggest a 'holding on' to some ideal, nor does it *only* imply a mere touching of the hand; it *can* imply something more intimate, such as the embraces of a lover (the primary verb, *hapto*, means "to fasten to, to kindle, to set on fire"). Mary is highly emotional and desperately wants to see Jesus, so when she finally realises he is there, seemingly well, her excitement nearly gets the better of her until Jesus reminds her to be cautious. Once again, we are led to believe that there is more of a physical, sexual relationship between Jesus and Mary.

One fact about the purification of women cries out to be included in our reassessment of the *"noli me tangere"* scene:

---

[6] Intriguingly, there is some current debate concerning the legitimacy of the Nazarite vow for women, as they are so frequently rendered impure due to menses. However, it has been argued that there are three times a female is not subject to this limitation: one who is prepubescent, elderly, or pregnant. This would, once again, point to Mary having taken on the Nazarite vow once she had conceived.

> If a woman conceives and bears a male child, she shall be ceremonially unclean seven days ... Her time of blood purification shall be thirty-three days; she shall not touch any holy thing, or *come into the sanctuary* until the days of her purification are completed.
> Lev 12:2, 4

If Mary has only recently given birth, which seems to be the case, her period of physical 'impurity' is far from over, hence the added phrase "not yet." *Jesus*' purification rite must not be jeopardised at this most critical stage.

Also, the 'tomb' has been Jesus' 'sanctuary', his Holy of Holies, recall; as mentioned earlier, those exiting the Holy of Holies of the tabernacle were still deemed imbued with the Shekinah, so Jesus is also 'off-limits' to being touched because of his recent 'close-encounter' with God. As he had anticipated all along, Jesus sees his survival as God's intervention within the Pool of Siloam; he has offered his soul up to death but has been redeemed at the last moment, just as Isaac was. He is truly a 'child of Abraham'!

This scene is the last in the sequence of seven structural parallels within the narrative linking the characters of Lazarus and Mary, i.e., they are elected in John 4; are brought to the attention of the Jews in John 8–9; are together for Lazarus' raising in John 11; are present as 'special guests' at the meal in John 12; represent Malchus and the 'gatekeeper' in John 18; are under the cross as Clopas and his wife in John 19; and are together at the tomb here, in John 20 (see also Appendices, 1; there are also theological parallels related to their respective Israel/Bride of God roles).

Escape Plan
In 2 Kgs 25:4 and Jer 39:4; 52:7, the siege of Jerusalem by the Babylonians during the reign of King Zedekiah is depicted; because the siege has created a famine in the city, the king and his soldiers flee through a breach in the wall and pass through the King's Garden" on their way to the desert and up to Jericho. They do this under cover of darkness. Just look at the *time* this flight is supposed to take place; the siege is said to begin in the "ninth year ... tenth month ... tenth day" of Zedekiah's reign, and the escape occurs on the *"ninth* day of the fourth month" of siege. The tenth month is Tebet, roughly January, and the *fourth* month, when the escape occurs, is Nisan, the month of Passover. So, we have *another* alluded to link to Passover *and* to the FG's "sixth hour" (i.e., the "ninth day"). This clue tells us that it is in the King's Garden and the "conduit" that Jesus and his two disciples are hiding after the crucifixion, and that the direction in which they will soon flee is toward the desert and beyond, towards the north.

Isaiah recounts the tale of a secret meeting at the "conduit of the upper pool on the highway to the Fullers Field" (Isa 7:3). A prophet is told to take his son and to meet the king there. He is warned to be careful, to go quietly and not to worry that he sees destruction around him, for everything will be all right. This is where it gets really interesting, for the prophet's son is called Shear-jashub, which means, of all things, "a remnant shall return." As a 'sign' to the house of David, for *its* failure to "stand firm in faith," a "virgin[7] shall bear a son, and shall name him Immanuel" (Isa 7:14), which means "God is with us." This birth will mark a new era for Judah, i.e., "such days as have not come since Ephraim departed from Judah,"—*bad* times. This is the citation Christianity takes as a prophecy of *Jesus'* birth but it is actually applied in the FG, implicitly, to Jesus' *son*.

> *Take with you the servants of your lord, and have my son ... ride on my own mule, and bring him down to Gihon. There let the priest ... and the prophet ... anoint him king over Israel ... over Israel and over Judah.*
> 1 Kgs 1:33–5

In this FG burial/resurrection scene there is Jesus the "king," Nicodemus the "teacher of Israel" (John 3:10, a 'prophet' in the old sense), his son Lazarus, who will now serve as the representative of the reconciled Israel (in Jesus' stead), and Mary the 'virgin' who gives birth to the first 'son' of the new kingdom of God. The waters of Spring Gihon, i.e., the waters of Siloam, become the place of the anointing of the king of a united Israel. *This* is what Jesus meant when Judas argued over Mary's use of the special anointing oil in John 12; it was, indeed, being kept for his 'burial'. Jesus will be in no fit state to walk too far, so there probably *is* a mule (or donkey) there. This is where the blind man, Lazarus, had received his symbolic cleansing after being elected and it is here that he receives his *own* sacred anointing, for he is now ascending ('rising' "again") to the status of high priest. As one of the theological parallels, Lazarus is depicted in a subtle and symbolic dual anointing scene with Jesus, just as Mary had been.

Neither can we ignore the tale in 2 Kgs 11–12, in which the sole survivor of the *Davidic* dynasty, a *male infant* called Jehoash ("God has given"), is secretly stolen away and *kept hidden* while *a priest acts as regent* until the boy is six. How much closer does the allusion to the usurpation of the throne of Judah by Jesus, Lazarus, and the child have to be?

Just as Hezekiah must go up to the "house of the Lord" on the "third day," in order to receive an additional fifteen years of life, so Jesus must return to the 'true' house of God in order to continue *his* life. This does not

---

[7] In the Hebrew, the term used for virgin is *'almah,* implying something kept out of sight (secret), as in a veiled young woman.

mean the temple at Jerusalem; this means the new house of God at Shiloh.

It is to this complex and subtle allusion to scripture that the 'confusion' in John 20:9 refers. As we realise several times throughout the FG, only a select few are privy to Jesus' schemes.

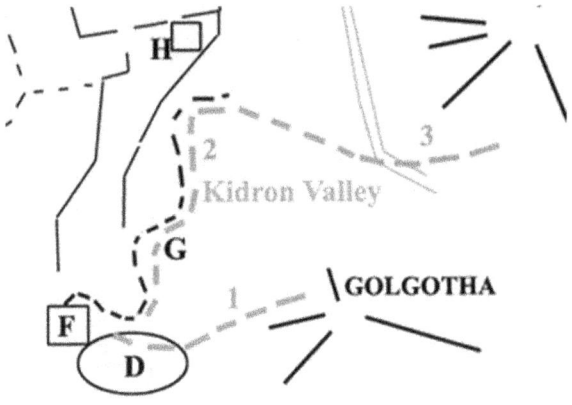

The Escape Route

D. King's Garden
F. Pool of Siloam
G. Spring Gihon (Hezekiah's Tunnel/"conduit")

The three men leave Golgotha **(1)** and re-enter the King's Garden they have become intimately familiar with; they know the entry and exit points, where they might be seen, where they will be safe. It is highly likely the resident gardener is one of Jesus' supporters, which is why the site becomes the group's hideout as they plan; he is probably there to assist. From there they access the Pool of Siloam, to let Jesus recover enough to be moved. When the time comes, they journey up the narrow Hezekiah's Tunnel[8] all the way to its end, down in the Kidron Valley **(2)**. The group heads north, towards the desert and onward to Shiloh **(3)**.

---

[8] The tunnel, in some modern photographs, has the most interesting shape—it looks like a woman's birth canal! Recall the allusion to the pain of childbirth, in John 16:20–2; might this be a subtle hint to the disciples of the 'plan' for the escape, i.e., a test, to see if anyone makes the connection (like Philip should have recognised "Arzareth", during the feeding sign)? This is, after all, the moment of Jesus' own spiritual 'rebirth' and, indeed, part of Lazarus'.

Turning Point

The inner niches and the tunnel leading from the Pool of Siloam *were*, at times, sealed with large stones, making 'tomb' and 'well' synonymous here. Recall that Lazarus was held captive in the cistern that had a stone (wheel) above it. This is why Mary can tell someone has already 'disturbed' the site; the stone has been moved.

In Genesis 29 (to which the scene with Mary at Jacob's Well alludes), Jacob suggests that the two women water their sheep and let them graze, for it is too early "for the animals to be gathered there." To this, the women respond by suggesting they cannot water the animals until "all the flocks are gathered together, and the stone is rolled from the mouth of the well (Gen 29:7–8). This is a very cryptic clue employed in the FG to the culmination of Jesus' mission; it can *only* be fully appreciated at the end of the gospel narrative, when things have come full circle, i.e., when the 'gathering' has been done (symbolically) and the stone is removed from the tomb/well from which Jesus will emerge King of Israel.

Then there is this:

> ...the prophet, having received an oracle, ordered that the tent and the Ark should follow with him ... he went out to the mountain where Moses had gone up and had seen the inheritance of God. Jeremiah came and found a cave dwelling, and he brought there the tent and the Ark and the altar of incense; then he sealed up the entrance. Some of those who followed him came up intending to mark the way, but could not find it. When Jeremiah learned of it, he rebuked them and declared: "The place shall remain unknown until God gathers his people together again and shows his mercy."
>
> 2 Macc 2:4–7

The mountain in this passage is in Moab, just across the Jordan, where Jesus spends time while he waits for Lazarus' initiation. The Ark, just like Jesus, is secretly concealed in a cave-like structure (for more on this, see "How Many Cubits" in the Appendix; the Samaritan tumult was said to be instigated by a rebel claiming to know that the Ark lay within Mount Gerizim but the only one who would know the location, traditionally, would be the Taheb, the "Restorer"). The gathering of God's chosen and the 'mercy' shown by Jesus' symbolic vindication on the "judgement seat," are indications that the hour has come to remove the obstruction and expose the the 'living waters'. The firstborn is returning to glory.

The Third Day

By the time evening comes (and note that no 'hours' are mentioned here, or in John 20:1), the disciples have reconvened in a room; we are not told where but the odds are strong it is somewhere in Shiloh, somewhere that can be secured against spies from the Jews. Shiloh is approximately thirty miles from Jerusalem, a distance conceivably traversed by mule in a day (like Josephus' trek from Cana) but with an injured man, who will need tending along the way, it makes sense to allow a longer journey. Jesus, like Hezekiah, however, must attend the "house of the Lord" "on the third day," if he is to see the new kingdom inaugurated. He arrives in Shiloh on the Tuesday, the third day *after* his 'burial' and consecration as "king" (i.e., on the Sabbath, his personal Day of Atonement), and the most special day of union with the divine; he *becomes* the "bridegroom."

Although some still argue that Jesus miraculously passes through a locked door in order to visit his disciples, there is nothing in the text to suggest this. All it says is that the doors are locked "for fear of the Jews" and that Jesus comes and stands "among them." Either he has been let in, or he gets there first (and this, actually, makes more sense, given what he says in John 13:36: "Where I am going, you cannot follow me now; but you will follow *afterward*." The point is, *he is there*; they did it!

The disciples say nothing at this point but Jesus says something so simple and so familiar to us today that it has been all but overlooked in even the most detailed analyses because the connection to Shiloh has never been made before. He says: "Peace be with you." This phrase was used by Jewish priests of the time, reiterating Jesus' priestly status but when we recall Jesus' words in John 16:33, i.e., "I have said this to you, so that *in me you may have peace*," we can appreciate the intended duality here. Jerusalem is known as the 'city of peace' but now we have another, for Shiloh *means* "peaceable, pacific," etc. Jesus is effectively pronouncing: "Shiloh be with you," or "Shiloh *is* with you." The messianic prophecy of Genesis 49 has been fulfilled! The sceptre has (according to Jesus) "departed from Judah."

There is no touching as Jesus is still unclean; the second and final ritual to remove his uncleanliness must take place on the seventh day (as alluded to by the use of the hyssop). Jesus does, however, confer the 'spirit' upon the disciples but he does so by breathing on them, not by the laying on of hands, as was the case with Lazarus, hinting yet again at Jesus' ritual impurity at this juncture). This is done as a reflection of Moses' conferring of "some of the spirit that is on" him on the "elders of Israel," so that they might "bear the burden of the people" along with him (Num 11:16f). It is this congregation of equals that was envisioned when the foot washing was performed.

The forgiveness of 'sins' is *not* the privilege of the Israelite priest, it is God's but the priest is the one *through* whom *atonement* is made (Lev 4:26, 31, 35; 5:6, 10, 13, etc.). Jesus would never refute this, so his statement in John 20:23 ("If you forgive the sins of any, they are forgiven them; if you retain the sins of any, they are retained") may seem incongruous but it is not, if it is read in the context of Moses' election of the "seventy," for the responsibility of such chosen men was to judge *as a court of law* (which is why the Sanhedrin claims its descent from this precedent group). It is the divine law that must be protected and maintained so that Israel can take its place in history once more, as the saviour of God's creation. Jesus sets up his own group of 'watchdogs' to make sure the commandments are followed. Besides, the English translation favours the word "forgive," whereas the Greek implies "release" and this is then paired with "retain"; the imagery of releasing/retaining emphasizes the 'atonement' aspect of the priestly duty (i.e., with the two goats on the Day of Atonement) and the legal context of Jesus' commission to the disciples.

Will Cephas Bow Down?

Those disciples receiving the spirit must consecrate themselves, just as the 'elders' must in Numbers 11. These new elect, however, are also to be *priests* and so their consecration must last seven days (Num 8:33), just as Lazarus' had. The NRSV says that a "week later" the disciples are once again in the locked room but in the Greek reference is made to "eight days," making the allusion to Num 9:1 perfectly clear: "On the eighth day" the priests must be ready, for on that day "the Lord will appear" (see also 1 Sam 10:8: "Seven days you shall wait, until I come to you and show you what you shall do"). Their seven days of confinement complete, the newly ordained priests are ready to come into the presence of the divine. Jesus' final rite of purification has, by now, taken place, and so he offers his wounds to be touched.

Thomas is conspicuously absent from the first meeting between Jesus and the disciples in the room in Shiloh; he obviously had not left Jerusalem with everyone else. We now know that Peter and Thomas are one and the same. At the moment of the betrayal, Peter had symbolically become 'Judas' but this was for the benefit of the reader, to make the connection between the Iscariot and Peter, his veritable 'twin'. Here, Peter/Thomas is about to revert, symbolically, to Cephas; the name *must* have been given to him for a reason.

Like Peter in the arrest scene, segregating himself from the community of disciples at a critical moment, Thomas is absent from the intimate gathering when Jesus presents himself. He is absent when the others receive the spirit and as there is no intimation that Jesus performs a special act *just* for him, we must assume that he is *not* granted the honour. Also, like Peter at the tomb, who must *see* everything for himself, so Thomas will not believe until he sees Jesus' wounds. Thomas reveals his ignorance three times (John 11, 14, 20), Peter denies Jesus three times.

The doors are shut, and the NRSV emphasizes this with the word "although," inferring (again) that Jesus must walk *through* the doors; it is simpler in the Greek and only implies that the room in which the disciples are gathered is, for the second time, shut. It is both for secrecy and for confinement, nothing more. Jesus repeats his declaration of "Shiloh (peace) be with you."

Knowing what this doubting disciple requires, Jesus offers himself for scrutiny: 'Look, here are my wounds, it really is me, touch me' he says but the disciple *does not* touch him. This is, you see, another test of Jesus'; in order for Peter to reach out and touch Jesus' side, he must lower his head, he must 'bow down' or 'curve', the action signified by his commission name Cephas. Yet he does not comply. As in every other case with Peter, this disciple offers instead a hyperbolic response: "My lord and my God." Jesus replies with yet another demeaning phrase for Peter/Thomas: "Blessed are those who have *not* seen and yet have come to believe."

> *I call to witness the gratitude of the people that is to come...*
> *though they do not see me with bodily eyes,*
> *yet with the spirit they will believe the things I have said.*
> 2 Esd 1:37

Although this is the humiliation Peter deserves, his being responsible, in part, for Jesus' betrayal and suffering, it is not enough to rid him of his pride; he *still* will not concede, and this is why the gospel's epilogue is added. Interestingly, in Luke 24:12, there is a deliberate 'reversal' of Peter's obstinacy, for he is said to "stoop down" (using the verb *parakuptó*) when he reaches Jesus' 'tomb' and sees the burial clothes; this verse is absent from several of the early versions, meaning it was probably added because the reputation of Peter from the FG needed to be addressed as Christianity arose.

The FG-proper ends with the closing statement of 20:30–1. The testament of Lazarus is complete.

22
EPILOGUE AND PROLOGUE

The Disciples

THE RISE OF PETER AND his importance to the Christian Church is not questioned; it is the lack of any *support* for his actions in the FG that I am interested in.

The "epilogue," so-called by most biblical scholars because it is so obviously a later addendum to the gospel-proper, consists entirely of John 21. The most common explanation for it is that Christians attempted to justify the FG with the Synoptic portrait of Peter, ensuring that its readers would have no doubt that Peter, and not the disciple "whom Jesus loved," was set up as Jesus' successor. Not only does this *imply* that the rivalry within the FG *is* substantial enough to warrant such a codicil, it is also a claim that actually *contradicts* the evidence of the epilogue text, yet few have questioned it. So, let us have a look at it, bearing in mind that this is written some time after the events of the FG-proper; both Jesus and Lazarus are dead by the time it is composed.

Jesus appears for the "third" time, making the meeting symbolic, for we have already been told that he "did *many other* signs in the presence of his disciples" (i.e., why is this one singled out?). The setting is the Sea of Tiberias, the site of two significant FG 'signs' (the feeding of the multitude and the 'rescue' of the disciples' boat). It is also the site of Bethsaida/Ain, the town of Peter, Andrew, and Philip, and of Capernaum, Jesus' earlier home.

Who is there? Look how they are grouped: "Simon Peter, Thomas called Didymus, Nathanael of Cana in Galilee, the sons of Zebedee, and two others." Peter is coupled with Thomas in the same way Mary Magdalene was coupled with 'Mary wife of Clopas'; it is a technique to reveal a synthesis of characteristics, the culmination of a single character's depiction.

Nathanael, whose name means "given of God," the man married to Jesus' daughter and the representation of the Remnant itself, is paired with the "sons of Zebedee" but who are they? We have no recourse to turn to extraneous texts for enlightenment; significance *must* be contained within the narrative of the FG (which introduces no new names without symbolic context) if it is to honour the original author's intent.[1] "Zebedee" is the Greek derivative of the Hebrew name Zabdi, meaning "gift of God." The Hebrew word *zebed* actually means "gift" and has the connotation of being a wedding gift, e.g., a dowry, making the allusion to the FG's divine marriage theme *and* the link to Nathanael clear. In the account of the return from exile in Neh 11:14, the *overseer of the priests* is called Zabdiel (note the *-el* ending), and in 1 Chr 7:21, one of the "sons" (descendants) of Ephraim is called Zabad. Thus, the name has three inherent elements that are of interest: priestly affiliation, marriage, and Josephite heritage. It is also very similar to Zebediah the Benjaminite in 1 Chr 8, and to a priest who marries an 'unsuitable' woman, in Ezra 10:20.

Intriguingly, and perhaps most profoundly, the name Shiloh is also often translated as "gift of God"! Jesus, when he speaks to Mary at Jacob's Well, says: "If you knew the gift of God ... he (it?) would have given you living water" (John 4:10). Both Jesus, the Ephraimite, and Lazarus, the Benjaminite represent the new, united kingdom of Israel at Shiloh. If the Samaritan woman only knew this (i.e., if the Samaritans had only kept the faith), she would have known the satiating "living water." Therefore, Jesus and/or Lazarus can be equated with Zebedee; the priests of the new house of God become the "sons of Zebedee" just as Aaron's 'sons' were the Aaronite priests.

Recall that in trying to decipher "Nazareth" in such a way that would support Jesus being a Josephite, preferably an Ephraimite, I came up with two potential sites, one of which was Naaran. The original "sons of Ephraim" (in the OT) are given certain cities, including Shechem, Beth-shean (on the border of the Manassites), Bethel, and a place 'eastward' called Naaran: "... in these lived the sons of Joseph son of Israel" (1 Chr 7:28–9). If we combine this name with "Zebedee", we can get "Jesus the Na(z)ar(e)an." Perhaps *this* is why the irony of the soldiers' words (and the "I AM" phrase of John 18:4–8) is so profound; they simply do not realise what they are saying!

So, the companions of Nathanael, the Remnant that is "given of God" and united in marriage to the Josephites (Jesus' daughter), are the "sons of Zebedee," i.e., the disciples who have been ordained as priests and are seen as the 'sons' of the "gift of God." Fitting.

The "two others" are not named but we can guess that one is Lazarus, for he is mentioned in John 21:7 as the "disciple whom Jesus loved" (*agapao*). The last is, I suggest, Philip, Jesus' other favourite (other son), so the pairing of these two is apt also. Apart from Judas, these are the only two

---

[1] Christian tradition suggests the sons of Zebedee are James and John, and that it is this John who authored the FG.

to be depicted without using their names (Philip in the tomb scene, and Lazarus when he was incognito).

153 Fish

There is a clear allusion to John 6 and the sudden appearance of Jesus on the Sea of Tiberias, bringing the disciples to their destination, for *this* is their final destination, i.e., the new priesthood in the new kingdom. Again, we see the men get into their boat, at 'night' this time, urged on by Peter's eagerness to "go fishing." This is not, however, a regular fishing trip; this is a proselytising trip, a recruiting campaign, i.e., Peter wants to expand the company. He wants more responsibility, more power perhaps. Nothing is caught. Jesus had twice referred to the work that must be done during daylight and to the fact that nothing can be done 'at night'; Peter is, once again, disobeying.

As Mary had not recognised Jesus in the garden, the disciples who are 'fishing' with Peter now fail to recognise him but this is purely for the purposes of continuity, i.e., Jesus' mysterious authority that comes from 'beyond'. When he affirms that they have nothing to "*eat*" (the NRSV translates this as "you have no fish," which is misleading at this point), thus alluding to the feeding scene in John 6; Jesus tells them to cast their nets on the 'right side of the boat'. If we are to compare this to the precedent scene in John 6, where fish again played a key role, the boat *should* be facing toward Capernaum, so the "right side" will be set against the backdrop of the Golan Heights. Jesus is telling them to find their catch to the east, beyond Bashan, for this is where Arzareth is, way beyond the Euphrates somewhere. The Israelites who have been scattered need to know of Shiloh. It is *not* an order to preach to the Gentiles, as many have suggested!

Lazarus, the disciple whom Jesus loves (*agapao*) tells Peter directly that this man on the shore *is* Jesus. A superficial reading would lead one to think that Lazarus is in the boat with the others but this is never implied. *He* would never have gone out 'at night' against Jesus' orders. No, Lazarus is on the shore, *with* Jesus.

The disciples gather the net and they find it filled to bursting but still Peter's response is slow; it is not until Lazarus calls out "It is the lord" (i.e., your master) that Peter reacts and he does so in much the same way as during the foot washing of John 13:9, that is, overzealously. He jumps out of the boat and into the water, about "two hundred cubits" off shore (see Appendices, 5). He is still trying to 'get there' before anyone else. I almost feel sorry for him at this stage (but not quite).

Although the text states that Peter is "naked," this does not mean that he has no clothes on, it simply means that he is clothed only in his linen undergarment; this *equates* to 'nakedness', especially for a priest. He actually puts *on* his outer garment before jumping into the water! Why? This obvious *lack* of vestments is an illustration of Peter's unsuitability for the office of high priest; he was not there when the others had received the spirit and he has undergone a public humiliation before his 'brothers' by being demoted. He is, in effect, a novice, working his way up. His lack of priestly robes, however, belies his keenness to take charge. He dons his outer garment to give a better show of himself (and this could be taken as an allusion to Peter's usurpation of the high-priestly status in the post-Johannine-community phase of the movement, i.e., he is donning the outer robe himself, rather than receiving it from his predecessor) but as he is concerning himself with *himself* the other disciples are left to haul the heavy fish to shore without his help.[2]

Jesus has prepared a "charcoal fire" on which to cook "breakfast";[3] a charcoal fire was seen earlier, outside the temple, when Jesus was arrested. It was used symbolically to signify the separation of the 'pure' from the 'wicked' and was the central image of Peter's denial scene. On this symbolic fire Jesus has placed both fish and bread, the two symbolic food items used in the feeding sign in John 6. Indeed, the Greek word for 'fish' in *both* instances is the same, *opharion*, which actually refers to dried, or pickled, *not* freshly caught fish, even though there is supposedly an abundance of them there. A *point* is being made.

This echo of the testing of Philip, which resulted in *his* demotion, anticipates the outcome of the scene in hand. Peter is about to be tested and is about to reveal his limitations and allegiances. There is to be another separation. The intention is *not* to convert anyone and everyone; Jesus is interested *only* in the Remnant, the devoted, those seeking the 'good old days' of Israel's intimacy with God. The 'book of signs', the FG, echoes this winnowing process by subverting its true message beneath layers and layers of clues. The hope was that the devout would recognise the 'signs' and would come to believe, though they could not be there, with Jesus, at Shiloh (hence the "Thomas" scenario). This is why Jesus rejected the crowd's attempt to make him 'king' in John 6; it was not the right time, place, or context but *some* of that crowd had understood.

Remember the very beginning of the gospel narrative, how the

---

[2] Would this not have made his swim more difficult and dangerous? One wonders, however, if this isn't a subtle reference to Peter's namesake, Jonah, who was thrown from the boat; this instigated his profound experiences, culminating in *his* humility and foreign duties.

[3] For the basis of the odd question in John 21:12, see 16:23, in the context of the metaphorical "child" being born (i.e., the new kingdom at Shiloh): "On that day you will ask me no question."

introduction of the disciples seemed to parallel the entry of the Israelites into Canaan and how there was division over the initial hailing of Jesus as "Messiah" and the subsequent clarification, "son of Joseph, King of Israel"? The FG's epilogue now conveys the consequences of this.

Jesus says to all the disciples, "bring me some of the fish." It is Peter who dashes forward to pull the net to him, i.e., Peter, on his own. The others have done all the work bringing them in, now Peter wants to get the praise for the haul. "Some" of the fish, not all of them, are brought to Jesus in a net that is not "torn." This phrase, too, has been heard before, with respect to the high priest's robe, giving the image a definite (high) priestly context.

There are a *specific* number of fish—153—and they are "large" fish. The FG does not include any numbers that are not symbolic, so this has to mean something.[4] Given the context of the entire scene, with the disciple-priests, the allusions to the sign of the 'gathering' (John 6), the keenness of Peter, and the allusion to the net being like the high priest's vestment, I suggest the 153 fish represent a specific group of people.

In the context set by the fire of separation, i.e., rejection, and the allusions to the 'miraculous' feeding sign in Bashan, we are led back to one very significant moment in the history of Moses and the Hebrews in the wilderness, i.e., Num 11:16f. The people have nothing to eat, are accused of having "rejected the Lord who is among" them, but are then given a surfeit of food. God instructs Moses: "gather for me seventy of the elders of Israel ... bring them to the tent of meeting, and have them take their place with you." These men are consecrated as priests, to act in concert with Moses, as legal advisors and defenders of the commandments. The number 153, then, is simply:

$$70 + 70 + 13$$

If Peter is being depicted consistently, what he is doing when he gathers up the net with the 'large' fish, is trying *again* to procure the double portion of the firstborn (as he had during the foot washing). Not only does he bring Jesus the required seventy, he tries to show that he can bring *twice* that many! They are 'large' because they are the "officers over" the people (Num 11:16).[5] We must also recall that there were "seventy born to Jacob"

---

[4] Interpretations over the years have included a) the number of varieties of fish in the area (!), b) the sum of the numbers one to seventeen (Augustine noticed this), the latter being the sum of seven and ten. Seven represents the Gentiles and ten the Jewish nation; the addition of the two suggests a worldwide mission, c) the 'non-Jews' who will enter the new community.

[5] I thought at one stage whether the 153 represented the daily course directors of the institutional priesthood. The number fluctuated around 156, and this would be in

(Exod 1:5); the family of legitimate Israelites are thus 'not enough' as far as Peter is concerned. Perhaps, if we judge Peter by his later behaviour, the extra are to be seen as 'willing Gentiles'?

The independent thirteen, then, are the twelve disciples plus one, presumably Peter, assuming precedence. Not only does this suggest Peter still sees himself as the high priest that *should* have succeeded Jesus, it anticipates his eventual split from the original community and his desire for his own, rivalling 'seventy'.

Testing Peter

Taking his cue from this show of pride and presumption, Jesus reverts to using Peter's other name, "Simon, son of Jonah," the name that insinuated his allegiance to Judas and his affiliation to Jonah in the OT. Again, things are coming full circle. This is the day of reckoning for Peter but how can Jesus test him? Looking back at John 14:23, where Peter was referred to as 'Judas', there was a threefold repetition of the word "love": "Those who love me will keep my word, and my Father will love them, and we will come and make our home with them. Whoever does not love me does not keep my words." Each of these 'love' words, is, in the Greek, *agapao*, not *phileo*. *Agapao* implies a sense of devotion that is a matter of principle, a reasoned, intellectual type of love that is, especially in the ancient world, extremely powerful and 'binding'. *Phileo*, on the other hand, suggests a more visceral kind of sentiment, one that is fed from the passions, not reason, and is thus used more to convey preferences (e.g., Philip as "lover of horses"), family bonds, or friendship; though strong, it is considered less profound.

When Lazarus is first seized ("ill") and the message is sent to Jesus, he is referred to as the one whom Jesus "loves" and this is the *phileo* verb, equating him to Philip, the "other disciple whom Jesus loved." This is to indicate that Mary and Martha are, at this juncture, unaware of Lazarus' profound significance to Jesus' plan; in keeping with their previous depictions, the women see things on a more pragmatic level, i.e., they *know* Jesus "loves" Lazarus as he loves them. In every other reference to Lazarus as the beloved disciple, however, whether explicit or implicit, he qualifies for *agapao*, e.g., 11:5, [13:23 is an addendum], 19:26, and here, in 21:7. As the blind man, he earned a threefold admission of devotion, following his threefold admission of belief. Jesus now demands a similar admission of

---

keeping with Peter's familiarity with the temple cultus but it would be too subtle a clue, perhaps, for those no longer in Palestine, and the number is not an approximation, it is quite precise. The 70 + 70 + 13 was my 'gut reaction' when I first worked on the FG, even before I had realised Peter's depiction.

'love' from Peter, to counter his three denials:

> Jesus: Do you love me more than these? (*agapao*)
> Peter: You know that I love you. (*phileo*)
> Jesus: Feed the lambs.

> Jesus: Do you love me? (*agapao*)
> Peter: You know that I love you. (*phileo*)
> Jesus: Shepherd my sheep.

> Jesus: Do you love me? (*phileo*)
> Peter: You know that I love you (*phileo*)
> Jesus: Feed my sheep.

In shifting to employ Peter's own term in the third and final question, Jesus provides an opportunity for this disciple to shift to the more intimate *agapao*. Peter fails to do so, remaining constant in his affirmation of *phileo*. This is, it would seem, as far as Peter is able (or willing?) to go, so he retains his arrogance and self-assuredness.

In Jesus' order for Peter to "feed ... shepherd ... feed" the lambs/sheep, is echoed the description of the 'reward' for devotion to God, described in Isa 40:9–11, with one vital amendment. The context of Isaiah's passage is the coming of God to redeem his people; its mood is optimistic and emphatic. A cry is heard: "Here is your God!" (John 21:7: "It is the Lord!"), and those who are to be rewarded are promised divine sustenance, tender care, and leadership. The original reads: "He will feed his flock like a shepherd; he will gather the lambs in his arms, and carry them in his bosom, and gently lead the mother sheep" (another aspect of the 'lamb' metaphor, of course).

The sequence here implies feeding, tending (shepherding, i.e., keeping together, safe, etc.), and *leading*. Although Peter is *potentially* granted the duty of feeding and shepherding, he is *not* granted the duty or honour of *leadership* in the now symbolically redeemed Israel. He is not ready. Peter has proven that he is still interested in leading a full order of priests but there is no physical temple in the new kingdom for them to function in. Besides, Jesus *has* his "ministers" already. If any more are to be elected, it will be Lazarus' duty, just as it had once been Jesus'.

Each time Jesus asks Peter if he 'loves' him and Peter says 'yes' but with the less significant *phileo*, Jesus responds with another test. How will Peter react to the first order "feed the lambs?" By this, Jesus means for Peter to teach the Israelites, to feed them with spiritual food, as he himself had done. If Peter answers the next question with *agapao*, he will prove that he now understands and that he is devoted to Jesus, the King of Israel, and to the 'lambs' that are scattered. The subsequent order uses the phrase, "my sheep," indicating *Jesus'* priesthood (e.g., the possessive 'my,' and the parallel of 'sheep' and 'large' fish, versus 'lambs' and smaller fish; the parallel to the sheep 'fold' as temple, etc.). Peter can, if he proves himself worthy, look after them and teach them while Lazarus is away (see below) but they are Jesus' *not* Peter's. By the time Jesus reaches the second level of the Isaiah 40 precedent, Peter has only one more chance to get it right, to bow down to the king and prove his humility. Again, he does not comply.

The next speech of Jesus' is a difficult one because of the addendum in 21:19 but if you think about it, an addendum is inserted at points where clarification by Christian scribes has been deemed a necessity for the general audiences of the Christian faith. The addendum is said to refer to the execution of Peter in c. 64 CE; this suggests that the FG epilogue *must* have been written prior to this, as 21:18 is interpreted by the addendum's scribe as some sort of prophecy. If the FG was written after this event, and was an intentional reference to the death of Peter in Rome, I think the entire epilogue would be redundant, for it would not matter to the followers of Peter whether the 'outlawed' gospel/community supported his ministry or not. It would only be effective, either as a deterrent or an invective, if Peter is still alive!

The mention of a "belt" being put around his outstretched arms implies 'binding', as in being a prisoner (cf. Paul in Acts 21:11–12). In Acts 12:6–11 Peter is in prison, bound by chains. An 'angel' comes to him and tells him to "get up" and "follow"; the chains fall off and he is freed. The angel instructs Peter to "fasten [his] belt," which he does (cf. "you used to fasten your own belt" in John 21:18). Peter then escapes and flees. The actual incident around which this tale is created is considered to be about ten to twelve years after the crucifixion. Notice, though how this scene echoes so well that of the 'raising of Lazarus' as explained earlier; there is the binding, the spoken command, etc., but notice, too, the echo of the 'lame man's' scene, where Peter is told to 'get up' and be free. It is no coincidence Peter's escape in Acts 12 is also a 'paschal release'.

It could be argued therefore that the FG epilogue was written after this event, as Peter's incarceration was clearly a matter of public knowledge (Acts 12:11), but before his death. This means, of course, that Peter outlives Lazarus (which may be why we see his depiction in light of his rival—everything Lazarus and Jesus did, Peter *copies*, whether history or fiction—and there seems to be a sense of security in the fact that no one is questioning this, either at the time or, indeed, today!). The Lazarus we see in John 21 is a posthumous characterization.

As the lame man, Peter was warned not to 'sin' any more, lest anything worse happen to him and later, he was remonstrated for his allegiance to the 'devil', so this final, third admonition in John 21 is fitting.[6] Indeed, Peter's representation as the impotent priest in John 5 foreshadows his ultimate failure to rise above his own expectations and desires; he feels 'safe' with what he knows but this will never bring him what he wants more than anything else, i.e., to be given the rights of the firstborn.[7]

This is where I wish to return to the topic of the Sheep Gate, discussed earlier with respect to the 'lame man's' scene in John 5. I pointed out that the word for "gate" doesn't appear in the Greek and that the link to the priestly gate was inferred. Imagine the scene: Peter is, metaphorically speaking, sitting on the ground, apathetic, complaining, unwilling to get up and do anything to better himself. The place he sits 'pertains to sheep' and is understood to be the place where the sheep are taken for sacrifice. When you look at the Hebrew, however, the name of the gate in Neh 3:28 (which was singled out for priestly consecration) is *Miphḳad*. This means "appointed place" but is rooted in *paqad*, which means "to attend, to appoint." The testing of Peter in the epilogue in terms of potentially appointing him to tend and feed the sheep is thus a taunting reminder that right from the start Peter has been unable to 'attend' to his duties.

With the new understanding of Lazarus' rather obscure use of Golgotha/Place of the Skull, i.e., as a personal castigation of Peter, it seems to make sense that as Peter began to make more of his 'perceived' role, and with stories of his success often almost plagiarising the scenes in the FG (e.g., this escape from prison, the healing of a lame man by just telling him to get up and walk [Acts 3:6], the conversion of the 'five thousand' [4:4], etc., and more in the Synoptics!), Lazarus' followers, or perhaps even his family, decided to write the epilogue. It becomes their way of reminding people, in no uncertain terms, how Jesus had struggled with Peter, and of making it clear that Jesus found him unsuitable as a leader. It reaffirms Lazarus' position as the chosen successor and most intimate disciple.

The only other time "follow me" is said as a command in the FG is to Philip, Jesus' first choice as successor but another who did not live up to expectations. As if he has not learnt by now, Peter delays and instead asks

---

[6] This threefold warning system is used to discipline erring members of the Qumran sect.

[7] There are three classes of disciples, according to the Talmud: "He ranks first who asks and answers when asked; he who asks but does not answer ranks next; but he who neither asks nor answers ranks lowest of all." The order of primacy is contingent upon action (e.g., responsibility, seeking knowledge, etc.), and reaction (humility, loyalty, etc.). This is just what we have seen displayed in the contrasting stories of Peter and Lazarus. The lame man, Peter, denies knowledge, denies responsibility but the blind man, Lazarus, both accepts responsibility and seeks further insight, therefore *he* ranks first.

Jesus about Lazarus, who is dutifully 'following' behind his spiritual father. "What about him?" he questions, as he looks over his shoulder. Jesus, as a teacher scolding a student, simply says, "What is it to you?" and repeats, probably more sternly and louder: "Follow me!" Just as with Thomas, who does not actually follow the order to touch Jesus' side, so Peter is not actually depicted as *following* Jesus; the tale of Peter ends with Jesus' rather emphatic order ... does he, or does he not 'follow'?

The concept of the charcoal fire, the obvious testing and Peter's failure, and the ambiguous ending suggest that Peter does not follow. He tries but cannot quite grasp the subtleties of Jesus' tactics. The entire purpose of John 21 seems to be a decisive *rejection* of Peter who, soon after Jesus' final departure from the community he founded, *assumes* the role of firstborn.

The misunderstanding of the 'brothers' (the 'community' of disciples who supposedly witness this confrontation between Peter and Jesus) who overhear Jesus say that it is his will that Lazarus "remain" until he "comes," evolves into a rumour that Lazarus will never die; presumably this is because they have no idea when, or if Jesus is going to return (see Acts 1:11). I have a problem with this, though.

The Greek word for "come" in this instance is *erchomai* and this can just as easily mean "go," depending on the context. Had the author of the epilogue wanted to depict Jesus as anticipating his return, why did he not omit the ambiguity and use the verb *epanerchomai* ("to return, come back again"), or even *heko* ("to come, be present"), which is used in John 2:4 and 8:42? Jesus, throughout the FG, is depicted as the one who has 'come' and the one time he mentions 'going' is when he tells his disciples (John 16:13–17) that he must "go away" so that the *parakletos* can guide them "into all the truth." In other words, Lazarus will reveal to them everything Jesus had kept secret (which, again, by the way, is an aspect of the mission described in 2 Esdras).

"I am going to the Father," Jesus explains in John 16, "A little while and you will no longer see me, and again a little while and you will see me," he adds but the disciples are confused. What Jesus is telling them is that soon he will be executed and none of them will see him (because he is hidden in the Pool of Siloam) but after a "little while," they will see him again. Indeed, they do, three days later, in the room in Shiloh. He finishes by declaring, in no uncertain terms: "I am *leaving* the world and am *going* to the Father" (16:28). There is no basis on which the translation of *erchomai* as "come," in 21:22, can be justified (in a pre-Christian context). It *must* be "go."

Lazarus, therefore, is to remain with Jesus until it is time for Jesus to 'go' to the Father, to die. This serves as the period of intimate training and verification that is implied in the description of the *parakletos*.

The rumour that has to be abated is simply another misunderstanding, a misinterpretation of some basic words, or, more likely, a preconception that Jesus will return to Galilee (or to public life?) when the messiah comes, perhaps. This would fit in with the idea expressed in the Messiah ben Joseph traditions, where the Davidic messiah would raise the slain Josephite messiah after "forty days" but this particular aspect, we must remember, is a post-Jesus phenomenon, not part of the ancient belief. It may well be, however, that the (augmented) Messiah ben Joseph tradition dates as far back as *this* period of indecision and rivalry, making the added FG epilogue even more understandable, if rumours such as this were prevalent.

Of course, though, Lazarus *does* die, as 21:23–4 makes clear, and this indicates the time when the epilogue is added. "This is the disciple who is *testifying* to these things and has written them, and we know that his *testimony* is true," the epilogue declares (cf. 19:35). 'This' disciple is the one just mentioned, walking with Jesus on the shore, i.e., Lazarus, the beloved. His testimony, a duty prescribed for the *parakletos*, *is* this gospel.

That there is not even the remotest mention of the calamitous War and the destruction of the temple, I am convinced the FG epilogue was added to the gospel sometime between c. 40 and 60 CE.

The FG Prologue

Now it is time to return to the very first eighteen verses of the gospel which, I claim, are written by someone other than Lazarus, indeed, other than the author who wrote the epilogue. Much has been written about the philosophy of the *logos*, especially from the Hellenistic perspective (e.g., from a presumed much later dating of the FG). In fact, the *logos* concept pervades the OT; it is a saviour and healer in Ps 107:20, and a 'messenger' that relays the divine will in Ps 147:15. Most significantly, in Isaiah 55 it becomes the agent through which God's plan is made manifest:

> ...everyone who thirsts, come to the waters ... listen so that you may live. ...my word shall not return to me empty, but it shall accomplish that which I purpose, and succeed in the thing for which I sent it. ...for you shall be led back in peace....
>
> Isa 55: 1, 3, 11–12

The 'word' is the 'voice' that is placed in the mouth of the prophet, the law that is granted to the 'children of God'; it is the inspiration of the Samaritan 'ancestral saints'. In this non-corporeal concentration of divine essence is the 'life' of which Jesus has been teaching throughout the FG; it is the creating force, it is the 'light' and the 'truth'.

Israel ... knew that Samuel was a trustworthy prophet of the Lord.

> *The Lord continued to appear ... to Samuel at Shiloh by the word....*
> *And the word of Samuel came to all Israel.*
> 1 Sam 3:20–4:1

John, the baptiser, although he heralded the coming of this 'light', was not to be the one to receive it, as we are soon told again; even though God ('he') made the world, we are told, and was in it, his own people, i.e., the Israelites, "did not know him" (cf. John 1:26, "Among you stands one you do not know," Jesus, God's representative in the 'flesh', in the 'world').

This 'word' of God, this 'spirit' became 'flesh' not once but many times, in the person of Adam, Abraham, Moses, Joshua, and then Jesus. The law was originally given through Moses but it was not adhered to; the people rejected it, they 'sinned'. Therefore, so the prologue asserts, through Jesus' mission the believers can return to God, can learn the truth, and can receive grace. "No one has ever seen God. It is the only son who is close to the Father's heart, who has made him known" (John 1:18). No one, *not even Jesus*, has 'seen' God; in the FG Jesus declares *only* that he has 'heard' God, i.e., the voice, the 'word' (John 14:24; 17:8, etc.).

Like the *parakletos*, the 'only son' acts as the messenger, the "angel ... ascending and descending." Who is the "Father's only son"? He is the representative, the heir; on one level this is Jesus but on the other, Israel: "[W]e your people, whom you have called your firstborn, only begotten (2 Esd 6:58); "Israel, whom you have named your firstborn (Eccl 36:17); "You are my son; today I have begotten you" (Ps 2:7); "I have become a father to Israel, and Ephraim is my firstborn" (Jer 31:9). Through the 'son of man' (a human not a deity) God is once again 'made known'.

Interestingly, one of the first appearances of the OT *logos* is recorded in Gen 39:21, where Joseph is incarcerated in Egypt; the 'word' (his 'wisdom?) remains with him during his ordeal, allowing him to befriend the jailer and improve his lot. The scenario culminates on the "third day," a festival, with the rise in status of the "cup bearer" and the execution of the "baker" by Pharaoh (sound familiar?).

The statement, "The light shines in the darkness, and the darkness did not overcome it," seems to be straight forward; with the added secretive theme of the inauguration of the new priesthood and the kingdom at Shiloh, however, the phrase takes on a more meaningful edge. The "light *shines*" uses a *present* tense verb but "the darkness did not overcome it" is a past tense phrase. The 'light' (the spirit) has been passed on to the son (of Jesus), via Lazarus the elected 'regent'; the priesthood and the divinely sanctioned monarchy *persists*, despite the 'darkness' that attempted to thwart it, that nearly killed Jesus and obliterated his followers. This perpetuation of 'life', i.e., the 'resurrection' of the spiritually 'dead' kingdom is the good news the gospel pronounces.

Therefore, the prologue, though written some time after the death of Lazarus and after the epilogue, maintains that the new kingdom Jesus (eventually) died for is still considered by the community to be the successful fulfilment of God's plan. The 'house of the Lord' at Shiloh still exists, at least at the time the prologue is added.

23
CONSIDERATIONS

THE GOSPEL ACCORDING TO JOHN is not such a mysterious text any more. It has historical corroboration; it apparently predates and therefore helps to lay the foundations for the Synoptic gospels. It profoundly exploits familiar traditions and themes from the Old Testament and its central claim regarding Jesus is one that is fully defensible using only the OT as supporting evidence. This means, in effect, that anyone in the Dispersion who has access to the Hebrew scriptures can 'find' the 'kingdom of God' as Jesus defines it. They can even find their way to the new *house* of God at Shiloh, if so inclined. The testimony of the *parakletos* was not just to make a statement that the divine kingdom was reinstated; it had to vindicate Jesus. For vindication one needs facts and they are supplied, beneath the more profound 'good news'.

Jesus, first hailed as the redeemer of Israel by a man who believed the end of an age was at hand, as with every other great historical figure who has sought conquest and position, has both followers and dissenters. With each passing year, and each public appearance, Jesus makes enemies. He is more and more misunderstood by the very people he has come to save; his mission has not been solely for the northern tribes but for *all* Israel, the nation of Israelites, God's 'beloved'. Without all twelve tribes, there is no future state of paradise; there is no 'bride'. Jesus makes clear during the foot washing and the meal that the twelve *are* to be equal, though there is still a 'master', a high priest, a king. The supremacy of the 'house of Joseph', must never be questioned again.

So, what of the more immediate implications of all of this? How does it relate to the Qumran discoveries, the Messiah ben Joseph tradition, and the other NT texts? What happened after the 'resurrection'? What happened to the child? There are so many new questions to ask, and still so much evidence to be found, but here are just a few considerations.

Aftershock
The audacity of the Jewish authorities during the Jesus incident is the reason, I think, why the Sanhedrin loses much of its power and prestige "about forty

years" before the War. The Jews have simply overplayed their hand and sent warning bells ringing for the Roman authorities. A modicum of tolerance is the Roman way—it simply makes life easier for all—but this presumption and outright scheming is just too much. The timing of momentous events in the history of Palestine during the brief span of c.35 to 37 CE is just too coincidental, i.e., one cannot discount the possibility that it was this messy business with Jesus that instigated the changes.

Vitellius, a more even-handed administrator than Pilate (whose hatred of the Jews is hardly a secret), arrives in Jerusalem once Pilate is dispatched to Rome. His gesture of granting the memorable paschal pardon is thus a well-planned compromise to keep relative stability in the region. He cannot simply reverse everything Pilate has done and return the Sanhedrin to their former glory, for this would be admitting publicly the error of a fellow officer of Rome (although we know Pilate's reputation was criticized). Instead, he offers the Jews something even more profound to them and less politically provocative, i.e., the return of the sacred vestments to the temple (plus, as any politician aiming to quell discontent, he offers to lower the taxes).

Meanwhile, there is an apparent parallel to the Jesus-Barabbas scenario; with one hand Vitellius grants the freedom of the vestments but with the other he deposes Caiaphas from the office of High Priest (Josephus, *Ant.* 18.4.3). It is *about* this time that the Sanhedrin seems to have lost its power to impose the death sentence, if the Talmud is to be believed. Could this be a retaliatory act against those who had dared to manipulate the ambassador of Rome?

Within a year of Pilate's extradition, Herod Antipas loses his position as tetrarch, after an ill-fated war with the king of Arabia, *and* Emperor Tiberius dies. Thirty years later, the temple is destroyed. Did Jesus become so famous because of this timely sequence of events? Did the augmented Messiah ben Joseph tradition arise soon after Caiaphas' downfall, or Herod's? It most certainly developed as a consequence of Jesus' perceived impact on the 'world' he had only recently left. No wonder some began to fear they had allowed a prophet to be killed.

The Qumran Quandary
As we have seen, there are several aspects in the FG that could be interpreted in light of the sect at Qumran. Even Josephus' account of the Essenes can shed light on Jesus' career to some extent. For instance, he claims that they are keen to 'administer' to one another on an equal basis, just as Jesus hopes will be the case when he washes his disciples' feet. Josephus also remarks that the Essenes prefer not to have children but to take on other people's

children as protégées; this is what seems to be the case with Jesus and Lazarus. Most intriguingly, for our interest in the historical veracity of the FG, the Essenes are armed (*Wars.* 2.8.4). Josephus suggests that they carry weapons for self-defence, which is just what the Samaritans claim, when petitioning against Pilate's unauthorized attack.

Essenes themselves were divided into at least two major sects, northern and southern, in c. 175 BCE. Judas the Alexandrian amalgamated his group of Essenes with the Pharisees, creating a community called the Ossaean Sect. It is primarily this group Josephus learns about during his spiritual quest, though he does mention the northern group, the *Nazoreans*. Some scholars have suggested Jesus may have been a member of this sect and this may be why Jesus is referred to as a Nazorean.

From our FG perspective, however, consider this: Just like the northern tribes who claimed to follow the original religion of Israel, the northern Nazoreans claimed fidelity to the original concept and tenets of the Essene faith. In other words, *both* saw themselves as the legitimate remnant of the original religion. Furthermore, the Nazoreans held a different view of the laws of Moses and did not comply with Jewish calendars or rituals. The most pronounced difference in the living practices of the two factions of Essenes was the concept of marriage. The southern, Pharisee-influenced Essenes believed in celibacy for initiates while the northern Nazoreans encouraged matrimony, perhaps even polygamy. It may be for this reason we hear John's disciples arguing against Jesus' suitability (i.e., purity) for the role of their long-anticipated messiah.

Preconceptions rule the day, however, with the majority of scholars deciding that the DSS documents which refer to the Teacher of Righteousness (or the "correct teacher") and the Wicked Priest *must* date to the Hasmonean period and, as such, they can have no bearing on matters pertaining to Jesus or John (even though some of the DSS date to at least c. 68 CE, perhaps even earlier, i.e., around the same period as the FG's epilogue).

With an open mind, however, one can see an interesting correlation of events and ideas pertaining to the DSS characters, and the FG's Jesus and John:

★ The Teacher of Righteousness is sent from God to instruct the Qumran sect after their segregation from Jerusalem. John, in the FG, is called a "man sent from God" to give "light" so that others might "believe" (in the delinquency of Jerusalem?).

★ The Qumran site, abandoned after the earthquake of 31 BCE, was re-inhabited around 6 CE, so it might have been this re-founding of the site that triggered the need for a new Teacher of Righteousness. No one *denies* that this might have been an office held by several successive persons, rather than just one individual.

★ Both the Teacher of Righteousness and John were priests.

★ It was the function of the Teacher to interpret and relate to his community the meaning of the visions and sayings of the Prophets. The first thing John really *says* in the FG relates to the prophet Isaiah. This is what Josephus has to say about such (Essene) 'leaders' (in the *plural*): "There are also among them [those] who undertake to foretell things to come, by reading the holy books, and using several sorts of purifications, and being perpetually conversant in the discourses of the prophets; and it is but seldom that they miss their predictions" (*Wars.* 2.8.12).

★ The Teacher and the Wicked Priest are said to have a confrontation on the Day of Atonement. When I first calculated the apparent chronology of the FG, I *had not* made this connection to the DSS but still arrived at the Day of Atonement for the initial encounter scenes between Jesus and John. There is some debate about how the Wicked Priest could travel on the Day of Atonement (being a strict Sabbath day) and the answer seems to be that he adhered to a slightly different calendar; Jesus and his disciples enter the house just in time for *their Sabbath.* The day of confrontation would thus have been just prior to this. As both the Samaritan and Jewish calendars, though divergent, allow for the Day of Atonement to fall on the prescribed *date* of 10th of Tishri, they do not necessarily (if ever) fall upon the same *day*. The fact that we are told of Jesus' compliance with the rules of the Day of Atonement and not John's, may suggest the two men are following alternative calendars.

★ It is further described that this confrontation takes place at, or very near the Teacher's place of 'exile', e.g., Qumran (unless there is another, as yet unknown site). At the beginning of the FG we have John just over the Jordan at Bethabara, and it is Jesus who makes the approach to John (not *vice versa*). He does so again later, at Aenon near Salim (i.e., Qumran).

★ The trouble between the Wicked Priest and the Teacher seems to be a difference of opinion regarding scriptural interpretation and, therefore, the law. In John 3, John's disciples are in a debate concerning "the one" their master was baptising with earlier, i.e., a debate about ritual purification.

★ The Wicked Priest is also referred to as the Man of Lies, though some scholars prefer to separate the two characters. Both are attributed the infamy of having caused the Teacher's downfall. The Man of Lies humiliates him through public demonstrations of superiority, and by leading the people 'astray', away from the Teacher's teaching. The Wicked Priest is said to "seek his death." The early sections of the FG relate the almost competitive nature of baptising, with Jesus persistently going to where John is, or has been, taking his disciples (though in the FG John *tells* them to follow Jesus) and baptising 'more disciples' than John. In John 1:20 the strength of the affirmation: "He confessed and did not deny it, but confessed" suggests something more sinister. There is definitely a competition of sorts going on here. Once disciples from John leave to be with Jesus, Jesus is referred to as "Teacher."

★ Also, this concept of 'lies' is a factor of the FG; Jesus is heard to reject the "father of lies"; Judas' name is linked to 'lying'; and Jesus himself is deemed, by the Jews, a madman who spouts nonsense. Josephus' reckoning of the Samaritan tumult leader, i.e., as "one to whom lying was a thing of little consequence" fits this impression (*Ant.* 18.4.1). Each side of the conflict of ideas accuses the other of 'lying' just as the Samaritans and the Jews each claim primacy and superiority, accusing each other of falsifying scripture.

★ In the end, John *does* get killed. Just as the FG fails to expand on the tumultuous events that lead to the deaths of many followers, so it refrains from elaborating on the death of John. I think it would be a natural response for the Qumran sect to blame the one person whose actions had caused so much of a stir that Herod had begun to feel threatened, i.e., Jesus.

★ Having begun his career 'in truth' and with the actual *support* of the sect, the Wicked Priest, according to the DSS, soon becomes ambitious, greedy and *violent*. His actions provoke the "men of violence" (the Galileans who hear Jesus at the temple and enforce their ambitions upon the gathering on Mount Gerizim?). He violates the sanctity of the temple in Jerusalem. He stirs up the anger of the people called 'Kittim' (presumed by most to be the Romans) and Jerusalem bears the brunt of their force; finally, he is handed over "into the hands of his enemies" to be "abused" then killed. I do not even have to explain the parallels, here.

★ The Wicked Priest is associated with the "wicked of Ephraim and Manasseh"; Jesus is an Ephraimite.

If Jesus is mentioned in the DSS, as I propose, he is *not* depicted as the Teacher of Righteousness. He *is* the Wicked Priest. This is not to say Jesus is evil; all it means is that he has proven *not* to be the messianic figure John (the Teacher) anticipated. After giving his public support of Jesus' claim to be Israel's 'redeemer' John, for some undeclared reason, apparently realises his mistake. Perhaps the unexpected interest in kingship, the rejection of the Jerusalem site itself, or the increased violence associated with Jesus' mission, leads John to denounce the entire affair as a false hope That John gathers his disciples in the desert and Jesus draws his primarily from the shores of the Sea of Galilee and the Dead Sea might offer further symbolic insight into the opposing mind-sets of these two preachers. Looking back on Matt 11:3, we can read more into John's query: *"Are* you the one who is to come, or are we to wait for another?"

Just as Jesus and Lazarus had publicly humiliated the Pharisees and the chief priests and were subsequently considered enemies and criminals, so Jesus has disappointed, embarrassed, and angered the Qumran sect, and as such, is preserved in *their* records as a foe. He is blamed for the death of their spiritual leader.

In contrast, Jesus' divine authority, his unquestioned victory, and his apparently 'peaceful' tactics immortalized by the FG's record of events are coloured by the affinity of its author to Jesus' cause. Such is the norm of 'History'.

The Holy Family

We hear of Mary and the child no more in the FG but in other documents, both biblical and historical, there are tantalizing clues that suggest she remains with Lazarus (until he dies), that she still protects the young child, and that her influence remains profound.

If we can now assume the FG to be a very early document, predating the Synoptics, so many of the conflicts, so much of the incongruence can be explained. Most interesting in this particular context, however, are the passages concerning the genealogy and infancy of Jesus, as depicted in Matthew's gospel. Luke sticks to the more traditional patriarchal genealogy, combining the Davidic *and* Josephite heritage, creating an air of doubt as to the patrimony through David.

According to Matthew (Matt 1:1–16) however, Jesus' lineage includes four outstanding women, an oddity in itself as women were seldom included in genealogies, unless the father was unknown. These females are depicted, almost to exclusion, in terms of their sexual or marital status:

- Tamar, the seducer of Judah
- Rahab the (foreign) prostitute
- Ruth the (foreign but subtle) seducer of Boaz
- Bathsheba, wife of Uriah, who committed adultery with David.

Note how Matthew's Joseph is explicitly referred to as the "son of David" to emphasize Davidic descent despite an unavoidable link to the name of Joseph. One has to question whether the Synoptic authors deemed

Jesus' lineage so suspect a pro-Davidic one had to be invented to correspond with the now hijacked movement after Jesus' disappearance. When we discuss Paul this does seem to have some rationale. The Davidic messiah was, after all, a much safer bet, a greater attraction to disheartened Jews and even Gentiles, than some obscure northern prophet who seemed to cause nothing but trouble!

In Matt 1:18–19, we find the story of Mary and Joseph, Jesus' alleged parents. After seeing the FG's version of events, however, it is easy to see Matthew's account as a distorted remnant of the Lazarus (Joseph)/Mary relationship (note how Joseph, below, is considered Mary's 'husband' even though they are 'betrothed'):

> Now the birth of Jesus the Messiah took place in this way. When his mother Mary had been engaged to Joseph, but before they lived together, she was found to be with child from the Holy Spirit. Her husband Joseph, being a righteous man and unwilling to expose her to public disgrace, planned to dismiss her quietly.

In the FG, it is *only* Jesus who is imbued with the Holy Spirit (and by *inheritance*, Joseph/Lazarus) and only he who can confer it, at least until the ministers are granted the authority in Shiloh, after the crucifixion.

Lazarus, *our* Joseph, is called to be Mary's husband, even though the child is not his. Because he is fully supportive of Jesus and his mission there is obviously no apprehension concerning his duty. As the *parakletos* and heir-elect, he accepts as his own everything Jesus passes on to him, e.g., name, knowledge, wife, child.

Remember that 'Lazarus' can be broken down into:

Laz	+	*'aras*
(from *levath/lavah*) "to unite"	+	"to engage for matrimony" or "betroth"

In fact, *levath/lavah* also suggests "borrowing" and/or "obligation," suggesting, perhaps, his obligation to Jesus, i.e., to look after *his* family.

The accusation of illicit behaviour against the 'mother' Mary, here and in other apocryphal texts, echoes that made against our Mary in the FG. In the early Christian text known as the *Protevangelion*, however, both Mary *and* Joseph are accused and put on trial by the priests; Joseph is accused of secretly marrying her, and of 'defiling a virgin', and Mary is considered to have betrayed her temple vows. They are ultimately vindicated, and the charges are dropped. This is *just* what happens in the FG!

Parallels between the Protevangelion and the FG

Protevangelion	FG
Mary is a young virgin who is favoured by God and therefore eminent	Mary, a virgin, becomes eminent and favoured by God
She has taken temple vows; she must not be defiled	She has taken the vows of the Nazarite and must not be compromised
Mary dwelt in the Holy of Holies (the reserve of the high priest)	She represents the Bride of God, the intimate partner of the Divine
She becomes pregnant while Joseph is away; the father is not known	She conceives during a time Jesus is often away but Lazarus is at hand; the father is ambiguous
The child is attributed the Holy Spirit	Only Jesus is associated with the Holy Spirit at the time Mary gets pregnant
Joseph delays his return	Jesus delays his return
He receives news *as he sleeps* of the significance of the child and his duty to marry Mary	Lazarus, as the 'blind man', with his eyes figuratively shut, receives the knowledge of Jesus' plan and accepts his duty to care for Mary and the child when Jesus is gone
Annas the scribe	Annas, one of the two high priests and heads of the Sanhedrin's Grand Council
The priest is said to have "placed so much confidence" in Joseph	Jesus, the priest in the adulteress' scene, has placed much confidence in Lazarus and this is purposely targeted by the authorities
Both Mary and Joseph are accused and put on trial by the priests	Mary is brought before the priest accused of adultery; Lazarus is brought before the Sanhedrin

In Matt 2:14, we see Joseph taking responsibility for Mary and her child, taking them out of Palestine during a time of great danger and threatened lives. They flee to Egypt, that mysterious land where Jesus, according to some, is supposed to learn his 'magic', but they remain there only until Herod is no longer a problem (cf. Jeroboam, the Josephite, flees to Egypt until Solomon dies).

After the crucifixion, all involved parties would be in fear of their lives, *especially* Joseph (Lazarus) and Mary (Magdalene). The Messiah ben Joseph tradition stipulated that the procurator would be 'slain' and this is how the extradition of Pilate was interpreted. The same thing applies here, for it is not long before Herod Antipas loses *his* hold on Judea and is forever banished, i.e., effectively, dead.

Does it not seem possible, then, that the Synoptic and subsequent accounts of the birth of a 'special' baby, of a 'Joseph' and a 'Mary' having been united in an arranged marriage, of uncertain but apparently sexually immoral acts, of a flight (perhaps only temporary) from danger, etc., might have been based on an obscured or skewed legend pertaining to the Lazarus/Joseph and Mary of the FG?

Origin, who first wrote of the existence of the *Protevangelion*, with its strangely pragmatic account of the betrothal and pregnancy of 'Mary', also stated that Jesus' 'brothers' were "sons of Joseph" by a former wife, which was naturally considered heresy. If, however, the FG predates the Synoptics, an alternative paradigm exists, e.g., it allows for Philip being the son from a 'previous marriage', for a start.

The original Holy Family, therefore, is *not* Jesus and his parents but Joseph of Arimathea (Lazarus), Mary Magdalene, and Jesus' son (and the notion that "Mary" married a much older man clearly reflects the ambiguity of her relationships with both the young Lazarus and the aging Jesus).

Mary Parody

Because of the limitations I set for myself while researching the FG, i.e., using only the information I thought an average first century Israelite abroad may possess, I used the OT as my primary reference, referring to Josephus only three or four years later, to confirm or reject certain ideas, etc. I then delved into his lengthy works, from time to time, to find snippets of background politics and potential insider information clarifying vague biblical passages and customs. Thinking I had finished adding new material, I was knocked for six when I accidentally stumbled across an amazing passage in Josephus, while looking for something completely unconnected. It tells of the assault on Jerusalem (c. 70 CE) that created a famine in the city:

> [A] certain woman that dwelt beyond Jordan, her name was Mary; her

father was Eleazar, of the Village Bethezub, which signifies the
House of Hyssop. She was eminent for her family and her wealth.

Wars. 6.3.4

The woman is starving (and obviously alone), and is harassed by soldiers who keep stealing her rations, so she is forced to succumb to the most heinous crime (cf. Lam 2:20, 4:10), i.e., that of eating her own child:

> [S]natching up her son, who was a child sucking at her breast, she said, 'for whom shall I preserve thee ...? ...be thou my food, and be thou a fury to these seditious varlets and a byword to the world, which is all that is now wanting to complete the calamities of us Jews.' As soon as she had said this, she slew her son; and then roasted him and ate one half of him.

You can see why this passage is so exciting, despite the fact that our Mary would be 'nearly fifty' by the time Jerusalem fell (presuming she was twelve or thirteen when first selected by Jesus) and probably didn't have a child young enough to suckle. Could this be an intended slur, a parody of the original Jesus-Mary-Lazarus-Child affair? There is a Mary, an Eleazar (Lazarus), a presumed 'father', the implied wealth of the family, the young son whom the woman is 'preserving', and the 'eating of the flesh' in order to be granted 'life'. There is also a village called Bethezub, rather than Bethany (but could *-zub* be a reference to 'Zebedee'?) and the 'House of *Hyssop.*' Hyssop was a factor in the FG's allusion to the rescue of Jesus by those of the house in Bethany.

It sounds *just* like the kind of misinformed invective against the rebellious group led by Jesus that one would *expect* from this Roman Jew, rather than the 'Christ' references I rejected from the start (e.g., *Ant.* 18.3) as being Christian addenda.

Coincidences?

The following are basically 'study notes' for (potential) future projects; they may be dead-ends or they may provide further insights. Decide for yourself.

Josephus relates the tale of Jesus, son of Ananus (*Wars.* 6.5.3), who denounces the city of Jerusalem just before the ultimate destruction of the temple itself. Described as a "plebeian, and an husbandman," this Jesus also prophesies doom and destruction in the temple. His first public display is at the Feast of Tabernacles.

He, also, speaks of "the bridegrooms and the brides," is arrested first by the 'eminent' men of the Jews, is subsequently sent to the Roman procurator (Albinus), is flogged, interrogated, asked who he is, where he comes from, and why he utters such words. He says little and is finally considered to be a 'madman'. This Jesus disappears from the public eye for several years but is found lamenting the fate of the temple when it is seized during the Jewish War. He is killed uttering his lamentations. The story is related in terms of the Jews' inability to see and comprehend the 'signs' that pointed to this destructive fate and the 'false prophets' who misguided many. It is unusual for Josephus to describe someone as a 'plebeian' suggesting that he may be countering any suggestion that the man was ... a priest? A 'husbandman'; was he a 'shepherd', by any chance?

One of the most intriguing comments, however, is the fact that Josephus provides a timeline, albeit confusing, for this man's "melancholy ditty", i.e., he made his voice heard at the Feast of Tabernacles "four years" before the War and continued for "seven years and five months." As the historian claims this Jesus was killed by a rock hurled by a siege engine during the closing stages of the Roman attack on the walls of the city (i.e., "he saw his presage in earnest fulfilled in our siege, when it ceased"), we must assume he dies sometime in September 70 CE, when the assault was nearly complete.

In Whiston's translation of Josephus there is a footnote to this account; a question arises pertaining to the comment that the Jews erected booths *within* the temple, i.e., has this reference to the celebrations been altered or misinterpreted? Let's consider both timeframes (this is a common theme in Josephus' works, making precise dating of events a bit of a nightmare!).

The War in Jerusalem, some argue, began with the revolt of the Jews against the Romans in August/September and the Roman (rather unimpressive) retaliation in October 66 CE. Though Christian tradition suggests the revolt started after the martyrdom of James the Just sometime in 62 CE, there is no satisfactory explanation why it took a further four years to spark an insurrection. Perhaps it didn't take that long.

If we accept that Jesus Ananus launched his mission at the Feast of Tabernacles in October 62 CE and his career spanned precisely *seven years and five months*, this would not lead us to the end of the attack in September 70 CE as Josephus records but to February, before the assault on the city began. Is this further blatant confusion on Josephus' part, or can we see the redactor's hand here? On the other hand, if we use Josephus' insistence that this Jesus began his campaign "four years before the War," this would, indeed bring us to September 62 CE and one might feel more inclined to accept that the murder of James triggered Ananus' tirade, especially if James *was* family.

Seven years and five months prior to the full-on siege would bring us to a date between the Festival of Dedication (December) 62 and Passover (April) 63, not the Feast of Tabernacles in October but the Dedication ceremony *does* take place *within* the temple. Furthermore, it takes place in December of 62, which is a perfect four years before what I and other scholars would deem the true beginning of the War against Jerusalem, i.e., in December 66 Vespasian began his subjugation of North and West Palestine (completing the takeover by December 68 CE).

So, rather than trying to solve the riddle of Josephus' two timeframes, which do not tally as they stand, all makes sense if we heed Whiston's cautionary note and use the dating rather than the spurious reference to 'Tabernacles' as the means to pinpointing Ananus' mission within the context of the War. How does this link to anything in our new perception of the historical Jesus and his legacy? Simply put, I think this character could be Jesus' now adult son, following in his father's footsteps (see below). I think his identity was, by the time Josephus came to write of him, somewhat vague, but the historian probably knew the tales of Jesus and superimposed pertinent details to fill out the narrative.

For those who wish to pursue this investigation I offer the following intriguing 'coincidences' and hope that someone with an open mind and a lot of research time can come up with an answer.

★ Josephus' "seven years and five months" just happens to be exactly the same duration as the "woes" described in Rev 8:13–13:16 (the first lasting five months, the next two both lasting forty-two months).

★ It is also the duration of the reign of King Ahasuerus (Artaxerxes) in Ezra 4:6, who ceased construction on the temple for the duration of his reign after a petition from the northern tribes who were refused inclusion by the Jews. Permission to continue was granted by King Darius of Persia sometime in his second year but the vagueness of the chronology here (e.g., the letter was devised in the king's 'accession year') one may be able to suggest the entire cessation of work lasted seven years and five months. It's a long shot perhaps but the fact that we are dealing with the raising of a 'new' temple in the context of hostilities between Samaritans and Jews is worth noting.

★ Simple numerology like that used in the FG gives us 7 + 5 = 12 (twelve), one of the most significant numbers in our Jesus' story.

★ In the discussion of John 7 we noticed an allusion to the original Dedication of the temple by Solomon at the Feast of Tabernacles and in John 10 we saw Jesus making his final public demonstration at the Festival of Dedication within the temple. Wouldn't it be rather uncanny for a complete stranger to begin his campaign in a confused context of Tabernacles/Dedication—and for him to endure almost identical consequences—and not be somehow connected to the FG Jesus and/or his son?

Paul's Protest

Paul's Letter to the Galatians preserves the most vivid evidence of a very early schism in the faith Jesus inspired. In Gal 1:6, Paul warns the Galatians to be wary of "a different gospel" that is circulating; then he contradicts himself, i.e., "not that there *is* another gospel" (1:7), but whatever he wishes to call it, he argues that it is "confusing" them. He is so adamant that this other gospel may contradict what he is preaching (i.e., "Jesus Christ, raised from the dead, a descendant of David—that is *my* gospel" [2 Tim 2:8]), that he says: "not even a messenger from heaven [should be believed if what he tells you is not the same as *I* have told you], let that one be accursed!" (Gal 1:9). That is pretty powerful! It was, I am convinced, the FG's story, the testament of Lazarus that was being denounced.

There may be a further clue in Paul's letters to Timothy, and it is a very cryptic one, perhaps intentionally, lest it get into the wrong hands. In the first letter, Timothy is in Ephesus, where he is told to "instruct certain people not to teach any different doctrine," and to warn them "not to occupy themselves with myths and endless genealogies that promote speculations, rather than the divine training" (1 Tim 1:3–4). In other words, Jesus' genealogy is again a matter of interest, perhaps concern, and Paul is adamant this has to be quashed. He is acting the spin-doctor, limiting any opposition to his own agenda.

A few passages later, Paul mentions two people who have, according to *his* ideals, "blasphemed," i.e., Hymenaeus and Alexander (1 Tim 1:20). Alexander I shall come back to in a moment, but Hymenaeus is referred to again, in the second letter to Timothy and there he is linked to a certain Philetus (2 Tim. 2:17). Philetus means "beloved" (in a brotherly sense); in the FG, two disciples were referred to in terms of being Jesus' *philetos* (a disciple whom Jesus 'loved'), i.e., Philip and Lazarus. Either one could be a thorn in Paul's side but it is Philip who first preaches openly in Samaria (only after it is proven safe does Peter follow!); it is he who is more readily associated with the *phileo* term. The name Hymenaeus means, "belonging to marriage"; "Lazarus," recall, also has a possible meaning of "unite for/in marriage."

What is this 'blasphemy' of which they are accused? They are accused of "claiming that *the resurrection has already taken place*" (***this is *astounding*!). If the two troublemakers are, indeed, Lazarus and Philip, this *would* be the 'good news' they would be teaching, i.e., that the Remnant *has* been reunited and the ideal Israel resurrected (at Shiloh)!

An Alexander is mentioned on five separate occasions, once in Mark, twice in Acts, and once in each of the two letters from Paul to Timothy. In Acts 19 he is a Jew elected as spokesman for the Ephesians but in 1 Timothy he is linked with Hymenaeus, and in 2 Timothy he appears as a "coppersmith" who apparently did Paul "great harm," and whom Paul indicates "the Lord will pay ... back for his deeds. You also must be aware of him, for he strongly opposed our message" (2 Tim 4:14–15). Sound familiar?

In Mark (15:21), Alexander is the son of Simon the Cyrene, who, I have claimed, is to be identified with Judas, i.e., the 'good thief' who ultimately realises he has to pay for his treachery. Thus:

Hymenaeus is Lazarus
Philetus is Philip
Alexander is Son of Judas

If we take "coppersmith" (*chalkeus*) to be a derogatory term in this context (*chalkeus* stems from *chalao*, "to lower down, to strike," a derivative of which appears in 1 Cor 13:1, where Paul suggests a soul without love can turn the words of angels into a meaningless, "noisy gong"), there is a further allusion to Judas. Copper in the OT (usually translated as brass or bronze) is used for making the utensils and vessels of the tabernacle (Exod 38), and later, those of the temple (put into the care of the chief priests, the treasurers, according to Ezra 8:27). Thus, this Alexander is indirectly linked to the general concepts of 'temple' and 'priesthood'. "Copper" is also a euphemism for 'money' (Mark 6:8; 12:41), making the possible allusion to the temple treasury, or even to Judas' 'blood money' an intriguing one.

In the FG's depiction of the arrest of Jesus, an odd little scene takes place that I seldom, if ever, see discussed in Johannine literature: "one of the police standing nearby struck Jesus on the face" (John 18:22). Two words are of interest here: 'police' and 'struck'. In the NRSV, the Greek word *hypēretōn* is translated as "police" but the term means an officer, a servant, an assistant, etc. In the FG it is used nine times, eight in connection with the "Jews," the chief priests, but one refers to Jesus' own 'ministers', who he says will fight for him if needed (John 18:36). The other term, translated as "struck" is *rhapisma*. This can mean a slap, with an open palm or a blow with an implement, like a stick.

Who is an officer of the high priest and has just fetched Peter into Annas' courtyard? Judas (as explained, i.e., "another disciple ... known to the high priest," in John 18:15). Who is the 'coppersmith' and thus has an etymological link to 'striking'? Judas. Who, then, strikes Jesus in John 18? Judas. Perhaps in frustration, or a pang of guilt that leads to panic, or a show of bravado to show that he has not 'turned native' and truly converted to Jesus' cause, Judas' slap in the FG morphs into the fated 'kiss' in the

Synoptics.

In Acts 4, just to make matters even more tantalizing, Alexander is said to be a member of the *family* of Annas, the (senior or retired) high priest! Is the Alexander of Paul's letter to Timothy the *son* of the FG's Judas? Any descendent of his would certainly be considered an opponent to Paul, the 'convert'; the 'son' must reflect his 'father' after all, so perhaps Judas Iscariot's son followed in his father's footsteps, just as Jesus' did.

To offer one last clue, the original biblical 'coppersmith' was Tubal-cain, a descendent of Cain, the arch-villain of the Hebrew Bible (Gen 4:22). The traditional arch villain of the New Testament is Judas.

Peter's Propaganda

As for Peter, if we allow him the benefit of the doubt, he does attempt to resign himself to Jesus' enforced abjection, for according to The Acts of the Apostles he does begin his public ministry with a call to his fellow "Israelites" and he does refer to Jesus as "Jesus of Nazareth." He then makes the fated error (two, in fact); he declares Jesus to be the Messiah ben David (Acts 2:29f) and he concerns himself with Gentiles (Acts 11). It seems that Peter does not 'follow' Jesus after all.

When Paul first encounters Peter, so he tells us in Gal 1:11, he "opposes him to his face" because Peter has been tempted into eating amongst the Gentiles, something Jesus would have strictly forbidden. What is interesting here, though, is the name Paul gives to Peter, i.e., "Cephas." Where did he get this name, if not from the community of disciples under Lazarus? The name does not appear anywhere else and it is obviously just as debasing in Paul's estimation as it was when Jesus first conferred it on Peter. Paul's ministry is dated very soon after that of Jesus' so this may yet another clue to the early foundations of the FG. (Of course, one can argue that Paul's usage came first and the FG echoed the name but given the information I present in "Paul's Protest," I think we can safely reject this argument.)

Many of the things Peter is reputed to have done after Jesus' departure echo his lifelong desire for position and authority, and his rivalry with Lazarus. As if to counter the testimony of the disciple "whom Jesus loved," Peter is also miraculously freed from imprisonment (as discussed), found to be living with his mother-in-law (as Lazarus lived with Martha), to have taken Jesus into his own home (as Lazarus did, at Bethany), and to have crowds come to see him because of his 'miraculous' deeds (as crowds had come to see Lazarus after he had been 'raised from the dead'). Peter performs 'miracles' very similar to Jesus' 'signs' but they are not linked by any underlying theological statement; it is as if they are performed (or rather attributed to him) simply for the sake of proving his status.

Take another look at the character Barsabbas, introduced in Acts 1:23. How close is this name to Barabbas, the "son of the high priest" (Judas)? Note, too, how this character has two other names: Justus and, of all things, Joseph. Commission names? In the new order ruled by Peter, rival to the young Joseph of Arimathea, lots are cast for a replacement for Judas; Joseph is rejected, echoing (perhaps in retaliation for) Peter's rejection from the small community Jesus took to Shiloh. It is almost childish, this 'tit-for-tat' echoing of the FG but it is so like the Peter we have come to know!

On the other hand, can Barsabbas be a 'son of' the FG Judas, nominated for a seat in the new order by Peter, whose previous alliance with the young man's father left him feeling obliged (but secretly hoping the lots will be cast against this Joseph, as Peter now wishes to 'move on'?) Remember, commission names change when a character shifts in nature or circumstance. Why else mention someone who was rejected? Recall, too, that Caiaphas' first name is Joseph; if Judas is a biological son of the high priest, it would be normal for him to name *his* son likewise.

One last intriguing question: Is "Barsabbas" a play on "Barabbas," the "son of the father"—"of lies" (Caiaphas)—pointing us, yet again, to Judas?

Given all this, the two letters attributed to Peter cannot be written by the same man (i.e., Peter) we have come to recognise in the FG. They are full of FG terminology, full of the sentiments and eloquence of the FG author, or perhaps someone taught by him (?). For instance: "Rid yourselves, therefore, of all malice, and all guile, insincerity, envy and all slander" (1 Pet 2:1); and "Humble yourselves therefore under the mighty hand of God, so that he may exalt you in due time" (5:6), i.e., something Cephas never did! He then goes on to say that the followers of Jesus are to emulate the disciples (just as *they* emulate Jesus), i.e., they are to see themselves as a "holy priesthood" in which malice, guile, etc., are washed away in a spiritual rebirth. This theme is central to the FG but was utterly lost on Peter.

Look at some of the other phrases in these letters:

- tend the flocks
- Do not lord it over those in your charge
- Do not be conformed to the desires that you formerly had in ignorance.
- You have been born anew
- Beloved
- Although you have not seen him, you love him (*agapao*)
- you are a ... royal priesthood
- Conduct yourself honourably among the Gentiles

- Women are also the 'heirs of the gracious gift'
- You have already spent enough time in doing what the Gentiles like to do ... passions, drunkenness
- as an elder myself and **a witness of the sufferings of Christ, as well as one who shares in the glory**
- **She who is in Babylon, *chosen together with you*, sends greetings**
- **and so does my son, Mark.**
- **Peace (Shiloh) to you**
- **brotherly affection, and brotherly affection with love (*phileo* and *agapao*)**
- **rescue the godly from trial**
- near-sighted and blind, and ... forgetful of the cleansing of past sins.
- escaped the defilements of the world

The Letter of James is also on a par with these Petrine Letters:
- servant
- twelve tribes in the Dispersion
- facing trials
- testing
- one who doubts is like a wave of the sea
- raised up
- a crown of life given to those who 'love' him (*agapao*)
- birth
- beloved
- 'gift' from above
- he gave us birth by the word of truth
- doers of the word, and not merely hearers
- those who look to the perfect law
- keep oneself unstained by the world
- 'fine clothes' vs. 'dirty clothes'
- heirs to the kingdom ... those who love him
- Abraham
- 'above' vs. 'below'
- Adulterers!
- friendship with the world is enmity with God
- humble ... submit yourself ... and [God] will exalt you
- Cleanse your hands
- will save the sick ... will raise them up
- the prayer of the righteous is powerful and effective
- death of the 'soul'

To be honest, the tone, message and style of the second letter attributed to Peter does bear the stamp of a different hand; that is, I think 1 Peter and 2 Peter have different authors. In all, I don't think Simon Peter wrote these, but that is just my opinion.

The three Letters of John are also worthy of closer scrutiny, *especially* the second letter! Also, reread the Synoptic gospels and see how their interpretations compare to what can now be seen in the FG. The transitions *are* better comprehended if we turn the dating around, placing the FG first, then perhaps, Luke/Acts, and/or Mark, then Matthew.

Increasingly powerful and popular Church authorities might well have appropriated the eloquent and profound writings of the seemingly defunct and outlawed sect led by Lazarus and attributed them to Peter, their aging and perhaps not-so-eloquent figurehead.

One can see how Peter would have *considered* himself an 'elder' and as one who 'shares in the glory' but doesn't that role better suit the younger Lazarus, considered an elder by virtue of his rank not his age. He was certainly one of the witnesses to Jesus' suffering, indeed a more intimate witness could not be found, except perhaps for Nicodemus. The plan devised by Jesus *necessitated* that Lazarus share in the glory of the new priesthood.

She who is in Babylon
In 2 Esd 3:2, we find Salathiel describing the "desolation of Zion and the wealth of Babylon" (cf. 3:38); in Zech 2:7, the prophet hears God say: "Escape to Zion, you that live with daughter Babylon ... the nations that plundered you." Arzareth, the land in which the Remnant is scattered, is not synonymous with Babylon, it is *within* it. That is, Babylon becomes a generic term for the Gentile, 'wicked' nations, while Arzareth is wherever the Remnant *are* within Babylon. It is a metaphorical place, recall, a 'limbo' of sorts.

In 2 John 1:1 we read: "From the Elder to the chosen lady and her children, whom I genuinely love, and not only I but also all who know the truth"; and in 2 John 1:13, "The children of your elect sister send you greetings." If this "she," "chosen lady," and "elect sister" is, in fact, Mary, we have a corroboration of the subsequent legends describing the exodus of Joseph and his charges to foreign lands.

With whom was 'she' chosen? According to 1 Peter 1:1, she was chosen together with the "exiles of the Dispersion who were destined by God the Father and sanctified by the Spirit to be obedient to Jesus Christ and to be sprinkled with his blood." There is a specific reference to Jesus' blood in the FG and this has specific meaning, in terms of the holy battle for the liberation and reunification of Israel. Jesus' blood signified his victory in that regard and this victory was itself signified by his entry into Jerusalem; the birth of his son in Ephraim is the linchpin of this perceived victory.

Similarly, those disciples who received the spirit did so after their ritual confinement up in Shiloh; they were then commissioned to transfer the spirit to the 'seventy', i.e., within the Dispersion. So, for there to be a female disciple 'chosen' at the same time as the other twelve ministers and for her to be deemed just as significant and authoritative—just as 'sanctioned'— this can only be Mary Magdalene, surely. That she was chosen 'together with' those in the Dispersion not so much because she was added to the inner circle after the disciples went to proselytise but because she is included as one of the scattered, the downtrodden, for she was a Samaritan, not a Jew, i.e. "together with" might suggest 'as well as' not 'at the same time as'.

In the legends that abound throughout the Middle Ages we hear of Mary (called the 'mother' of Jesus of course) travelling to France either by design or under coercion. She is beyond the land of Israel, i.e., within Babylon. There is no way to know how long the fugitive group (Mary, Martha, Lazarus, and child) are absent from their homeland but there are some intriguing clues to suggest they return to Palestine a few years later.

Magi and Murder
Matthew's tale of the magi seeking out the 'star rising in the east' (Matt 2:1-18) does have a potential link to the FG.

In Num 24:17, it is predicted that a "star shall step forth out of Jacob" and this implies a princely ruler, a messianic figure: The Messiah ben Joseph is referred to as "the star." Could it not be possible for news of Jesus' campaign against the establishment in Jerusalem to reach distant shores, where spiritual leaders and philosophers perceive a potentially radical shift in Israel's theological and therefore political status? In other words, Jesus is seen as the potential 'star' whose profile is steadily 'rising'. Remember that John expects such a man and, at least in the beginning, sees in Jesus the "light" of such a 'star'. Matthew uses the Greek word *anatolé*, which is commonly translated as "east" but this is an inferred meaning, an extrapolation, for *anatolé* means "a rising," e.g., "of light," so, though *suggesting* "dawn" and therefore the "east," it *can* be translated without any geographical allusions.

Although many set themselves up as royal pretenders, or make themselves notorious by their bandit ways, Jesus seems to be the only figure in this historical setting who shakes Jerusalem to the very core. Ironically, he does so in a posthumous sense, for it is only when the chain reaction of his rebellion is seen with hindsight (after his eventual disappearance from the main stage) that we see the Messiah ben Joseph legend suddenly becoming far more detailed and uncannily similar to the events surrounding Jesus' final days.

On the other hand (and I think this more likely), perhaps it is the birth of Jesus' *son and heir*, i.e., the realised hereditary kingdom that triggers panic for Herod *Antipas*. The word Matthew uses to describe the figure known as Herod in his narrative is *basileus*, which means "ruler, commander of the people," etc. It doesn't *necessarily* mean "king" as in 'royal lineage'. Herod the Great *was* the last king of his line but Antipas could just as well be a *basileus*. Has the Christian tradition intentionally or erroneously interpreted an earlier context for this Herod?

Consider:

- ★ Herod demands to know the exact date of birth of the boy (Matt 2:16); astrologers (the magi) suggest the child would have to be **two years old or under.**

- ★ Jesus' son, between the lines of the FG, is born just before **Passover, 36 CE.**

- ★ The tenure of Herod Antipas' authority in the region becomes uncertain in the summer of **37 CE**, when Herodias' (the disputed second wife of Herod) brother Agrippa inherits control of the territories once held by Philip (Antipas' half-brother, who had died in 34 CE).

- ★ If Herod is beginning to feel uneasy, threatened, and at risk of losing his position, the last thing he would want is another 'upstart' causing a problem for him. It turns out that Herodius is the instigator of a petition to make Herod king, but Agrippa plays dirty and convinces Caligula, now Emperor, that Herod is a traitor. Could it be at all possible that Herodius, allegedly behind the murder of John (the baptiser), was the one who put the idea of killing the "star" into Herod's mind?

- ★ The child, if he was considered a threat to Herod's security, must have been born before March **37 CE**, when Tiberius dies and the political situation changes.

- ★ March/April, 36 CE to March 37 CE, means Jesus' son would be about **one year old**, or about **17-18 months**, if his concerns peak with the inauguration of Agrippa as King in the summer.

- ★ Rumours of a secret army being raised lead Caligula to exile Herod in the summer of **39 CE.**

Because of Herod's rash response to Jesus' apparent success in securing a new, hereditary and apparently 'legitimate' priesthood, Lazarus, Mary, Martha, and the child leave Jerusalem until it is safe to return; *this* is the root of all those subsequent legends of the family group travelling to distant lands.

It is also a rationale for the gospel's ambiguity surrounding the identity of the husband/father, the "I'm Spartacus" feel to Mary's trial scene, etc. The FG is devotedly clandestine about the child *because* he is under a death sentence, just as Lazarus and Jesus were; he is incognito, just as his father and step-father had been in times of danger, hidden beneath the storyline—but he is most certainly there. Lazarus' duty as the *parakletos* included telling the truth about Jesus' mission; the child is the pinnacle of that mission (i.e., as the first hereditary, Ephraimite high priest of the new kingdom), so he *must* exist between the lines. It's just a matter of looking a bit deeper!

John Mark

This mysterious child, the new 'star' rising, is, I suggest, the other mysterious young boy from the New Testament, John Mark.

Consider the following intriguing usage of the name Mark in the early Christian texts:

★ The Petrine letters that I argue to be very Johannine include the name Mark as the 'son' of the author.

★ There is a tradition that the Gospel of Mark was written by John Mark (I do not agree).

★ The Secret Gospel of Mark potentially contains the tale of Lazarus, though couched in slightly different terminology (e.g., the young boy going through a ritual ordination that lasts seven days, paralleling Lazarus' internment).

★ In Acts 12:12 Peter finds himself in much the same predicament as Lazarus does, i.e., hunted by the authorities, his life in jeopardy. He appears "as if from the dead" at the house of a certain Mary, the mother of John Mark.

★ John Mark's father is allegedly not known.

★ In Col 4:10 John Mark is said to be a 'cousin' to Barnabas (but this can also read as "nephew"); Barnabas' actual name is Joseph.

The Testament of Lazarus

★ Peter takes John Mark under his wing just as Jesus did Lazarus.

★ Later, John Mark and Paul fall out and Mark leaves with Barnabas but in 2 Tim 4:11, Paul demands the previously disowned John Mark be brought to him in Rome even though this would put the youth in danger.

How intriguing that in subsequent NT documents (the 'Petrine' letters) we hear of the *equality* of women within the new community;[1] the direct mentioning of one woman in particular (some translations assume this to be a sister church) who is somewhere in Babylon; the pro-Shiloh blessing; and the name of a 'son', Mark, whose position is obviously significant if he is sending his greetings to the intended recipient of the letter (1 Pet 5:13).

According to Acts 12:12, Peter is freed from prison in a manner that echoes Lazarus' break-out and arrives at the home of John Mark's mother Mary, in Jerusalem. The Catholic Encyclopaedia suggests this Mary is Peter's "old friend" and a "prominent member" of the early church in Jerusalem. Is this *yet another* Mary, or is she the Magdalene, the mother of Jesus' son, returned from 'Babylon'?

The fact that our Mary would give lodgings to Jesus' least favourite disciple shouldn't really be an issue here, for Peter's story subsequent to the FG is replete with instances of usurpation; he is depicted as taking over all that was Jesus', even his home and family, in a blatant bid for the rights of the firstborn. Recall the site referred to as Jesus' Cradle at the south-eastern corner of Temple Mount, i.e., not only do legends pertaining to 'Mary and her child' make this site significant to both Christians and Muslims, there is also a link to Peter: "… close to The Templar's building, to the east of the city walls was Simon the Zaddik's place of dwelling. It is told that here he customarily hosted Miriam and Jesus in great honour, and gave them to eat."[2] Yet again, Peter's largess is at the forefront here;[3] he goes down in

---

[1] See Appendices, 3 (Gospel of Thomas), where Peter's attitude to women is quite the reverse, perhaps corroborating the argument here that the so-called Petrine letters were not composed by this man but by someone with an affinity for the status of Mary. As other traditions do place the young Mark with Peter at some point, it would be an 'honest error' to assume 1 Peter was, indeed his composition. The fact that it speaks of 'Jesus Christ' rising 'from the dead, etc.,' might well have been an *ex post facto* (i.e., Pauline) Christian addition to a previously discovered missive, i.e., it was too good not to use, so they commandeered it for their cause.

[2] Tuvia Sagiv, "Solomon's Stables and the Southern Gates," http://www.templemount.org/solstables.html. 1996).

[3] Rabbi Yehuda HaChasid (1150–1217 CE) in *Sefer Chasidim* (Section 191) writes: "If a Jew converts to Christianity, we refer to him with a derogatory nickname. For example, if his name was Avraham, we call him Afram ('from afar, dust'), or

history as being the one who cares for Mary and the child.

Another little clue intrigues me here; the passage in Acts 12:12–17 suggests that Mary's home is rather substantial, having room enough for several members of the community to gather there. She is a wealthy woman it seems, in keeping with the family status of Nicodemus and Lazarus. There is also the mention of an 'outer gate' and a female gatekeeper! It is interesting that in this instance the gatekeeper is given a name, i.e., Rhoda (meaning "one from Rhodes"). A purely Greek name, this may suggest that Mary is in a wealthy enough home to afford Greek slaves. Look what Rhoda does, though; instead of opening the gate, she runs to tell those inside that Peter is there. Who is the FG's 'gatekeeper'? Mary. What was Mary's first entry into the FG narrative? She was the character of the (foreign) Samaritan woman who ran back to her people to tell them about Jesus, the man at the well. On the morning of Jesus' so-called resurrection, she runs to tell the disciples. Are we seeing a strange blend of the truth here, in such a way that echoes the FG founding narrative, yet replaces Jesus with Peter and blurs the distinction between Mary Magdalene and the now esteemed mother of John Mark? So many apparent coincidences cannot be ignored.

The Catholic Encyclopaedia also says:

> In the preface to his Gospel in manuscripts of the Vulgate, Mark is represented as having been a Jewish priest: "Mark the Evangelist, who exercised the priestly office in Israel, a Levite by race." Early authorities, however, are silent upon the point, and it is perhaps only an inference from his relation to Barnabas the Levite (Acts 4:36).

Thus, many have considered the evangelist Mark to be the same "Mark" of Peter's letter. I cannot agree with this identification (as will become evident shortly), but the 'priestly' aspect intrigues me. Further, according to the Encyclopaedia:

> Early in the third century Hippolytus ... refers to Mark as *ho kolobodaktulos*, i.e. "stump-fingered" or "mutilated in the finger(s)," and later authorities allude to the same defect. Various explanations of the epithet have been suggested: that Mark, after he embraced Christianity, *cut off his thumb to unfit himself for the Jewish priesthood*; that his fingers were naturally stumpy; that some defect

---

something similar. We do this even to a *tzaddik*, if the Christians venerate him—like Shimon Kipah, who was a righteous man but the Christians approbated him—venerated him as one of their saints, and gave him the surname (Simon) Peter. Even though he was a righteous man (a *tsaddik*), the Jews gave him the nickname of Peter Chamor ("Firstling donkey," a play on Exod 13:13). Avraham Ya'akov Finkel, *Sefer Chasidim* (Jason Aronson, 1997), 85.

in his toes is alluded to.

Lazarus was maimed in an attempt to prohibit his role as a functioning priest of course, under his commission name Malchus. This is all tantalizing, to say the least, but there is even more to consider.

Many scholars are not sure what to make of the relationship between Peter/Paul and this young man and seem happy to suggest that John Mark was merely a fairly insignificant assistant. When Paul first sets out with Barnabas around 46 CE, John Mark, if we assume him to be Jesus' son, would be about eleven/twelve years old, nearing the age Lazarus was when he was first introduced to Jesus. Within the next two years, i.e., as *he* becomes 'of age', John Mark is seen to be 'assisting' within the group led by Barnabas, the Cypriot Levite. The Levite connection certainly fits our once priestly Lazarus but the link to Cyprus?

We have already discussed western legends pertaining to the expulsion, or escape, of Mary, Martha, and Lazarus to France but the Eastern Orthodox Church teaches that Lazarus and his 'sisters' went to Cyprus! He was supposedly appointed bishop at Kition by Paul and Barnabas. He is said to have died there in 63 CE.

We are never told who the boy's father is (Col 4:10);[4] when we also notice that the other name for John Mark's 'cousin/uncle' Barnabas is Joseph, we can be forgiven in thinking that we are reading about Lazarus, whose final commission name in the FG is Joseph. The name Barnabas is often translated as "son of comfort" but could this be stretched to "son of the Comforter"? This was Jesus' role as the Samaritan Taheb, recall. It also translates as "son of Nabas" or 'son of prophecy/the prophet." Now that *is* interesting, i.e., the 'prophet' is Jesus!

So, is Barnabas Lazarus?

It would make sense, if we imagine that after Jesus' death the new order at Shiloh is not as strongly secured as had been the plan, splinters of disciples having broken away, like Peter, to take up their own agenda. Mary and Lazarus are more vulnerable than ever and see the need to leave when Herod orders the death of the children. When the political situation in Judea changes they return, Lazarus takes on a new commission name (Barnabas), and takes control of the primary group of Jesus-followers that has grown in his absence; at some stage he is sent out with Paul to Antioch (and this would explain why he is not at home with Mary when Peter supposedly stays at his house and takes the young boy under his wing).

One may ask why Lazarus would condone to preach to the Gentiles

---

[4] Christian tradition holds that John Mark was born in Cyrene, of all places, which would be a link to Judas in this analysis.

with Paul, when he is fully aware of Jesus' lack of interest in non-Israelites. The answer seems to come in the words of Acts 13:46: "It was necessary that the word of God should be spoken first to you (i.e., the "Jews"). Since you reject it and judge yourselves to be unworthy of eternal life, we are now turning to the Gentiles." It would appear that the lofty aspirations of the original Jesus movement simply peters out, or gets railroaded by the onslaught of messiah-seeking, Rome-hating, power-hungry alternatives. Lazarus loses his seat as the 'right-hand-man', the *parakletos*, etc., and becomes an accessory to be flaunted about on Paul's own promotional campaigns. Lazarus, perhaps, has little choice left, if he wishes to 'preach' about his beloved Jesus.

In Antioch, Paul, Barnabas, and John Mark come face to face with a man called Bar-Jesus, i.e., Son of Jesus, whose other name is Elymas (Acts 13:6–11); curiously, an addendum suggests this second name is a translation of the first name, which is odd because Elymas is not used anywhere else (and is thus not a common 'translation', if readers have to be told), and it *does not* mean "son of Jesus" but something akin to "wisdom, or power." Acts 13:6 uses the term *magos*, i.e. magus/magi, in a parallel to the FG's Thomas Didymus, i.e., Bar-Jesus is called, in effect, "Magician, the magician," just as Thomas is called "Twin, the twin." The author of Acts is thus presenting a hidden meaning, an invitation to think twice. Could it be that Bar-Jesus is actually Peter?

Paul pronounces Bar-Jesus a heretic; in Acts 8:9–24, however, there is a certain Simon (Peter's other name), who is also a "magician" (*magos*), who is going about Samaria "saying that he was someone great," using the Greek word *megas*, which means "great," e.g., "large" (as in the "large" 153 fish of John 21 that were interpreted as higher-status officers/priests), or "powerful," i.e., the meaning of Elymas (and perhaps a play on *magos*).

Consider the level of vitriol in this scene; Paul is scathing, seething, i.e., "... will you not *stop* making crooked (i.e., *diastrephó*, thus "distorting, perverting, misinterpreting") the straight paths of the Lord?" he implores, with the inference that this 'magician' is known to him already, i.e., "will you *not stop* ...?" implies persistence. He calls Bar-Jesus, the "son of the devil," using the same word, *diabolos*, as in John 6 and 13, which linked Peter and the established temple priesthood. Notice how he also uses the word "straight," which is *euthus* in Greek; the same term is used as a name for the place where Paul is to receive a miraculous reversal of his blindness thanks to a disciple called Ananias (Acts 9:10–19). This place is a "street called Straight" (cf. "crooked" in Paul's invective, above) but more intriguingly, Paul is to be found in "the house of Judas" (i.e., which can mean the abode of, or the 'family of').

Although commentators are keen to assert that this Ananias is not the same as the one mentioned in Acts 23:2, who is the high priest at the time (i.e., son of Nebedæus, *Ant.* 20.5.2), I think there *is* a possible connection, in that there is a subtle allusion to the relationship between Peter, Judas, and the temple cultus—with Paul right in the middle, initially, as the 'adversary' of the growing Christian church. Peter has branched out on his own but Paul seems to be sitting comfortably in the bosom of Judas' family home, i.e., a home within the high-priestly domain (as Judas was the 'son' of Caiaphas, so Paul is here seen to be under the influence of the 'high priest' Ananias). The use of the same name for two apparently very different people in the same storyline suggests either an uncanny 'coincidence' with regard to the names of people involved, a mistranslation somewhere, or an intended signpost to some deeper meaning. As I am convinced that most biblical texts were written by highly skilled scribes, with a profound knowledge of the literary and lexical legacy of their Hebrew ancestors, I posit it is the last of these suggestions.

As we have also seen, Paul is utterly unimpressed with Peter and thinks he is wrong and misleading in his preaching. Is Peter now openly claiming to be Jesus' successor (his 'son')? Nothing has changed, it seems (and see Peter's claim to be Jesus' 'chosen one' to preach to the Gentiles in Acts 15:7) but here, Paul does just what Peter does in the Synoptics, i.e., he commandeers Jesus' 'signs' to give him the upper hand. The two, fairly closely depicted 'signs' that define Paul's conversion relate to 'blindness', i.e., his being struck blind on the Damascus road, and then the laying on of hands to 'remove' that blindness; this is precisely what happens with Lazarus, as the 'blind man'.

Jesus' son, the young John Mark was not, I suggest, already with Paul and Barnabas, as Acts 13:6 suggests; this is, indeed, an addendum, to help justify his presence later in the narrative. The relationship with Peter comes first. It would be feasible for Lazarus to travel to Antioch with Paul, having left his family in the 'care' of Peter (at Bethany); remember John 21 and Peter's testing by Jesus, i.e., he was granted a position of responsibility to tend and care for the 'flock' but not *lead* them. In his ever-noticeable over-exuberance, however, Peter might seize the opportunity to go on another of his 'fishing trips' with the young John Mark in tow, in a show of status (e.g., "Look, Jesus entrusted his son to me!").

In Acts 13:13, just after the scene with Bar-Jesus, John Mark splits from the group and returns to Jerusalem; it is probable Peter takes him home. In 15:37, however, Barnabas requests that John Mark be allowed to join them on campaign but Paul adamantly refuses. Why? Because, to Paul, the boy had clearly 'sided' with Paul's adversary, Peter—but he is just a boy, under the influence of a "powerful" man. At this point, Lazarus/Barnabas is probably realising that he has been neglecting his duty as John Mark's protector, as his 'step-father', and not wishing to leave the lad alone again with the scheming Peter, takes him (*and* Mary and Martha) to Cyprus (no one knows for how long).

When Paul is in dangerous Rome, however, he insists that Mark come to him because he might prove "profitable" (i.e., useful as bargaining leverage? Warning echoes of Caiaphas, here). Why? There is much speculation about this unexplained schism but when we later hear Paul speaking of the gospel that is not to be listened to, we can see how this might be explained in terms of Barnabas (Lazarus) and John Mark refusing to accept the changes to Jesus' vision that Paul is demanding. Could it be, therefore, that it is Paul's ulterior motive to see Mark and indeed Lazarus captured in Rome and thus removed from his side, painful thorns as they probably becoming? Why else would he wish to put the young Mark at risk after they have separated under discordant circumstances? (Recall the outright rejection of Hymenaeus and Philetus, aka Lazarus and Philip, i.e., old wounds?). So, John Mark's safety again becomes an issue for Lazarus, his regent, his protector.

I had long suspected that the attribution of the FG to "John" was a later phenomenon. Now I see that it *was* originally given this 'title', at least once the epilogue was added, for Lazarus was dead by then and John Mark needed to reiterate the standing within what was left of the community, i.e., a clear rejection of Peter was needed. Thus Lazarus' personal testament became the official 'good news' when John came of age and put his name to it, via the epilogue. (The use of the Greek (sur)name "Mark" in 1 Peter 5:13 is, for me, the 'smoking gun' that proves this otherwise very Johannine-sounding letter was appropriated for a more Hellenized audience.)

The Road to Shiloh

So, what of Jesus after the escape? There is no way of knowing *how* long he manages to stay alive but the fact that he hints at an imminent death when he speaks to his disciples suggests his remarkable 'recovery' was always expected to be temporary. Though his emulation of Hezekiah had sparked a hope for many more years of life, the unexpected, serious injury from the Roman soldier has taken its toll. He has fought so hard for his kingdom; I think he would wish to die in his own land.

Only a *very* few places in the OT are given precise locations, the most obvious and clear is, coincidentally or not, Shiloh. At the end of the Book of Judges, the Benjaminites are in need of wives, so they are told to go to the yearly festival at Shiloh to procure them, and they are given explicit directions: "Shiloh, which is north of Bethel, on the east of the highway that goes up from Bethel to Shechem, and south of Lebonah" (Judg 21:19).

Between Jerusalem and Bethel, enroute to Shiloh, is a place called Ramah; an inhabitant of Ramah is referred to as *Ramathiy*. Joseph of Arimathea (Lazarus) is thus intrinsically (symbolically) linked with this site.

The Ramah mentioned in Joshua 18:25 is allotted to the tribe of Benjamin (Nicodemus and Lazarus' tribe) and is close enough to Jerusalem to serve as a resting place before entering, or in the FG's case, leaving, the city (cf. Judg 19:13). The Ramah mentioned in 1 Samuel on the other hand is the home of Samuel, in the hill country of Ephraim (where Samuel was offered up as a Nazarite). The two sites are in such close proximity, both being about four or five miles north of Jerusalem, it is probable they are one and the same. Such a dual identification, though, is common, as we have seen, and once again it suits the FG author's purpose for, in keeping with tradition, there is *also* a Ramah on the border of the tribal lands of Asher (Josh 19:29, 36), a tribe that figured largely in Jesus' initial gathering of disciples (see Appendices, 5).

As a child, Lazarus lives with his father, Nicodemus, in Capernaum (which is probably where Jesus and Nicodemus *first* meet, being both men's home). Then, as Jesus' protégée, he moves with his spiritual father down to Bethany, about one and a half miles from the city of Jerusalem, into a house acquired perhaps by the wealthy Nicodemus, which is why Lazarus hints at it being 'his' house. Once Jesus is crucified, the Bethany home becomes defunct and this is when the Ramah site comes into play. Perhaps, though, there is a more intimate connection to be made, one more in keeping with Lazarus' role as the 'beloved' adopted 'son'.

Jeremiah recounts a dream in which he hears weeping from Ramah—the weeping of Rachel, the mother of Benjamin and Joseph, who is buried there. She mourns for her lost Josephite children, who are scattered and have been without their God (Jer 31:15). The name Bethany also invokes a sense of mourning, so the continuity is enlightening; it links Bethany to Ramah/Arimathea but more importantly, it provides a potential fulfilment of the Josephite tradition, i.e., the cyclical theme that has its origins in the FG's allusions to the Remnant of Joseph returning to the Promised Land.

Joseph of Arimathea returns the 'son of Joseph' to his "own nation" just as Joshua returns the bones of Joseph to Shechem. It is the duty of the 'son' to bury the father and one that is foreshadowed by the premature burial scene of John 19. Likewise, both Eleazar and Joshua (OT) are buried in the "hill country of Ephraim" but each within territory owned by their respective tribes; the duality of the Ramah site seems to satisfy this requirement for a consistent parallel. The more traditional translation of *ramah* is "high, exalted," making it both an apt reflection of Jesus' now exalted status as the King of Israel.

It is here, in Ramah, a peaceful coign of vantage on the plateau overlooking the territory of Ephraim, with Shiloh in the distance that Samuel, the last divinely chosen defender of the covenant *before* Jesus, had been laid to rest. I think this is probably where Jesus is truly laid to rest by his beloved disciple, Lazarus. It would be exciting to think Lazarus is duty-bound to bury Jesus' bones *with* the Ark; remember that the Hebrew word for both Joseph's ossuary and the Ark of the Covenant is the same for both. How fitting an end that would be!

> *For the righteous are taken away from calamity.*
> *And they enter into PEACE (Shiloh).*
> Isa 57:1

With Jesus gone, Lazarus and Mary, along with Martha and the young John Mark, head for distant shores, whether by choice or by force (both are inferred by various traditions). It does seem that they return not to Samaria but to Jerusalem. The son's inheritance, Jesus' legacy, clearly plays heavily in John Mark's later life (if he is, indeed, Josephus' Jesus Ananus) but there is an element of doubt, perhaps a sense of defeat in the fact that the young family is not residing in the north. If Peter and Paul do attempt to 'convert' the young man to their respective ways of thinking, it must be that the kingdom at Shiloh was not a long-term success, even as a subversive sect.

That there is no claim to the Ark by Peter or Paul suggests there must have been good reason not to disclose its (inferred) whereabouts after Jesus' death (see Appendices, 5). Without these two men and their personal agenda, however, it may be that Jesus' mission would have faded into obscurity within a few years and all we might know of him today would be a handful of obscure references to the 'madman' who managed to disrupt Jerusalem more than any other rebel of his day. The rise of Christianity created a vast audience hungry for details about their figurehead but in the rush to make Jesus their 'king' perhaps something special was lost.

I like to think that Lazarus, the ever-faithful adopted son, the erudite and ingenious author of the FG-proper, continued to spread his own version of events, as was his calling. I can accept that many years away from home might have diluted the zeal he felt at the height of the excitement by his master's side. The resurrection of the Remnant ideal, however, had, for all intents and purposes, slipped into obscurity in Lazarus' absence, so Paul's protest either worked, or was no longer required. For a time, there was an attempt to 'let bygones be bygones' and work together but clearly the two men could not agree and we all know who prevailed.

Excursus: Nothing New Under the Sun?

OTHERS HAVE BEATEN ME TO at least some of my conclusions! Rather than being disappointed, I am thrilled because it means that I have been on the right track and not just 'out there' on my own.

The following brief analyses of just two examples demonstrate that there is potential evidence to support a long-term understanding of the Jesus story presented here, preserved subversively in the FG.

Leyden's Secret
Hinting at biblical interpretations that would have been considered heretical in their day, depictions of the Holy Family provided plenty of scope for the motivated (and brave) artist skilled at concealing, for want of a better analogy, a tree within a forest.

Madonna and Child with Mary Magdalene and Donor
by Lucas van Leyden (1521/22)

Interestingly, Leyden was an acquaintance of Albrecht Dürer and claimed to have been influenced by his work. Much of Dürer's painting is profoundly symbolic, inspiring generations of art historians to delve into the many layers of meaning depicted by the subtlest of details.

The donor in Leyden's painting kneels on the right-hand side facing the woman on the left, who is, we assume, holding the infant Jesus.

Traditionally, a woman holding a jar (in New Testament artistic depictions) has always implied Mary Magdalene. Other familiar attributes of this character include long hair and a red dress or cloak. She is often depicted looking pensive, as if showing remorse for her 'sinful ways'.

As a rule, Mary, the mother of Jesus, wears a garment that is blue and she has her head covered to signify her modest and/or married status. This mother figure is commonly referred to as the 'Queen of Heaven' and often she wears a little crown or is seated on a throne.

What do we see in this picture? Everything is mixed up. The woman on the right appears older and more refined. She is wearing a dress that is predominantly blue with just a little red; she has a headdress on, and is looking at the infant with a stern expression and her finger stretched out, as if telling him to behave, as a mother might. However, *she* is holding the alabaster jar!

The other woman, on the left, wears a blue dress that is overwhelmed by her red cloak. She has the long hair but it is lightly *veiled*—almost imperceptible at first glance but symbolising the status of wife—it is she who holds the child. Look at where her left hand is rested; it holds the *foot* of Jesus, just as Mary Magdalene had when she anointed it.

Look very closely and you will see a vine growing from the left side of the women in red (seated to the left). It seems to come from her body, through her dress. Might it suggest a blood lineage through this woman (remember the 'vine' symbolism of Jer 6:9, where the 'vine' is equated with the Remnant)? Ivy is commonly associated with death (can we assume Mary's closer link to Jesus' death/burial by virtue of her anointing him?) but often it implies *undying* devotion, like that of the Magdalene.

The chair under the woman on the left is golden and ornate and above it is the cupola or dome of a throne. If the woman on the right is supposed to be Mother Mary, perhaps letting the other female hold the infant for a moment, why is *she*, i.e., the *supposed* Queen of Heaven, *not* the one sitting on the throne?

The confusion is all but eradicated if we assume the left-hand female to be Mary Magdalene and the right not Mary the 'mother' of Jesus but Martha, his wife, (mother of Philip). *She* was in the house when Mary was anointing Jesus' feet so she has at least a contextual right to be holding the jar. Indeed, she would have more of a claim, being Jesus' wife; perhaps this is the artist's meaning. The red accents in the right-hand woman's attire link her to Mary, e.g., as "sisters." She wags the finger just as Martha does, metaphorically, in the FG (i.e., as fastidious, serious, responsible).

What makes this interpretation even more probable is the fact that the scenery behind the figures is split into two quite distinct landscapes. On the right, behind the supposed 'Mother Mary' the land is relatively barren, desert-like. Stark, rocky hills and a dry path dominate. On the left, however, everything is far more lush and green. Considering the analysis of the FG I propose here, this is exciting, as it may suggest exactly what I have claimed, i.e., that Mary Magdalene (the fertile woman) is the mother of the child Martha (the barren one) is too old to bear.

Those rocky hills in the background (to the right) hold a little secret of their own. If you look *very* carefully, the artist has implied a hollow in the first one, i.e., a cave, or a tomb. There is a roughly sketched D-shaped chamber with the suggestion of an internal floor, and a large, flat, round stone lies on the ground just in front, to the left. Amazingly, however, the artist has included an open window, or hole in the side wall, suggesting an alternative exit point (i.e., no tomb would have a window).

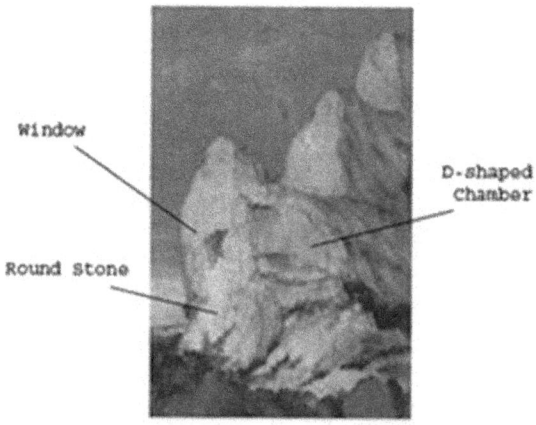

The three hills resemble three cloaked figures walking away from the tomb, perhaps hinting at the three men (Jesus, Nicodemus, and Lazarus) who left the empty tomb via an exit at the back of the Pool of Siloam and went out to the desert.

The donor is the only figure that is in any way ordinary, uncomplicated, and conventional. He holds the lilies associated with the Virgin Mother, the cross of Jesus, and hanging from that, the tools of a carpenter. As he was the one commissioning the painting, he probably dictated such items on his list of 'must haves'. Did he *know* that he was depicted as paying homage to Mary Magdalene and the *son* of Jesus?

As with any symbolic interpretation, however, you have to acknowledge that it is always subjective and, in the end, only the artist really knew what he/she meant to say in any given work (visual or written). The details in the painting I have mentioned are all there for anyone to see but *you* may find an alternative explanation for why Leyden chose to turn tradition on its head and flout the accepted biblical symbolism of his age. A couple more details to consider:

What of the broken fence/wall? Fences bind things, enclose things, limit access. Does this symbolise a truth set free? In standard Christian symbolism an enclosed garden, i.e., one that is fenced/walled-in, represents virginity and is normally associated with the mother of Jesus. Is the artist suggesting there was no Immaculate Conception?

This last detail intrigues me. The child is holding what *looks* to be a rolled-up sheepskin. In traditional Christian iconography, the infant Jesus is seen with a live lamb; I have never seen this rolled up fleece before. I wonder if this is a symbol of the rolling-up and receiving of the mantle of office we saw in the so-called 'resurrection' scenario in the FG. That is, the mantle *and* identity of Jesus as the 'lamb of God' is now handed to his son (via Lazarus, the regent). This image may suggest the 'lamb' is already dead when this scenario supposedly 'takes place', i.e., this is *not* Jesus as a baby, but the young John Mark, taking on the legacy of his father.

I have long wondered why artists depicted Mary Magdalene with a *baby* Jesus in the same image, as in all the gospels both she and Jesus are adults. I think many guessed their true connection but had to be very discrete about depicting it.

King Arthur and the FG Story

The Arthurian romances have a complex and ancient genealogy, blending lore and history from the earliest kings of England and Wales, to the influence of the Romans, to the machinations of the Medieval Church. This is not a discussion of which parts of the story came from which source (though the majority of the list below stems from Sir Thomas Mallory's *Le*

Morte d'Arthur) but how the overall legend of Arthur, the Round Table, the quest for the Holy Grail, and the escapades of the chief characters *appear* to have an uncanny correlation to the FG's rendition of the Jesus movement, as described in this book (give or take a few more traditional allusions).

I must admit, however, this was a late addition to my work, even though I have had an interest in Arthur all my life. Once I felt familiar with this new version of the gospel, I began to make these connections with the tales of Camelot. I offer the following parallels as a springboard for further and more comprehensive analyses. This is an abridged list!

Arthur – Jesus
Merlin – Lancelot – Tristan – Perceval – Lazarus
Guinevere – Mary Magdalene
Morgan le Fay – Martha / Mary Magdalene
Galahad – John Mark
Avalon – Shiloh
Excalibur – Ark
Gawain – Peter
Mordred – Peter[1]

Arthur Legend	**FG**
The birth of Arthur is steeped in supernatural lore and his father is concealed in mystery	Jesus' birth is mysterious and his genealogy is of great import in the FG. Jesus' own perception of his 'father' is a matter of contention
The 'miracle' of Arthur removing the sword from the stone occurs on several 'feast days', culminating at Pentecost	Jesus' mission is concentrated around the feast days; Lazarus, as the 'sick young boy', first enters the gospel at Pentecost
Merlin's identity begins as a wild-	John the baptiser is the wild-man

---

[1] This identification is a bit confusing, as the identity of Mordred as Arthur's son really does have a parallel in the FG interpretation but later, we see Mordred being Arthur's enemy, jealously breaking up the court, getting the queen and Lancelot in trouble, and seizing Guinevere, which makes him the image of Peter (as demonstrated in the list). The only way of justifying the two depictions is to assume Mallory saw Peter as the 'intended' son, which, in a way Peter could have been (if, perhaps, he had just got up and walked, when Jesus first told him to) and certainly wanted to be. With his character sealed in the parallel of Gawain, maybe we should see 'Mordred' as a play on 'more dread'!

man prophet and then changes	prophet; focus shifts to Jesus' protégée, Lazarus
He is later identified as Ambrosius, the youth picked for sacrifice by King Vortigern but who rises to a seat of honour because of his visions	The young Joseph (OT) was reprieved due to his skills at interpreting dreams and rises in status; Lazarus is 'sacrificed' in order to be raised to a seat of honour
Arthur first meets Merlin in the guise of a 14-year-old boy	Jesus first meets Lazarus as a 12–13-year-old boy
He becomes an advisor to the king; he is called a 'king maker'	Joseph (OT) serves this role but so too does Nicodemus, and probably Lazarus to an extent; in the Pool of Siloam Lazarus and/or Nicodemus anoint Jesus King
In Sir Thomas Mallory's *Le Morte d'Arthur*, Merlin leaves the storyline quite early (the fourth book)	The character of Lazarus is limited to one scenario in the FG but with the use of commission names we find him elsewhere in the gospel
Arthur's first major battle is against eleven kings, whom he never really defeats; there is allusion to a three-year period; Arthur is accompanied by two right-hand men, also kings; at the end of battle, Arthur falls for a young maiden of high descent and they conceive a son (Borre)	Jesus is symbolically isolated from the eleven other tribes; his mission lasts about three years; his two right-hand men are Lazarus and Nicodemus; early in his undertaking he meets a young woman of impeccable descent and they conceive a son
A man approaches Arthur on the road and begs for his son Tor to be taken by the king as a Knight of the Round Table	Lazarus is the 'sick' boy whose father meets Jesus on the road and begs of him to take his son into the new order, as a protégée
Sir Gawain also wished to be a knight. On Arthur's wedding day the king makes both men knights but he honours Tor first and gives	Peter is jealous of Jesus' favouritism toward Lazarus, bemoaning his lack of advancement in favour of this youngster; he attacks Lazarus with a

him pride of place at the Table; Gawain reveals his jealousy by threatening to attack Tor with a sword; he is discouraged by another but swears revenge	sword/dagger; this ploy fails but Peter persists in defying Jesus' plan
Arthur is injured and Merlin rescues him by making his opponent 'sleep' though he seems dead; he takes Arthur to a hermit who is knowledgeable in salves – after three days Arthur is deemed fit enough to 'ride and go'	Both Lazarus and Jesus are, at some point, rendered asleep but not dead; after the crucifixion Lazarus retrieves Jesus' body and Nicodemus tends his wounds with salves; on the 'third day' Jesus must be fit enough to ride to Shiloh
Arthur receives Excalibur from the Lady of the Lake; there is talk of water and a mysterious future 'gift' from the man to the woman	Jesus, in effect, receives verification of his commission when he meets Mary at Jacob's Well in Samaria. There is talk of water and the 'gift' Jesus claims she would receive if she asked
Merlin advises that Excalibur's scabbard is more valuable to Arthur than the sword itself; so long as the king keeps it by his side he cannot be vanquished; it offers protection but it also signifies concealment	There is a necessary degree of secrecy in Jesus' mission, especially with regard to the location of the Ark and the lineage of the child; so long as Jesus maintains the mystery, the heir remains safe; so long as the Ark remains hidden, the legitimacy of the new order cannot be challenged
Merlin had prophesied that the one destined to kill Arthur would be born on that May Day; all children born on that day are sentenced to death; Mordred, Arthur's son, born on May Day, escapes	Herod (Antipas, I suggest) is nervous about the rise of the 'star', the blessed child, and orders all children two and under slain; Jesus' son escapes
The first mention of the Sangreal (holy blood) is in the context of the interment of twelve kings, with Arthur's image (holding his sword) standing 'above' them;	Jesus is the figurehead over and above the twelve disciples, each a representative of a tribe; Jesus is the light, figuratively, but he claims that when he is gone, another, the

Merlin lights tapers for each king and professes that when he dies the lights will go out and the 'adventures of the Sangreal shall come among [them] and be achieved'	*parakletos* (Lazarus), and by extension the child, will come and teach them the mysteries of the new kingdom; the Sangreal, the bloodline of the new priestly dynasty, will be achieved
Two knights kill each other, not realising they are brothers until it is too late. Their battle is referred to as the Dolorous Stroke, which renders the Waste Lands barren and the quest for the restorative Grail necessary; the knights are buried together by Merlin, who makes one sword from their two and this sword is destined for Galahad, cast in stone and retrieved, in the manner Arthur received his first sword (not Excalibur), echoing the succession of leadership	At the start of Jesus' mission Israel is in a forlorn state; tribes who should be brothers are alienated and are killing each other (Samaritans vs. Jews); the quest for the new divine kingdom is necessary to restore Israel to its former glory; the pinnacle of the mission is to seat the child (John Mark) on the throne
The young Galahad is given the special seat at the Round Table called the Siege Perilous; only the purest and holiest of knights has the right to sit here; another knight (Brumart) attempts to seize the position and is killed by mysterious forces	John Mark is the focus of the new kingdom; as Jesus' successor he is the purest and holiest of the community; those priests who attempted to approach the original Ark without permission were killed by its power; Peter, in attempting to come too close to Jesus (equated to the Ark) after the resurrection, is reprimanded and punished
The Grail is hidden within the Palace Adventurous, which lies deep within the Castle of Carbonek	The Ark was housed in the Holy of Holies, deep within the temple complex, then hidden in a cave
Merlin's demise in *Le Morte d'Arthur* is strange; he falls in love with the Lady of the Lake, Nimue, teaches her everything he knows,	Lazarus' depicted 'demise' is just as strange; he may or may not be in love with Mary but he is bound to her; Mary is taught by Jesus and

and is rewarded by her casting a spell on him that seals him within a cave (or tower) under a rock	Lazarus; Lazarus' duty to Jesus/Mary leads to his capture; he is held within the cistern (tomb/cave) beneath a 'stone'
An attempt is made to rescue Merlin from under the rock but Merlin himself says he can only be released by the woman who put him there; this would only happen once Arthur returns (after his 'death') to sit on the throne	Lazarus is rescued from his imprisonment in the cistern and Mary is specifically called to be there; there is confusion in the FG epilogue as to Lazarus' position after the crucifixion but also the future 'return' of Jesus
A branch of a 'holy herb' became the Sign of the Sangreal	In the FG the herb (branch) associated with the crucifixion, and thus the blood of Jesus, is hyssop
Arthur is involved in many skirmishes but perhaps the most disturbing is the battle with the five kings in the "North" (Wales); Arthur and his knights are set upon by these men, several knights are killed but Arthur escapes; miraculously, Arthur returns to claim victory, slaying 30,000 of the enemy almost singlehanded	The level of violence in Jesus' mission is somewhat disconcerting; in the symbolism of the FG the number five represents the southern tribes, i.e., the "Jews"; the Samaritan tumult takes place in the north; the Samaritans claim they are set upon; in the ensuing massacre many are killed, including some of Jesus' followers but Jesus himself escapes; he soon declares victory over the 'world'
Morgan le Fey is one of the most puzzling of the Arthurian characters; she is Arthur's half-sister in Mallory's tale but niece in earlier texts; she is taught the sacred mysteries by Merlin (Mallory) or nuns (earlier sources); she is a shape-shifter, said to fly with dragons (or to become one); she is lover to Arthur's nephew and serves as Guinevere's lady-in-waiting;	Martha is the FG's most misunderstood character; she is Jesus' wife but acts, in effect, as Mary's lady-in-waiting; Martha is linked with dragons in French legend; could it be possible that Martha's jealousy of Mary leads her to be, if even unwittingly, party to Lazarus' and Mary's arrest for adultery?; her behaviour in John 11 suggests she is not on the same 'wavelength' as Jesus; on the other

Mallory suggests that a jealous Morgan instigates the rumours about the queen and Lancelot; she is known as Arthur's 'healer' (associated with ointments and potions) but she almost kills him with her treachery; in Geoffrey Monmouth's story she helps free a knight accused of adultery by turning the tables on the accusers; she ends up in Avalon

hand, it is Mary who is associated with the oils of 'healing'; she is the alleged lover of Jesus' adopted son; it is she who is involved in the 'adulteress' scene which results in the accusers being reproached; (neither woman can be seen as being treacherous, but it is interesting that the Cistercians marginalized Morgan le Fey in the romances, contrasting her against the piety of the Virgin Mary; is this a sign that they likened her to the Magdalene, whom they also marginalized, i.e., Morgan the evil sorceress and Mary the harlot?)

Arthur is sent twelve ambassadors from Rome; they honour him as King but demand taxes on pain of death and destruction; many lords and kings support Arthur in denying any tribute to Rome; they also provide many troops; Arthur leads the battle with nine knights by his side; Emperor Lucius is guarded by giants—Arthur goes up a mountain and is confronted by one; the giant wears a coat embroidered with the beards of those who seek his 'protection' but it also has sewn within it many precious stones; Arthur and his men slay the giant; meanwhile, a senator escapes the battle and informs Lucius of Arthur's prowess; a great battle ensues and 100,000 Romans are killed

The emphasis on accepting Roman sovereignty reminds us of Jesus' walking on the Sea of Tiberias; the Samaritan tumult involves Galileans who come armed and ready to force their anti-Roman agenda on Jesus' supporters; Roman troops appear and many are killed; there are nine 'northern' tribes (the tumult takes place in Samaria); we know Jesus escapes but so too does the spy, the one who runs back to Pilate to tell him where Jesus is hiding; the coat of precious stones echoes the breast piece of the high priest (recall that it is Caiaphas who fears repercussions from the Romans) perhaps the beards in the giant's coat relate to the humiliation of the Jews (de-bearded to weaken them) as they cow-tow to the Romans; the 'giant' could be Pilate

Lucius is killed, Arthur injured; Arthur is made Emperor by the

Jesus is mocked as a pretender to the throne but he does become a king; he

The Testament of Lazarus

will of the people; he returns to England	effectively slays the Roman prefect and eventually returns to his homeland (Samaria)
From the moment Merlin leaves the story Lancelot takes precedence; he passes tests of honour and loyalty, declares his devotion to Guinevere and becomes Arthur's right-hand-man	After John 11, Lazarus disappears from the gospel but the character lives on in Joseph; he affirms his loyalty to Mary (and Martha) and becomes Jesus' deputy high priest
Immediately after Lancelot's adventures are over, Tristram /Tristan takes the limelight; as a young man he enters the service of his uncle, King Mark. He is wounded but is healed by Iseult; Iseult is intended for the king but thanks to a magical potion Tristan and Iseult fall for each other; their relationship is kept secret but on one occasion Tristan's blood is found in her bed and she is tried for adultery	Lazarus enters the service of Jesus, King of Israel, as a young man; Mary is specifically called to be with him when he is released from his incarceration; she is openly chosen by Jesus to bear *his* child but Lazarus and Mary are united in a 'secret' ceremony; the focus on blood in a bed is fascinating, cf. the revealing of the blood-stained bridal sheet I discuss in the analysis of the adulteress in the FG
Tristan disguises himself as a beggar in order to be there for her when she swoons; he is wounded and believes only Iseult can heal him, so he sends for her; Tristan dies before Iseult does; various legends suggest Tristan and Iseult have a son	Remember that the 'blind man' was seen as a beggar; Lazarus is 'ill/dead' and Mary is sent for; the potential allusions to Mary in Josephus' accounts of the fall of Jerusalem and the reference to the death of Lazarus in the FG's epilogue suggest that Mary outlives Lazarus; Lazarus and Mary raise the child, John Mark
Lancelot descends from Joseph of Arimathea; His original (first) name is Galahad; he is said to have a son called Galahad (born in Britain); this is *Sir* Galahad; Lancelot witnesses the Holy Grail	This inclusion of Joseph of Arimathea is the strongest and perhaps the only *direct* link with the FG; The name of the father is handed down to the son; Lazarus reaches a certain degree of

but Galahad becomes the holiest of knights, occupying the Siege Perilous; he takes a sword from a stone, just as Arthur had; Galahad is one of three knights who eventually find the Grail	authority/status and is, figuratively, in touching distance of spiritual perfection; it is John Mark, the wonder-child, born in Ephraim, who attains the supreme position; the equivalent of 'three knights' could be John Mark, Lazarus, and Nicodemus; John Mark follows in his father's footsteps
Galahad is conceived out of wedlock and by enchantment; his mother is Elaine; Arthur has a niece by the same name who falls in love with Perceval	John Mark is conceived in unorthodox circumstances; his parents may or may not be married and the sheer symbolic/ritualistic nature of Jesus' plan makes the entire situation unconventional; Mary is Jesus' adopted daughter in a symbolic sense; she is united with Lazarus (Perceval); A confusion of Elaines there and a confusion of Marys here!
The introduction of Galahad begins with the account of him being fed from the Holy Grail; he consumes the Sangreal	Jesus specifies the symbolic significance of 'eating his flesh and drinking his blood'
Galahad is reared by twelve nuns in secret and when he is 'of age' a messenger is sent for Lancelot to come and dub the youth knight; when Lancelot gets there, he asks if this is the boy's own desire, and this is affirmed; Lancelot has the authority to create knights	John Mark is reared by the sacred inner circle of the twelve united tribes, symbolically represented by Mary and Lazarus; Lazarus' father goes out to ask Jesus to take the boy into his circle; as the blind man, his parents affirm he is 'of age' to speak for himself; Lazarus has the same authority as Jesus, in that he is his counterpart in the office of High Priest
On the day Galahad is made knight, i.e., Pentecost, gold letters appear on the Siege Perilous and	Lazarus' ascension to Jesus' new order occurs at Pentecost (as the sick boy); the high priest's breast piece

the sword in the stone (encrusted with precious stones) appears hovering above a river; Gawain attempts to pull the sword but fails; Galahad follows a ritual 'choosing', just as do Arthur and Lancelot	bears the stones that represent the tribes; Peter is constantly striving to attain a higher position and greater authority; John Mark will undergo the same ritual initiation as Jesus and Lazarus (cf. Secret Gospel of Mark)
Arthur tells the knights that they will see greater marvels than this; an 'ancient' dressed in white brings the young Galahad to the Table; he says 'peace be with you'; he mentions the boy's lineage through the line of Joseph of Arimathea, and declares that the glory of the court will be accomplished through Galahad	Jesus tells the people who witness the young Lazarus being offered to Jesus (as the sick boy) that they shall see 'greater things than this'; white clothing symbolises purity of office, e.g., a (high) priest; Jesus' symbolic phrase alluding to Shiloh is 'peace be with you'; Lazarus is the key to Jesus' glorification and John Mark is the key to the glorification of Shiloh and the new order
The old man transfers his mantle to the young Sir Galahad and says "Follow me"	Jesus transfers his mantle to (the regent) Lazarus in the Pool of Siloam; Jesus says "Follow me"
The tale is related of Joseph of Arimathea landing in Britain only to be thrown into prison by an adversary; supporters of Joseph break him out and the people are converted	Lazarus is held prisoner by the Sanhedrin; he is freed by Jesus and his allies; many are converted as a consequence
Galahad visits a tomb; he lifts the lid and is almost overwhelmed by the stench of the body inside; he is told that the body symbolises the "duress of the world" and the "wretchedness" of the world that made Jesus' mission necessary and inevitable	Lazarus is within the 'tomb', symbolising the dejected and sorrowful Israel, awaiting the intervention of Jesus; the stone is 'lifted off'; Martha presumes there will be a stench, equating to presumed guilt and thus 'wretchedness'
Galahad is likened to Jesus directly, in the context of his	Women are vital to Jesus' mission; his support for the falsely accused

championing the rescue of and respect for women, especially those who are mistreated	'adulteress' could be the inspiration for the 'Castle of Maidens' scene in *Le Morte d'Arthur*
Galahad ascends a mountain and hears a divine voice telling him what to do in his quest for the Grail	Jesus hears the voice of God; he ascends mountains to be closer to the divine
Gawain is told he must do penance for his sins but he refuses and seeks out further adventures with two of his comrades	Peter must 'bow down' and be humbled but he refuses; eventually he leaves the initial community with a band of followers, to start his own mission in Jesus' name
With the end of Lancelot, we see Perceval enter the story; when he sets out on his quest the world is in a sorry state; only with the completion of his tasks can the world be put to rights; He visits the cave of the Fisher King[2] twice—	When the gospel begins the world is in a bad way; only with the completion of Jesus' mission can it be set to rights; Lazarus visits the Pool of Siloam twice—once when he is 'blind' and once when he is enlightened; he rises in status and

---

[2] The character of the Fisher King is worthy of a chapter of its own but here I just want to mention this: The Fisher King (Pellam in Mallory) is one of the oldest of the Arthurian characters, with his roots in twelfth-century Celtic mythology but he echoes the FG's Peter to a tee! Generally known as the 'Wounded King', it was said that he was lame, due to a wound that made him 'impotent' (described as a 'thigh wound' but implying a wound to the genitals). This wound was described as the 'Dolorous Stroke' which was delivered with a sword and seen as divine vengeance for sin (Jesus warns the 'lame man' not to sin any more). Is this a parody of the sword wound inflicted on Malchus? That is, Peter attempted to thwart the young Lazarus' rise to high priest, but the Fisher King is made unable to procure sons—one of the most important duties of Israelite males, but especially of a priest! In some versions the Fisher King *is* a priest, so the inability to continue the line negates his purpose as priest. This impotency is later taken up to imply his metaphorical impotency, due to his being swayed too much by power and the 'benefits' of that power. He is said to sit in a boat, fishing, awaiting someone special to help/heal him! How much closer does it have to get?! That he is the guardian of the Grail bothered me at first, until the John Mark link and the subsequent tales of Peter being so magnanimous to Mary and her child.

In 1909, Wm. A. Nitze ("The Fisher King in the Grail Romances," *Proceedings of the Modern Language Association* 24 (3):365–418, doi:10.2307/456840) posited a theory that the Fisher King could be Peter but he left the idea dangling, claiming (earlier) that although certain characters in the Arthurian legends echoed those of

once in ignorance, once in full awareness; he undergoes spiritual enlightenment and rises in status, becoming the guardian of the Grail	becomes guardian to the child, John Mark
Excalibur is the symbol of the ultimate ruler, the purest of heart, 'the once and future king'; it is unconditionally Arthur's and when he is mortally wounded, he makes certain it is cast into the Lake from whence it came—its hiding place; no pretender to the throne would take possession of it	The Ark is the ultimate symbol of the new, pure priesthood, the holy Remnant chosen by God; it is Jesus' and the new order's claim to legitimacy now and forever; he keeps it well hidden throughout the mission but it seems it is kept concealed after his death; the world is not ready?
Lancelot is 'set up' by Mordred and some of the knights and is found in the queen's chamber; he is arrested for treason and Guinevere is accused of adultery	Mary and Lazarus are clearly 'set up' by false witnesses, one of whom is probably Peter, in his bid to get the young protégée ousted
There is a sort of sad malignancy in Mordred; he has always sought the king's favour and desires power and position; he usurps the throne and abducts Guinevere while Arthur is away fighting in Rome	Peter is a pathetic, manipulating man who has ambitions along a similar line; he promotes himself as Jesus' successor, copying the 'signs', even trying to take responsibility for Mary and the young John Mark; he takes the lad away while Lazarus is away with Paul
Camelot is the ideal kingdom, the seat of the Knights of the Round Table	Shiloh is the ideal kingdom, the seat of the new priestly order

---

the gospels, all attempts to unify the separate identities into one convincing theory had failed. He went on to list other 'coincidental' echoes of the FG that he didn't relate to Peter at all: 1) the Fisher King's "suffering reflected the barrenness of his land" (378; in the FG the 'lame man' illustrates the state of Israel), 2) he has a "companion or double from whom he cannot be disassociated" (378; Peter and Judas), and 3) he is symbolically linked to 'water' (395; as the lame man, Peter is introduced by the pool, and he jumps into the sea in the epilogue).

Avalon is the mysterious place to which Arthur recedes after he is mortally wounded.	After his crucifixion, having been mortally wounded, Jesus explains that he must go to the Father
It is said Arthur will return one day	Rumour spreads that Jesus will return one day
The numbers 3, 5, 7, 9, 12 are frequently used throughout the legends	3, 5, 7, 9, 12 are the FG's symbolic/special numbers

APPENDICES

1. Chief Characters

Jesus
    Samaritan
    Son of Joseph; represents tribe of Ephraim
    Samaritan Taheb
    Josephus' Samaritan rebel
    High Priest
    King
    Emulates Joshua (Exodus)

Lazarus (3rd stage)
    Official's son (1st stage)
    "The one"
    Blind man (2nd stage)
    parakletos (4th stage)
    Malchus (5th stage)
    Clopas (6th stage)
    Joseph (7th stage)
    Deputy High Priest
    Angel (at head)
    Represents tribe of Benjamin
    Represents the new Israel / "rod of Judah"
    Regent to child
    Gospel (co)author
    Emulates Eleazar (Exodus)

Mary (3rd stage)
    Samaritan woman (1st stage)
    Woman accused of adultery (2nd stage)
    Nazarite (4th stage)

Female gatekeeper (5th stage)
Wife of Clopas (6th stage)
Magdalene (7th stage)
Represents tribe of Joseph (Ephraim) / "rod of Ephraim"
Emulates ascending Bride of God (Ezekiel 16)
Wife of Lazarus, mother of Jesus' child

Simon Peter
Lame man
Cephas
Son of Jonah
The other Judas
Thomas (twin)
Represents tribe of Simeon / established priesthood
Rival to Lazarus
Emulates Jonah (Jonah)

Judas
Unnamed disciple (John 1, 18)
The Iscariot
Son of Simon
Barabbas
Represents tribe of Judah / Temple institution / Scapegoat killed
Infiltrator /spy
Emulates Simon, Captain of the Temple (2 Macc)

Nicodemus
Royal official
Servant of the high priest (John 18:26)
Angel (at feet)
Represents tribe of Benjamin
Father of Lazarus
Temple Priest / Pharisee
Parallels Ezra (2 Esdras)

Nathanael
Bridegroom at Cana
Son-in-law of Martha and Jesus
Represents tribe of Asher / The Remnant

Martha
Wife of Jesus and mother of Philip

Acts as a foil
Formally adopts Lazarus at crucifixion
(Tribe of Manasseh or Ephraim)

Philip
Son of Jesus and Martha
The 'other' disciple (John 20:3)
Represents those 'lost' / Hellenized
(Tribe of Ephraim)

Andrew
Messenger / Assistant
Represents tribe of Levi
Emulates Caleb (loosely)

John
Baptiser
Herald
Qumran community leader
(Tribe of Levi)

2. Proposed FG Historical Timeline

Citation	Scene	Inferred Special Day	Month (Jewish)	Month	Year CE
John 1:2	First meeting with John	Day of Atonement	Tishri	Sept/Oct	33
2	wedding in Cana	"third day"	Nisan	April	34
2:12	Capernaum	"remained"			34
2:13–21	temple tirade	Passover	Nisan	April	34
3:22	Second meeting with John	Day of Atonement	Tishri	Sept/Oct	34
4:35	Samaritan woman	Passover	Nisan	April	34
4:46–54	official's son	Pentecost	Siwan	June	34
5:1	lame man	New Year	Tishri	Sept/Oct	34
7:1	Jesus arrives at festival 'in secret'	Tabernacles	Tishri	Sept/Oct	34

7:38	"the one" called	Tabernacles	Tishri	October	34
9	Blind man	After Tabernacles	Tishri	October / November	34
10:22	Portico of Solomon	Dedication	Kisleu	December	34
10:40	Bethabara	"remained" / Mary gets pregnant			35
6:1–12	feeding 5000 (shifted timeframe)	Passover	Nisan	April	36
Josephus	*mountain top tumult*	*Passover*	*Nisan*	*April*	*36*
11:1	Lazarus held	Passover	Nisan	April	36
11:54	child born in Ephraim	"remained"	Nisan	April	36
12:12–18	entry into Jerusalem	Passover	Nisan	April	36
12f	Crucifixion and establishment of 'kingdom' at Shiloh	Passover / (symbolic Day of Atonement)	Nisan	April	36
External sources	*Pilate leaves*	*(Start of sailing season)*	*Shebat*	*February*	*37*
	Emperor Tiberius dies		*Adar*	*March*	*37*
Josephus	*Vitellius arrives*	*Passover*	*Nisan*	*April*	*37*
Matthew 2	Herod gets nervous / orders death of children		*Nissan – Av/Elul*	*April – July/Aug*	*37*

3. External References

A.

"Let us lie in wait for the righteous man, because he is inconvenient to us and opposes our actions; he reproaches us for sins against the law, and accuses us of sins against our training. He professes to have knowledge of God, and calls himself a child of the Lord. He became to us a reproof of our thoughts; the very sight of him is a burden to us, because his manner of life is unlike that of others, and his ways are strange. We are considered by him as something base, and he avoids our ways as unclean; he calls the last end of the righteous happy, and boasts that God is his father. Let us see if his words are true, and let us test what will happen at the end of his life; for if the righteous man is God's child, he will help him, and will deliver him from the hand of his adversaries. Let us test him with insult and torture, so that we may find out how gentle he is, and make trial of his forbearance. Let us condemn him to a shameful death, for, according to what he says, he will be protected."

Wisdom of Solomon 2:12–20

B.

"Yeshu is to be stoned because he practised sorcery and seduced Israel and led them away from God. Anyone who can provide evidence on his behalf should come forward to defend him." When, however, nothing favourable about him was found, he was hanged on the Sabbath of the Passover. Ulla commented: "Do you think that he belongs among those for whom redeeming evidence is sought?" Rather, he was a seducer [of whom] the All-merciful has said: "Show them no pity ... and do not shield them" (Deut 13:8). In Yeshu's case, however, an exception was made because he was close to those who held [political/religious] authority.'

Baraitha Sanhedrin 43a (3–4 Century CE)

This passage intrigues me because of the references to the legal debate surrounding Jesus' execution. Remember, Peter's role as witness (in John 18) comes immediately after Jesus' audacious request that the *zugot* find evidence in support of his innocence; if none was found, Peter's testimony must have been damning (it may also suggest a greater time laps between Jesus' arrest and crucifixion, for by law the procedure to procure evidence could last up to forty days).

Note, too, how the debate, above, is one concerning innocence/guilt, *not* whether or not the Sanhedrin has the right to pass the death sentence; clearly, they do. Can we take the final sentence to mean that even this lip-service to legality was carried out because of Jesus' *apparent* high status, e.g., his highly visible priestly/kingly status (that obviously confused many; recall how Peter first reacted, as the 'lame man', i.e., he saw Jesus as an authoritative figure, a superior), or perhaps a status he acquired by recruiting powerful Pharisees and priests? It has been shown that there is reason to question Jesus' several escapes from the temple officers, and his ability to break Lazarus out; who, in high places, were helping him?

C.

> Yeshu came and learned the letters of the Name, he wrote them upon the parchment which he placed in an open cut on his thigh and then drew the flesh over the parchment ... when he came to his house he reopened the cut ... and lifted out the writing ... and obtained the use of the letters. ...Then the sages selected a man named Judah Iskarioto and brought him to the Sanctuary where he learned the letters of the Ineffable Name as Yeshu had done ... Iskarioto attempted to force Yeshu down to earth but neither of the two could prevail against the other for both had use of the Ineffable Name. However, Iskarioto defiled Yeshu, so that they both lost their power and fell down to earth, and in their condition of defilement the letters of the Ineffable Name escaped from them.
>
> *Toledot Yeshu* (6–14 Century CE)

A controversial Jewish polemic against the legitimacy of Jesus' mission, this strange tract describes how Judas and Jesus compete for supremacy before Queen Helene, by performing magic tricks (e.g., flying, a magical feat explained in the Kabbalah). How clearly it echoes the Barabbas scene, though, with Judas (the representative of the institution) and Jesus the rebel who uses the divine 'Name' to verify and validate his actions; both are 'brought down to earth' simultaneously, i.e., Barabbas (Judas Iscariot) is crucified when Jesus is.

The *Toledot Yeshu*, which I discovered toward the end of my research, proves to be highly significant, in fact, for it:

> ★ states Jesus was *conceived* in adultery on the **Day of Atonement;** the FG mission begins on this day and ends on it, symbolically.

> ★ claims that the followers of Yeshu celebrated the **Feast of the Circumcision** *instead* of the Day of Atonement; I suggested the final meal was possibly a *bris*!

> ★ claims that Mary and Joseph were **adulterous**; in the FG, this is Mary Magdalene and Lazarus/Joseph.

★ asserts that Jesus **changed the names** of his disciples and confirms the use of new names to **hide identity** e.g., "we returned here and we switched our names that no one would recognise us" (Midrash *Toldoth Yeshu* of Rabbi Yohanan ben Zakai); i.e., commission names.

★ links Peter's name-change to "a Torah law regarding redeeming **the firstborn**" (Zakai); Peter's jealousy in the FG is rooted in his desire to claim the inheritance of the firstborn. This is one of the most profound links, as the concept is peculiar to the FG and is subtle enough to be overlooked, yet here it is considered vital.

★ reveals the **ambition of Peter**, who makes the sages promise that he will get a significant place in the new world order, in exchange for helping to trap Jesus; the FG demonstrates how Peter's disloyalty is considered on a par with, if not worse than Judas', for Judas was 'hired' to betray Jesus, Peter chose to.

★ emphasizes Jesus' **northern interests** (in some versions he claims to be the "Messiah Ephraim"), placing his campaign solidly in Upper Galilee (where he finds refuge against allegations that his genealogy is 'unsuitable'), just as the Messiah ben Joseph tradition does.

★ has **five** disciples (suggesting the source is the FG: Andrew, Peter, Philip, 'the unnamed', and Nathanael).

★ mentions purposefully assigned infiltrators, **spies sent** out as disciples to follow Jesus and report back to the Sanhedrin so that they can devise a **trap that will bring Jesus into Jerusalem** and into their grasp; in one version of the *Toledot* Judas is specifically sent to infiltrate the disciples.

★ places Jesus' capture in a **synagogue in Tiberias**, a city mentioned only in the FG, and when asked his name, he gives at least four variations, echoing the "**I AM**" ambiguity.

★ suggests the **sages appoint Simeon Kepha** to convince the new sect to separate from Judaism altogether and thus end the internal conflict.

★ suggests "Simeon, having gained the secret of the Ineffable Name, healed a leper and a **lame man** by means of it and thus found acceptance as a true disciple" (Zakai); this is a prime example of Peter usurping the 'signs' of Jesus (note the fact that he was accepted as a 'true disciple' only after this, suggesting he was previously considered an outsider).

The *Toledot Yeshu* was never part of my original MA Thesis research. No one ever mentioned it and I can honestly say I never investigated it. When I did finally read it, I was stunned to see so many parallels. The so-called parody, the sarcastic and denigrating alternative history of Jesus, may well have deep within its core, ironically, several elements of truth! That my own, independent analysis of the gospel should come up with so many similar ideas suggests that there *is* a common denominator, e.g., the FG itself.

Then I found this:

D.

[Jesus] was buried next to some aqueduct, and some Jew was entrusted with his custody. At that very night, however, the aqueduct was suddenly flooded. By Pilate's order, (Jesus) was sought for twelve months but never found.

Agobard, *De Judaicis superstitionibus*
(*On the Superstitions of Jews*, 826 CE),[1]

Agobard, Bishop of Lyon (c.769–840 CE), was the first to make reference to the *Toledot* as a Jewish text. Notice what he is suggesting here, though! Jesus was "*buried next to some aqueduct*"; the body disappears suddenly (due to a *flood*). This gives us the Pool of Siloam/conduit link. That is, there must have been a thread of legend suggesting Jesus was buried in a watery, cave-like place, rather than a 'tomb'. I have never heard of any other source that mentions anything remotely like this.

E.
Gospel of Thomas and Gospel of Mary
Again, these two Gnostic documents were read *very* late in this analytical journey, as I really wished to see if the FG could be understood fully, in isolation and in historical context.

---

[1] PL 104, pp. 87–8. As cited in Michael Meerson and Peter Schäfer, eds. and trans. *Toledot Yeshu: The Life Story of Jesus Two Volumes and Database: Volume I Introduction and Translation* (JCB Mohr: 2014), 3 (note 4).

They do, however, offer support for the depiction of Peter presented in this book, i.e., the image of Peter as the antagonist of the FG narrative.

> Simon Peter said to him, "Let Mary leave us, for women are not worthy of life." Jesus said, "I myself shall lead her in order to make her male, so that she too may become a living spirit resembling you males. For every woman who will make herself male will enter the kingdom of heaven."[2]
>
> Gospel of Thomas, 114

What this excerpt demonstrates is an animosity toward Mary that reveals Peter's true colours; to the Gnostics, Peter represented the epitome of orthodoxy—just as he does in the FG. This animosity, however, escalates in the Gospel of Mary, where Peter comes across as jealous, snide, and bitter, denouncing Mary's version of Jesus' "truth." It seems she, like Lazarus (the "beloved disciple") was privy to secrets (and of course, the FG shows this to be the case); Peter is incensed, just as in the FG, i.e., that 'others' have seemingly received more than their share, perhaps—or have 'got there before him'. He is openly rebuked as being "hot-tempered" and for treating women as if they were the enemy, against Jesus' wishes. Peter's apparent claim to have resided with Mary and the young John Mark earlier, when Lazarus (Barnabas) was away with Paul, might just be further support for this domineering, self-imposing man (Mary probably never stood a chance of declining his offer to 'move in' and then take her son away with him!).

It would seem the early Gnostic Christians might have formed their opinion of Peter from his less than gracious representation in the FG.

4. Mary and Lazarus Parallels

Mary Magdalene	**Lazarus**
Associated with water; Jacob's Well	Associated with water; Pool of Siloam

---

[2] Scholars debate the meaning of this enforced gender-transition by Jesus but within the assumed Egyptian context of early Gnosticism, it may simply be a reference to the Osirian belief concerning the deceased soul requiring to adhere to the prescribed prayers, spells, rites, etc., in order to be reborn. All the Osirian rites were set down in masculine terminology so, especially towards the end of the first century CE, many Egyptian females appropriated/absorbed masculine traits for their funerary art, texts, etc., in order to comply and thereby ensure *their* 'life' in the hereafter.

Declares belief in Jesus and brings Samaritans to him	Declares belief in Jesus and is the cause of many of the Jews converting
Associated with third day motif	Associated with third day motif
Living in Bethany house	Living in Bethany house
Accused of adultery and brought to trial	Arrested and brought before Sanhedrin / implicated in adultery case
Anointed / Physical contact with Jesus via a (liquid) substance (*oil*)	Anointed / Physical contact with Jesus via a (liquid) substance (*spittle/clay*)
Mourns Lazarus	Mourned by Mary by virtue of her being indoors
Rises in status throughout gospel; seven symbolic stages	Rises in status throughout the gospel; seven commissions
Commission name (Magdalene) means "tower" indicating both a married woman and one that is raised up to a high place	Commission name (Lazarus) means "united in marriage" and (Arimathea) suggests an already 'high place' with its root in *ramah*
Only disciple to touch Jesus (feet)	Only disciple to be touched by Jesus (eyes)
"Stone removed from the well" scene anticipates the 'raising of Lazarus' scene	The stone is removed from his 'tomb' and his emancipation heralds the rise of the new temple/kingdom
Gatekeeper of the new kingdom by virtue of motherhood	Regent/protector until the son is of age but also 'gatekeeper' i.e., assists Jesus (the 'gate') in conversions from the priesthood.
Rod of Ephraim	Rod of Judah
Represents Bride of God / Israel	Represents the new, revived Israel

5. How Many Cubits?

One of the more difficult issues to deal with in the FG is the meaning of specific distances but I think there is a plausible interpretation that can include each of the three instances:

John 6:19 25-30 stadia 10-12000 cubits
John 11:18 15 stadia 6000 cubits
John 21:8 200 cubits 200 cubits

The common denominator is cubits, but the last 200 are different because they are in the gospel's epilogue, and are therefore employed to emphasize an issue germane to this section's unique message.

We also need to know the following information:

★ 4000 cubits = (approx.) 1 (Jewish) mile

★ According to Josh 3:4, the Ark of the Covenant and the congregation were to remain at a respectful distance of "about two thousand cubits." (This developed into the 'Sabbath day's journey'.)

In John 6, Jesus has just celebrated the Passover out on the Golan Heights. The disciples row on the Sea of Galilee for a distance of 'about' 25–30 stadia, or 10–12000 cubits (about two and a half to three miles). If we take the average of this, i.e., 11000 cubits, and divide it by 2000 (the distance determined for the Ark and the congregation), we get 5.5. Thus, Jesus, I suggest, is (roughly) 5.5 times this distance away from the Ark (wherever he thinks, or knows, it is) at the moment he leaves the shores of Bashan. This would be a total of 17–18 miles. How is this significant? The northern Ramah is roughly 17–18 miles away, as the crow flies, from the eastern shore of the Sea of Galilee.

Now, in John 11, we learn that Bethany is 15 stadia away from Jerusalem, though no direction is specified but, as suggested earlier, it must lie to the south or east. Tradition *has* placed it neatly southeast, and there is no real reason to argue a few degrees either way; 15 stadia equal 6000 cubits, or about 1.5 miles, i.e., three times the Ark-congregation distance. At this point, then, just as Jesus is about to enter Jerusalem (where Martha meets him), he would have to travel 3 times the distance mentioned to get to the Ark, i.e., about 4.5 miles. This is the approximate distance to the Benjaminite Ramah, north of Jerusalem!

What I think may be inferred here, is that the Ark is (according to Jesus) in Ramah prior to its planned transportation to Shiloh, where it belongs. Whether the Ark was first in the northern town, then transported to the southern one, is anyone's guess, and my calculations may be purely coincidental but the fact that both measurements can even *allude* to a 'Ramah' is enough for me to think there may be something to this idea.

One might also see a link to the reference in 2 Macc 2:4–7, i.e., to the Ark being hidden in a "cave-dwelling" after Jeremiah had "assessed" the territory from the vantage point of Moab. Jesus had spent a year there, too. Remember that Ramah also means "high, exalted" and that there had been a strange and inaccurate rumour about the Samaritan rebel leading people to the Ark that was supposedly under *Mount Gerizim*. Rumours are usually based on *something*, if prone to exaggeration and error. Can it be that Jesus figured out where the Ark was hidden by following in the footsteps of Jeremiah? When he stood before the Samaritan throng and pointed across to the holy site of Shiloh, was he also indicating that the Ark lay in a cave up at Ramah?

In Peter's final scene in the FG's epilogue, however, the emphasis has changed. I tried to find a Ramah (geographical) connection but, although I couldn't, I think there is something analogous going on here. If we maintain the idea of the respectful distance from the Ark (2000 cubits), 200 cubits represents one-tenth, echoing the ten portions of anointing oil we saw earlier (which discounted Judas and Peter); each of the disciples would have to travel that distance to get to Jesus and thus all *he* represents, e.g., the Ark, the true temple, the kingdom of God. The disciples in the boat are the ones who are said to be at this distance, not Peter, who is eagerly swimming ashore. He is still not one of the "ten."

Peter has jumped into the sea, wearing the shift of a novice; in his over-enthusiasm to be recognised and receive Jesus' approval, he is not respecting the prescribed distance rules. He has not learned much. The epilogue's use of distance is thus another attempt to castigate and distance Peter from Lazarus and the inner circle loyal to Jesus' ideals.

6. Siloam Tower

One of the potentially enlightening tangents other investigators may wish to pursue is the mention of the fall of the Siloam Tower in Luke 13:1–2. Not only is this the only other mention of Siloam in the NT, it is brimming with symbolism in its own right.

Siloam = Pool where Jesus escapes certain death; representation of the divine Remnant; analogous to Shiloh

Tower = A fortified place usually associated with a gate; the symbol for Mary Magdalene; the symbol for a married woman

Luke says that when the Tower fell, eighteen people died. The number 18 is sacred in Judaism. It signifies CHAI or Life (being 10 or *yud* + 8 or *ches*). It is the representation of Eve.

Josephus does mention (*Wars*. 5.4) a tall wall that stood above the Pool and he mentions several towers within the walls of Jerusalem but nowhere does he mention the Siloam Tower nor its fatal collapse. Surely such a tragedy, such a fracture to the defences of the city, would be recorded? Could it be that Luke, the one evangelist who seems to have an affinity for the FG's tale, however subversive or confused, is here referring to the small Johannine community that was thwarted and vilified by Paul? Surely those involved were not 'evil' as Paul had claimed, Luke seems to suggest.

Might the number 18 also be a symbolic reference to the core community? Thus: Jesus (Life); Mary (Tower/Eve); Lazarus; Martha; Philip; John Mark, and the circle of twelve disciples.

7. Jesus/Lazarus Parallels to the Story of Joseph

Joseph	Jesus/Lazarus
Sent by God (Gen 45:5, 7)	John 3:34, 4:34, etc.
As the Son of God ("Joseph and Aseneth," early second century text of Egyptian-Judaism)	John 1:34, 3:35, 10:36, etc.
"Israel loved Joseph" (Gen 37:3)	Jesus loves Lazarus (John 11:3, 5)
Receives *kethoneth* as sign of status (Gen 37:3)	Wears a *chiton* which is described in terms relating to the priestly *kethoneth* (John 19:23), but is also given outer robe as sign of royalty (19:2)
Conspired against and thrown into pit (Gen 37:4–11, 18f)	Lazarus held in cistern/prison; conspiracy to kill him (John 11)
Stripped of garment (Gen 37:23) No hand laid on him (Gen 37:22)	John 19:23 John 7:44, 8:59, 10:39
Honorary member of royal household (Gen 39:2)	Lazarus is honorary 'son' of the King of Israel (John 1:49)

The Testament of Lazarus

Claims knowledge of God's will (Gen 40:8, 41:45)	John 7:44, 8:59, 10:39
Steward over house (Gen 41:40)	John 2:19–22, 10:2, etc.
"arrayed in garments of fine linen" (Gen 41:42) (Josephus, in *Ant.* 2.5.7, says "to wear Purple")	"they dressed him in a purple robe" (John 19:5)
"Do what he says" (Gen 41:40)	"Do whatever he tells you." (John 2:5)
Master not greater than servant (Gen 39:9)	John 13:16, 15:20
Brother returns to pit to find Joseph gone (Gen 37:29)	Disciples return to tomb to find Jesus gone (John 20:1f)
Good shepherd vs. bad (Gen 37:2)	John 10:11–14
God as 'helper' (Gen 49:25)	Lazarus means "God has helped"
One 'set apart' (Gen 49:26)	Nazarite, 'anointed,' etc. (also John 15:18–19)
Attributes power to God (Gen 41:16)	Jesus constantly refers to his authority/power from God the Father
Advised of his father's illness and goes to him / the covenant is reiterated / Joseph's sons are made 'heirs' (Gen 48:1ff)	Jesus receives a message that his 'son' is ill and goes to him / initiation rite of heir to priesthood follows, emphasizing the new covenant / Lazarus and John Mark becomes heirs
Joseph marries daughter of priest	Lazarus is betrothed to Mary, in Samaritan tradition daughter of a priest
Joseph wrongly accused of adultery	Jesus/Lazarus/Mary wrongly accused of adultery

On	Jesus sits on 'throne' that symbolically rejects On as part of the heritage (e.g., the solar worship of the early Israelites who set themselves up in Jerusalem), and sets up the new Israel as a purely Israelite nation faithful to the god of Abraham
Asks Pharaoh for body of 'father' (Gen 50:17–19)	Joseph of Arimathea asks Pilate for body of father (John 19:38)
Joseph's bones buried in Shechem	Jesus' body finally buried at Ramah?

8. Joseph the Priest

An interesting footnote to the Egyptian heritage of Israel, is the fact that whereas the Book of Genesis is full of praise for Joseph, in its list of the original twelve tribes (Gen 49:1–27), later texts, such as Numbers (1:5–15) and Deuteronomy (33:1–29), have omitted this name altogether. The dominant tribes of Israel leave only a fleeting glimpse of Joseph and his religion.

We must remember that Joseph married the daughter of a priest of On, the central locus of Atum-Ra worship at the time. It is highly likely that Joseph was a priest himself, first of the El Elyon religion, then, through his marriage and later position in Egypt, of the Atum-Ra cult. Such a role would clarify his significance and authority, and is supported by a few details not stricken from the record:

(Gen. 37:3)
Joseph receives the *kethoneth* from his father, Jacob, which sets him apart from and above his siblings. *Kethoneth* is the term given to the linen tunic of the priestly vestments.

(Gen. 40:8)
Joseph claims to be able to discern the will of God: "Do not interpretations belong to God? Please tell them to me" he requests. This claim is made even before Joseph's rise to power, suggesting he has a certain authority in his own right. According to Josephus (*Wars*. 3.8.3), the interpretation of dreams is a priestly skill/function.

(Gen. 41:45)
Joseph marries the daughter of a priest. Levitical law (Lev 21:13–15) prescribes that priests and the daughters of priests should marry in order to preserve the sacred blood of the priesthood.

(Gen. 44:15)
Joseph practices divination: "Do you not know that one such as I can practice divination?" (See also 44:5). Through the 'Urim and Thummim' the high priest (Egyptian/Israelite) divines the will of God.

(Gen. 47:20f)
The persistent reference to the priests being allowed to retain their land despite the general purchase of arable land for the Pharaoh's reserves is followed, immediately, by the statement: "Thus Israel settled in the land of Egypt ... and they gained possession in it, and were fruitful and multiplied exceedingly" (v.27). The adverbial 'thus' must refer back to this advantageous retaining of land and must, therefore imply that Joseph was exempt from the limitations which forced many into poverty, i.e., he was a priest. He is granted Goshen as his own territory (cf. 47:11–12). Is this reflection of Joseph the basis for the tradition that Jesus acquired his 'magical' (and thus priestly) abilities in Egypt?

9. Basic Parallels to the Exodus Story

Exodus	FG
Moses goes up a mountain to commune with God	Jesus goes up a mountain (Josephus; to reveal he knows where the Ark is)
When he descends, he sees the people have not understood and he destroys the stones	There is misunderstanding and violence
A covenant takes place on the third day	A covenant takes place on the third day
Joshua renewed the covenant at Shechem	Jesus plans to renew the covenant at Shiloh
The initial priesthood is comprised of twelve priests, one	Jesus initiates twelve disciples, one from each tribe, and insists the new

representing each tribe, and one high priest; it is hereditary	priesthood be dynastic
Eleazar leads the majority of Israel south to Jerusalem; he is one of two high priests, the other being Joshua	Lazarus is of a southern tribe and becomes the deputy high priest to Jesus.

10. Carpenter

Nothing is mentioned in the FG of Jesus being a carpenter but this is just another example of how our new understanding of the FG can shed light on the Synoptics, for in Matt 13:55, Jesus is the "son of the carpenter" and in Mark 6:3, he is "the carpenter, son of Mary."

All the four major figures in the anticipated Jewish *eschaton* are referred to as 'carpenters' *including* the Messiah ben Joseph:

> And the Lord showed me four carpenters (Zech 1:20) ... they were Messiah the son of David, Messiah the son of Joseph, Elijah, and the Priest of Righteousness.
> Succah 29.2

The passage in Zechariah suggests that the four 'carpenters' ('blacksmiths' in the NRSV) are sent by God to challenge all who have scattered his people.

Suggested Reading

Secondary sources were not used for this analysis, beyond those presented in my MA thesis in the 1990s. Below are a few works that may assist you develop your own interpretation of the FG and the historical Jesus but my advice would be to start from scratch. You can utilise Biblehub's Interlinear Greek/Hebrew Bibles online; these will provide a solid cross-section of translations and commentaries.

Anderson, P. Ed. *John, Jesus and History* Atlanta: SBL, 2016.

Bauckham, Richard. *Gospel Women: Studies of the Named Women in the Gospels*. Grand Rapids: Eerdmans, 2002.

———. *Jesus and the Eyewitnesses: The Gospels as Eyewitness Testimony*. Grand Rapids: Eerdmans, 2017.

Blomberg, Craig L. *The Historical Reliability of John's Gospel: Issues & Commentary*. Downers Grove: IVP Academic, 2014.

Brodie, Thomas, L. *The Quest for the Origin of John's Gospel: A Source-Oriented Approach*. Oxford: Oxford UP, 1993.

Culpepper, R. Ed. *John and Judaism*. Atlanta: SBL, 2017.

Dawes, Gregory W., Ed. *The Historical Jesus Quest: Landmarks in the Search for the Jesus of History*. Louisville: Westminster John Knox Press, 2000.

Fowler, William G. and Michael Strickland. *The Influence of Ezekiel in the Fourth Gospel*. Intertextuality and Interpretation, Volume 167. Leiden: Brill, 2018.

Herrstrom, David Sten. *The Book of Unknowing: A Poet's Response to the Gospel of John*. Eugene: Wipf & Stock, 2012.

Horsley, Richard, A. *Bandits, Prophets, and Messiahs: Popular Movements in the Time of Jesus*. Harrisburg: Trinity, 1999.

Knoppers, Gary N. *Jews and Samaritans: The Origins and History of Their Early Relations*. Oxford: Oxford UP USA, 2013.

Köstenberger, Andreas J. *Encountering John: The Gospel in Historical, Literary, and Theological Perspective.* Encountering Biblical Studies. Grand Rapids: Baker Book House, 2013.

Martin, Raymond. *The Elusive Messiah: A Philosophical Overview of the Quest for the Historical Jesus.* Boulder: Westview, 1999.

Mitchell, David. C. *The Origins of Messiah ben Joseph.* Newton Mearns, Scotland: Campbell Publication. 2016.

Numada, J. *John and Anti-Judaism.* Atlanta: SBL. 2021.

Orton, David E. *The Composition of John's Gospel: Selected Studies from Novum Testamentum* (Brill's Readers in Biblical Studies). Leiden: Brill, 1998.

Penwell, Stewart. *Jesus the Samaritan: Ethnic Labeling in the Gospel of John*, Biblical Interpretation Series, Vol 170. Leiden: Brill, 2019.

Perrin, Nicholas. *Jesus the Priest*, London: SPCK, 2018.

Reed, Jonathan L. *Archaeology and the Galilean Jesus: A Re-Examination of the Evidence.* Harrisburg: Trinity, 2000.

Tabor, James D. *The Jesus Dynasty*, London: HarperElement, 2006.

Index

2 Esdras, 31, 59, 60, 61, 67, 68, 90, 115, 116, 117, 118, 142, 147, 155, 163, 164, 165, 167, 170, 180, 232, 270, 289

2 Esdras (comparison list), 61

Aaron, 2, 3, 22, 27, 116, 159, 176, 181, 243, 256, 281

abandon, 211, 250

Abarim, 19, 121

Abraham, 3, 16, 29, 32, 37, 38, 72, 79, 81, 111, 139, 141, 148, 152, 158, 164, 166, 175, 210, 291, 309, 353

Abraham (children), 63, 139, 141, 166, 210

Abraham rejoiced, 141

Adam, 291

adoption, 247

adulteress, 10, 44, 55, 85, 98, 129, 131, 132, 133, 135, 140, 162, 164, 183, 244, 245, 300, 331

adultery, 43, 53, 55, 98, 128, 129, 130, 160, 162, 163, 164, 165, 167, 171, 176, 237, 298, 300, 326, 330, 344, 347, 348, 351, 352

Aenon near Salim, 72, 296

agapao, 56, 159, 201, 267, 281, 282, 285, 286, 308, 309

Ahijah, 49

Ain, 26, 280

alabaster jar, 253, 323

Alexander, 234, 305, 306, 307

aloes, 253, 257

ambiguity, 27, 56, 60, 85, 108, 109, 135, 158, 184, 217, 225, 227, 228, 241, 245, 289, 300, 313, 345

amen, 99

Amram, 129

Ananias, 317

Andrew, 22, 23, 24, 27, 81, 96, 104, 186, 189, 199, 210, 280, 345

angels, 269, 270

Anna (prophetess), 8, 37, 39

Annas, 95, 121, 215, 218, 219, 225, 226, 300, 306, 307

anointed, 182, 211

anointing, 33, 81, 122, 146, 147, 161, 183, 184, 185, 211, 244, 253, 255, 256, 257, 264, 274, 323, 347, 352

Antioch, 316, 317, 318

aqueduct, 346

Arimathea, 247, 270, 301, 308, 348, 353

Ark, 9, 10, 11, 12, 45, 81, 82, 111, 113, 114, 115, 116, 155, 177, 190, 204, 206, 239, 256, 276, 321, 326, 328, 329, 336, 349, 350, 354

armed, 97, 112, 113, 114, 119, 196, 210, 211, 217, 221, 232, 237, 295, 331

arrest, 21, 198, 204, 213, 224, 302, 306

Arzareth, 30, 31, 32, 61, 63, 104, 149, 154, 256, 282, 310

Asher, 8, 32, 37, 38, 39, 87, 320

asleep, 165

author (my house), 163

Babylon, 310, 314

bandit, 113, 153, 211, 228, 311

baptism (Jesus'), 20

Barabbas, 42, 118, 228, 229, 230, 231, 232, 233, 234, 243, 251, 259, 294, 308, 344

Bar-Jesus, 317

Barnabas, 313, 316, 317, 318, 319

barren, 324, 326

Barsabbas, 308

Bashan, 100, 101, 103, 111, 117, 120, 122, 168, 282, 284, 349

begging, 145, 148, 163, 326

believe, 61, 88, 122, 126, 145, 152, 166, 173, 174, 190, 191, 195, 199, 268, 269, 278, 279, 283, 295

belly, 251

beloved, 22, 43, 70, 158, 159, 193, 194, 211, 244, 247, 249, 252, 285, 290, 305, 309, 320, 321, 347

belt, 287

Benjamin, 3, 69, 91, 136, 281, 319, 320

Bethabara, 18, 19, 26, 39, 155, 162, 164, 168, 296

Bethany, 18, 19, 20, 26, 39, 53, 56, 160, 161, 163, 164, 165, 167, 181, 186, 206, 253, 256, 302, 318, 320, 347, 348, 349

Bethel, 28, 184

Bethesda, 99

Bethezub, 302

Bethlehem, 32

Bethsaida, 23, 24, 26, 96, 280

Beth-zatha, 98, 99, 159, 262

betrothal, 43, 130, 161, 162, 169, 184, 299, 301, 352

blasphemy, 46, 97, 217, 224, 305

blemish, 92, 211

blind man, 17, 20, 37, 54, 64, 89, 131, 134, 144, 145, 146, 147, 148, 149, 151, 157, 158, 160, 162, 165, 166, 171, 174, 176, 182, 185, 196, 201, 202, 203, 225, 261, 274, 285, 288, 300, 318, 332, 333

Index

blindness, 17, 79, 92, 93, 144, 145, 146, 147, 148, 150, 152, 158, 191, 309, 317, 318

blood, 24, 114, 118, 120, 121, 132, 219, 243, 249, 251, 310, 323, 326, 330, 332

blood money, 235, 306

boat, 107, 282

boat), 111

body, 252, 256, 265, 269, 353

bones (Joseph's), 12, 76, 115, 239, 320, 351

bones (valley of), 165

bound, 116, 175, 209, 254, 287

bow down, 25, 262, 263, 264, 279, 287, 335

bread, 101, 102, 103, 120, 194, 283

breastpiece, 241

bridal sheet, 132

bride, 245

Bride of God, 18, 42, 43, 44, 45, 75, 76, 83, 91, 128, 133, 160, 181, 182, 183, 185, 244, 293, 300, 302, 347

bridegroom, 39, 74, 75, 121, 182, 267, 277, 302

bris, 182, 185, 344

brothers, 24, 27, 173

burial, 78, 171, 175, 184, 253, 254, 257, 259, 260, 271, 277, 320, 323

Caiaphas, 48, 95, 153, 178, 179, 198, 209, 215, 217, 218, 219, 225, 228, 231, 233, 234, 235, 266, 294, 318, 319, 331

Cain, 307

Caleb, 3, 24

Caligula, 312

Cana, 37, 38, 39, 87, 160, 280

Capernaum, 42, 46, 57, 87, 89, 90, 107, 111, 120, 127, 149, 151, 280, 282, 320

captive, 170, 171, 172, 175, 230, 246, 319

carpenter, 355

Cephas, 25, 26, 122, 172, 200, 215, 262, 264, 278, 279, 307, 308

Chamber of Approved Offerings, 216

Chamber of Hewn Stone, 171, 218, 219

Chamber of the Captivity, 172

Chamber of the Official, 218

Chamber of the Vestments, 219

Chamber of the Well, 172, 218

Chamber of Wood, 172, 218, 219

chief priests, 94, 126, 186, 198, 226, 227, 234, 235, 306

child, 130, 135, 136, 162, 182, 184, 185, 187, 189, 202, 213, 218, 244, 246, 247, 273, 274, 283, 293, 298, 299, 300, 301, 302, 313, 314, 323, 324, 325, 328, 329, 332, 333, 335, 336

children of God, 155, 193, 236, 290

choice, 27, 42, 59, 61, 84, 90, 146, 148, 151, 218, 219, 230, 233, 238, 243, 251

Chronicle of Abu'l Fath, 129, 133

circumcision, 47, 124, 182, 344

cistern, 172, 257, 276, 330, 351

City of David, 187, 205, 259, 261

clay, 131, 134, 146, 147, 150, 165, 174, 348

Clopas, 244, 245, 247, 252, 280

Comforter, 5, 316

commission name, 7, 18, 29, 58, 89, 91, 95, 96, 128, 152, 157, 163, 173, 179, 183, 193, 197, 201, 203, 210, 246, 247, 252, 261, 262, 264, 279, 308, 316, 327, 345

conceive, 162

conceive (not), 162

conduit, 259, 265, 273, 274, 346

consummation, 161

conversion, 12, 64, 89, 90, 93, 116, 126, 144, 148, 149, 150, 153, 157, 158, 186, 245, 288, 318, 326, 348

coppersmith, 306, 307

Court of Israel, 179, 218

Court of the Priests, 179

covenant, 3, 4, 6, 38, 39, 43, 45, 48, 61, 76, 77, 88, 97, 107, 168, 175, 183, 191, 195, 321, 351, 352, 354

crime, 151, 186, 223, 233, 236, 237, 302

crown, 12, 28, 61, 188, 241, 242, 309, 323

crucifixion, 21, 237, 259, 260, 265

crucifixion nails, 234, 235

cubits, 177, 206, 282, 349

cup, 194, 212, 249, 264

Cyprus, 316, 319

Cyrene, 234, 316

Damascus Gate, 258

daughter-in-law, pure, 245

Davidic messiah, 2, 5, 16, 30, 32, 50, 57, 105, 107, 113, 126, 144, 151, 155, 187, 188, 226, 227, 284, 290, 299, 307, 355

Day of Atonement, 21, 33, 34, 35, 38, 125, 182, 192, 218, 220, 231, 241, 242, 243, 255, 266, 268, 270, 277, 278, 296, 344

death sentence, 97, 100, 124, 128, 129, 165, 167, 180, 193, 221, 222, 223, 224, 226, 230, 233, 252, 270, 294, 313

deceit, 29, 42, 48, 64, 92, 140

dedication, 123, 154, 188

Dedication, 144, 154, 161, 188, 303, 304

demon, 124, 140

deputy, 182, 194, 209, 210, 212, 219, 231, 247, 250, 269, 355

destruction, 197, 232, 261, 274

devil, 113, 122, 139, 140, 196, 198, 226, 288, 317

diabolos, 197, 226, 317

Didymus, 199, 280, 317

dipped, 194

disguised, 201, 252, 270, 326

Dispersion, 309, 310, 311

dividing garments, 6

donkey, 187, 188, 274

dove, 22, 61, 74, 146

drunkards, 77

Dung Gate, 260, 261

dust, 132, 134, 147

ear, 211

ear, pierced, 212

earthquake, 73, 78, 295

eat, 79, 83, 103, 105, 113, 120, 121, 181, 282, 284, 302

eighteen, 351

eighth day, 278

Eleazar (Jerusalem), 302

Eleazar (Lazarus), 159, 211, 302

Eleazar (OT), 2, 3, 4, 24, 91, 99, 159, 256, 320, 354

election, 22, 44, 74, 104, 146, 147, 150, 154, 166, 169, 181, 182, 198, 212, 231, 261, 264, 278

Eli, 82, 210

Elijah, 16, 82, 102, 103, 167, 170, 230, 268, 355

Elisha, 103

Elymus, 317

emancipation, 39, 49, 87, 88, 89, 92, 97, 101, 107, 108, 174, 181, 229, 230, 252, 348

ephod, 241, 242

Ephraim, 3, 4, 7, 9, 11, 22, 69, 70, 77, 78, 82, 91, 100, 129, 141, 160, 161, 180, 183, 186, 188, 229, 230, 274, 281, 291, 297, 311, 320, 321, 333, 345, 347

escape, 117, 119, 155, 174, 175, 186, 190, 205, 207, 230, 231, 237, 239, 250, 273, 287, 288, 319, 344

eschaton, 56, 169, 195, 355

Essenes, 6, 15, 39, 46, 125, 166, 184, 259, 269, 270, 294, 295

excommunication, 120, 151, 157, 257

exodus, 11, 24, 39, 88, 89, 101, 103, 108, 190, 214, 230, 310

Ezekiel 16, 43, 44, 76, 83, 86, 128, 183

Ezra, 31, 58, 59, 60, 61, 67, 164, 232

falling to ground, 208

false charges, 128, 130, 131, 132, 141, 165, 173, 176, 224, 264, 299, 352

false chargess, 129

father, 55, 69, 114, 129, 135, 146, 182, 198, 228, 245, 291, 300, 302, 313, 316, 326, 351, 353

father of lies, 48, 139, 153, 197, 198, 209, 228, 230, 297

father/son, 22, 25, 87, 158, 175, 193, 202, 270, 307, 320, 332

feet, 183, 184, 192, 206, 207, 213, 241, 269, 270, 347

female servant, 213

fence, 325

festival, 39, 46, 92, 168, 215, 216, 218, 219, 229, 266, 291

fig tree, 28, 65, 80

Filio Dei, 237

filthy clothes, 174, 177, 209, 309

fire, 82, 116, 197, 214, 216, 283, 284, 289

first fruits, 89, 123

firstborn, 4, 6, 11, 13, 22, 24, 27, 63, 69, 70, 82, 84, 95, 111, 121, 150, 159, 169, 173, 179, 180, 190, 192, 200, 210, 212, 219, 225, 227, 237, 247, 249, 264, 267, 276, 284, 288, 289, 291, 314, 345

fish, 103, 187, 282, 283, 284

fish (dried), 102, 103

Fish Gate, 186, 187

fish, 153, 282, 284, 317

fish, dried, 120, 283

fish, house of, 26

fish, large, 284, 287, 317

Fisher King, 326

five husbands, 79, 81

five loaves, 102

five plus two equals seven, 102

five sons of Judah, 102

flesh, 120, 121, 302

flesh and blood, 118, 120, 121, 333

floor, 131, 132, 195

follow me, 277, 288, 326

Follow me, 27

forty, 222

forty-six years, 50, 51, 142

Fountain Gate, 260

Friday, 266

fruit, 186, 189

fuller, 259

Fullers Field, 259, 274

Gabbatha, 238, 239, 240

Galileans, 113, 114, 118, 178, 225, 297, 331

Galilee, 5, 16, 32, 36, 37, 53, 76, 126, 127, 149, 290, 345

gall, 249

garden, 204, 205, 207, 215, 217, 270, 325

gardener, 207, 270, 271, 275

gate, 126, 131, 132, 153, 187, 213, 214, 217, 219, 220, 244, 260, 270, 288, 315, 348, 350

Gate of Ephraim, 187, 189

Gate of the Firstborn, 219

Gate of the Offering, 217

Gate of the Sacrifice, 217

Gate of the Scapegoat, 220

Gate of the Song, 217, 218

Gate of Women, 217, 218

gatekeeper, 212, 213, 217, 244, 270, 273, 315, 348

gematria, 13, 34

genealogy, 7, 10, 23, 31, 57, 61, 68, 74, 94, 128, 298, 305, 325, 326, 345

Genesis 24, 79, 84, 86

Genesis 29, 79, 84, 172, 276

Genesis 49, 277

Gentiles, 101, 189, 194, 282, 284, 285, 307, 308, 316

Gethsemane, 204

Gibeah, 3

gift, 13, 281, 309, 326

giftd, 281

Gihon, 172, 205, 259, 261, 265, 274

giving birth, 189, 274

giving birth, 60, 180

giving birth, 275

glorification, 17, 18, 61, 159, 189, 190, 202, 264, 334

Golan, 100, 120, 282, 349

Golgotha, 233, 257, 258, 261, 263, 264, 288

Gospel of Mary, 346

Gospel of Nicodemus, 252

Gospel of Thomas, 70, 346

great Sanhedrin, 224, 225

Greeks, 154, 187, 189, 198

hair, 165, 184, 185, 323

Hallel, 218

hands and feet, 175, 254, 263

Hasmonean Palace, 240

head, 183, 269

healing, 18, 49, 62, 87, 90, 99, 106, 124

help, 61, 69, 94, 97, 157, 160, 164, 201, 203, 335, 351

Herod, 6, 14, 15, 50, 51, 106, 107, 196, 220, 254, 294, 297, 301, 312, 313, 316, 328

Hezekiah, 319

Hezekiah's Tunnel, 265, 275

hiding, 107, 111, 113, 118, 123, 180, 252, 273, 326, 331

hieron, 47, 51

high priest, 11, 33, 48, 75, 95, 110, 128, 133, 134, 139, 153, 159, 176, 178, 180, 182, 185, 189, 192, 193, 198, 203, 209, 210, 211, 212, 214, 215, 218, 219, 220, 224, 225, 228, 229, 230, 231, 232, 234, 241, 242, 243, 250, 256, 264, 267, 268, 270, 274, 283, 284, 285, 293, 294, 300, 306, 307, 308, 318, 331, 332, 333, 335, 354, 355

high priests, two, 209, 271

Hindu, 114

Hinnom, 205, 260

Holy Family, 298, 301, 322

Holy of Holies, 241, 243, 268

horses, 26, 27, 285

House of Hyssop, 302

house of Joseph, 70, 76, 179, 187, 190, 227, 293

The Testament of Lazarus

hunger, 100, 102, 103, 105, 248

husband, 45, 79, 80, 83, 128, 132, 162, 245, 269

Hymenaeus, 305, 306, 319

hyoscine, 248

Hyrcanus, 81, 83, 139

hyssop, 248, 249, 250, 272, 277, 330

I AM, 108, 109, 110, 138, 141, 208, 281, 345

icthyus, 187

illness, 88, 158, 159, 160, 165, 351

Immaculate Conception, 325

inheritance, 61, 70, 82, 137, 142, 192, 228, 247, 248, 264, 299, 321, 345

insurrection, 118, 233

intertextuality, ii

intoxicated, 42, 77, 185

invalids, 93

Iscariot, 186, 196, 198, 199, 200, 278, 307, 344

Israel (Lazarus as, 172

Israel (Lazarus as), 165, 169, 172

ivy, 323

Jacob, 3, 6, 24, 28, 29, 33, 37, 61, 63, 76, 79, 91, 120, 121, 152, 184, 225, 252, 270, 284, 311, 353

Jacob's Well, 78, 79, 84, 85, 91, 161, 172, 218, 276, 281, 328, 347

jars, 40, 45

javelin/lance, 248

jealous, 53, 136, 172, 173, 264, 326, 327, 347

Jehoash, 274

Jeremiah, 117, 258, 276, 350

Jerusalem, 43, 92, 96, 123, 145, 147, 164, 168, 169, 173, 187, 190, 205, 206, 230, 234, 259, 265, 275, 297, 301, 302, 303, 311, 313, 318, 320, 321, 349

Jesus (married)), 53

Jesus (priest), 96

Jesus (priestly benediction), 104

Jesus Ananus, 303

Jesus' father, 299, 300, 344

Jesus' mother, 132, 261, 299, 300, 301, 325

Jesus, son of Ananus, 302

Jesus' birthplace, 32

Jesus' Cradle, 261, 314

Jesus' daughter, 39

Jesus' marital status, 85, 162

Jesus' mother, 55, 57, 129, 323

Jethro, 225

Jews (as title), 8

Jews, as title, 7, 16

John (baptiser), 14, 15, 20, 33, 73, 74, 75, 155, 189, 198, 231, 291, 296, 297, 311

John Mark, 309, 313, 317, 318, 319, 329, 333, 334, 335, 336, 351

Jonah, 25, 26, 283, 285

Joseph (Acts), 308

Joseph (Barnabas), 313, 316

Joseph (OT), 2, 4, 12, 22, 69, 76, 115, 136, 142, 172, 173, 187, 239, 247, 252, 257, 291, 320, 327, 351, 353

Joseph of Arimathea, 173, 177, 247, 252, 253, 320, 326, 332

Josephus, 114, 116

Joshua, 2, 3, 4, 7, 10, 19, 24, 33, 47, 77, 78, 91, 101, 113, 142, 159, 206, 230, 239, 291, 320, 354

Judah, 3, 8, 12, 13, 24, 26, 27, 32, 43, 69, 70, 77, 91, 131, 160, 161, 185, 196, 197, 199, 200, 206, 207, 239, 241, 274, 277, 348

Judah (five tribes), 99

Judas, 118, 183, 185, 186, 193, 196, 197, 198, 199, 200, 201, 204, 207, 208, 209, 211, 212, 213, 214, 217, 226, 232, 233, 234, 235, 256, 257, 261, 263, 264, 274, 278, 281, 285, 297, 306, 307, 308, 316, 317, 318, 336, 344, 345

judgement seat, 239

Kerioth, 196, 197, 234

Kidron, 187, 204, 205, 206, 207, 260

king, 110, 227, 239, 274, 277, 293

King Arthur, 195, 325

King David, 142, 184, 204, 209

King Herod, 95, 229, 312

King Hezekiah, 259, 265, 274

King of Israel, 5, 12, 17, 29, 33, 80, 85, 87, 135, 138, 139, 188, 202, 208, 228, 237, 239, 252, 255, 276, 284, 287, 320, 332, 351

King of the Jews, 226, 240

King Zedekiah, 273

King's Garden, 207, 261, 265, 273, 275

King's Pool, 260, 261

kingship, 1, 12, 29, 106, 240, 242

kiss, 306

lamb, 20, 21, 34, 101, 216, 219, 231, 249, 250, 325

lame man, 36, 66, 93, 94, 95, 96, 97, 123, 145, 146, 148, 152, 171, 172, 173, 195, 200, 210, 215, 225, 262, 267, 287, 288, 335, 336, 343, 346

laughingstock, 197

Lazarus, 91, 126, 129, 135, 136, 139, 145, 147, 148, 149, 150, 151, 152, 157, 158, 159, 160, 161, 162, 163, 164, 165, 166, 167, 168, 169, 170, 171, 172, 173, 174, 175, 177, 179, 181, 182, 183, 184, 185, 186, 188, 192, 193, 194, 195, 200, 201, 202, 203, 204, 209, 210, 211, 212, 215, 217, 221, 245, 246, 247, 249, 250, 252, 253, 254, 256, 261, 264, 265, 267, 268, 269, 270, 271, 272, 273, 274, 276, 278, 281, 282, 285, 287, 288, 289, 290, 291, 298, 299, 300, 305, 306, 307, 310, 313,

314, 316, 317, 318, 319, 320, 321, 326, 330, 347, 351

Lazarus, official's son, 90, 152

leadership, 286, 318

Leah, 85, 136, 161

legal, 22, 39, 47, 56, 87, 99, 121, 127, 129, 130, 134, 145, 152, 153, 174, 201, 214, 215, 223, 224, 225, 226, 247, 252, 278, 284, 296, 343

legs, 250

lesser Sanhedrin, 223

Letter to the Hebrews, 219

Levi, 24, 27

Levite, 315, 316

Leyden, Lucas van, 322

lifted up, 49

lifting up, 17, 63, 70, 138, 160, 169, 171, 175, 179

light, 9, 17, 18, 22, 42, 61, 62, 67, 108, 137, 142, 149, 166, 169, 191, 200, 290, 291, 295, 311, 328

liquid, 41, 185, 194, 248, 255, 256, 347, 348

litra, 253, 255, 256, 262

living waters, 8, 20, 40, 93, 125, 131, 147, 173, 251, 281

locked door, 277

logos, 290, 291

lots, 232, 243, 263, 308

mad, 121, 124, 140, 141, 146, 303

magi, 311, 312

magician, 317

Malchus, 208, 209, 210, 211, 212, 214, 264, 270, 273, 316, 335

Mallory, Sir Thomas, 325

Man of Lies, 296

mandrake, 248

mantle, 103, 268, 325, 326, 334

market place, 153, 186, 232

Martha, 9, 53, 56, 63, 65, 85, 136, 160, 161, 164, 167, 169, 171, 173, 183, 194, 247, 267, 269, 271, 285, 307, 313, 316, 323, 324, 326, 330, 332, 334, 351

Martha (mythology), 54

Martha (wife), 55, 56

Martha, wife, 56, 170

Mary (Jerusalem), 301, 313, 314

Mary (Jesus' mother), 311, 323, 344

Mary Magdalene, 53, 55, 85, 86, 88, 91, 128, 129, 132, 133, 135, 136, 152, 156, 160, 162, 169, 172, 173, 180, 182, 183, 184, 185, 213, 217, 245, 246, 247, 250, 253, 256, 264, 266, 267, 269, 270, 271, 272, 273, 274, 276, 280, 281, 285, 298, 301, 310, 311, 313, 314, 315, 316, 322, 323, 324, 325, 326, 328, 329, 331, 333, 344, 347, 350, 351

Mary Magdalene (elevated), 244

Mary, Jesus' aunt, 57

Index

meal, 181, 192, 193, 194, 212, 267, 293, 344

Melchizedek, 12, 68, 72, 116, 139, 209, 210, 257

mercy seat, 239

Messiah ben Ephraim, 5, 32

Messiah ben Joseph, 4, 5, 6, 10, 20, 32, 36, 38, 49, 111, 117, 118, 122, 127, 164, 180, 230, 272, 290, 293, 294, 301, 311, 312, 345, 355

messianic secret, 2

mikvah, 20, 40, 147, 148

ministers, 102, 154, 192, 193, 203, 207, 209, 286, 299, 306, 311

Miryam (OT), 183

Moab, 196, 197, 276, 350

Mordred, 326

Moses, 2, 3, 4, 7, 30, 38, 47, 68, 70, 76, 108, 112, 113, 114, 117, 118, 121, 124, 159, 168, 176, 177, 184, 224, 225, 276, 277, 278, 284, 291, 354

Moses (to Samaritans), 9

Mount Gerizim, 8, 9, 11, 78, 80, 81, 82, 83, 111, 113, 114, 116, 118, 120, 122, 179, 189, 210, 212, 221, 225, 229, 250, 251, 276, 297, 350

Mount of Destruction, 260, 261

Mount of Olives, 204, 205, 207, 258, 259, 260

mountain, 8, 31, 38, 61, 64, 66, 67, 101, 102, 103, 108, 111, 112, 113, 114, 115, 116, 117, 118, 119, 121, 122, 232, 237, 276, 326, 354

mourning, 56, 61, 163, 165, 170, 176, 178, 179, 184, 204, 219, 267, 269, 320, 347

myrrh, 249, 253, 257

Naaran, 33, 281

Naarath, 33

nail wounds, 255

naos, 47, 51, 142, 216

Nathanael, 12, 27, 28, 29, 30, 38, 39, 40, 46, 63, 64, 80, 87, 88, 105, 152, 280, 281, 345

Nazareth, 17, 27, 28, 30, 31, 32, 33, 37, 63, 66, 208, 281, 307

Nazarite, 33, 39, 88, 128, 185, 244, 267, 272, 300, 320, 352

Nazorean, 109, 208, 240, 295

Nazoreans, 295

Nehushtan, 70

New Year, 92

Nicodemus, 58, 59, 60, 61, 63, 64, 67, 68, 71, 80, 88, 89, 90, 95, 124, 126, 127, 145, 146, 148, 149, 151, 152, 154, 157, 159, 164, 201, 214, 224, 253, 255, 256, 270, 271, 274, 310, 320, 327, 328

Nicodemus, priest and Pharisee, 90

night, 23, 59, 61, 67, 145, 158, 166, 196, 215, 216, 217, 218, 256, 259, 260, 282, 346

nine, 61, 167, 232, 326, 331

nine tribes, 31, 61

not yet fifty, 141, 142

nothing may be lost, 103

numerology, 4, 41, 102, 304

occult passage, 220

of age, 146, 151, 201, 202, 247, 316, 319, 326, 333

oil, 183, 184, 185, 253, 255, 256, 257, 262, 264, 274, 347

On, 239, 353

ordinary priest, 241, 242

ordinary priests, 94, 96, 216

ordination, 168, 169, 174, 177, 181, 184, 256, 313

ossuary, 12, 115, 235, 321

Palace of Herod, 240

palm boughs, 188

parakletos, 62, 201, 202, 203, 209, 270, 289, 290, 291, 293, 299, 313, 329

paschal pardon, 228, 294

Passover, 8, 21, 33, 34, 39, 47, 51, 84, 89, 100, 101, 102, 103, 104, 105, 111, 112, 113, 114, 117, 118, 120, 121, 122, 180, 181, 192, 194, 205, 212, 217, 218, 226, 229, 231, 240, 249, 250, 265, 266, 273, 303, 343, 349

Paul, 177, 231, 305, 307, 314, 317, 318, 319, 321, 351

peace, 13, 28, 61, 72, 113, 116, 277, 279, 290, 321, 326

Pentecost, 8, 89, 102, 326, 333

Peter, 23, 24, 25, 26, 27, 65, 66, 96, 97, 99, 104, 114, 122, 148, 149, 155, 157, 172, 173, 176, 179, 186, 192, 193, 195, 196, 198, 199, 200, 201, 202, 207, 208, 210, 211, 212, 213, 214, 215, 216, 217, 225, 226, 238, 249, 256, 262, 264, 267, 268, 269, 278, 279, 280, 282, 283, 284, 285, 286, 287, 288, 289, 305, 306, 307, 308, 310, 313, 314, 315, 316, 317, 318, 319, 321, 326, 327, 329, 334, 335, 336, 343, 345, 346, 347, 350

Peter (letters), 308

Peter's denials, 212, 214

Petros, 25

Pharisees, 26, 59, 71, 75, 80, 94, 96, 113, 125, 126, 127, 132, 144, 148, 149, 151, 152, 153, 154, 158, 164, 172, 173, 174, 176, 178, 216, 226, 295

phileo, 26, 27, 159, 267, 285, 286, 305, 309

Philetus, 305, 306, 319

Philip, 23, 24, 26, 27, 28, 104, 126, 159, 187, 189, 198, 199, 247, 267, 269, 280, 281, 283, 285, 288, 305, 306, 319, 345, 351

piercing wound, 250

Pilate, 6, 23, 66, 112, 113, 114, 116, 118, 119, 142, 210, 211, 215, 217, 219, 220, 221, 223, 226, 227, 228, 229, 230, 231, 232, 233, 236, 237, 238, 239, 240, 252, 257, 264, 294, 295, 301, 331, 346, 353

Place of the Fire, 216, 217, 219

Place of the Hearth, 216

Place of the Skull, 263, 264, 288
police, 306
polygamy, 53, 133, 134, 295
Pool of Beth-zatha, 92
Pool of Shelah, 261
Pool of Siloam, 147, 150, 165, 174, 176, 201, 203, 259, 261, 265, 267, 268, 275, 276, 289, 324, 327, 334, 335, 346, 347
portico of Solomon, 154
pregnancy, 132, 185, 301
pregnant, 130, 156, 162, 170
priest, 137, 198
priesthood, corrupt, 45, 48, 70, 93, 131, 138, 173, 216, 228, 232
prisoner, 167, 175, 223, 226, 228, 229, 287, 334
prophet, 9, 16, 21, 49, 98, 103, 108, 110, 127, 138, 141, 149, 169, 214, 246, 250, 274, 290, 294, 316, 326, 327
protégée, 27, 88, 90, 91, 103, 126, 129, 145, 148, 157, 190, 295, 320, 327, 336
Protevangelion, 132, 299, 301
purification, 17, 46, 48, 64, 73, 82, 84, 135, 177, 182, 206, 207, 220, 229, 245, 249, 251, 258, 265, 272, 273, 277, 278, 296, 334
purification of women, 272
purification water, 40, 73
purification waters, 73
purple, 242, 352

purse, 183, 186, 236
Queen of Heaven, 323
Qumran, 7, 14, 20, 22, 36, 46, 73, 75, 222, 269, 288, 293, 294, 295, 296, 297, 298
Rachel, 4, 12, 32, 85, 136, 161, 320
raising, 139, 160, 171, 177, 179, 287
Ramah, 320, 349, 350, 353
rebirth, 60, 88, 138, 145, 148, 151, 153, 157, 164, 165, 181, 182, 308, 309
reclining, 193, 194
red heifer, 258
regent, 247, 291, 348
remnant, 274, 295
Remnant, 2, 3, 4, 9, 10, 11, 17, 18, 29, 30, 31, 38, 39, 40, 45, 46, 49, 58, 63, 64, 65, 66, 69, 70, 78, 79, 80, 103, 121, 138, 141, 152, 153, 154, 189, 228, 230, 280, 281, 283, 305, 310, 320, 321, 323, 350
Restorer, 44, 46, 82, 84, 138, 152, 276
resurrection, 50, 157, 165, 166, 169, 246, 268, 291, 293, 305, 321
Rhabbouni, 271
right hand, 22, 69, 70, 148, 169, 252, 270
rival, 136, 149, 161, 173, 176, 192, 193, 200, 210, 280, 287, 290, 307
rivers of living water, 251

robe, 241

rods, 91, 129, 134, 160, 169, 183, 347

rolled up, head cloth, 268

rolled up, headcloth, 270

Rome, 80, 106, 107, 112, 118, 119, 178, 179, 195, 217, 221, 229, 236, 237, 238, 240, 287, 294, 314, 319, 326

royal official, 61, 87, 164

Sabbath, 34, 92, 124, 125, 148, 168, 223, 224, 226, 250, 265, 266, 267, 268, 270, 271, 277, 296, 343, 349

Sabbath of Sabbaths, 266

Sabbaths, two double, 266

sacrifice, 46, 120, 121, 122, 158, 166, 175, 184, 217, 218, 219, 233, 242, 250, 288, 326

Salathiel, 31, 61, 67, 68, 90, 142, 155, 310

Samaria, 3, 16, 18, 32, 43, 49, 76, 77, 80, 81, 83, 89, 102, 111, 154, 173, 178, 182, 227, 305, 317, 331

Samaritan, 8, 46, 101, 120, 167, 206

Samaritan (background), 8

Samaritan (Jesus as), 1, 140

Samaritan Passover, 101, 102

Samaritan tumult, 66, 110, 112, 116, 117, 122, 135, 143, 178, 179, 189, 225, 229, 233, 237, 297, 330, 331

Samaritan woman, 10, 44, 55, 76, 79, 81, 85, 91, 104, 128, 136, 180, 183, 185, 245, 281, 315

Samaritat tumult, 210

Samson, 185

Samuel, 88, 320, 321

Sanhedrin, 90, 164, 165, 167, 171, 172, 174, 222, 223, 225, 226, 264, 271, 278, 293, 294, 300, 334, 343, 345, 348

Sanhedrin, great, 176, 178

Sanhedrin, lesser, 151

Sarah and Hagar, 136

sash, 241

Satan, 122

scapegoat, 21, 179, 219, 220, 225, 230, 231, 233, 246, 264, 272

sceptre, 12, 111, 241, 257, 277

schism, 3, 4, 6, 9, 27, 46, 81, 91, 99, 190, 305, 319

Sea of Galilee, 26, 106, 298, 349

Sea of Tiberias, 100, 106, 107, 280, 282, 331

secret, 30, 59, 63, 67, 69, 80, 123, 148, 149, 150, 157, 170, 204, 225, 252, 259, 261, 267, 269, 274, 276, 279, 289, 291, 299, 324, 326, 332, 346, 347

Secret Gospel of Mark, 169, 313, 334

Seder, 181, 192, 194

servant (blind), 152

servant of the high priest, 209

servant of the king, 89, 146, 164, 270

servants, 61, 87, 193, 209, 212, 213, 214, 216, 218, 245

seven, 19, 36, 40, 42, 45, 55, 61, 63, 65, 79, 86, 87, 89, 92, 101, 103, 124, 168, 173, 174, 182, 212, 218, 223, 229, 273, 278, 284, 313, 347, 348, 381

seven thousand (Remnant), 103

seven years and five months, 303, 304

seventh day, 89, 125, 168, 169, 181, 212, 249, 250, 272, 277

seventy, 224, 278, 284, 285, 311

Shear-jashub, 274

Shechem, 3, 10, 76, 77, 78, 82, 319, 320, 351, 354

sheep, 17, 21, 79, 84, 93, 104, 120, 126, 153, 154, 155, 172, 173, 222, 232, 276, 286, 287, 288

Sheep Gate, 93, 96, 99, 155, 173, 221, 288

Shekinah, 82, 116, 155, 177

shepherd, 286, 351

Shiloah, 147

Shiloh, 10, 11, 12, 13, 49, 50, 65, 66, 81, 82, 91, 111, 116, 136, 147, 148, 153, 155, 188, 189, 190, 191, 193, 200, 202, 203, 210, 227, 241, 244, 246, 256, 267, 275, 277, 278, 279, 281, 282, 283, 289, 291, 292, 293, 299, 305, 308, 309, 311, 314, 316, 319, 321, 326, 328, 334, 336, 349, 350, 354

Shimon Kipah, 315

Sicarii, 196, 210, 234

sign, 19, 20, 26, 28, 33, 36, 40, 41, 47, 48, 55, 59, 60, 65, 71, 73, 87, 89, 90, 102, 103, 105, 107, 108, 118, 120, 133, 139, 142, 145, 149, 151, 160, 166, 167, 168, 170, 177, 179, 187, 188, 190, 206, 214, 221, 222, 239, 242, 250, 251, 252, 269, 274, 280, 283, 284, 307, 318, 331, 336, 346, 351

signs and wonders, 62, 88, 89, 101, 105, 123, 206, 222

Siloam, 274

Siloam Tower, 350

Simeon, 24, 196, 199, 200, 346

Simeon Kepha, 345

Simon, 24, 186, 196, 199, 201, 280, 285, 315, 317, 347

Simon the Cyrene, 233, 306

Simon the Zaddik, 314

Simon, Captain of the Temple, 186, 197, 217, 232, 236

sin, 94, 96, 97, 131, 133, 140, 145, 146, 150, 158, 174, 231, 238, 250, 266, 287, 335

sisters, 57, 85, 136, 160, 161, 316, 324

skull, 257, 260, 263

solar worship, 3, 230

soldiers, 208, 210, 216, 242, 243, 260

Solomon, 123, 154, 236

Solomon's portico, 188

Solomon's Stables, 261

Son of God, 236

son of Joseph, 7, 10, 19, 27, 239, 284, 301, 320, 355

Son of Joseph, 5, 7

son of man, 68, 69, 70, 110, 121, 138, 152, 175, 190, 236, 291

Song of Solomon, 183, 244

Sons of Light, 167

soul, 17, 73, 154, 170, 190, 228, 246, 306, 309, 347

spikenard, 253

spirit, 16, 19, 20, 22, 43, 60, 61, 67, 74, 75, 82, 141, 150, 155, 159, 201, 250, 268, 277, 278, 283, 291, 299, 300, 310, 311

spittle, 61, 64, 146, 147, 348

star, 311, 313, 328

stench, 9, 173, 174, 334

stone, 79, 171, 172, 173, 239, 265, 267, 276, 324, 326, 330, 334, 347, 348

stone pavement, 64, 239

storm, 117

strong drink, 185

struck, 306

stumbling stone, 172

successor, 7, 103, 142, 145, 149, 150, 159, 193, 201, 202, 210, 214, 264, 267, 268, 280, 288, 318, 329, 336

suffering servant, 16, 17, 18, 21, 29, 30, 154, 219, 266

Sunday, 266, 267

survival, 17, 190, 206, 233, 239, 245, 249, 254, 265, 266, 269

survivors (Remnant), 30

Susanna, 128

sword, 326

sword/dagger, 114, 196, 209, 210, 211, 326, 328, 335

Sychar, 72, 76, 77, 78, 79, 115, 185

synagogue, 90, 118, 120, 151, 157, 345

tabernacle, 83, 132

Tabernacles, 8, 92, 102, 123, 125, 144, 147, 154, 168, 174, 178, 188, 191, 251, 302, 303, 304

Taheb, 4, 9, 44, 82, 109, 111, 113, 115, 206, 276, 316

teacher, 60, 90, 124, 125, 137, 149, 150, 151, 228, 286

Teacher, 193, 271, 297

teacher of Israel, 58, 124, 150, 274

Teacher of Righteousness, 295, 297

temple, 41, 47, 48, 49, 50, 51, 59, 61, 66, 81, 82, 83, 92, 118, 120, 121, 123, 132, 137, 142, 153, 154, 155, 164, 172, 179, 188, 195, 216, 217, 218, 219, 220, 221, 222, 229, 230, 236, 237, 239, 275, 283, 285, 286, 287, 290, 294, 302, 303, 304, 348, 350

Temple Court, 179

Temple of Jupiter Hellenius, 83

test, 79, 91, 104, 129, 131, 132, 152, 198, 201, 214, 275, 279, 283, 285, 286, 288

testament of Lazarus, 319

the light, 230

the one, 63, 66, 126, 145, 168, 174, 192, 193

thief, 232, 234

thieves, 153, 176, 197, 216, 228, 232, 234

third day, 38, 39, 49, 61, 67, 84, 90, 124, 168, 173, 177, 179, 188, 249, 250, 265, 266, 272, 274, 277, 291, 328, 347, 348, 354

thirsty, 42, 106, 125, 173, 248, 251, 290

thirteen (bar mitzvah), 39, 87, 88, 90, 126, 145

thirty years, 61, 67, 116, 142, 294

thirty-eight years, 94, 95, 211

Thomas, 199, 200, 250, 278, 280, 317

three attestations, Lazarus, 149, 285

three denials, 20, 196, 278

three disqualifications, 176

throne, 123, 206, 239, 257, 274, 323, 326, 329, 331, 353

Tiberias, 37, 106, 107, 111, 118, 345

Tiberius, 14, 221, 229, 237, 294, 312

Tiberius Caesar, 106

time/hour, 33, 79, 84, 89, 231, 273

Timnath-serah, 3, 78, 115

Tirathaba, 112, 114, 115

titulus, 240, 260

Tobit, 79

Toledot Yeshu, 344

tomb, 9, 164, 165, 166, 168, 171, 173, 185, 252, 255, 265, 267, 268, 269, 271, 272, 273, 276, 282, 324, 326, 334, 346, 348, 352

torches, 217

torn, 242, 284

torrent, 78, 147, 205, 206, 207, 261

touch, 146, 185, 250, 272, 273, 277, 279, 289, 347

tower, 244, 347

traders, 46, 47, 48, 49, 186, 222, 232

transference, 19, 150, 176, 248, 267, 268

treasury, 137, 186, 221, 235, 306

trial, 23, 43, 100, 128, 132, 133, 162, 164, 167, 168, 223, 224, 225, 259, 299, 300, 309, 347

tribute, 12

Tuesday, 38, 267, 277

tunic, 241, 242, 243

turban, 12, 176, 177, 241, 243, 268, 270

twelve, 7, 23, 61, 66, 101, 103, 122, 145, 166, 167, 193, 195,

200, 206, 226, 241, 285, 287, 293, 304, 309, 311, 326, 328, 333, 346, 351, 353, 354

twelve baskets, 102

twin, 199, 201, 317

Twin, Judas', 200

two 'wives', 53

two days, 35, 38, 84, 90, 164, 167

two fish, 102

two goats, 21, 231, 232, 278

two sons of Joseph, 102

two worlds, 61

two" day, 84

undergarment, 241

unnamed, 22, 23, 24, 198, 209, 210, 226, 281, 345

Upper Market-place, 222

Uriel, 59, 60, 61, 67, 90, 164

Urim and Thummim, 82, 354

Valley Gate, 261

Valley of Slaughter, 260

veil, 176, 177, 180

Vespasian, 304

vestments, 2, 209, 215, 219, 229, 230, 241, 243, 267, 268, 269, 283, 284, 294, 353

vine, 28, 61, 63, 69, 70, 323

violence, 1, 48, 105, 110, 112, 122, 124, 135, 179, 196, 201, 208, 210, 211, 227, 228, 297, 330, 354

virgin, 57, 79, 86, 132, 160, 161, 274, 299, 300, 325

Vitellius, 112, 229, 294

voice, 15, 18, 26, 65, 108, 154, 166, 190, 290, 291, 303, 326, 335

vow, 185, 267, 272, 299, 300

walking on water, 107, 115, 117

War, 31, 222, 290, 294, 303, 304

washing, 192, 193, 194, 195, 207, 241, 277, 282, 284, 293, 294

water (wound), 250

waters of bitterness, 131

wedding, 36, 38, 45, 55, 79, 182, 251, 267, 281

weep, 170, 270

weeping, 170, 190, 269, 320

wheel, 171, 172, 276

white, 61, 84, 101, 169, 176, 215, 241, 243, 259, 268, 269, 270, 271, 326, 334

Wicked Priest, 295, 296, 297

wicked tenants, 70, 225

widow, 170, 247

wilderness, 205

wilderness/desert, 15, 18, 19, 21, 43, 44, 47, 61, 72, 93, 94, 97, 101, 125, 205, 222, 231, 233, 273, 275, 324

wild-man, 326

wine, 36, 40, 41, 42, 59, 77, 248, 249

winnowing, iii, 36, 91, 98, 121, 189, 214, 262, 283

witness, 89, 132, 140, 161, 214, 223, 225, 226, 264, 265, 309, 310, 334, 343

word of God, 140, 141

world, 13, 16, 26, 58, 61, 64, 138, 152, 164, 165, 174, 195, 200, 225, 227, 250, 264

Zabdi, 281

Zarethan, 32

Zealots, 1, 196

Zebedee, 280, 281, 302

Zebediah, 281

zugot, 224, 225

SHE BROUGHT THE ART OF WOMEN
A Song of Solomon, Nabonidus, and the Goddess

By Janet Tyson

Of interest to

★ **BIBLICAL STUDIES**

★ **ANCIENT NEAR EASTERN AND EGYPTIAN STUDIES**

★ **FEMINIST STUDIES**

★ **ESOTERICA/OCCULT**

The Song of Solomon was written by a woman; it tells the story of the marriage between King Nabonidus of Babylon and the Egyptian princess, Nitocris. Set during the seven years they lived at Tayma, Arabia, the Song is a surprisingly personal testimony from one who knew the couple intimately. This book challenges all preconceptions about the Song, and provides a strong argument for it being a historical, unified narrative.

ISBN Paperback 978-1-7393154-4-3
    Hardcover 978-1-7393154-3-6
    Digital 978-1-7393154-5-0

www.ingramcontent.com/pod-product-compliance
Lightning Source LLC
Chambersburg PA
CBHW040240130526
44590CB00049B/4012